The Earthscan Reader in Business and Sustainable Development

The Earthscan Reader in Business and Sustainable Development

Edited by Richard Starkey and Richard Welford

London and Sterling, VA

First published in the UK and USA in 2001 by
Earthscan Publications Ltd

Reprinted 2004, 2005

ISBN: 1 85383 639 7 paperback
          1 85383 659 1 hardback

Typesetting by Composition and Design Services
Printed and bound by Creative Print and Design (Wales), Ebbw Vale
Cover design by Andrew Corbett

For a full list of publications please contact:

Earthscan
8–12 Camden High Street
London, NW1 0JH, UK
Tel: +44 (0)20 7387 8558
Fax: +44 (0)20 7387 8998
Email: earthinfo@earthscan.co.uk
Web: www.earthscan.co.uk

22883 Quicksilver Drive, Sterling, VA 20166–2012, USA

A catalogue record for this book is available from the British Library

Library of Congress Cataloging-in-Publication Data

The Earthscan reader in business and sustainable development / edited by Richard Welford and Richard Starkey.
      p. cm.
   Includes bibliographical references and index.
   ISBN 1-85383-659-1 (hardcover : alk. paper) – ISBN 1-85383-639-7 (pbk : alk. paper)
   1. Industrial management–Environmental aspects. 2. Economic development–
   Environmental aspects. 3. Sustainable development. I. Welford, Richard,
   1960- II. Starkey, Richard.

HD30.255 .E17 2000
658.4'08–dc21   00-059306

Earthscan publishes in association with WWF-UK and the International Institute for Environment and Development

This book is printed on elemental chlorine-free paper

To mum, dad and Ruth – once again with love and thanks

Richard Starkey

For my family

Richard Welford

The world has enough for everyone's need, but not for everyone's greed.

Mahatma Gandhi

Contents

Introduction

Section 1   Overview

Section 2   Business Opportunities

Section 3   Environmental and Social Accounting

Section 4   Critical Perspectives

Section 5   Trade and Sustainable Development

Conclusion: Win–Win Revisited: a Buddhist Perspective

List of Illustrations

Boxes

Tables

Figures

About the Authors

Carol Adams is a professor of accounting at the University of Glasgow. She is a member of the Council of the Institute of Social and Ethical AccountAbility and is on the panel of judges for the joint Institute for Social and Ethical AccountAbility (ISEA)/Association of Chartered Certified Accountants (ACCA) Social Reporting Awards. Carol's research is concerned with comparative international social and ethical disclosures and the processes by which companies decide what to report. She has received funding from the Association of Certified Accountants, the Chartered Institute of Management Accountants and has been awarded two academic fellowships by the Institute of Chartered Accountants of England and Wales. Her work has been published in several academic journals of international standing, books and professional monographs. She has presented her work at international conferences and has held visiting appointments to academic institutions in Australia, Hong Kong and the USA.

Dr Sharon Beder is an associate professor in the Science, Technology and Society Programme at the University of Wollongong. She is the author of many articles and books, including *Toxic Fish and Sewer Surfing* (Allen & Unwin, 1989), *The Nature of Sustainable Development* (Scribe, 1996), *Global Spin: the Corporate Assault on Environmentalism* (Green Books, 1997) and *The New Engineer* (Macmillan, 1998). Her web page is at http://www.uow.edu.au/arts/sts/sbeder/.

Sharon worked as a professional engineer for several years before returning to university to do a PhD in Science and Technology Studies. She has been environmental education co-ordinator at the University of Sydney, chairperson of the Environmental Engineering Branch of the Institution of Engineers, Sydney, president of the Society for Social Responsibility in Engineering, a director of the Earth Foundation and a recipient of a Michael Daley Award for excellence in science, technology and engineering journalism.

Jem Bendell is a social and environmental researcher, writer, activist and consultant with five years of experience working on business responsibility for sustainable development. In that time he has been instrumental in the development of a number of certification schemes for responsible business. Previously a visiting professor at Universidad Nacional in Costa Rica, he is currently an associate of the New Academy of Business and is completing a PhD in International Policy at the University of Bristol. He is the editor of *Terms of Endearment: Business, NGOs and Sustainable Development* (Greenleaf Publishing, 2000). For more information visit http://www.jembendell.com.

Martin Bennett is principal lecturer in accounting and financial management at Gloucestershire Business School, Cheltenham and Gloucester College of Higher Education, UK. He previously worked in the accountancy profession, as a financial manager in industry, in management development, and in higher education and research.

He researches, writes and consults on environmental accounting and performance measurement. His publications, with co-authors, include *Sustainable Measures: Evaluating and Reporting on Environmental and Social Performance* (Greenleaf Publishing, UK, 1999), *Eco-Management Accounting: report on the EU's ECOMAC research project* (Kluwer Academic Publishers, 1999), *The Green Bottom Line: Environmental Accounting for Management: Current Practice and Future Trends* (Greenleaf Publishing, UK, 1998), and *Environment Under the Spotlight: Current Practice and Future Trends in Environment-related Performance Measurement for Business* (Association of Chartered Certified Accountants, UK, 1998), as well as several articles and working papers. He runs seminars and courses on environmental accounting and performance measurement and is a founder-member and current chair of the Environmental Management Accounting Network.

Colin Dey is lecturer in accounting at the University of Dundee. He has recently completed his doctoral thesis which centred on the development of social accounting and bookkeeping at the UK fair trade organization, Traidcraft plc. His other research interests include the development of qualitative research methodologies, including critical ethnography, in the design of new accounting and information systems. He is currently working on the development and application of corporate 'silent' social accounts with colleagues at the Centre for Social and Environmental Accounting Research.

Paul Ekins has a PhD in economics from the University of London and is reader in environmental policy in the Department of Environmental Social Sciences of Keele University. He is also a programme director of the sustainable development charity Forum for the Future, directing its Sustainable Economy Programme, Senior Consultant to Cambridge Econometrics and a member of the UK's National Consumer Council. He is also a specialist adviser to the Environmental Audit Committee of the House of Commons.

Paul Ekins' academic work focuses on the conditions and policies for achieving an environmentally sustainable economy, and he has extensive experience consulting for business, government and international organizations. He is the author of numerous papers and articles, and has written or edited six books. In 1994 he received the United Nations Environment Programme (UNEP) Global 500 award 'for outstanding environmental achievement'.

John Elkington is a founder and now chairman of SustainAbility Ltd, one of Europe's leading consultancies focusing on business strategies for sustainable development, and has worked in the environmental field for over 20 years. He has consulted with government organizations (including the European Environment Agency, the Organisation for Economic Co-operation and Development (OECD), the

United Nations Development Programme (UNDP), the United Nations Environment Programme (UNEP) and the World Bank), non-governmental organizations (NGOs) (including European Partners for the Environment, Greenpeace International and World Wide Fund For Nature (WWF)) and companies (among them BAA, BP, British Gas, BT, Dow, Electrolux, IBM, ICI, Ford, Novo Nordisk, Procter & Gamble, ScottishPower, Shell and Volvo).

A regular columnist for *The Guardian* and *Tomorrow* magazine, he is the author or co-author of a dozen books. These include a number one bestseller, *The Green Consumer Guide* (Victor Gollancz, 1989), with Julia Hailes. His two latest books are *Cannibals With Forks: The Triple Bottom Line of 21st Century Business* (Capstone Publishing Ltd, 1997) and, again with Julia Hailes, *New Foods Guide* (Victor Gollancz, 1999). He has also authored or co-authored more than 20 published reports – the latest being *The Internet Reporting Report* (SustainAbility, 1999). He is chairman of the Environment Foundation and a member of a number of committees, including the Board Environment Committee at Anglian Water plc and the Consultative Forum on the Environment and Sustainable Development, convened by the European Commission. In 1989, he was elected to the UN Global 500 roll of honour for his 'outstanding environmental achievements'.

Richard Evans has a Master's degree in Business Administration (MBA). After ten years in industrial sales he joined Fritz Schumacher's Intermediate Technology Group. In 1985 he became marketing director of Traidcraft plc, the UK's leading 'fair trade' business. In 1991 Traidcraft plc started to develop an annual report to its stakeholders measuring systematically its performance against its development objectives and corporate values. Since Traidcraft plc published the first externally audited 'Social Account' in 1993, he has been active in developing social and ethical accounting and, through his consultancy *ethics etc…*, in advising an international portfolio of clients in the corporate sector, government and development. He is retained by The Co-operative Bank plc as social and ethical auditor. Richard Evans is a Council member and founder of the Institute of Social and Ethical AccountAbility and has contributed to papers and books on social accounting, including *Building Corporate AccountAbility* (Zadek, Pruzan and Evans, Earthscan, 1997), *Business Ethics: Principles and Practice*, (Moore (ed), EBEN and Business Education Publishers, 1997) and in *The Journal of Business Ethics* and *Accounting, Auditing and Accountability Journal*.

Carl Frankel is a writer, journalist, consultant and entrepreneur specializing in business and sustainable development. From 1990 to 1994 he was the editor and publisher of the trade newsletter *Green Market Alert*, which he founded. From 1996 to 1999 he was North American editor for *Tomorrow* magazine, which specializes in business and sustainability. He is currently a contributing editor to that same magazine and a contributing editor to *Green Futures*, a UK-based environmental magazine. His regular column, Integrate This!, appears on http://www.radiowoodstock.com. He is currently working on a book, with the working title: *Triad: A Conversation with the Past About the Future*, that he expects to be published in 2001. Frankel is a founding director of The Story and Strategy Alliance, which develops sustainability-related visions, scenarios and strategies. Frankel can be contacted at frankel@storyandstrategy.com, and for more information about his activities and The Story and Strategy Alliance see http://www.storyandstrategy.com.

H Landis Gabel is professor of economics and management and associate dean for the MBA Programme at INSEAD in Fontainebleau, France. He holds a BSc (engineering), MBA and PhD (economics) from the University of Pennsylvania and an MSc (economics) from the London School of Economics.

Professor Gabel's research focuses on microeconomics and public policy, in particular industrial, trade and environmental policy. He has written or edited five books, most recently *Frontiers of Environmental Economics* (Edward Elgar, 2000), *European Casebook on Industrial and Trade Policy* (Prentice-Hall, 1995), and *The Principles of Environmental and Resource Economics* (Edward Elgar, 1996). He has published papers in economics, legal, environmental and business journals such as the *Journal of Environmental Economics and Management, Southern Economic Journal, Antitrust Journal, The Energy Journal, Antitrust Law Journal, Journal of Industrial Economics, Sloan Management Review* and *Harvard Business Review*.

Professor Gabel founded INSEAD's Centre for the Management of Environmental Resources in 1989 and co-directed it until 1995.

Rob Gray is professor of accounting at the University of Glasgow and director of the Centre for Social and Environmental Accounting Research. He was formerly the Mathew professor of accounting and information systems at the University of Dundee. He is the author or co-author of nearly 200 books, monographs, articles and papers, the majority of which are in the areas of accountability, social accounting and environmental reporting and accounting. He is a member of ten editorial boards of academic and professional journals and a founder member of the ACCA environmental reporting awards and the ACCA/ISEA Social Reporting Awards schemes.

Stuart L Hart is professor of strategic management and director of the Sustainable Enterprise Initiative at the University of North Carolina's Kenan-Flagler Business School. Previously, he taught corporate strategy at the University of Michigan Business School and was the founding director of Michigan's Corporate Environmental Management Program. Professor Hart's research interests centre on strategy innovation and change. He is particularly interested in the implications of environmentalism and sustainable development for corporate and competitive strategy. In 1999, he was recognized nationally as a 'faculty pioneer' by the World Resources Institute for his work in integrating environmental and social issues into the management education curriculum. He has published over 40 papers and authored or edited four books. His article 'Beyond Greening: Strategies for a Sustainable World' won the McKinsey Award for Best Article in the *Harvard Business Review* for 1997.

Paul Hawken is an environmentalist, educator, lecturer, entrepreneur, journalist and bestselling author. He is known around the world as one of the leading architects and proponents of corporate reform with respect to ecological practices. His writings and work have caused chief executive officers (CEOs) to transform their internal corporate culture and business philosophy towards environmental restoration. His six books have been published in over 50 countries, in 27 languages and include *The Ecology of Commerce* (Harper Collins, 1993) which was voted in 1998 as the number one college text on business and the environment by professors in 67 business schools. He has just completed *Natural Capitalism: Creating the Next Industrial Revolution* (Earthscan, 1999) with Amory and Hunter Lovins. He has served on the board of many environmental organizations including Point Foundation, Center for Plant Conservation, Conservation International, Trust for Public Land, Friends of the Earth and National Audubon Society.

Peter James is professor of environmental management at the University of Bradford and director of a consultancy business. His publications, with co-authors, include *Sustainable Measures: Evaluation and Reporting of Environmental Performance* (Greenleaf Publishing, 1999), *The Green Bottom Line: Environmental Accounting for Management* (Greenleaf Publishing, 1998), *Driving Eco-Innovation* (FT Pitman, 1997), *Corporate Environmental Management in Britain and Germany* (Anglo-German Foundation, 1997) and *Environment under the Spotlight: Current Practice and Future Trends in Environment-related Performance Measurement in Business* (ACCA, 1998) as well as many articles on environmental benchmarking, environmental accounting, performance evaluation and product evaluation for environmental and business journals. He can be contacted at sustainablebusiness@compuserve.com.

Dr David C Korten is the author of *When Corporations Rule the World* and *The Post-Corporate World: Life After Capitalism*, board chair of the Positive Futures Network, publishers of *Yes! A Journal of Positive Futures* (http://www.futurenet.org), and founder and president of The People-Centered Development Forum (http://www.iisd.ca/pcdf).

Dr Korten earned his MBA and PhD degrees at the Stanford Graduate School of Business and served for five and a half years as a faculty member of the Harvard University Graduate School of Business. He devoted his early career to setting up the College of Business Administration at Haile Selassie I University in Addis Ababa and serving as academic director of the Central American Management Institute (INCAE) in Managua. He has also served as Ford Foundation staff in Manila and Asia regional adviser on development management for the US Agency for International Development.

L Hunter and Amory B Lovins are co-chief executive officers of Rocky Mountain Institute (RMI) (http://www.rmi.org), an independent, entrepreneurial, nonprofit resource policy centre which they co-founded in 1982 in Old Snowmass, Colorado. RMI's 50 staff foster the efficient and restorative use of resources as a path to global security. The Institute's message is summarized in the Lovinses' book with business author Paul Hawken, *Natural Capitalism: Creating the Next Industrial Revolution* (Earthscan, 1999). This influential synthesis shows how new business and market models can use integrative technical design to make sustainability into a new core source of competitive advantage and put the private sector in the vanguard of restorative practices.

Hunter Lovins is a political scientist, sociologist, lawyer, forester, and cowboy. Co-author of many of the couple's 27 books and several hundred papers, she has shared with Amory Lovins two visiting academic chairs, the 'Alternative Nobel', Mitchell, and Nissan Prizes and the Lindbergh Award.

Amory Lovins, originally a consultant experimental physicist, has received an Oxford MA (by virtue of being a don) and six US honorary doctorates, briefed 11 heads of state, and received the Onassis Prize, the Heinz Award, a MacArthur Fellowship and the 1999 World Technology Award (Environment). He founded and chairs Hypercar, Inc., which is RMI's fourth for-profit spinoff company; the third, E SOURCE (http://www.esource.com), was sold in 1999 to the *Financial Times* group.

The Lovinses consult extensively for the private sector, especially on advanced resource productivity for the electricity, water, real-estate, car, chemical, oil, and semiconductor industries. *The Wall Street Journal*'s Centennial Issue named Amory Lovins among 39 people in the world most likely to change the course of business in the 1990s; *Car* magazine, the 22nd most powerful person in the global automotive industry; *Newsweek*, 'one of the Western world's most influential energy thinkers'. The impact of *Natural Capitalism* is already being compared to that of *Silent Spring*.

Damian Miller received his MPhil in environment and development from the Geography Department at Cambridge University and then went on to pursue his PhD in affiliation with the Judge Institute of Management Studies. His PhD concentrated on entrepreneurship in the off-grid solar power sector in developing countries. In particular, his fieldwork was conducted in India and Indonesia where he shadowed separate entrepreneurs in their efforts to establish financially viable solar businesses. He graduated with his PhD from Trinity College Cambridge in the summer of 1998 and joined Shell Renewables where he is a now a business developer in the rural electrification market segment. Since joining Shell, Damian Miller has established two separate renewable energy companies, in India and Sri Lanka respectively, called Shell Renewables India and Shell Renewables Lanka. The companies are focusing initially on selling solar photovoltaic home lighting and water pumping systems to rural households that suffer from chronic shortages of grid power or have not yet received an electricity connection. Eventually these companies will expand into other renewable sectors including, but not limited to, biomass and wind applications. Damian Miller has published several articles based on his PhD research and subsequent commercial activities. He will be writing a book provisionally entitled *Selling Solar: Entrepreneurship and Sustainable Change* which will be available from Earthscan in 2001.

Titus Moser presently works for the Sustainable Development Group at Shell International. He is also a senior associate at the Judge Institute of Management Studies, University of Cambridge. He has a PhD in management studies from the University of Cambridge and an MBA from McGill University, Canada. He has worked for the environmental consultancy Environmental Resources Management, for Ecover, a producer of environmentally friendly cleaning products, and consulted to a range of private sector, governmental and non-governmental organizations.

His academic and professional work focuses on understanding the role that transnational corporations play in the sustainable development of less-developed countries. He has published a number of related articles and his book: *Transnational Corporations and Sustainable Development: The Case of the Colombian and Peruvian Petroleum Industries* will shortly be published by Earthscan. He can be contacted at tjm20@hermes.cam.ac.uk.

David F Murphy joined the New Academy of Business in early 1998 as its senior researcher following four years at the School for Policy Studies, University of Bristol, where he worked on various research projects. These included: an Economic and Social Research Council (ESRC)-funded project on corporate social responsibility policies in UK companies; a policy brief on corporate codes of conduct for The World Conservation Union (IUCN); and his PhD on business–NGO partnerships for sustainable development. Recent work has included research on corporate responses to HIV/AIDS in South Africa for the International Labour Organization and an international review of business–NGO partnerships in the forest products sector for WWF-International. From 1983 to 1992, he coordinated various community education and health programmes for CUSO, a Canadian development NGO, in both West Africa and Canada. David is the co-author of *In the Company of Partners: Business, Environmental Groups and Sustainable Development Post-Rio* (The Policy Press, 1997). He is currently responsible for the New Academy's programmes on human rights and partnerships.

Dave Owen is professor of accounting and head of the Management School at the University of Sheffield. He has previously held academic appointments at the Universities of Salford, Manchester, Leeds and Huddersfield.

Dave has published widely in the area of social and environmental accounting. Among his notable publications is the leading text *Accounting and Accountability: Changes and Challenges in Corporate Social and Environmental Reporting*, co-authored with professors Rob Gray and Carol Adams and published by Prentice-Hall International in 1996. His current research interests centre on recent developments in social and ethical accounting, auditing and reporting, with current projects in this area funded by the Institute of Chartered Accountants in England and Wales and the Chartered Institute of Management Accountants.

Forest Reinhardt is an associate professor at Harvard Business School. He is the author of *Down to Earth: Applying Business Principles to Environmental Management* (Harvard Business School Press, 2000). His other recent work includes 'Market Failure and the Environmental Policies of Firms', in the *Journal of Industrial Ecology* and 'Sustainability and the Firm', forthcoming in the interdisciplinary journal *Interfaces*. Reinhardt has also written numerous classroom cases on firms' management of environmental problems, all of which are available from Harvard Business School Publishing. Raised in western Montana, Reinhardt holds a PhD in Business Economics from Harvard University, an MBA with high distinction from Harvard Business School and an AB, *cum laude*, from Harvard College.

Sarah Roberts is an associate at the International Institute for Environment and Development where she manages projects on business and sustainable development. Three of her current major work themes are: managing supply chains for sustainable development; developing more sustainable North–South trade; and assessing the impact of environmental and social certification schemes. Sarah is currently studying for an MBA and has a Masters degree in Environmental Technology from Imperial College in London and a Chemistry degree from Manchester University.

Nick Robins has more than ten years', experience with international environment and development issues, focusing on European Union (EU) policy-making and business practice. He is currently the director of IIED's new Sustainable Markets Group. His work aims to find practical ways of delivering the transformation in global markets – in trade, investment, corporate responsibility and consumption patterns – that sustainable development requires. He is co-author of a number of recent IIED publications, including *Sustaining the Rag Trade, The Reality of Sustainable Trade, Who Benefits?, Unlocking Trade Opportunities, Consumption in a Sustainable World, Rethinking Paper Consumption* and *Incentives for Eco-Efficiency*. In the past two years, Nick Robins has also worked as an adviser/consultant to the UK Department of Environment, Transport and the Regions, the Department for International Development and the British Council; the EU Directorate-General for the Environment; the Norwegian Ministry of the Environment; the Environment Directorate of the OECD; and the UN Department for Economic and Social Affairs. He is also a member of the advisory council of Forum for the Future's Sustainable Economy Unit, the new NPI/WWF 'Companies of the Future' investment fund and is a board member of European Partners for the Environment.

Bernard Sinclair-Desgagné is professor of technology economics and management at the Ecole Polytechnique de Montreal, where he is associated with the Jarislowsky Chair on International Business and the National Sciences and Engineering Research Council of Canada (NSERC) Chair on Site Remediation and Management. He is also research director of the Organizational Design and Incentives Group at the Interuniversity Research Center for the Analysis of Organizations (CIRANO) in Montreal. He holds a PhD in management science from Yale University, was granted visiting professorships at Boston University and the Ecole Polytechnique de Paris, and was a faculty member of INSEAD in France for seven years before moving to Montreal. One of his main research areas is the regulation and management of major technological and environmental risks. He has published extensively on those subjects in first-rate academic journals. He also acts regularly as a consultant for government and business.

Richard Starkey is Senior Researcher at the Centre for Corporate Environmental Management at the University of Huddersfield and along with the Centre's Director, Richard Welford, co-edited *The Earthscan Reader in Business and the Environment*. He is an expert member of the ISO subcommittee responsible for producing ISO 14031, the international standard on environmental performance evaluation, and has recently edited a handbook for the European Environment Agency entitled

Environmental Management Tools for SMEs – A Handbook. Richard sits on the editorial board of the journals *Eco-Management and Auditing* and *Business Strategy and the Environment* and has consulted for organizations such as Samsung, TXU Europe, The British Standards Institution and Forum for the Future. His current work includes research exploring the potential for greenhouse gas emissions trading at the level of the individual citizen (see http://www.dtqs.org).

Dr Ernst von Weizsäcker is president of the Wuppertal Institute for Climate, Environment and Energy, director of the Institute for European Environmental Policy (IEEP) in Bonn and a member of the Club of Rome. Since October 1998 he has been a member of the German Parliament and in March 2000 he was appointed Chairman of the Parliamentary Enquete Commission on 'Globalisation of the World Economy – Challenges and Answers'. He was director at the United Nations Centre for Science and Technology for Development. In 1989 Dr von Weizsäcker, together with the Norwegian prime minister Gro Brundtland, received the Italian Premio De Natura and in 1996 he was awarded the WWF Conservation Medal. In addition to *Factor Four* (Earthscan, 1998) co-authored with Amory and Hunter Lovins, his books include *Ecological Tax Reform: Policy Proposal for Sustainable Development* (with Jochen Jesinghaus, 1992) and *Earth Politics Year*, both published by Zed Books (1994).

Richard Welford is professor of Corporate Environmental Management and director of the Centre for Corporate Environmental Management at the University of Huddersfield. He is also visiting professor of Sustainable Management at the Norwegian School of Management in Oslo. He has written widely on the subject of corporate environmental management and along with Richard Starkey co-edited *The Earthscan Reader in Business and the Environment*. He is editor of the leading academic journal *Business Strategy and the Environment* and the practitioner-based journal *Eco-Management and Auditing*. Richard is a director of ERP Environment, a member of the Advisory Board of the Greening of Industry Network and a member of the ESRC Global Environmental Change Programme Committee. He undertakes consultancy work and training for selected companies and organizations.

Dr Simon Zadek is chair of the international professional body for social auditing, the Institute of Social and Ethical AccountAbility, having been development director of the New Economics Foundation and chair of the Ethical Trading Initiative until the end of 1998. He is on the Steering Committee of the Global Reporting Initiative, the Operating Council of the Global Alliance for Workers and Communities, and the International Advisory Committee of the Copenhagen Centre.

Simon has contributed to the development and practice of corporate responsibility and accountability as a practitioner, adviser and external verifier, in building multi-stakeholder alliances to promote good practice and through his writing. He has co-edited several books, including *Building Corporate AccountAbility* (with Peter Pruzan and Richard Evans, Earthscan, 1997), and more recently *Mediating Sustainability: Growing Policy from the Grass Roots* (with Jutta Blauert, Kumarian Press, Inc., 1998). He has written on diverse topics such as the environment and trade, indicators for sustainable development, Buddhist economics, social entrepreneurs, utopia and economics, ethical trade, civil regulation, new social partnerships, disability and sustainable consumption.

Chapter Sources

Section 1
Overview

1   Stuart L Hart (1997) 'Beyond Greening: Strategies for a Sustainable World', *Harvard Business Review*, January–February 1997
2   John Elkington (1998) 'The "Triple Bottom Line" for 21st-century Business', in *Companies in a World of Conflict*, edited by John Mitchell, Earthscan, London

Section 2
Business Opportunities

3   Forest Reinhardt (1999) 'Bringing the Environment Down to Earth', *Harvard Business Review*, July–August 1999
4   Ernst Ulrich von Weizsäcker, Amory Lovins and L Hunter Lovins (1997) 'The Imperfect Market', *Factor Four: Doubling Wealth, Halving Resource Use*, Earthscan, London – Section 1.20: Profitable Energy and Waste Savings in a Louisiana Factory and Section 4.2: The Imperfect Market
5   Amory Lovins, L Hunter Lovins and Paul Hawken (1999) 'A Road Map for Natural Capitalism', *Harvard Business Review*, May–June 1999
6   H Landis Gabel and Bernard Sinclair-Desgagné (1998) 'The Firm, its Routines and the Environment', in *The International Yearbook of Environmental and Resource Economics 1998–1999: A Survey of Current Issues*, edited by T Tietenberg and H Folmer, pp89–118 (revised version)

Section 3
Environmental and Social Accounting

7   Rob Gray, Dave Owen and Carol Adams (1996) 'What is Social Accounting?', Prentice-Hall, London – extract from Section 1.2
8   Martin Bennett and Peter James (1998) 'The Green Bottom Line', in *The Green Bottom Line*, edited by Martin Bennett and Peter James, Greenleaf Publishing, Sheffield

Section 4
Critical Perspectives

Section 5
Trade and Sustainable Development

Acknowledgements

We would like to thank Jason Eligh for his extremely helpful comments on our drafts of the general introduction, section introductions and conclusion. We would also like to thank Horace Herring for his thoughts on the 'win–win' debate, which greatly assisted the writing of the introduction to Section 2 and Simon Bullock who, at very short notice, provided us with information on 'environmental space' for the introduction to Section 1. Thanks too to Barbara Starkey whose insightful comments on the various drafts of the conclusion were much needed and appreciated. David Jones also provided us with helpful comments on the conclusion.

Our job as editors was made considerably easier by a number of publishers who were kind enough to send us articles in electronic form, so our thanks to Greenleaf Publishing, New Society Publishers, MCB University Press and Green Books.

In addition, we are very grateful to Academic Typing Services at the University of Huddersfield who helped us out of a number of tight spots by transferring various articles on to disk at short notice. And a big thank you to CCEM's secretary, Linda Orwin who has done a considerable amount of work on the Reader over the course of its preparation.

We would also like to express our thanks to Jonathan Sinclair Wilson at Earthscan for the opportunity to edit a second Earthscan Reader, which has been a rewarding experience. And finally our thanks go to Akan Leander at Earthscan who supervised the production of this Reader. The Reader has taken rather longer than planned to finish and, throughout its preparation, Akan has shown a patience and good humour far beyond the call of duty.

Acronyms and Abbreviations

ABB	Asea Brown Boveri
ABC	activity-based costing
ACCA	Association of Chartered Certified Accountants
AFPA	American Forest and Paper Association
ARM	Asset Recycle Management
ARR	Alliance for Reasonable Regulation
ASTM	American Society for Testing Materials
BCSD	Business Council for Sustainable Development
BT	British Telecommunications
CAB	Central African Batteries
CAFE	corporate average fuel economy
CAI	Confederation of Australian Industry
CEAC	Corporate Environmental Advisory Council
CEE	Central Eastern Europe
CEO	Chief Executive Officer
CEP	Council of Economic Priorities
CEPAA	Council of Economic Priorities Accreditation Agency
CER	corporate environmental report
CERES	Coalition for Environmentally Responsible Economies
CFC	chlorofluorocarbon
CIRANO	Interuniversity Research Centre for Sustainable Development
CITES	Convention on International Trade in Endangered Species
CMA	Chemical Manufacturers Association
CO_2	carbon dioxide
CSR	corporate social reporting
CVD	countervailing duty
DFE	design for the environment
EDF	Environmental Defense Fund
EEA	European Environment Agency
EIBE	European Institute of Business Ethics
EMAS	Eco-Management and Audit Scheme
EPA	Environmental Protection Agency
ESRC	Economic and Social Research Council
EU	European Union
FAO	Food and Agriculture Organization
FDI	foreign direct investment
FOE	Friends of the Earth

FSC	Forest Stewardship Council
GAAP	generally accepted accounting principles
GAAT	General Agreement on Tariffs and Trade
GCIP	Global Climate Information Project
GDP	gross domestic product
GM	General Motors
GNP	gross national product
GRI	Global Reporting Initiative
HCFC	hydrochlorofluorocarbon
HDI	Human Development Indicator
HDPE	high-density polyethylene
HFC	hydrofluorocarbon
ICC	International Chamber of Commerce
IEA	Institute for Educational Affairs
IEEP	Institute for European Environmental Policy
IIED	International Institute for Environment and Development
IIP	Investors in People
IISD	International Institute for Sustainable Development
ILO	International Labour Organization
INCAE	Central American Management Institute
IRIS	International Research Institutes
ISDW	Index of Sustainable Development Welfare
ISEA	Institute of Social and Ethical Accountability
ISO	International Standards Organization
IUCN	The World Conservation Union
LCA	life-cycle assessment
LDC	less developed country
LPI	Living Planet Index
MDI	metered dose inhaler
MEA	market efficiency audit
MNC	multinational corporation
MTBE	methyl tertiary butyl ether
NAFTA	North American Free Trade Agreement
NEF	New Economics Foundations
NIS	Newly Independent States of the Former Soviet Union
NGO	non-governmental organization
ODS	ozone-depleting substance
OECD	Organization of Economic Cooperation and Development
OPEC	Organization of Petroleum Exporting Countries
ORAP	Organization of Rural Associations for Progress
OSHA	Occupational Safety and Health Administration
P&L	profit and loss
PAC	Political Action Committee
PCB	polychlorinated biphenyls
PCP	polyvocal citizenship perspective
PET	polyethylene terephthalate

PPM	process and production method
PVC	polyvinyl chloride
RAG	Rainforest Action Group
RITE	Research Institute for Innovative Technology for Earth
RMI	Rocky Mountain Institute
ROI	return on investment
SEAAR	social and ethical accounting, auditing and reporting
SEC	Securities and Exchange Commission
SEI	Sustainable Enterprise Initiative
SOP	standard operation procedure
TEAP	Technology and Economic Assessment Panel
TNC	transnational corporation
TQM	Total Quality Management
TRI	Toxic Chemical Release Inventory
TX	Traidcraft Exchange
UNCED	United Nations Conference on Environment and Development
UNCTAD	UN Conference on Trade and Development
UNDP	United Nations Development Programme
UNEP	United Nations Environment Programme
UNRISD	United Nations Research Institute for Social Development
WBCSD	World Business Council for Sustainable Development
WCED	World Commission for the Environment and Development
WHO	World Health Organization
WRI	World Resources Institute
WTO	World Trade Organization
WWF	World Wide Fund For Nature

Introduction

In 1997 the *Harvard Business Review* published an article by Stuart L Hart entitled 'Beyond Greening: Strategies for a Sustainable World' (see Chapter 1). That a discussion of sustainable development found its way on to the pages of such an established business publication was clear confirmation that the corporate community was beginning to consider the business implications of sustainable development. In addition, the issue has received increasing attention from the academic, consultancy and non-governmental organization (NGO) communities and the time therefore seemed to us to be right to put together this Reader. Our aim has been to compile a selection of what we consider to be the most important recent contributions on the subject of business and sustainable development. The pieces here present the views of experts from the varied worlds of business, academia, consultancy and NGOs, and all but one (first published in 1996) date from 1997 onwards.

As this is a Reader about sustainable development, it is necessary to briefly say something about this much discussed term. The most well-known and influential definition is that set out in the so-called *Bruntland Report*[1] (1987) and from it – to quote Tom Gladwin (1999) – *'hundreds of derivative definitions have followed'* (a large number are set out in Murcott, 1997). The term was used in the report to denote a morally defensible form of economic and social development and it is this notion that most subsequent definitions have sought to embody.[2] For if it is anything, sustainable development is above all a moral concept – a concept which seeks to define a development which is fair and just. In short, then, sustainable development is about social justice.

Debates about what constitutes a fair or just distribution of wealth, rights and opportunity within society have occurred throughout history – from those in ancient Greece about the justification for slavery[3] to the current debate about lowering the age of consent for gay men. In fact it could be said that politics has principally been – and still is – a debate about what constitutes social justice. In the past, debates about social justice have tended to focus on distributional issues *within* a particular generation (*intra*generational justice). However, with the rise of concern about environmental issues over the last decades, increasing attention has been given to future generations and considerations of *inter*generational justice – that is, justice *between* generations.

The environment is the basis of all economic activity, indeed of life itself. It provides us with food and water and with the raw materials for the production of goods and services. In addition, it acts as a sink for our wastes and provides 'life support services' such as maintaining climate and ecosystem stability. Given its critical importance, it is surely only right that the quality and integrity of the environment be maintained for future generations. Surely (to use the language of rights and duties) future generations have a right to inherit – and we, the current generation, have a concomitant duty to ensure that they do inherit – an environment equal in quality to our own.[4] As Robert Costanza and Herman Daly have put it:

> *An important motivation behind the sustainable development discussion is that of a just bequest to future generations. Utility cannot be bequeathed but natural capital can be. Whether future generations use the natural capital we bequeath to them in ways which lead to happiness or misery is beyond our control. We are not responsible for their happiness or utility – only for conserving for them the natural capital that can provide happiness if used wisely* (1992, p39).

So are we as a society maintaining environmental quality? Are we meeting our obligations to future generations – to our children and our children's children? The evidence suggests that we are not and that the global ecosystem is being progressively degraded. For instance, in its 1998 *Human Development Report* looking at the effects of consumption on human development, the United Nations Development Programme (UNDP) points out that our consumption patterns have brought about two environmental crises '*that are nudging humanity towards the "outer limits" of what the earth can stand*':

> *First are the pollution and waste that exceed the planet's sink capacities to absorb and convert them. Reserves of fossil fuels are not running out, but use of these fuels is emitting gases that change the ecosystem – annual carbon dioxide (CO_2) emissions quadrupled over the past 50 years. Global warming is a serious problem, threatening to play havoc with harvests, permanently flood large areas, increase the frequency of storms and droughts, accelerate the extinction of some species, spread infectious diseases – and possibly cause sudden and savage flips in the world's climates. And although material resources may not be running out, waste is mounting, both toxic and non-toxic. In industrial countries per capita waste generation has increased almost threefold in the past 20 years.*

> *Second is the growing deterioration of renewables – water, soil, forests, fish, biodiversity:*

> - *Twenty countries already suffer from water stress, having less than 1000 cubic metres per capita a year and water's global availability has dropped from 17,000 cubic metres per capita in 1950 to 7000 today.*
> - *A sixth of the world's land area – nearly 2 billion hectares – is now degraded as a result of overgrazing and poor farming practices.*
> - *The world's forests – which bind soil and prevent erosion, regulate water supplies and help govern the climate – are shrinking. Since 1970 the wooded area per 1000 inhabitants has fallen from 11.4 square kilometres to 7.3.*
> - *Fish stocks are declining, with about a quarter currently depleted or in danger of depletion and another 44 per cent being fished at their biological limit.*
> - *Wild species are becoming extinct 50–100 times faster than they would naturally, threatening to tear great holes in the web of life* (UNDP, 1998, p4).

The *Living Planet Report* published by the World Wide Fund For Nature (1999) paints a similar picture. The report presents a Living Planet Index (LPI), a measure of the change in the health of the world's natural ecosystems since 1970, focusing on the Earth's forest, freshwater and marine biomes – those that contain most of the world's biodiversity. The report shows that the LPI has declined by about 30 per cent relative to its reference point in 1970, which can be interpreted as meaning that the world has lost nearly a third of its natural wealth in that time.

In Chapter 1, Stuart L Hart argues that although things are bad elsewhere, *'we may be approaching ecological recovery in the developed world'* as a result of *'stringent environmental regulations, the greening of industry and the relocation of the most polluting activities (such as commodity processing and heavy manufacturing) to the emerging market economies'.* Whilst it may be true that the state of the environment is in general better in the developed world, even Hart's cautious assessment may be overly optimistic. Take, for instance, the European environment. In its report *Environment in the European Union 1995*, the European Environment Agency (1995) stated that:

> *The European Union is making progress in reducing certain pressures on the environment, though this is not enough to improve the general quality of the environment and even less to progress towards sustainability. Without accelerated policies, pressures on the environment will continue to exceed health standards and the often limited carrying capacity of the environment. Actions taken to date will not lead to full integration of environmental considerations into the economic sectors or to sustainable development.*

Its 1999 report *Environment in the European Union at the Turn of the Century* (EEA, 1999) tells much the same story. In the Foreword to the report, the agency's executive director writes:

> *The Agency has previously reported that despite more than 25 years of Community Environmental Policy – which has been successful in its own terms – general environmental quality in the EU is not recovering, and in some areas it is worsening. This present report confirms both that situation and the fact that the unsustainable development of some economic sectors is the major barrier to improvement* (p4).

So it is quite clear that society is not meeting the demands of intergenerational justice. Does it fare any better in relation to intragenerational justice? Whilst views about what constitutes social justice vary considerably, it is clearly the case that the current distribution of wealth, rights and opportunities in society today does not come close to conforming with any reasonable conception of social justice. Consider, for instance, the hundreds of millions of people who do not enjoy the rights set out in that benchmark of social justice, *The Universal Declaration of Human Rights*, adopted by the UN General Assembly in 1948.

Take, for example, the right set out in Article 25 to a standard of living adequate for health and wellbeing (United Nations, 1999). As the UN's 1998 *Human Development Report* (UNDP, 1998) quoted earlier makes very clear, despite rising global consumption, there are tens of millions whose standard of living still falls way below this level. The report quite rightly points out that the increase in world consumption – from US$1.5 trillion in 1900 to US$24 trillion in 1998 – has in many ways been greatly beneficial:

> *The benefits of this consumption have spread far and wide. More people are better fed and housed than ever before. Living standards have risen to enable hundreds of millions to enjoy housing with hot water and cold, warmth and electricity, transport to and from work – with time for leisure and sports, vacations and other activities beyond anything imagined at the start of this century (p1).*

However, it goes on to say that this growth in consumption *'has been badly distributed, leaving a backlog of shortfalls and gaping inequalities'*. Again, it is worth quoting extensively from the report (see also Box I.1 and Table I.1):

> *Today's consumption is undermining the environmental resource base. It is exacerbating inequalities. And the dynamics of the consumption–poverty–inequality–environment nexus are accelerating. If the trends continue without change – not redistributing from high-income to low-income consumers, not shifting from polluting to cleaner goods and production technologies, not promoting goods that empower poor producers, not shifting priority from consumption for conspicuous display to meeting basic needs – today's problems of consumption and human development will worsen…*

> *Consumption per capita has increased steadily in industrial countries (about 2.3 per cent annually) over the past 25 years, spectacularly in East Asia (6.1 per cent) and at a rising rate in South Asia (2.0 per cent). Yet these developing regions are far from catching up to levels of industrial countries, and consumption growth has been slow or stagnant in others. The average African household today consumes 20 per cent less than it did 25 years ago.*

> *The poorest 20 per cent of the world's people and more have been left out of the consumption explosion. Well over a billion people are deprived of basic consumption needs. Of the 4.4 billion people in developing countries, nearly three-fifths lack basic sanitation. Almost a third have no access to modern health services. A fifth of children do not attend school to grade 5. About a fifth do not have enough dietary energy and protein. Micronutrient deficiencies are even more widespread. Worldwide, 2 billion people are anaemic, including 55 million in industrial countries. In developing countries only a privileged minority has motorized transport, telecommunications and modern energy.*

> *Inequalities in consumption are stark. Globally, the 20 per cent of the world's people in the highest-income countries account for 86 per cent of total private consumption expenditures – the poorest 20 per cent a miniscule 1.3 per cent. More specifically, the richest fifth:*

> *   • Consume 45 per cent of all meat and fish, the poorest 5 per cent.*
> *   • Consume 58 per cent of total energy, the poorest fifth less than 4 per cent.*
> *   • Have 74 per cent of all telephone lines, the poorest fifth 1.5 per cent.*
> *   • Consume 84 per cent of all paper, the poorest fifth less than 1 per cent.*
> *   • Own 87 per cent of the world's vehicle fleet, the poorest fifth less than 1 per cent (pp1–2).*

Box I.1 The Ultra-rich

New estimates show that the world's 225 richest people have a combined wealth of over $1 trillion, equal to the annual income of the poorest 47 per cent of the world's people (2.5 billion).

The enormity of the wealth of the ultra-rich is a mind-boggling contrast with low incomes in the developing world:

- The three richest people have assets that exceed the combined gross domestic product (GDP) of the 48 least developed countries.
- The 15 richest have assets that exceed the total GDP of sub-Saharan Africa.
- The wealth of the 32 richest people exceed the total GDP of South Asia.
- The assets of the 84 richest exceed the GDP of China, the most populous country, with 1.2 billion inhabitants.

Another striking contrast is the wealth of the 225 richest people compared with what is needed to achieve universal access to basic social services for all. It is estimated that the additional cost of achieving and maintaining universal access to basic education for all, basic health care for all, reproductive health care for all women, adequte food for all and safe water and sanitation for all is roughly $40 billion a year. This is less than 4 per cent of the combined wealth of the 225 richest people in the world.

The country with the biggest share of the world's 225 richest people is the US, with 60 (combined wealth of $311 billion), followed by Germany, with 21 ($111 billion), and Japan, with 14 ($41 billion). Industrial countries have 147 of the richest 225 people ($645 billion combined), and developing countries 78 ($370 billion). Africa has just two ($3.7 billion), both from South Africa.

Source: Forbes Magazine, 1997

Table I.1 *The Ultra-rich, by Origin, 1997*

Region or country group	Distribution of the 225 richest people	Combined wealth of the ultra-rich (US$ billions)	Average wealth of the ultra-rich (US$ billions)
OECD	143	637	4.5
Asia	43	233	5.4
Latin America and the Caribbean	22	55	2.5
Arab States	11	78	7.1
Eastern Europe and CIS	4	8	2.0
Sub-Saharan Africa	2	4	2.0
Total	**225**	**1015**	**4.5**

Source: Forbes Magazine, 1997

And, of course, it hardly needs saying that there are millions who do not enjoy many of the other rights set out in the Declaration – for example, the right not to be held in slavery or servitude (Article 4), not to be subjected to torture or to cruel, inhuman and degrading treatment or punishment (Article 5) and not to be subjected to arbitrary arrest, detention or exile (Article 9).

So where does business fit into all this? Surely, as Forest Reinhardt argues in Chapter 3 '*companies aren't in business to solve the world's problems*'. Quite so. But, as Reinhardt also acknowledges, neither can questions of social responsibility be ignored. If, as has been argued above, we as a society have a duty to pursue social justice, then business – a prominent and powerful actor within society – has a duty to collaborate with other actors in pursuit of this goal. Put simply, the pursuit of profit must go hand in hand with the pursuit of social justice. This is what John Elkington in Chapter 2 refers to as accounting against 'the triple bottom line' – the fact that business must consider not only its own economic wellbeing but also its contribution to environmental and social wellbeing. Or, as the World Business Council for Sustainable Development has put it (WBCSD, 1999), the role of business is:

> the delivery of competitively priced goods and services that satisfy human needs and bring quality of life, while progressively reducing ecological impacts and resource intensity throughout the life cycle, to a level at least in line with the Earth's estimated carrying capacity.

The role of business is examined further in Section 1 of the Reader which provides an introduction to the various issues relating to business and sustainable development. One such issue, the effect on the business bottom line of improving environmental performance is examined in Section 2 whilst the issues of environmental and social accounting are covered in Section 3. We have argued here that business activities must be consistent with the demands of social justice but just how committed is business to sustainable development? The views of a number of writers who question the extent of business commitment are set out in Section 4. The final section examines the contentious issues of trade and sustainable development as it relates to business and the Reader finishes with a short conclusion.

We are very grateful for having had the opportunity to edit this Reader and very much hope that we have provided a representative and stimulating selection of readings that will provoke serious reflection and discussion on the crucially important issue of business and sustainable development.

References

Bowra, C (1996) *Classical Greece*, Time-Life International, The Netherlands

Costanza, R and Daly, H (1992) 'Natural Capital and Sustainable Development', *Conservation Biology*, vol 6, no 1, pp36–46

European Environment Agency (1995) *Environment in the European Union 1995*, EEA, Copenhagen

European Environment Agency (1999) *Environment in the European Union at the Turn of the Century*, EEA, Copenhagen

Galbraith, J K (1987) *A History of Economics: The Past as the Future*, Penguin Books, London

Gladwin, T (1999) 'A Call of Sustainable Development', *'Mastering Strategy' supplement, Financial Times*, 13 December, p3

Hawken, P (1995) *The Ecology of Commerce*, Phoenix, London

Mayhew (1997) 'Fading to Grey: the Use and Abuse of Corporate Executives' Representational Power', in *Hijacking Environmentalism: Corporate Responses to Sustainable Development*, edited by Richard Welford, Earthscan, London

Murcott, S (1997) http://www.sustainableliving.org/appen-a.htm [13/01/00]

United Nations Development Programme (1998) *Human Development Report 1998*, Oxford University Press, New York

United Nations (1999) *The Universal Declaration of Human Rights*, http://www.un.org/rights/50/decla.htm [1/12/99]

World Business Council for Sustainable Development (1999) http://www.wbcsd.ch/aboutdfn.htm [1/12/99]

World Commission for the Environment and Development (1987) *Our Common Future*, Oxford University Press, London

World Wide Fund For Nature (1999) http://panda.org/livingplanet/lprreport.html [1/12/99]

Notes

1   *Our Common Future*, the 1987 report by the World Commission for the Environment and Development, is commonly referred to as the *Brundtland Report* (after the commission's chair, Gro Harlem Bruntland). The report defines sustainable development as development *'that meets the need of the present without compromising the ability of future generations to meet the needs of others'* (WCED, 1987, p8)

2   It has been argued (see, for instance, Mayhew, 1997) that, motivated by considerations of profit rather than the common good, some in the corporate world have sought to define sustainable development simply to justify 'business-as-usual'. Jonathon Porritt (2000) notes that *'sceptics are already asking if sustainable development isn't just another linguistic fudge to shore up inherently unsustainable systems'*

3   Most citizens of ancient Greece were in favour of slavery. Aristotle's justification was that *'The lower sort are by nature slaves, and it is better for them as for all inferiors that they should be under the rule of a master'* (Galbraith, 1987). However, there were a small number of Athenians who believed slavery to be wrong. One of them, the playwright Euripedes, wrote (Bowra, 1966):

> Slavery,
> That thing of evil, by its nature evil,
> Forcing submission from man to what
> No man should yield to.

4   Indeed the global environment is now so degraded in many parts of the world that there is a strong case for improving rather than merely maintaining environmental quality for future generations. What many would like to see is what Paul Hawken, in his wonderful book *The Ecology of Commerce*, refers to as a 'restorative economy' – an economy where *'restoring the environment and making money would be the same process'* (Hawken, 1995, p12)

Section 1

Overview

Introduction

The chapters in this section provide an overview of many of the issues relating to business and sustainable development and introduce a number of themes that are examined further in subsequent sections. The section begins with a chapter by Stuart L Hart who argues that *'sustainable development will constitute one of the biggest opportunities in the history of commerce'*. To make the most of this opportunity, argues Hart, business needs to do two things: to understand the problems posed by society's current unsustainable patterns of behaviour and to develop a strategy for providing solutions. Hart explains the problems society faces with reference to what he calls 'the three economies' – the market economy, the survival economy and nature's economy – and their interaction. These three economies have, he explains, become *'worlds in collision, creating the major social and environmental challenges facing the planet: climate change, pollution, resource depletion, poverty and inequality'*.

To explain the role of business in providing solutions, Hart makes use of Paul Ehrlich and Barry Commoner's famous equation $EB = P \times A \times T$: environmental burden equals the product of population, affluence (consumption per capita) and technology (environmental burden per unit of consumption).[1] Environmental burden can, in theory, be reduced by reductions in population and affluence or improvements in technology. However, Hart points out that the global population is set to increase substantially and argues that reducing affluence is not an option in the developing world as it is precisely here where poverty is greatest and where living standards need to be raised. This leaves technology. Hart estimates that in order to provide basic amenities to an increased global population, the world economy may have to increase in size by as much as ten times and for this to happen without any increase in environmental burden, technology would have to improve by the same factor of ten. And this is where business comes in for, as Hart puts it, *'Although population and consumption may be societal issues, technology is the business of business'*.

It is the delivery of these improvements that will constitute the massive business opportunity referred to above. But in order to deliver them Hart believes that companies need to evolve through three stages of environmental strategy: pollution prevention, product stewardship and clean technology. This evolution will only be possible, he argues, if the company has an overall guiding vision, a sustainability vision that directs the firm towards the solution of social and environmental problems. In conclusion, Hart argues that the responsibility for ensuring a sustainable world falls largely on business because *'corporations are the only organizations with the resources, the technology, the global reach and ultimately the motivation to achieve sustainability'* – this motivation deriving from the fact that '*in the final analysis it makes good business sense to pursue strategies for a sustainable world'*.

Hart's chapter raises a number of important issues, one of which is the role of technology in halting environmental degradation. Some very rough, 'back-of-an-envelope' calculations using Ehrlich and Commoner's equation will be useful here. If we assume (in line with UN estimates)[2] that the richest 20 per cent of the global population are responsible for 80 per cent of consumption, this means that, on average, the richest 20 per cent consume 16 times as much per capita as the rest of the population. And if we also assume (again in line with UN estimates)[3] that the population in the richest countries will remain stable until 2050, with the three billion increase in global population occurring in the other countries, then by how much would global production have to increase if, by 2050, the entire population was to have living standards equivalent to that in the highest income countries?

If the economies of the richest countries did not grow at all during this period (meaning per capita income remained unchanged), then global production would still have to increase six times.[4] However, if they were to continue to grow as they have done over the last 25 years – that is at an average of 2.3 per cent per year – then by 2050 they would have increased roughly three times in size (as will average per capita affluence). Therefore in order for the rest of the world to have such living standards, the global economy would have to grow by a massive 18 times. So in order to keep environmental burden constant, the resource efficiency of technology would also have to increase 18-fold. However, if the average rate of growth in the richest countries increased to 3 per cent a year, then by 2050 the economy would have increased in size by a factor of 24 and so the resource efficiency of technology would have to improve 24 times. And if this 3 per cent growth continued to 2100, then resource efficiency would have to increase a staggering 96 times as the economy would be almost 100 times bigger than it is today!

However, it is not enough merely to maintain the current environmental burden for, as the various data set out in the Introduction and in Chapter 1 show, the current environmental burden is not sustainable. We argued in the Introduction that sustainable development requires the maintenance of environmental quality, or – to use the terminology developed by Friends of the Earth (FoE) – that we live within 'environmental space'. Environmental space is defined as:

> *the global total amount of environmental resources: such as absorption capacity, energy, non-renewable resources, agricultural land and forests that humankind can use without impairing the access of future generations to the same amount* (FoEE, 1995, p5).

FoE's detailed research has suggested that in order to live within environmental space, it will be necessary to reduce our environmental burden very roughly by a factor of two.[5] If this is the case, then under the scenario of a 2.3 per cent growth rate referred to above, living within environmental space by 2050 will require the resource efficiency of technology to improve 36 times and under the 3 per cent scenario a 48-fold increase will be required. And with 3 per cent growth up to 2100 a mind-boggling 192-fold improvement in resource efficiency would be necessary to keep within environmental space limits!

What the above calculations suggest is that it is not enough simply to assume that technology will be able to deliver both ongoing economic growth *and* the maintenance of environmental quality. For a start, there is no guarantee that the resource efficiency of technology can improve by the 50, 100 or 200 times that would be required. And of course there is also no guarantee that whatever increases in resource efficiency do occur will not be outrun by increased consumption. If business is serious about pursuing sustainable development, then whilst a commitment to pursuing resource efficiency is necessary and to be welcomed, it cannot be deemed sufficient. What is needed in addition is an unequivocal commitment to maintaining environmental quality. In other words, business must commit itself to a system of production that absolutely respects environmental limits. Living within environmental space means that there are limits to the quantity of raw materials that can be extracted from, and the amount of waste that can be released into, the environment and so the task of business is to use technology to maximize the value that can be created within these limits. If this means that some economic growth is possible, all well and good, but if, as the above calculations suggest, *continuing* growth is not possible, then our moral obligation to future generations means that it is growth and not environmental quality, that has to be forgone.

Another issue raised by Hart is that of business attitudes towards sustainable development. Whilst it is undoubtedly true that the corporate sector wields a tremendous amount of power in today's global economy – David Korten points out in Chapter 12 that, of the world's largest 100 economies, only 49 are countries, the rest being corporations – there are many who question whether business is inclined to use this power to help bring about the transition to sustainable development. It is not therefore so much a question of whether, as Hart believes, corporations are the *only* organizations with the motivation to achieve sustainable development, but whether the majority of corporations actually have *any* such motivation. This issue is explored in some detail by the chapters in Section 4.

In Chapter 2, John Elkington looks at the way in which, as a result of public pressure, the corporate environmental agenda is evolving into a broader sustainable development agenda. Traditionally, he argues, businesses have been judged on their financial performance. But increasingly these days their environmental performance is also taken into account and in the future their social impact will also be considered. In other words, they will be measured against what he refers to as 'the triple bottom line' – that is, on their ability to deliver profit, to contribute to the preservation of the environment and to act in accordance with the demands of social justice. As he puts it: '*Business people – who are increasingly alert to some of the major market opportunities that the sustainability transition will open up – must increasingly recognize that the challenge now is to help to deliver economic prosperity, environmental quality and social equity simultaneously*'.

Companies are far more familiar with the economic accounting than they are with the environmental and social accounting, and Elkington points out that accounting for one's impact on the natural environment and on social wellbeing is complicated by the fact that it is not just a question of being accountable to shareholders. Companies have a much broader constituency – society – to whom they have to account. Indeed, one of the lessons that Elkington draws from the Brent

Spar incident is that companies can no longer ensure societal approval for their activities merely by dealing with government policy-makers and regulators. Instead, companies will need to enter into dialogue with, and be accountable to, their whole constituency of stakeholders if they are to maintain their licence to operate. We are, entering, believes Elkington, a new era of 'stakeholder capitalism'. Stakeholder capitalism is discussed further in Chapter 16 and environmental and social accounting are the subjects of Section 3.

If businesses are to meet the requirements of the triple bottom line, argues Elkington, there is a need to *'turn conventional markets – and conventional business thinking – on their heads'.* What is needed is a *'values revolution'.* He approvingly quotes Jane Nelson of the Prince of Wales Business Leaders Forum who emphasizes the importance of mobilizing in *'the millions of people who work in the business sector ... a greater sense of innovation, entrepreneurship, individual responsibility and social and environmental awareness'.* For both her and Elkington *'The core issue is about changing attitudes, values and approach'.*

References

Carley, M and Spapens, P (1998) *Sharing the World: Sustainable Living and Global Equity in the 21st Century*, Earthscan, London

Friends of the Earth Europe – FoEE (1995) *Towards Sustainable Europe: A Summary*, Friends of the Earth Europe, Brussels

McLaren, D, Bullock, S and Yousuf, N (1998) *Tomorrow's World: Britian's Share in a Sustainable Future*, Earthscan, London

United Nations Development Programme (1998) *Human Development Report 1998*, Oxford University Press, New York

United Nations Population Division (1999) *Briefing Packet: World Population Estimates and Projections, 1998 Revision*, http://www.popin.org/pop1998/1.htm, [23/11/99]

Notes

1   As affluence (A) is defined as per capita consumption (C/P) and technology as environmental burden per unit of consumption (EB/C), the equation can be rewritten as $EB = P \times C/P \times EB/C$. By simplifying the right-hand side of the equation it can be seen that it is indeed equivalent to the left-hand side

2   The UNDP's 1998 *Human Development Report* (UNDP, 1998, p2) states that the 20 per cent of the world's population in the highest income countries account for 86 per cent of private consumption expenditure

3   See United Nations Population Divison, 1999

4   Our estimate differs somewhat from that of Hart's

5   For instance, they argue for a reduction in CO_2 emissions of 50–60 per cent and a reduction in the flow of non-renewable resources through the global economy of 50 per cent – see, for example, McLaren et al, 1998, p88, 212 and Carley and Spapens, 1998, pp79, 86

1

Beyond Greening: Strategies for a Sustainable World

Stuart L Hart

The environmental revolution has been almost three decades in the making and it has changed for ever how companies do business. In the 1960s and 1970s, corporations were in a state of denial regarding their impact on the environment. Then a series of highly visible ecological problems created a groundswell of support for strict government regulation. In the United States, Lake Erie was dead. In Europe, the Rhine was on fire. In Japan, people were dying of mercury poisoning.

Today, many companies have accepted their responsibility to do no harm to the environment. Products and production processes are becoming cleaner; and where such change is under way, the environment is on the mend. In the industrialized nations, more and more companies are 'going green' as they realized that they can reduce pollution and increase profits simultaneously. We have come a long way.

But the distance we've travelled will seem small when, in 30 years, we look back at the 1990s. Beyond greening lies an enormous challenge – and an enormous opportunity. The challenge is to develop a sustainable global economy; an economy that the planet is capable of supporting indefinitely. Although we may be approaching ecological recovery in the developed world, the planet as a whole remains on an unsustainable course. Those who think that sustainability is only a matter of pollution control are missing the bigger picture. Even if all companies in the developed world were to achieve zero emissions by the year 2000, the earth would still be stressed beyond what biologists refer to as carrying capacity. Increasingly, the scourges of the late 20th century – depleted farmland, fisheries and forests; choking urban pollution; poverty; infectious disease and migration – are spilling over geopolitical borders. The simple fact is this: in meeting our needs, we are destroying the ability of future generations to meet theirs.

The roots of the problem – explosive population growth and rapid economic development in the emerging economies – are political and social issues that exceed the mandate and the capabilities of any corporation. At the same time, corporations are the only organizations with the resources, the technology, the global reach and, ultimately, the motivation to achieve sustainability.

It is easy to state the case in the negative: faced with impoverished customers, degraded environments, failing political systems and unrevealing societies, it will be increasingly difficult for corporations to do business. But the positive case is even more powerful. The more we learn about the challenges of sustainability the clearer it is that we are poised at the threshold of an historic moment in which many of the world's industries may be transformed.

To date, the business logic for greening has been largely operational or technical; bottom-up pollution-prevention programmes have saved companies billions of dollars. However, few executives realize that environmental opportunities might actually become a major source of *revenue growth*. Greening has been framed in terms of risk reduction, re-engineering or cost cutting. Rarely is greening linked to strategy or technology development and, as a result, most companies fail to recognize opportunities of potentially staggering proportions.

Worlds in Collision

The achievement of sustainability will mean billions of dollars in products, services and technologies that barely exist today. Whereas yesterday's businesses were often oblivious to their negative impact on the environment and today's responsible businesses strive for zero impact, tomorrow's businesses must learn to make a positive impact. Increasingly companies will be selling solutions to the world's environmental problems.

Envisioning tomorrow's businesses, therefore, requires a clear understanding of those problems. To move beyond greening to sustainability, we must first unravel a complex set of global interdependencies. In fact, the global economy is really three different overlapping economies.

The *market economy* is the familiar world of commerce comprising both the developed nations and the emerging economies.[1] About a billion people – one-sixth of the world's population – live in the developed countries of the market economy. Those affluent societies account for more than 75 per cent of the world's energy and resource consumption and create the bulk of industrial, toxic and consumer waste. The developed economies thus leave large ecological footprints – defined as the amount of land required to meet a typical consumer's needs (see Figure 1.1).

Despite such intense use of energy and materials, however, levels of pollution are relatively low in the developed economies. Three factors account for this seeming paradox: stringent environmental regulations, the greening of industry and the relocation of the most polluting activities (such as commodity processing and heavy manufacturing) to the emerging market economies. Thus to some extent the greening of the developed world has been at the expense of the environments in emerging economies. Given the much larger population base in those countries, their rapid industrialization could easily offset the environmental gains made in the developed economies. Consider, for example, that the emerging economies in Asia and Latin America (and now Eastern Europe and the former Soviet Union) have added nearly two billion people to the market economy over the past 40 years.

With economic growth comes urbanization. Today one of every three people in the world lives in a city. By 2025, it will be two out of three. Demographers predict that by that year there will be well over 30 megacities with populations exceeding eight million and more than 500 cities with populations exceeding one million.

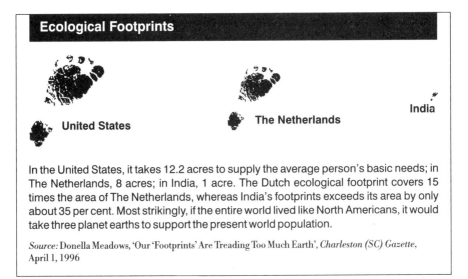

Ecological Footprints

United States

The Netherlands

India

In the United States, it takes 12.2 acres to supply the average person's basic needs; in The Netherlands, 8 acres; in India, 1 acre. The Dutch ecological footprint covers 15 times the area of The Netherlands, whereas India's footprints exceeds its area by only about 35 per cent. Most strikingly, if the entire world lived like North Americans, it would take three planet earths to support the present world population.

Source: Donella Meadows, 'Our 'Footprints' Are Treading Too Much Earth', *Charleston (SC) Gazette,* April 1, 1996

Figure 1.1 *Ecological Footprints*

Urbanization on this scale presents enormous infrastructure and environmental challenges.

Because industrialization has focused initially on commodities and heavy manufacturing, cities in many emerging economies suffer from oppressive levels of pollution. Acid rain is a growing problem, especially in places where coal combustion is unregulated. The World Bank estimates that by 2010 there will be more than one billion motor vehicles in the world. Concentrated in cities, they will double current levels of energy use, smog precursors and emissions of greenhouse gas.

The second economy is the *survival economy*: the traditional, village-based way of life found in the rural parts of most developing countries. It is made up of three billion people, mainly Africans, Indians and Chinese who are subsistence oriented and meet their basic needs directly from nature. Demographers generally agree that the world's population, which is currently growing by about 90 million people per year, will roughly double over the next 40 years. The developing nations will account for 90 per cent of that growth and most of it will occur in the survival economy.

Owing in part to the rapid expansion of the market economy, existence in the survival economy is becoming increasingly precarious. Extractive industries and infrastructure development have in many cases degraded the ecosystems upon which the survival economy depends. Rural populations are driven further into poverty as they compete for scarce natural resources. Women and children now spend, on average, four to six hours per day searching for fuelwood and four to six hours per week drawing and carrying water. Ironically, those conditions encourage high fertility rates because, in the short run, children help the family to garner needed resources. But in the long run, population growth in the survival economy only reinforces a vicious cycle of resource depletion and poverty.

Short-term survival pressures often force these rapidly growing rural populations into practices that cause long-term damage to forests, soil and water. When wood becomes scarce, people burn dung for fuel, one of the greatest – and least well-known – environmental hazards in the world today. Contaminated drinking water is an equally grave problem. The World Health Organization estimates that burning dung and drinking contaminated water together cause eight million deaths per year.

As it becomes more and more difficult to live off the land, millions of desperate people migrate to already overcrowded cities. In China, for example, an estimated 120 million people now roam from city to city, landless and jobless, driven from their villages by deforestation, soil erosion, floods or droughts. Worldwide, the number of such 'environmental refugees' from the survival economy may be as high as 500 million people and the figure is growing.

The third economy is *nature's economy*, which consists of the natural systems and resources that support the market and the survival economies. Non-renewable resources, such as oil, metals and other minerals, are finite. Renewable resources, such as soils and forests, will replenish themselves, as long as their use does not exceed critical thresholds.

Technological innovations have created substitutes for many commonly used non-renewable resources – for example, optical fibre now replaces copper wire. And in the developed economies, demand for some virgin materials may actually diminish in the decades ahead because of reuse and recycling. Ironically, the greatest threat to sustainable development today is depletion of the world's *renewable* resources.

Forests, soils, water and fisheries are all being pushed beyond their limits by human population growth and rapid industrial development. Insufficient fresh water may prove to be the most vexing problem in the developing world over the next decade as agricultural, commercial and residential uses increase. Water tables are being drawn down at an alarming rate, especially in the most heavily populated nations, such as China and India.

Soil is another resource at risk. More than 10 per cent of the world's topsoil has been seriously eroded. Available cropland and rangeland are shrinking. Existing crop varieties are no longer responding to the increased use of fertilizer. As a consequence, per capita world production of both grain and meat peaked and began to decline during the 1980s. Meanwhile, the world's 18 major oceanic fisheries have now reached or actually exceeded their maximum sustainable yields.

By some estimates, humankind now uses more than 40 per cent of the planet's net primary productivity. If, as projected, the population doubles over the next 40 years, we may outcompete most other animal species for food, driving many to extinction. In short, human activity now exceeds sustainability on a global scale (see Figure 1.2).

As we approach the 21st century, the interdependence for the three economic spheres is increasingly evident. In fact, the three economies have become worlds in collision, creating the major social and environmental challenges facing the planet: climate change, pollution, resource depletion, poverty and inequality.

Consider, for example, that the average American today consumes 17 times more than his or her Mexican counterpart (emerging economy) and hundreds of times

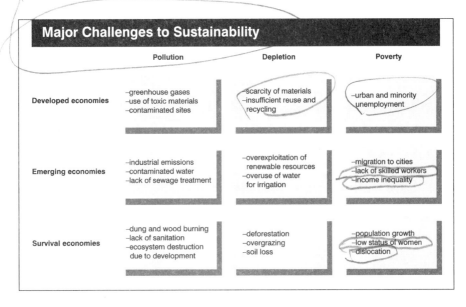

Figure 1.2 *Major Challenges to Sustainability*

more than the average Ethiopian (survival economy). The levels of material and energy consumption in the United States require large quantities of raw materials and commodities, sourced increasingly from the survival economy and produced in emerging economies.

In the survival economy, massive infrastructure development – for example, dams, irrigation projects, highways, mining operations and power generation projects – often aided by agencies, banks and corporations in the developed countries, has provided access to raw materials. Unfortunately, such development has often had devastating consequences for nature's economy and has tended to strengthen existing political and economic élites, with little benefit to those in the survival economy.

At the same time, infrastructure development projects have contributed to a global glut of raw materials and hence to a long-term fall in commodity prices. And as commodity prices have fallen relative to the prices of manufactured goods, the currencies of developing countries have weakened and their terms of trade have become less favourable. Their purchasing power declines while their already substantial debt load becomes even larger. The net effect of this dynamic has been the transfer of vast amounts of wealth (estimated at US$40 billion per year since 1985) from developing to developed countries, producing a vicious cycle of resource exploitation and pollution to service mounting debt. Today developing nations have a combined debt of more than US$1.2 trillion, equal to nearly half of their collective gross national product.

Strategies for a Sustainable World

Nearly three decades ago, environmentalists such as Paul Ehrlich and Barry Commoner made this simple but powerful observation about sustainable development: the total environmental burden (EB) created by human activity is a function of three factors. They are population (P); affluence (A), which is a proxy for consumption; and technology (T), which is how wealth is created. The product of these three factors determines the total environmental burden. It can be expressed as a formula: $EB = P \times A \times T$.

Achieving sustainability will require stabilizing or reducing the environmental burden. That can be done by decreasing the human population, lowering the level of affluence (consumption), or changing fundamentally the technology used to create wealth. The first option – lowering the human population – does not appear feasible short of draconian political measures or the occurrence of a major public-health crisis that causes mass mortality.

The second option – decreasing the level of affluence – would only make the problem worse because poverty and population growth go hand in hand: demographers have long known that birth rates are inversely correlated with level of education and standard of living. Thus stabilizing the human population will require improving the education and economic standing of the world's poor, particularly women of child-bearing age. That can be accomplished only by creating wealth on a massive scale. Indeed, it may be necessary to grow the world economy as much as tenfold just to provide basic amenities to a population of eight billion to ten billion.

That leaves the third option: changing the technology used to create the goods and services that constitute the world's wealth. Although population and consumption may be societal issues, technology is the business of business.

If economic activity must increase tenfold over what it is today just to provide the bare essentials to a population double its current size, then technology will have to improve 20-fold merely to keep the planet at its current levels of environmental burden. Those who believe that ecological disaster will somehow be averted must also appreciate the commercial implications of such a belief: over the next decade or so, sustainable development will constitute one of the biggest opportunities in the history of commerce.

Nevertheless, as of today few companies have incorporated sustainability into their strategic thinking. Instead, environmental strategy consists largely of piecemeal projects aimed at controlling or preventing pollution. Focusing on sustainability requires putting business strategies to a new test. Taking the entire planet as the context in which they do business, companies must ask whether they are part of the solution to social and environmental problems or part of the problem. Only when a company thinks in those terms can it begin to develop a vision of sustainability – a shaping logic that goes beyond today's internal, operational focus on greening to a more external, strategic focus on strategic development. Such a vision is needed to guide companies through three stages of environmental strategy.

Stage one: pollution prevention

The first step for most companies is to make the shift from pollution control to pollution prevention. Pollution control means cleaning up waste after it has been created. Pollution prevention focuses on minimizing or eliminating waste before it is created. Much like total quality management, pollution prevention strategies depend on continuous improvement efforts to reduce waste and energy use. This transformation is driven by a compelling logic: pollution prevention pays. Emerging global standards for environmental management systems (ISO 14000, for example) also have created strong incentives for companies to develop such capabilities.

Over the past decade, companies have sought to avoid colliding with nature's economy (and incurring the associated added costs) through greening and prevention strategies. Aeroquip Corporation, a US$2.5 billion manufacturer of hoses, fittings and couplings, saw an opportunity here. Like most industrial suppliers, Aeroquip never thought of itself as a provider of environmental solutions. But in 1990, its executives realized that the company's products might be especially valuable in meeting the need to reduce waste and prevent pollution. Aeroquip has generated a US$250 million business by focusing its attention on developing products that reduce emissions. As companies in emerging economies realize the competitive benefits of using raw materials and resources more productively, businesses like Aeroquip's will continue to grow.

The emerging economies cannot afford to repeat all the environmental mistakes of Western development. With the sustainability imperative in mind, BASF, the German chemical giant, is helping to design and build chemical industries in China, India, Indonesia and Malaysia that are less polluting than in the past. By colocating facilities that in the West have been geographically dispersed, BASF is able to create industrial ecosystems in which the waste from one process becomes the raw material for another. Colocation solves a problem common in the West, where recycling waste is often infeasible because transporting it from one site to another is dangerous and costly.

Stage two: product stewardship

Product stewardship focuses on minimizing not only pollution from manufacturing but also all environmental impacts associated with the full life cycle of a product. As companies in stage one move closer to zero emissions, reducing the use of material and production of waste requires fundamental changes in underlying product and process design.

Design for Environment (DFE), a tool for creating products that are easier to recover, reuse or recycle, is becoming increasingly important. With DFE, all the effects that a product could have on the environment are examined during its design phase. Cradle-to-grave analysis begins and ends outside the boundaries of a company's operations – it includes a full assessment of all inputs to the product and examines how customers use and dispose of it. DFE thus captures a broad range of external perspectives by including technical staff, environmental experts, end customers and even community representatives in the process. Dow Chemical Company has pioneered the use of a board-level advisory panel of environmental experts and external representatives to aid its product-stewardship efforts.

By reducing material and energy consumption, DFE can be highly profitable. Consider Xerox Corporation's Asset Recycle Management (ARM) programme which uses leased Xerox copiers as sources of high-quality, low-cost parts and components for new machines. A well-developed infrastructure for taking back leased copiers combined with a sophisticated remanufacturing process allows parts and components to be reconditioned, tested and then reassembled into 'new' machines. Xerox estimates that the ARM savings in raw materials, labour and waste disposal in 1995 alone were in the US$300 million to US$400 million range. In taking recycling to this level, Xerox has reconceptualized its business. By redefining the product-in-use as part of the company's asset base Xerox has discovered a way to add value and lower costs. It can provide continually its lease customers with the latest product upgrades, giving them state-of-the-art functionality with minimal environmental impact.

Product stewardship is thus one way to reduce consumption in the developed economies. It may also aid the quest for sustainability because developing nations often try to emulate what they see happening in the developed nations. Properly executed, product stewardship also offers the potential for revenue growth through product differentiation. For example, Dunlop Tyre Corporation and Akzo Nobel recently announced a new radial tyre that makes use of an aramid fibre belt rather than the conventional steel belt. The new design makes recycling easier because it eliminates the expensive cryogenic crushing required to separate the steel belts from the tyre's other materials. Because the new fibre-belt tyre is 30 per cent lighter, it dramatically improves fuel economy. Moreover, it is a safer tyre because it improves the traction control of antilock breaking systems.

The evolution from pollution prevention to product stewardship is now happening to multinational companies such as Dow, DuPont, Monsanto, Xerox, ABB, Philips and Sony. For example, as part of a larger sustainability strategy dubbed A Growing Partnership with Nature, DuPont's agricultural products business developed a new type of herbicide that has helped farmers around the world to reduce their annual use of chemicals by more than £45 million. The new Sulfonylurea herbicides have also led to a £1 billion reduction in the amount of chemical waste produced in the manufacture of agricultural chemicals. These herbicides are effective at 1–5 per cent of the application rates of traditional chemicals, are non-toxic to animals and non-target species and biodegrade in the soil, leaving virtually no residue on crops. Because they require so much less material in their manufacture, they are also highly profitable.

Stage three: clean technology

Companies with their eye on the future can begin to plan for and invest in tomorrow's technologies. The simple fact is that the existing technology base in many industries is not environmentally sustainable. The chemical industry, for example, while having made substantial headway over the past decade in pollution prevention and product stewardship, is still limited by its dependence on the chlorine molecule. (Many organochlorides are toxic or persistent or bioaccumulative.) As long as the industry relies on its historical competencies in chlorine chemistry, it will have trouble making major progress toward sustainability.

Monsanto is one company that is consciously developing new competencies. It is shifting the technology base for its agriculture business from bulk chemicals to biotechnology. It is betting that the bioengineering of crops rather than the application of chemical pesticides or fertilizers represents a sustainable path to increased agricultural yields (see Magretta, 1997).

Clean technologies are desperately needed in the emerging economies of Asia. Urban pollution there has reached oppressive levels. But precisely because manufacturing growth is so high – capital stock doubles every six years – there is an unprecedented opportunity to replace current product and process technologies with new, cleaner ones.

Japan's Research Institute for Innovative Technology for Earth (RITE) is one of several new research and technology consortia focusing on the development and commercialization of clean technologies for the developing world. Having been provided with funding and staff by the Japanese government and more than 40 corporations, RITE has set forth an ambitious 100-year plan to create the next generation of power technology which will eliminate or neutralize greenhouse gas emissions.

Sustainability vision

Pollution prevention, product stewardship and clean technology all move a company toward sustainability. But without a framework to give direction to those activities, their impact will dissipate. A vision of sustainability for an industry or a company is like a road map to the future, showing the way products and services must evolve and what new competencies will be needed to get there. Few companies today have such a road map. Ironically, chemical companies, regarded only a decade ago as the worst environmental villains, are among the few large corporations to have engaged the challenge of sustainable development seriously.

Companies can begin by taking stock of each component of what I call their 'sustainability portfolio' (see Figure 1.3 and Box 1.1). Is there an overarching vision of sustainability that gives direction to the company's activities? To what extent has the company progressed through the three stages of environmental strategy – from pollution prevention to product stewardship to clean technology?

Consider the car industry. During the 1970s, US government regulation of exhaust emissions forced the industry to focus on pollution control. In the 1980s, the industry began to tackle pollution prevention. Initiatives such as the Corporate Average Fuel Efficiency requirement and the Toxic Release Inventory led car companies to examine their product designs and manufacturing processes in order to improve fuel economy and lower emissions from their plants.

The 1990s witnessed the first signs of product stewardship. In Germany, the 1990 'take-back' law required car manufacturers to take responsibility for their vehicles at the end of their useful lives. Innovators such as BMW have influenced the

---

Box 1.1 Aracruz Celulose:
A Strategy for the Survival Economy

'*Poverty is one of the world's leading polluters*', notes Erling Lorentzen, founder and chairman of Aracruz Celulose. The US$2 billion Brazilian company is the world's largest producer of eucalyptus pulp. '*You cannot expect people who don't eat a proper meal to be concerned about the environment.*'*

From the very start, Aracruz has been built around a vision of sustainable development. Lorentzen understood that building a viable forest-products business in Brazil's impoverished and deforested state of Espirito Santo would require the simultaneous improvement of nature's economy and the survival economy.

First, to restore nature's economy, the company took advantage of tax incentives for tree planting in the late 1960s and began buying and reforesting cut-over land. By 1992, the company had acquired over 200,000 hectares and planted 130,000 hectares with managed eucalyptus; the rest was restored as conservation land. By reforesting what had become highly degraded land, unsuitable for agriculture, the company addressed a fundamental environmental problem. At the same time, it created a first-rate source of fibre for its pulping operations. Aracruz's forest practices and its ability to clone seedlings have given the company advantages in both cost and quality.

Aracruz has tackled the problem of poverty head-on. Every year, the company gives away millions of eucalyptus seedlings to local farmers. It is a pre-emptive strategy, aimed at reducing the farmers' need to deplete the natural forests for fuel or lumber. Aracruz also has a long-term commitment to capability building. In the early years Aracruz was able to hire local people for very low wages because of their desperate situation. But instead of simply exploiting the abundant supply of cheap labour, the company embarked on an aggressive social-investment strategy, spending US$125 million to support the creation of hospitals, schools, housing and a training centre for employees. In fact, until recently, Aracruz spent more on its social investments than it did on wages (about US$1.20 for every US$1 in wages). Since that time, the standard of living has improved dramatically, as has productivity. The company no longer needs to invest so heavily in social infrastructure.

* Marguerite Rigoglioso, 'Stewards of the Seventh Generation', *Harvard Business School Bulletin*, April 1996, p55

---

design of new cars with their design for disassembly efforts. Industry-level consortia such as the Partnership for a New Generation of Vehicles are driven largely by the product stewardship logic of lowering the environmental impact of cars throughout their life cycle.

Early attempts to promote clean technology include such initiatives as California's zero-emission vehicle law and the UN Climate Change Convention which ultimately will limit greenhouse gases on a global scale. But early efforts by industry incumbents have been either incremental – for example, natural-gas vehicles – or defensive in nature. Electric-vehicle programmes, for instance, have been used

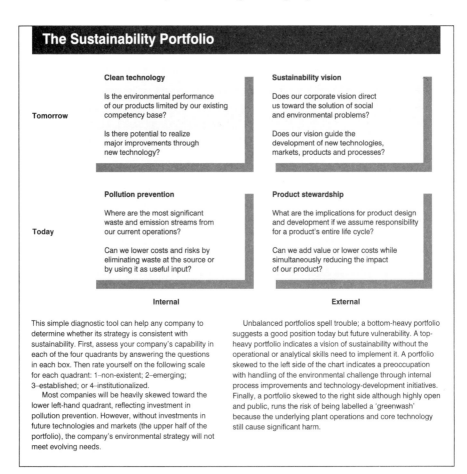

Figure 1.3 *The Sustainability Portfolio*

to demonstrate the infeasibility of this technology rather than to lead the industry to a fundamentally cleaner technology.

Although the car industry has made progress, it falls far short of sustainability. For the vast majority of car-producing companies, pollution prevention and product stewardship are the end of the road. Most executives in the car industry assume that if they close the loop in both production and design, they will have accomplished all the necessary environmental objectives.

But step back and try to imagine a sustainable vision for the industry. Growth in the emerging markets will generate massive transportation need in the coming decades. Already the rush is on to stake out positions in China, India and Latin America. But what form will this opportunity take?

Consider the potential impact of cars on China alone. Today there are fewer than one million cars on the road in China. However, with a population of more than one billion, it would take less than 30 per cent market penetration to equal the current size of the US car market (12–15 million units sold per year). Ultimately,

China might demand 50 million or more units annually. Because China's energy and transportation infrastructures are still being defined, there is an opportunity to develop a clean technology yielding important environmental and competitive benefits.

Amory Lovins of the Rocky Mountain Institute has demonstrated the feasibility of building hypercars – vehicles that are fully recyclable, 20 times more energy efficient, 100 times cleaner and cheaper than existing cars. These vehicles retain the safety and performance of conventional cars but achieve radical simplification through the use of lightweight, composite materials, fewer parts, virtual prototyping, regenerative braking and very small, hybrid engines. Hypercars, which are more akin to computers on wheels than to cars with microchips, may render obsolete most of the competencies associated with today's car manufacturing – for example, metal stamping, tool and die making and the internal combustion engine.

Assume for a minute that clean technology like the hypercar or Mazda's soon-to-be-released hydrogen rotary engine can be developed for a market such as China's. Now try to envision a transportation infrastructure capable of accommodating so many cars. How long will it take before gridlock and traffic jams force the car industry to a halt? Sustainability will require new transportation solutions for the needs of emerging economies with huge populations. Will the giants in the car industry be prepared for such radical change, or will they leave the field to new ventures that are not encumbered by the competencies of the past?

A clear and fully integrated environmental strategy should not only guide competency development, it should also shape the company's relationship to customers, suppliers, other companies, policy-makers and all its stakeholders. Companies can and must change the way customers think by creating preferences for products and services consistent with sustainability. Companies must become educators rather than mere marketers of products (see Figure 1.4).

For senior executives, embracing the quest for sustainability may well require a leap of faith. Some may feel that the risks associated with investing in unstable and unfamiliar markets outweigh the potential benefits. Others will recognize the power of such a positive mission to galvanize people in their organizations.

Regardless of their opinions on sustainability executives will not be able to keep their heads in the sand for long. Since 1980, foreign direct investment by multinational corporations has increased from US$500 billion to nearly US$3 trillion per year. In fact, it now exceeds official development-assistance aid in developing countries. With free trade on the rise, the next decade may see the figure increase by another order of magnitude. The challenges presented by emerging markets in Asia and Latin America demand a new way of conceptualizing business opportunities. The rapid growth in emerging economies cannot be sustained in the face of mounting environmental deterioration, poverty and resource depletion. In the coming decade, companies will be challenged to develop clean technologies and to implement strategies that drastically reduce the environmental burden in the developing world while simultaneously increasing its wealth and standard of living.

Like it or not, the responsibility for ensuring a sustainable world falls largely on the shoulders of the world's enterprises, the economic engines of the future. Clearly, public policy innovations (at both the national and international levels)

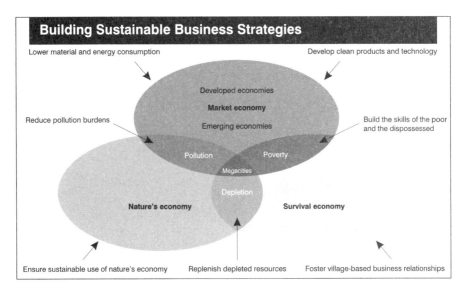

Figure 1.4 *Building Sustainable Business Strategies*

and changes in individual consumption patterns will be needed to move toward sustainability. But corporations can and should lead the way, helping to shape public policy and driving change in consumers' behaviour. In the final analysis, it makes good business sense to pursue strategies for a sustainable world.

References

Magretta, J (1997) 'Growth Through Global Sustainability: an Interview with Monsanto's CEO Robert B Shapiro', *Harvard Business Review*, January–February 1997

Notes

1   The terms 'market economy', 'survival economy' and 'nature's economy' were suggested to me by Vandana Shiva, *Ecology and the Politics of Survival* (1991), United Nations University Press, New Delhi

2

The 'Triple Bottom Line' for 21st-century Business

John Elkington

Introduction

This chapter looks at some of the ways in which the environmental agenda for business is now evolving into a broader agenda based around sustainable development. This process is likely to see a new challenge at board level, requiring companies to focus increasingly on what is described as the 'triple bottom line' of sustainable development: economic prosperity, environmental quality and – the element which business had tended to overlook – social justice. The chapter looks at each of the three 'bottom lines' in turn, discussing definitions, accountability, accounting, auditing and reporting.

Contrary to the apparent views of many media editors, public concern about environmental issues remains at much higher levels than was the case in the 1980s. Indeed, as we approach the third millennium, public opinion polls show high and growing levels of public concern about some key aspects of the environmental agenda. For example, a majority of people in all but one of 17 countries studied in a recent international survey of 15,000 people believed that environmental problems now significantly affect their health. In most countries with comparative data, these health concerns are significantly deeper than was the case five years ago.[1]

The closing years of the 1990s saw another wave of international environmental pressure building, driven by such factors as global warming, drought and the impact of globalization.[2] Some of the corporate casualties included Shell (issues: Brent Spar, Nigeria), Nike (issue: social conditions of labour in the developing world) and Monsanto (issue: denial of consumer choice in relation to the introduction of genetically modified foods).

The sustainability agenda, long understood as an attempt to harmonize the traditional financial bottom line with emerging thinking about the environmental bottom line, is turning out to be much more complicated than some early business enthusiasts imagined. Increasingly, we include social justice in a 'triple bottom line', along with economic prosperity and environmental quality.

Some of the more thoughtful business leaders are beginning to accept that to refuse the challenge implied by the 'triple bottom line' is to risk major reverses in key markets and, if things go really wrong, commercial extinction. Nor is this simply a threat for major transnational corporations: increasingly, they will be forced to pass the pressure on down their supply chains, to smaller suppliers and contractors.

These changes flow from a profound reshaping of society's expectations and, as a result, of the local and global markets that business serves. Anyone who has worked in this area for any time knows that there are waves of change. Some of these waves are driven by 'triple bottom line' factors – most particularly in recent decades by environmental pressures. To accept the challenge is to embark on a process that is likely to be both intensely taxing and – potentially – highly rewarding. The transition to sustainable capitalism will be one of the most complex our species has ever had to negotiate.

As we move into the third millennium, we are embarking on a global cultural revolution. Business, much more than governments or NGOs, will be in the driving seat. This will be partly because of the widely recognized retreat of governments and partly because business will increasingly find itself with no option but to help coevolve global governance systems appropriate to the 21st century. Paradoxically, this will not make the transition any easier for business people. Some will take to this new business environment like the proverbial ducks to water. But for many others, the transition will prove gruelling, if not impossible. For others, performing against the 'triple bottom line' will come to seem like second nature.

It was in the year 1995 that key elements of the new agenda began to crystallize, particularly around the problems experienced by Shell in relation to the disposal of the Brent Spar and human rights issues in Nigeria. At the time, we drew three conclusions from the Brent Spar controversy (Elkington, 1996).

The first is that companies that believe that dealing with government policymakers and regulators alone is enough to ensure broader societal approval for environmentally controversial decisions are riding for a fall. Such companies will need to consult a growing range of environmental 'stakeholders'. Indeed, it is no accident that SustainAbility has just completed a major two-volume report, entitled *Engaging Stakeholders*, for the United Nations Environment Programme (UNEP) and 16 international corporations (SustainAbility, 1996).

Historically, Shell may have been successful in developing 'scenarios' – or pictures of possible futures – to guide its business decisions. But while it had networked assiduously with conservationists and some environmentalists, it had not been a leader in the emerging field of stakeholder dialogue. Since Brent Spar and the Nigeria débâcle, however, the company has been racing to make good this gap.

Successful companies of the future will have to work out ways of engaging even groups like Greenpeace in the evolution of their corporate environmental strategies.

Lesson two is that all industrial products – be they detergents, cars or oil platforms – must be subjected to a life-cycle environmental assessment at an early stage in their development and the results must be made public. New product designers may now talk more comfortably about 'cradle-to-grave' assessments of consumer products, but industry still finds it hard to think, communicate and consult in similar terms about oil platforms, let alone nuclear power plants.

Lesson three struck me when I was in Denmark, two days before Shell made its Brent Spar U-turn. Denmark was one of the most vigorous opponents of Shell's dumping plans and there had been intense media interest in the reactions of environmentally proactive Danish companies to the issue. We were helping to organize

Table 2.1 *Engaging Stakeholders: Ten Transitions*

Established focus		Emerging focus
1 One-way, passive communication	→	Multi-way, active dialogue
2 Verification as option	→	Verification as standard
3 Single company progress reporting	→	Benchmarkability
4 Management systems	→	Life cycles, business design strategy
5 Inputs and outputs	→	Impacts and outcomes
6 Ad hoc operating standards	→	Global operating standards
7 Public relations	→	Corporate governance
8 Voluntary reporting	→	Mandatory reporting
9 Company determines reporting boundaries	→	Boundaries set through stakeholder dialogue
10 Environmental performance	→	'Triple bottom line' economic, environmental and social performance

Source: SustainAbility, 1995

the fifth annual visit of environmentalists and other stakeholders from across the EU to the Danish biotech company Novo Nordisk, which makes enzymes and healthcare products like insulin. The media asked Novo what its stance was on Brent Spar. Having signed the International Chamber of Commerce's Business Charter for Sustainable Development which, among other things, requires signatory companies to challenge the environmental performance of suppliers, Novo Nordisk decided that it could not remain silent.

The implication is that companies taking difficult decisions can no longer count on each other to stay silent if their consciences dictate a stand. In effect, Novo Nordisk concluded that environmental commitment can no longer be simply a question of investment and technology. Increasingly, it is about ethics and values. Once only a few companies – notably The Body Shop, which recently published its first *Values Report* – were prepared to speak in public about environmental and sustainability issues, but the number is expected to grow.

We stand on the threshold of a new era, an era of 'stakeholder capitalism' which has massive implications for major corporations. Table 2.1, taken from volume 1 of our *Engaging Stakeholders* report, highlights ten major building trends in the field of corporate environmental accounting, reporting and communication.

Apart from a new focus on impacts and outcomes (rather than simply on the provision of raw data), we are seeing the spotlight shifting towards issues related to areas such as verification, benchmarking (and the benchmarkability of reported data) and corporate governance. No wonder so many boards are beginning to get a little edgy about where the environmental agenda is headed.

But perhaps the key messages come through 'Transitions' 9 and 10. Transition 9 suggests that companies seeking to build up social capital, including stakeholder trust, will need to involve stakeholders in setting the boundaries of life-cycle assessment and environmental reporting processes alike. Only if stakeholders are turned, in effect, into a new category of customers and consulted right down the line will they believe that the company itself is trustworthy.

This challenge becomes even more urgent now that the sustainability agenda is formally opening up to embrace not only environmental and economic dimensions as, for example, in the concept (developed by the World Business Council on Sustainable Development and others) of eco-efficiency, but also the social and ethical dimensions. This is why we increasingly talk of the 'triple bottom line' of sustainable development. Business people – who are increasingly alert to some of the major market opportunities that the sustainability transition will open up – must increasingly recognize that the challenge now is to help to deliver economic prosperity, environmental quality and social equity simultaneously.

What is interesting, as anyone who regularly reads business magazines like *Business Week* and *Fortune* will already have recognized, is that the language of business is itself changing in advance of the necessary transitions. Given the role of language in facilitating thought, this is important. Among the new concepts joining the business lexicon are:

- value migration (failure to maintain leadership in the personal computer market cost IBM as much as US$70 billion, according to Adrian Slywotsky in *Value Migration*) (Slywotsky, 1996);
- coevolution and business ecosystems (in *The Death of Competition*, James Moore notes that the new business paradigm *'requires thinking in terms of whole systems'* and coevolving with customers, suppliers, competitors and other stakeholders) (Moore, 1996);
- the democratization of strategy creation (for, as Gary Hamel put it in *Competing for the Future*, it is *'imagination, not resources, that is scarce'*) (Hamel and Prahalad, 1994);
- and, yes, the triple bottom line of sustainability (Elkington, 1997).

Put all of this together and what do we have? An impending sustainability transition that will shake established markets and business relationships to their core, triggering massive value migration. Successful companies will have to focus growing attention on the business ecosystems of which they are part, seeking to coevolve with a much wider array of stakeholders – including environmental organizations.

The 'Triple Bottom Line'

When the *Harvard Business Review* turned its spotlight on to the sustainability agenda in 1997, Stuart L Hart noted that: *'Beyond greening lies an enormous challenge – and an enormous opportunity. The challenge is to develop a sustainable global economy: an economy that the planet is capable of supporting indefinitely'* (Hart, 1997). This represents a profound challenge. Although some parts of the developed world may be beginning to turn the corner in terms of ecological recovery, the planet as a whole is still seen to be on an unsustainable course. *'Those who think that sustainability is only a matter of pollution control are missing the bigger picture',* explained Hart, director of the Corporate Environmental Management Program at the University of Michigan.

Even if all the companies in the developed world were to achieve zero emissions by the year 2000, the earth would still be stressed beyond what biologists refer to as its carrying capacity. Increasingly, the scourges of the late 20th century – depleted farmland, fisheries and forests; choking urban pollution; poverty; infectious disease and migration – are spilling over geopolitical borders. The simple fact is this: in meeting our needs, we are destroying the ability of future generations to meet theirs.

And these problems are not simply economic and environmental, either in their origins or nature. Instead, they raise social, ethical and, above all, political issues. The roots of the crisis, Hart concluded, are *'political and social issues that exceed the mandate and capabilities of any corporation'.* But here is the paradox: *'At the same time, corporations are the only organizations with the resources, the technology, the global reach and, ultimately, the motivation to achieve sustainability'.*

There is no question that some of these issues can have – indeed, already have had – a profound impact on the financial bottom line. Think of the companies and industries making or using such products as asbestos, mercury, PCBs, PVC and CFCs and it is clear that the long-term sustainability of major slices of any modern economy is already being called into question.

Worryingly, at least on current trends, things can only get worse. *'It is easy to state the case in the negative,'* as Hart pointed out. *'Faced with impoverished customers, degraded environments, failing political systems and unravelling societies, it will be increasingly difficult for corporations to do business. But,'* he stressed, *'the positive case is even more powerful. The more we learn about the challenges of sustainability, the clearer it is that we are poised at the threshold of a historic moment in which many of the world's industries may be transformed.'*

The level of change implied by the transition to sustainability is extraordinary. As the Worldwatch Institute put it in a recent *State of the World* report:

> *We are only at the beginning of this restructuring. New industries are emerging to re-establish natural balances – based on technologies that can produce heat and light without putting carbon into the atmosphere; on metals made out of the scrap of past buildings and cars; on papers made out of what was once considered wastepaper. Some homes and offices are heated entirely by the sun or from electricity generated by the wind* (Kane, 1996).

But sustainable capitalism will need more than just environment-friendly technologies and, however important these may be, markets that actively promote dematerialization. We will also need to address radically new views of what is meant by social equity, environmental justice and business ethics. This will require a much better understanding not only of financial forms of capital but also of natural and social capital.

Business leaders and executives wanting to grasp the full scale of the challenge confronting their corporations and markets will need to carry out some form of sustainability audit against the emerging requirements and expectations driven by sustainability's 'triple bottom line'. In the spirit of the management dictum that what you cannot measure you are likely to find hard to manage, we should ask whether it is possible to measure progress against the 'triple bottom line'.

The answer is yes, but the metrics are still evolving in most areas – and need to evolve much further if they are to be considered in an integrated way. In the following pages, we briefly focus on the relevant trends in relation to the economic, environmental and social bottom lines. In each case, we headline some of the current thinking on accountability, accounting, performance indicators, auditing, reporting and benchmarking. But we also look at the new concepts and requirements emerging at the interfaces between each of these great agendas, in the 'shear zones'.

The economic bottom line

Let's kick off in the area where business should feel most at home. Given that we are using the 'bottom line' metaphor, however, we need to understand exactly what it means in its traditional usage. A company's bottom line is the profit figure after deduction of costs and depreciation of capital, part of standard accounting practice. In trying to assess a company's conventional bottom line performance, accountants pull together, record and analyse a wide range of numerical data. This approach is often seen as a model for environmental and social accounting, but the challenge can be even tougher in these emerging areas of corporate accountability.[3]

Economic capital

So how should a would-be sustainable corporation assess whether its business operations are economically sustainable? Obviously, a critical first step is to understand what is meant by economic capital. In the simplest terms, equity capital is the total value of a corporation's assets minus its liabilities. In traditional economic theory, capital as a factor of production can come in two main forms: physical capital (including machinery and plant) and financial capital. But as we move into the knowledge economy, the concept is gradually being extended to include such concepts as human capital – a measure of the experience, skills and other knowledge-based assets of the individuals who make up an organization. There is an important difference between the statement of capital in the accountant's balance sheet and the valuation that an investor places on the capital worth of the company. The first looks backward, towards costs and an allowance for depreciation. The second looks forward, to the expected future value of profits which the company is likely to generate. Concepts of sustainability can enter into both measures: depreciation and depletion in the backward-looking balance-sheet measure and deteriorating (or sustaining and growing) earning power in the case of the forward-looking valuation.

Among the questions investors such as fund managers already ask a firm in estimating its forward-looking value are the following: *Are your costs competitive – and likely to remain so? Is the demand for your products and services sustainable?*

Is your rate of innovation likely to be competitive in the longer term?' In short, *'Are your profit margins sustainable?'* (Rubenstein, 1994). In the longer term, too, the concept of economic capital will need to absorb much wider concepts, such as natural capital and social capital, both of which are discussed below.

Economic accountability

So how are companies held accountable? In most countries, companies have an obligation to give an account of their financial performance. In the case of limited companies, directors are accountable to shareholders. This responsibility is partly discharged by the production and – in the case of public companies – publication of an annual report and accounts. An annual general meeting provides shareholders with an opportunity to oversee the presentation of audited accounts, the appointment of directors and auditors, the fixing of their remuneration and recommendations for the payment of dividends. Companies are also responsive to the 'investment community' – pension and other investment fund managers, stockbrokers' analysts, credit agencies and investment banks – whose main concern is the forward-looking value of the company – the sustainability of its bottom line.

Typically, there has been little, if any, overlap between the areas covered by financial analysts in serving the interests of shareholders and the issues of interest to other stakeholders in terms of the environmental and social bottom lines. But one area where we see a growing degree of overlap between a company's economic and environmental performance is 'eco-efficiency'. As policies to protect and sustain the environment in its broadest sense grow in strength, business profits will be affected by their ability to anticipate and respond to those policies efficiently. At the same time, too, there are early signs that, as the sustainability agenda becomes a board-level issue, we will see growing overlaps with the whole corporate governance agenda.

Economic accounting

By the very nature of their work and training, most traditional accountants are shortsighted. Typically, the so-called accounting period is 12 months. Internal accounts are often prepared on a monthly or quarterly basis, with full results produced annually. However, the pressure to perform on a quarterly basis is intensifying worldwide as 'Anglo-Saxon' approaches to investment management and stock valuation spread.

In preparing their accounts, accountants are guided by a range of reasonably well-established concepts. These include the ongoing concern concept (with assets not stated at break-up value, unless there is evidence that the company is no longer viable), the consistency concept (which calls for accounts to be prepared on a consistent basis, allowing accurate comparisons between quarters or years), the prudence concept (accounts should be prepared on a conservative basis, recording income and profits only when they are achieved and making provision for foreseeable losses) and depreciation (with the value of most assets progressively written off over time). Despite 500 years – some people, counting early clay tablets would say at least

5000 years – of evolution in mainstream accounting, there remain huge controversies over how companies account for acquisitions and disposals, record extraordinary and exceptional items, value contingent liabilities, capitalize costs and depreciate their assets. One of the most thought-provoking books of the 1990s was *Accounting for Growth*, in which Terry Smith stripped away the camouflage of 'creative accounting' and helped shareholders, analysts and others to assess how strong a particular company's finances really are (Smith, 1992).

We have tended to see the bottom line as the hardest of realities, representing the unappealable verdict of impartial markets (Caulkin, 1996). But it is increasingly clear that such accounting concepts are human-made conventions that change over space and time. Bottom lines are the product of the institutions and societies in which they have evolved. And, because accounting inevitably involves compromises, the bottom line turns out to be influenced by subjective interpretations, quite apart from 'creative' accounting. So, for example, when Rover was taken over by BMW and subjected to Germany's stricter valuation criteria, a 1995 'profit' of £91 million became a £158 million 'loss' (Caulkin, 1996).

Economic issues and indicators

These are key tools of the trade. Among the items you would expect to see in a company's report and accounts would be a profit and loss account, a balance sheet and a statement of total recognized losses and gains. When it comes to wider economic sustainability, however, there is a surprising lack of generally acceptable indicators. Key considerations here might include the long-term sustainability of a company's costs, of the demand for its products or services, of its pricing and profit margins, of its innovation programmes and of its 'business ecosystem'.

Economic auditing

Once we know what we should be measuring, the next question is how are we doing against the agreed benchmarks. Internal audits aim to ensure that management controls are working effectively. External audits involve an independent examination of, and an expression of an opinion on the financial statements of an organization. The evidence collected draws on such sources as the company's accounting systems and the underlying documentation, its tangible assets and interviews with managers, employees, customers, suppliers and other third parties having some knowledge of the company. Only in exceptional circumstances are the key social and environmental issues fully on the radar screen.

Economic reporting, risk rating and benchmarking

Audits are designed to produce information for internal consumption and to provide reassurance to investors, but there are growing demands for much greater levels of transparency. How far should a company be expected to go? Levels of reporting by companies vary widely, partly reflecting different accounting regimes and partly different opinions on what it is appropriate to report. The information generated by such reports, by management presentations to analysts and credit agencies and available from other sources, is used to evaluate and predict performance and calculate risks. Financial analysts are interested, for example, in working out expectations of share prices, premiums for insurance policies or security for loans. Even today, environmental and social risks are not high on the agenda for most companies, with the result that very few annual reports yet contain a robust section on social and/or environmental performance.

Another use for the reported data is benchmarking, which involves comparisons of processes and products, both within an industry and outside it, to identify and then meet or exceed best practice. Most benchmarking exercises in this area, however, now involve in-depth, in-company research and intercompany comparisons, rather than simply relying on published reports. And it would be rare indeed in today's world for a company to spend much time on other aspects of the 'triple bottom line', unless it happened to be operating in a highly sensitive industry like waste disposal or nuclear power.

Environmental Bottom Line

The social agenda for business probably has a longer history than the environmental agenda. Think of the early controversies around slavery, child labour and working conditions. But, following a flurry of interest in social accounting and auditing in the 1970s, the environmental agenda has tended to attract greater attention. The result, paradoxically, is that many business people these days feel happier being challenged on environmental issues than on social issues. This fact has had a marked impact on the way the sustainability agenda is defined by business.

Natural capital

How can a would-be sustainable corporation work out whether it is environmentally sustainable? Again, a critical first step is to understand what is meant by natural capital. The concept of natural wealth is both complex and still evolving. If you try to account for the natural capital embodied in a forest, for example, it is not simply a question of counting the trees and trying to put a price-tag on the lumber they represent. You have to account for the underlying natural wealth which supports the forest ecosystem, producing – as just one stream of benefits – timber and other commercial products. Wider forest functions that need to be added into the equation include contributions to the regulation of water (in the atmosphere, water table, soils and surface waters) and of greenhouse gases like carbon dioxide and methane (Rubenstein, 1994). And then there are all the flora and fauna, including commercial fisheries, whose health is linked to the health of the forest.

Natural capital can also be thought of as coming in two main forms: 'critical natural capital' and renewable, replaceable or substitutable natural capital. The first form embraces natural capital which is essential to the maintenance of life and ecosystem integrity. The second form is natural capital which can be renewed – for example, through breeding or relocation of sensitive ecosystems – repaired – for example, environmental remediation or desert reclamation – or substituted or replaced – for example, the growing use of human-made substitutes, such as solar panels in place of limited fossil fuels (Bebbington and Gray, 1996). Among the questions business people will need to ask are the following: 'What forms of natural capital are affected by our current operations and will they be affected by our planned activities?' 'Are these forms of natural capital sustainable given these, and other likely pressures?' 'Is the overall level of stress properly understood and likely to be sustainable?' 'Is the "balance of nature" or the "web of life" likely to be affected significantly?'

Environmental accountability

In many countries, companies are held accountable by regulators for aspects of their environmental performance. In the United States, the Toxic Release Inventory requires companies producing more than certain threshold limits of over 600 chemicals to report their emissions. Some countries, like The Netherlands, also back up their regulations with voluntary programmes designed to push companies towards sectorally agreed targets.

Just as often, however, business is held to account by environmentalist and media campaigns, which may bear little relation to regulated or voluntarily agreed targets. And as companies begin to challenge their supply chains, a new dimension of pressure is being introduced. Recently, for example, this author was invited by Volvo to help facilitate their first environmental conference for supplier companies. The company's top management told the 500-plus audience that Volvo had started off by focusing on safety and then added quality. Now, they said, environmental performance was increasingly in the spotlight and suppliers would find environmental aspects being covered in Volvo's regular supplier audits.

Environmental accounting

The field of environmental accounting is relatively embryonic, but is generating a growing literature (Gray, Bebbington and Walters, 1993, and van Dieren, 1995). Among other things, it aims to rebalance the treatment of environmental costs and benefits in conventional accounting practice; separately identify environment-related costs and revenues within the conventional accounting systems; devise new forms of valuation which encourage better management decisions and increased investment in environmental protection and improvement; develop new performance indicators to track progress; and experiment with ways in which sustainability considerations can be assessed and incorporated into mainstream accounting (Grey et al, 1993).

Environmental issues and indicators

The sheer number of potential issues and hence the expanding range of possible environmental risks, is reflected in the potential indicators. These include: legal compliance; provisions for fines, insurance and other legally related costs; landscaping, remediation, decommissioning and abandonment costs; performance against forthcoming laws and standards; public complaints; emergency and contingency plans; life-cycle impacts of products; energy, materials and water usage at production sites; potentially polluting emissions; environmental hazards and risks; waste generation; consumption of critical natural capital, and performance against best-practice standards set by leading customers and by green and ethical investment funds.

The task is being made somewhat easier by the development and publication of international environmental management standards. Globally, there is ISO 14001, developed by the International Standards Organization (ISO) in the wake of the 1992 Earth Summit (Sheldon, 1997). In Europe, there is the Eco-Management and Audit Scheme which takes a step beyond ISO 14001 by requiring companies to produce an annual environmental statement for each registered site. Both of these schemes are voluntary, but the expectation is that market forces will drive them down through value chains in the same way as the Total Quality Management approach has spread.

Environmental auditing

The purpose of audits is to assess the state of a company's management systems and progress against a range of indicators and targets. Environmental audits have a long history in the United States, but really took root in Europe in the 1990s. Indeed, SustainAbility helped to spur the trend with *The Environmental Audit*, an early report published jointly with the World Wide Fund For Nature (WWF), (Elkington, 1990). Typically, such audits focus on the environmental impact of the audited organization, but more particularly they review such areas as compliance against regulations and other standards, the performance of internal management systems, energy usage, waste production and recycling and the use of eco-efficient technologies.

Environmental reporting, risk rating and benchmarking

The environmental reporting and benchmarking trends have been, and very likely will continue to be enormously significant. The first few corporate environmental reports (CERs), or environmental annual reports, were published in 1990, and their number has subsequently mushroomed to many hundreds. Most of these reports have been prepared on a voluntary basis, with the result that the indicators used and the presentation of performance data are highly diverse, complicating comparisons. Most are not yet much help for those trying to assess the risks associated with the operations of given companies.

These problems, however, are slowly being addressed as reporting companies begin to relate their performance against such indicators as emissions or waste arising to the volume or value of production. So, for example, an oil company might link its environmental performance to a barrel of oil produced, while a water utility might compare its performance against sector averages. But few, if any, companies have willingly reported on their performance against the sorts of indicators found at the interface between the environmental and social bottom lines. These include the challenging issue of 'environmental justice', which in recent years has proved a painful thorn in the side of the US chemical industry.

Social Bottom Line

Some in the sustainable development community insist that sustainability has nothing to do with social, ethical or cultural issues. A sustainable world, they argue, could equally well be more equitable or less equitable than today's world. The real issues, they say, relate to resource efficiency. Like King Canute, they are trying to hold back the tide by sheer force of will or prejudice. Their views may be a useful counterbalance to attempts to turn sustainability into a new form of communism, but in the end our progress against the social bottom line is going to be critically important in determining the success or failure of the sustainability transition.

Environmental justice is an area where environmentalists and human rights campaigners, traditionally two separate communities, have been finding common cause. To begin with, the focus was on the question of whether certain groups of deprived Americans were also selectively disadvantaged through exposure to environmental problems. Many companies fought the environmental justice lobby, but subsequent research found that economically and socially deprived groups *are* also more likely to be environmentally disadvantaged. '*On average, 230 times more toxic waste was emitted in neighbourhoods near the plants of the fifty largest industrial toxic polluters than in the communities of the CEOs responsible for the waste,*' noted Stephen Viederman of the US Jessie Smith Foundation (Viederman, 1996). The agenda is now expanding to embrace such issues as the rights of the Ogoni people of Nigeria or the global-warming-related threats to the livelihoods of the peoples of countries like Bangladesh (IISD, 1996).

Social capital

So how should a would-be sustainable corporation think about social capital? One of the best discussions of social capital can be found in Francis Fukuyama's book *Trust: The Social Virtues and the Creation of Prosperity* (Fukuyama, 1995). He says that social capital is '*a capability that arises from the prevalence of trust in a society or in certain parts of it*'. It is a measure of '*the ability of people to work together for common purposes in groups and organizations*'. This ability is likely to be critical to the sustainability transition. It can be developed (or eroded) at every level in a society, from the basic family unit to the major institutions of international government. It depends on the acquisition and maintenance of such virtues as loyalty, honesty and dependability.

The central benefits flow from a lowering of social friction. So, for example, Fukuyama notes that '*if people who have to work together in an enterprise trust one another because they are all operating according to a common set of ethical norms, doing business costs less. Such a society will be better able to innovate organizationally, since the high degree of trust will permit a wide variety of social relationships to emerge'*. In the same way, the degree of trust between a corporation or industry and its external stockholders is likely to be a key factor determining long-term sustainability. Conversely, *'widespread distrust in a society imposes a kind of tax on all forms of economic activity, a tax that high-trust societies do not have to pay'*.

A key assumption in the work SustainAbility has done in recent years is that sustainable development is most likely – and will be achieved at the lowest overall cost to the economy – in those societies where there are the highest levels of trust and other forms of social capital.

Among the questions business people will need to ask are: 'What are the crucial forms of social capital in terms of our ability to become a sustainable corporation?' 'What are the underlying trends in terms of the creation, maintenance or erosion of these forms of capital?' 'What is the role of business in sustaining social capital?' 'To what extent are such concepts as environmental justice and intra- and intergenerational equity likely to change the way in which we define and measure social capital?'

Social accountability

Whatever its critics may choose to believe, business is part of society. Governments try to regulate and otherwise control the social impacts associated with industry and commerce, but history is full of examples where the political agenda was created outside the intertwined worlds of government and business. Whether it was the crusade to end slavery or the various campaigns to end child labour in European and North American factories, business people have long found their freedom of action being increasingly constrained by emerging social movements.

As globalization gathers steam, the interface between the economic and social bottom lines becomes increasingly problematic. Consider the abortive attempt by Germany's Krupp Hoechst to take over its rival Thyssen. This represented an attempt to make the German steel industry more competitive in the face of intensifying international competition. But, faced with mass rallies by tens of thousands of Ruhr steelworkers concerned about the implications for their jobs, protesting about 'casino capitalism' and calling for 'people before profit', Krupp – and its partner banks, Deutsche, Dresdner and Goldman Sachs – backed down (Woodhead, 1997). The decision was widely hailed by German politicians as evidence that the country's social consensus economy works, that 'social responsibility' had prevailed. But there are short-term definitions of responsibility and longer term definitions. The two companies may achieve the necessary efficiencies without redundancies, but if globalization continues Germany may simply have postponed the day of reckoning. In doing so, it may be ensuring that the inevitable economic and social quakes are worse than they need have been.

It is against this background that we see a new stirring of interest in such concepts as social accounting and auditing. The evolution of social auditing, in particular, has more or less paralleled that of environmentalism, but with wilder swings between its 'boom and bust' periods. In the United States, the pioneers in the late 1960s and early 1970s included Ralph Nader and organizations such as the Council on Economic Priorities. In the UK the charge was led by the late George Goyder with books including *The Responsible Company* and, later, by the likes of the Consumers' Association, Social Audit Ltd and Counter Information Services (Goyder, 1973).

The idea was to expand the range of stakeholders involved in industry's deliberations. To begin with, the focus was on consumers and those directly affected by a company's products, but the new, more inclusive models of stakeholder capitalism have progressively drawn the boundaries so as to include an ever-widening range of stakeholders. The social statement produced by The Body Shop as part of its 1995 *Values Report* provides a striking illustration of the trend.

Social accounting

Social accounting aims to assess the impact of an organization or company on people both inside and outside. Issues often covered are community relations, product safety, training and education initiatives, sponsorship, charitable donations of money and time, and the employment of disadvantaged groups. '*Socio-economic sustainability*', says Professor Tom Gladwin of the Leonard N Stern School of Business, New York University, involves '*poverty alleviation, population stabilisation, female empowerment, employment creation, human rights observance and opportunity on a massive scale*' (Gladwin et al, 1995). Like environmental accounting, this is an area where a great deal of further work is needed.

Social issues and indicators

Among the issues for which performance indicators have been developed are animal testing, armaments or other military sales, community relations, employment of minorities, human rights, impacts on indigenous peoples, nuclear power, irresponsible marketing, land rights, oppressive regimes, political contributions, trade union relations, wages and working conditions and women's rights. National surveys in countries like Norway have shown a disturbing trend: the perceived quality of life grew until some time in the late 1960s or early 1970s, but has been falling almost constantly since. In the UK, too, the perceived quality of life deteriorated substantially between 1975 and 1990, according to the country's first index of 'real' social wealth, even though money incomes continued to rise. According to the New Economics Foundation, despite a 230 per cent increase in gross national product (GNP) over the period and a near-doubling in consumer spending, the costs of commuting, pollution, policing and cumulative environmental damage all rose significantly (Viederman, 1996).

Emerging indicators include the Human Development Indicator (HDI) and the Index of Sustainable Development Welfare (ISDW), the second of which adjusts normal measures of welfare by subtracting, for example, the costs of unemployment, commuting, road traffic accidents and all forms of environmental pollution. Increasingly, companies will need to use such measures to assess their net contributions to society's real wealth. The health and safety reports issued by some companies are a step in this direction.

Social auditing

Social auditing is usually considered as covering the non-financial impact of companies. In this sense, environmental audits are often seen as a form of social audit. The purpose of social auditing is for an organization to *assess* its performance in relation to society's requirements and expectations. Like it or not, sustainability auditing and reporting will be all about 'triple bottom line' performance, and social and ethical accounting, auditing and reporting in particular are likely to come up the curve like so many rockets (Elkington and Stibbard, 1997).

It is now over 20 years since pioneering organizations including Britain's Social Audit Ltd started to put companies such as Avon Rubber, Coalite and Tube Investments under the microscope. Then things went horribly quiet for about 15 years. Now it is almost possible to watch the penny dropping in some CEO brains. Reading the forewords of recent CERs, for example, shows that social issues are clearly back on the sustainability agenda.

'*It's now clear that the doubling of world population over the next 40 years will place unprecedented pressure on social and biological systems,*' noted Monsanto chairman and CEO Bob Shapiro in the company's 1995 *Environmental Annual Review*. '*This means that we have to broaden our definition of environmental and ecological responsibility to include working towards "sustainable development" – "sustainable" because countless generations will need to live on this planet, "development" because they shouldn't be condemned to live in poverty.*'

These ideas are echoed on the other side of the Atlantic. According to the 1995 *NatWest Group Environment Report*, Derek Wanless, the giant bank's then chief executive: '*At NatWest we are convinced that the triangle of society, economy and the environment are the determinants of the future and we will continue to take account of that fact in the way we run our businesses.*'

Social reporting, risk rating and benchmarking

But how do we get from words to action? The Danish health care and enzymes company Novo Nordisk, whose environmental reporting has consistently won plaudits internationally, is one of the companies that has been thinking through how to tackle the social reporting agenda. These areas are even more complex and political than the environmental agenda. But such companies are beginning to see *social* auditing as potentially offering a vitally important way of managing complexity.

The problem, says Dr Chris Tuppen, who led British Telecom's (BT) charge in the area of environmental reporting, is that all of this is '*rather like learning a new language*'. And when you are learning a new language, nothing slows things down as fast as different teachers speaking different dialects and disagreeing publicly on how the new language is to be used, and what it means. Unfortunately, this is exactly what has been happening, although a degree of turmoil is to be expected in any area undergoing rapid evolution. More positively, Professor Peter Pruzan of the Copenhagen Business School is fairly optimistic, noting that there is currently '*a strong convergence in terminology, methodology and practice*'.

The financial community remains largely unconvinced of the value of all of this, however. '*Environmental issues are bottom line sensitive*', comments Tessa Tennant of the National Provident Institution, a leading UK pension fund, '*but the bottom line implications of social issues are not clear. It would be difficult to justify why a company should produce a social report, although information on the level of absenteeism and employee turnover rates would be very relevant*'. That said, she acknowledges that '*we are interested is seeing what companies are producing. Social reporting by most companies is quite incoherent. There may be sections on community relations and perhaps charitable giving, but getting comprehensive data on social issues is still very difficult.*'

So how to make things more coherent? Luckily, there is a new Institute of Social and Ethical AccountAbility, dedicated to the task of keeping an eye on the latest trends in social and ethical accounting and auditing worldwide. Welcoming the institute, BT chairman Sir Iain Vallance said that he believed that '*in today's society, companies not only need to operate in an ethical manner, but also need publicly to demonstrate they are doing so*' (Institute of Social and Ethical AccountAbility, 1996).

Indeed, the 134-page Social Statement which formed part of The Body Shop's 1995 *Values Report*, is the report to beat (The Body Shop, 1995). This document figured large in SustainAbility's decision to rank this company as the world leader in sustainability, as they reported in the UNEP report *Engaging Stakeholders*. But if there is one report that might be viewed from a 21st-century perspective as the seed of an impending accounting revolution, it could well be 'Visualizing Intellectual Capital' in *Skandia*, a supplement to the Swedish financial services company's 1994 Annual Report (Skandia, 1994).

Skandia argues that a company's value consists of more than what is traditionally shown in the income statement and balance sheet. Hidden assets, which they see as including employees' competence, computer systems, work processes, trademarks, customer lists and so on are increasingly important in determining the value of a company. Concluding that '*our intellectual capital is at least as important as our financial capital in providing truly sustainable earnings*', Skandia provides some 'out-of-the-box' ideas on how a company's brainpower might be valued.

The company's 1996 report was entitled *The Power of Innovation* and concluded: '*Our responsibility is to turn the future into an asset.*' In trying to assess the contribution that various forms of social capital could make to value creation, Skandia concludes that '*organizational capital is generated by packaging competence and increasing the use of information and communication technology*'. This, the company concludes, '*contributes to long-term sustainability*' (Skandia, 1996). Longer term, could a mutated version of Skandia's approach be used to value the 'triple bottom line' relationships and credibility a company has developed?

Accounting for the 'triple bottom line'

It is clear that progress, or the lack of it, can be measured against a wide range of indicators associated with each of the three bottom lines of sustainability. But the next step will be to tackle this agenda in an integrated way. Key tools will be sustainability accounting, auditing and reporting. In many respects these concepts are still 'black boxes', more talked about in generalities than defined in precise terms, but there is now fascinating work under way in each of these areas.

Ultimately, as Professor Rob Gray and his colleagues put it, sustainability reporting '*must consist of statements about the extent to which corporations are reducing (or increasing) the options available to future generations*' (Gray et al, 1993). This is an extremely complex task, but one which will probably look much easier once we have worked our way through a decade or two of experimentation in sustainability accounting, auditing and reporting. A key area of activity in this respect will be 'full cost pricing', underpinned by new forms of full cost accounting. The idea of full cost pricing is that all the costs associated with a product or service should be internalized, and, as a result, reflected in its price.

Very often we will be unable to say whether or not a particular company or industry is 'sustainable', but we will become increasingly sophisticated in terms of our ability to assess whether or not it is moving in the right direction. The 'triple bottom line' approach clearly complicates matters. It is one thing to suggest, as some do, that a sustainable corporation is one which 'leaves the biosphere no worse off at the end of the accounting period than it was at the beginning', but when we include the social and ethical dimensions of sustainability the range of sustainability-related issues and impacts grows dramatically. This does not mean that we should not try to move in this direction, simply that we should be very careful about over-hyping the likely early benefits or pace of progress. Most medium-term progress, in fact, is likely to be made against the first and second bottom lines (economic and environmental), although the rate of progress in social accounting, auditing and reporting suggests that at least a core set of indicators could be available and in use within a matter of years. Meanwhile, the concept of the 'sustainable corporation' is still evolving.

Our Common Future, the Report of the Brundtland Commission, gave at best anecdotal suggestions on what a sustainable corporation might look like, although we can retain some of the principles applied to countries (Rubenstein, 1994). In the most general terms it would not only conserve and use nature and natural resources for the benefit of present and future generations, but also respect a range of human rights, including the right to a clean, safe environment, in the process. And it would contribute to progress against a range of new human welfare indicators which are currently still in development.

Conclusion

Challenge to business leaders

Many of today's business leaders come from a generation that was acutely aware of markets and, to a degree, of corporate governance issues. But they have tended to be less concerned about values, corporate transparency, product life cycles or really long-term thinking. Growing competitive pressures and the ever-increasing requirements of the financial markets are making an already grim situation worse. Nor are the hitherto neglected issues particularly high on the agenda for many of the business schools training their successors. But things are changing in ways which would hardly be guessed from looking at the business news. And there are good reasons. Too many of today's business leaders continue to lay off thousands of people while taking massive pay rises themselves. Their ability to communicate the future they are driving towards varies between poor and disastrous. Too often, it seems, they also have little understanding of the social consequences of their actions. As Peter Drucker has put it: *'Few top executives can even imagine the hatred, contempt and fury that has been created – not primarily among blue-collar workers who never had an exalted opinion of the "bosses" – but among their middle management and professional people. I don't know what form it will take, but the envy developing from their enormous wealth will cause trouble'* (Lenzner and Johnson, 1997).

These side-effects of markets and human greed have the potential to undermine any embryonic trust society may have in business leaders, and, as a result, the capacity of the business world to make the necessary contributions to the sustainability transition.

Markets depend on new business concepts for their evolution. The 'triple bottom line' of sustainable development will spawn huge numbers of new business concepts, many of them successful. But to get to this point we need vigorously to stir the pot of business thinking, education and training. Thinking and practices which for the most part still remain on the periphery of the business mainstream need to be folded firmly into the emerging heartland of 21st-century business.

It is always tempting, when challenged on the question of how far we have come, to focus on 'green industries' or 'green exports'. There are important growth sectors here, certainly. US exports of environmental technology alone grew by 50 per cent between 1993 and 1995, for example, reaching US$14.5 billion. But the sustainability transition requires a great deal more than clean-up technology and environmental consulting. We also need to turn conventional markets, and conventional business thinking, on their heads. It is clear that this is a mainstream challenge which must impact all sectors of industry and commerce, and we should be responding to it with an appropriate level of imagination and energy. One of the most useful reviews of business progress to date in dealing with a range of 'triple bottom line' issues is *Business as Partners in Development*, a report by Jane Nelson of the Prince of Wales Business Leaders Forum (Nelson, 1996). She argues that:

> *The greatest opportunity for harnessing the power and potential of business as a partner in development lies firstly, in motivating and mobilising the talents and energies of the millions of people who work in the business sector and secondly, in mainstreaming a greater sense of innovation, entrepreneurship, individual responsibility and social and environmental awareness into their daily working lives.*

Nelson also speaks for many when she concludes that:

> *We know what the economic, environmental and social problems are. The need now is to focus on solutions. At one level the solutions are technology, finance and institutions. Ultimately, however, these are just the 'mechanics'. The core issue is about changing attitudes, values and approach. It is about thinking and acting in non-traditional ways. It is about a new way of governance – at both societal and corporate level.*

The values revolution has only just begun to stir the corporate pot, and the effects will intensify as growing numbers of companies respond and require their corporate partners to do likewise. Ethical challenges are surfacing more than they used to. So, for example, France's Lyonnaise des Eaux faced tough ethical scrutiny during its initially hostile bid for the UK's Northumbrian Water (Jack, 1996). The French group had been the subject of allegations about its links with politicians during the 1980s. Instead of ducking the challenge, however, Lyonnaise des Eaux set up three new board subcommittees, one of which took charge of ethical policies. An executive director was made solely responsible for ethical matters, codes of conduct were drafted for both the group and its subsidiaries and wrongdoers were fired.

The group's directors, as the *Financial Times* reported, '*have attempted to embrace a wider range of values, stressing duties not only to shareholders, but to employees, customers and to the community at large – particularly in environmental matters and urban affairs*' (Jack, 1996). Greater transparency, on everything from environmental performance to the stock options payable to the chairman, has been a key part of the new order.

Interestingly, at the time of the changes, 43 per cent of this group's turnover was generated outside France and 30 per cent of its shareholders were foreign, mainly from Switzerland and the Anglo-Saxon countries. In those countries, according to René Coulomb, who took over as group director responsible for ethics, '*people are much more serious*' about corporate governance and ethics issues. In many countries, clearly, corruption is still the name of the game. Refuse to play by these rules and you are not in the game. Over time, however, the transparency revolution will help to spread 'triple bottom line' values around the world.

Markets to match

But transparency and values are of little help when the markets are structured in the wrong way, so that all the pressures force companies to behave in ways which they know are unsustainable. The world's fisheries provide a topical example. The world's media regularly run stories on how overfishing is emptying the seas and oceans of their most important commercial fish stocks (Emerson, 1997). This amounts to a real test-case of sustainability.

Commercial fishing is an example of a massive industry with often conflicting economic, social and ecological objectives. Today's methods of controlling vessel numbers, mesh sizes, quotas for catches and by-catches, and so on are hugely complex, but it does not take the proverbial brain surgeon to know that many of our great fisheries, and the industries and communities that depend upon them, are unsustainable. It is an extraordinary fact, too, that the world's governments currently spend over US$50 billionn a year to subsidize a fishing industry worth US$70 billion. The proverbial Martian would certainly conclude that we are mad.

No one disputes that universal solutions to such problems are unlikely. The most effective remedies will vary from country to country. But those fisheries that have introduced market mechanisms have generally done well. These typically work in the following way. Fishermen acquire a share (quota) of the resource and harvest it in the most desirable manner, generally trying to maximize returns on their investment, subject to whatever legal constraints the government has implemented. Since the fishermen own or lease the quota, each share owner has an incentive to ensure that the stocks are harvested in such a way as to ensure future sustainability. Moreover, in cases where these stocks are transferable – that is, they can be sold on – the system can also favour the most efficient fishermen. So far, of course, such market approaches cannot be used on the high seas, where no individual country has exclusive jurisdiction, so access to the resource cannot be limited. But this is another challenge for the future. How do we put in place (and then effectively police) regimes which help to conserve and rebuild our natural resources? Market approaches will be a key part of the answer, with the added benefit that they can, when properly designed, ensure a healthy degree of self-policing.

In other areas, a wide range of new initiatives are being developed to test sustainable business concepts out in the real world. In the United States, for example, the Management Institute for Environment and Business is working with large corporations and business schools to develop knowledge and methods for integrating environmental and social goals into business planning and decision-making. Through its Sustainable Enterprise Initiative (SEI), it aims to deepen its relationships with a select number of companies as they jointly explore ways to integrate economic, environmental and social objectives through every aspect of their businesses. Three areas on which SEI is focusing are: design for the environment; profit and loss management; and performance indicators and measurement.

Since engineers estimate that 80–90 per cent of the cost of a typical product, and some 80 per cent of its environmental impact, is determined at the design stage, this is the logical place to start. Key focus areas will include designing for optimum material, energy and water efficiency and designing for disassembly, remanufacturing and recycling. The profit and loss (P&L) statement is a basic management tool used by general managers to guide operations, investments and sale projections. Hence, building environmental, health and safety considerations into the P&L is a powerful means of ensuring that a business unit seriously addresses the integration issue. And the axiom that 'you manage what you measure' also holds true in the environmental, health and safety area, and will also inevitably hold true right across the 'triple bottom line' agenda. As a result, there will be a growing demand for sustainability indicators which have been pilot-tested and debugged to the point where they perform well in the real world.

A new focus on value chains

Markets operate through value chains, and companies now need to work with their value chains to deliver sustained 'triple bottom line' performance through the product life cycle. As the centre of gravity of the economy shifts, new industrial sectors suddenly appear under the spotlight. Remanufacturing is one example. In the United States, this unglamorous, little noticed industry which returns discarded durable products to as new condition, involves over 70,000 small to medium-sized companies employing nearly 500,000 people (Lund, 1996). Similar unsuspected opportunities will pop up all over the place as the sustainability transition takes hold, offering new markets for companies large and small.

Or consider the relatively unsexy area of office carpeting. A US commercial flooring company has launched an innovative programme aimed at selling 'functionality' rather than any particular product: a true life-cycle business concept. Working closely with fibre producers, Interface has developed a new product line by remanufacturing products, converting 'old' products into new carpeting or floor tiles. The customer then 'leases' the product – or, to put it another way, leases the comfort the carpeting provides. Once the carpet reaches the end of its useful life, a new floor covering is supplied to replace the old and the 'spent' product is remanufactured and reintroduced into the market after refurbishing, remanufacturing or a fashion facelift (Falkman, 1996).

Value chains can also be used as powerful levers for change in industries which have not yet decided to make the necessary adjustments. When corporate customers get agitated about 'triple bottom line' issues, they can often exert enormous influence on their suppliers. As *Business Week* reports: '*Shin Won Honduras is cleaning up its washrooms.*' The South Korean clothing subcontractor in San Pedro Sula is buying fire extinguishers, installing emergency exits and checking the ventilation – all in the hope of winning business from J C Penney & Co. '*Penney wants so many things,*' says manager Heung-Tae Kim. Meanwhile, other customers, among them Reebok International and Sears Roebuck, have laid down the law: no underage workers (Malkin, 1997).

This is the emerging business reality. '*Thirteen people came to check us from Levi's,*' noted a lawyer for Seolim, a Korean–Honduran joint venture aiming for a contract with the US company. '*You cannot fool these people.*' Campaigning organizations know that they can use the combination of consumer pressure and value chains to bring intense pressure to bear on some industries. At the same time, however, companies are beginning to realize that they must use consumers and value chains to 'pull through' life-cycle improvements in 'triple bottom line' performance, just as brands like Intel and Nutrasweet have been pulled through in areas such as personal computers and soft drinks. In some cases, this will be one more reason for business people and campaigners to work together.

In steering the sustainable business debate into the mainstream, we will also need to recognize that it is often much more effective to get a 20 per cent solution to a particular problem into 20 millon homes than to get an 80 per cent solution into 100,000. Of course, these options may not be mutually exclusive but, as Microsoft has shown, if the basic platform is brought into people's lives it can then be continuously improved. However, only if people use the more sustainable technologies and systems instead of the less sustainable alternatives will the promised advantages be realized.

Innovation and initiatives

Technology is now evolving very fast. Brian Arthur, Citibank Professor at the Santa Fe Institute in New Mexico, carried out some rough-and-ready calculations and estimated that the pace of technological evolution is currently running '*at roughly 10 million times the speed of natural evolution: Hurricane speed. Warp speed*' (Arthur, 1997). Clearly, the sustainability community is going to have to invade the world's research and development laboratories, and fast.

Table 2.2 *The Sustainability Agenda*

Corporate citizenship → *Competition*
Eco-agenda handled by:
Board, strategists, investor relations (mid-1990s)
↑
Process and product designers, marketers (mid-1980s)
↑
Corporate environment managers, planners (early-1970s)
↑
Public relations, legal advisers (late-1960s)

Source: SustainAbility, 1995

Some of the best work will be done outside the giant labs, in 'skunkworks' or in institutes which are currently outside the mainstream. Consider the Rocky Mountain Institute (RMI). In an interesting metaphor, the inventor Paul MacCready once likened Amory Lovins of RMI to a grain of sand in an oyster, the irritating catalyst that causes pearls to form. As RMI itself notes, '*Free and fair markets often produce the best pearls: they just need a little sand to get them started. By putting the right information into the right hands at the right time, the Institute stimulates technologies and techniques that work better and cost less. That those pearls also happen to benefit the environment need not concern the oysters*' (Rocky Mountain Institute, 1996).

The resulting pearls may be 'hypercars' that offer dramatic improvements in fuel efficiency and emissions per kilometre, or they may be garments made in safe factories employing reasonably paid people. But whether we work in traditional labs or in new ones, the aim will be the same: to build sustainability thinking into the entire life cycle, from conception to resurrection. In the process, we must trigger a process of value migration which will dwarf what happened to the car industry when the Organization of Petroleum Exporting Countries (OPEC) oil shocks hit or to the mainframe computer industry when personal computers came along.

So, in summary:

- Reservoirs of public support for key elements of the environmental agenda remain at much higher levels than is currently recognized by the media.
- A 'third wave' of public pressure on business looks likely during the period 1997–2001.
- The agenda for business is opening out into a much broader 'triple bottom line' challenge, which embraces currently accepted areas like eco-efficiency, but also increasingly will include such issues as environmental justice and human rights.
- The economic implications are profound, with an implied restructuring of markets, industries and economies over the next few decades.
- As a result of all of these interlocking factors, the sustainability agenda will increasingly become the preserve of the board, a trend illustrated in Table 2.2.

References

Arthur, W B (1997) 'How Fast is Technology Evolving', *Scientific American*, February 1997

Bebbington, J and Gray, R (1996) 'Sustainable Development and Accounting: Incentives and Disincentives for the Adoption of Sustainability by Transnational Corporations', in *Environmental Accounting and Sustainable Development: The Final Report*, Limperg Institute, The Netherlands

Body Shop, The (1995) 'International Social Statement', *Values Report*, The Body Shop

Caulkin, S (1996) 'When Black Means Red', *The Observer*, 14 April

Elkington, J (1997) *Cannibals With Forks: The Triple Bottom Line of Sustainable Development*, Chapstone Publishing

Elkington, J and Stibbard, H (1997) 'Socially Challenged', *Tomorrow*, vol 7.2 March/April

Elkington, J (1996) 'The Triple Bottom Line for 21st Century Business', Greenpeace Business Conference 'Brent Spar and After', 25 September

Elkington, J (1990) *The Environmental Audit*, SustainAbility and WWF, London

Emerson, W (1997) 'Can Private Property Rescue Fisheries?', *The OECD Observer*, no 205, OECD, Paris, April/May

Falkman, E G (1996) *Sustainable Production and Consumption: A Business Perspective*, World Business Council for Sustainable Development

Fukuyama, F (1995) *Trust: The Social Virtues and the Creation of Prosperity*, Hamish Hamilton London

Gladwin, T N, Kaouse, T and Kennelly, J J (1995) 'Beyond Eco-Efficiency: Towards Socially Sustainable Business', *Sustainable Development*, vol 3, pp 35–43

Goyder, G (1973) *The Responsible Company*, Blackwell, Oxford

Gray, R, Bebbington, J and Walters, D (1993) *Accounting for the Environment*, Paul Chapman Publishing, London

Hamel, G and Prahalad, C K (1994) *Competing for the Future: Breakthrough Strategies for Seizing Control of your Industry and Creating the Markets of Tomorrow*, Harvard Business School Press, Cambridge, MA

Hart, S L (1997) 'Beyond Greening: Strategies for a Sustainable World', *Harvard Business Review*, January/February

IISD (1996) 'Environmental Justice', *Developing Ideas*, issue 3, International Institute for Sustainable Development

Institute of Social and Ethical Accountability (1996) *Lunch Brochure*, Institute of Social and Ethical Accountability

Jack, A (1996) 'The Water Music', *Financial Times*, 2 February

Kane, H (1996) 'Shifting to Sustainable Industries', *State of the World*, Worldwatch Institute

Lenzner, R and Johnson, S S (1997) 'Seeing Things as They Really Are', *Forbes Magazine*, 10 March

Lund, R T (1996) *The Remanufacturing Industry: Hidden Giant*, reviewed in *Business and the Environment*, March

Malkin, E (1997) 'Cleanup at the Maquiladora', *Scientific America*, February

Moore, J F (1996) *The Death of Competition: Leadership and Strategy in the Age of Business Ecosystems*, John Wiley & Sons, Chichester

Nelson, J (1996) *Business as Partners in Development: Creating Wealth for Countries, Companies and Communities*, The Prince of Wales Business Leaders Forum, in collaboration with the World Bank and UNDP

Rocky Mountain Institute (1996) 'Playing the Market: Using Competition to Get Others to Practice What We Preach', *Rocky Mountain Institute Newsletter*, vol 7, no 1, spring 1996

Rubenstein, D B (1994) *Environmental Accounting for the Sustainable Corporation: Strategies and Techniques*, Quorum Books

Sheldon, C (ed) (1997) *ISO 14001 and Beyond: Environmental Management Systems in the Real World*, Greenleaf Publishing, Sheffield

Skandia (1994) 'Visualising Intellectual Capital', in *Skandia*, (supplement to 1994 Annual Report), Skandia, Sweden

Skandia (1996) *Intellectual Capital Development*, Skandia, Sweden

Skandia (1996) *The Power of Innovation* (supplement to 1996 Interim Annual Report), Skandia, Sweden

Slywotsky, A J (1996) *Value Migration: How to Think Several Moves Ahead of the Competition*, Harvard Business School Press, Cambridge, MA

Smith, T (1992) *Accounting for Growth: Stripping the Camouflage from Company Accounts*, Century, London

SustainAbility (1996a) *Engaging Stakeholders, Vol 1: The Benchmark Survey*, United Nations Environment Programme

SustainAbility (1996b) *Engaging Stakeholders Vol 2: The Case Studies*, United Nations Environment Programme

van Dieren, W (ed) (1998) *Taking Nature into Account: Towards a Sustainable National Income*, a report to the Club of Rome, Copernicus, New York

Viederman, S (1996) 'From Prudent Man to Prudent Person: Sustainability and Institutional Investment for the 21st Century', Harvard Seminar on Environmental Values, Cambridge, MA, 12 December 1996

Woodhead, M (1997) 'A Pyrrhic Victory for Germany', *The Sunday Times*, 30 March

Notes

1   The proportions of respondents feeling that things had got worse showed significant increases between 1992 and 1996 in countries as diverse as Switzerland (up 31 points), Chile (up 21 points), Japan (up 28 points), Portugal (up 7 points), Great Britain (up 7 points), Canada (up 7 points) and The Netherlands (up 5 points). People living in developing countries and Southern Europe are by far the most likely to believe that their health has been affected by environmental problems, but citizens of the developed world are also likely to believe it. High-scoring countries include Finland (75 per cent), Germany (69 per cent), the United States (66 per cent), Spain (65 per cent), Australia (63 per cent) and Great Britain (60 per cent). Data from International Research Institutes (IriS), '*More people today than ever before believe their health is being affected by environmental problems*', press release from IriS and the *International Environmental Monitor*, 14 February 1997

2   Globalization is a powerful driver because of the economic, social and environmental fall-out it causes and because of the major uncertainties it introduces into many people's lives

3   Many of the definitions under the 'economic bottom line' section are based on the *Oxford Dictionary of Business*, Oxford University Press, 1996

Section 2

Business Opportunities

Introduction

In Chapter 1, Stuart L Hart refers to the substantial business opportunities that he sees arising from the transition to sustainable development. This section contains a number of pieces that examine the opportunities for so-called 'win–win' initiatives – initiatives which improve a firm's environmental performance whilst enhancing its business performance.

In Chapter 3, Forest Reinhardt cautions against seeing the win–win issue in black-and-white terms, arguing that it is as untrue to claim that there are no win–win opportunities as it is to claim that all environmental initiatives will result in some increase in competitive advantage. Reinhardt outlines five approaches – product differentiation, managing competitors, cost savings, managing environmental risk and redefining markets – that companies can use to integrate the environment into their business thinking and which *may* in certain circumstances yield business benefits. However, like all other business initiatives, environmental initiatives should be assessed on a case-by-case basis and implemented only if it is believed that they will have a positive business impact. As Reinhardt puts it: '*Environmental problems are best analyzed as business problems. Whether companies are attempting to differentiate their products, tie their competitors' hands, reduce internal cost, manage risk, or even reinvent their industry, the basic tasks do not change when the word "environmental" is included in the proposition.*'

In his section on cost savings, Reinhardt refers to what he calls the 'free lunch' debate. Although the saying tells us there's no such thing, there are those who argue that this is most definitely not the case when it comes to improving environmental performance within companies. They argue that many opportunities exist for improving environmental performance not just at zero cost but in ways that can actually save a firm money, sometimes substantial amounts. In short, there are numerous opportunities not just to lunch for free but to be paid to do so. This view has been hotly contested by those who believe that opportunities for cost-saving environmental improvements are very much the exception rather than the rule and that by and large lunch has to be paid for.[1] (Reinhardt himself takes the view that '*the free lunch advocates overstate their case*'.) A number of the key articles in this debate were included in the *Earthscan Reader in Business and the Environment* (Welford and Starkey, 1996) and, given its continued prominence, the remaining chapters in this section are devoted to exploring the debate further.

It is worth pointing out that assessing whether an environmental initiative truly generates a business benefit requires that *all* costs associated with that initiative be accounted for. One such cost is management time. As Reinhardt argues, improvements in environmental performance '*can only be gathered after an investment of management time and that resource is hardly free*'. Frances Cairncross points out that there is always an opportunity cost attached to managerial time: '*If a bright young manager must look for ways to reduce waste output he or she is not available for developing new markets or streamlining production*' (various authors, 1994, p41). Whilst transferring a manager to work on an environmental initiative may result in a process modification that makes the process both cheaper and more environmentally friendly, if the cost savings achieved represent a smaller sum than the manager could have earned for the company carrying out his or her original activity, then we do not have a truly win–win situation. This clearly demonstrates Reinhardt's key point – namely, that firms should be seeking to maximize the efficiency of their entire business system (an ever-changing combination of resources, labour and capital) and that maximizing the efficiency of one part of the system – such as energy or resource use – will not necessarily be compatible with that aim.

Chapter 4 by Ernst von Weizsäcker and Amory and Hunter Lovins (taken from the book *Factor Four*) argues against those who hold that genuine win–win opportunities – those where savings exceed *all* costs – are the exception rather than the rule. Those who hold this view believe that there cannot be numerous win–win opportunities that have laid undiscovered for years because by and large firms spot and snap up all genuine cost-saving opportunities *as soon as they become available*. In other words – and to use that well-worn analogy – firms tend to pick up pretty much immediately any \$10 bills that appear on the ground. However, the authors argue that firms just do not behave in this way and that those who believe they do, do so not on the basis of empirical evidence but on the basis of a mistaken assumption about the validity of the neoclassical economic model of the firm. Neoclassical economics represents the firm as a single, rational decision-maker with perfect knowledge of all technological options and their attendant costs, and in a world populated by such firms, genuine cost-saving measures would of course be put in place at the earliest possible moment rather than lying around unexploited for long periods. The authors argue that those who hold that win–win opportunities seldom exist, do so precisely because they simply assume a priori that the behaviour of firms in the real world resembles the behaviour of the firm in the neoclassical model. Or, as they put it: '*The assumption that the way things already are is indistinguishable from an economic optimum is an unexamined article of faith more than a reasoned conclusion.*'

However, the authors go on to argue that in reality this assumption about perfect knowledge '*is an empirical proposition subject to experimental test*' and that the many examples of the discovery of previously unexploited win–win opportunities they describe in their book constitutes strong empirical evidence that this assumption is false. The numerous examples of firms discovering '*huge and juicy savings ... [that] have lain about untapped for all these decades*' shows that firms are not the omniscient entities described by the neoclassical model and that there are plentiful win–win opportunities in today's economy.

In Chapter 5, Amory and Hunter Lovins, along with Paul Hawken, set out what companies need to do to make the most of such unexploited win–win opportunities. They call their approach 'natural capitalism' which they describe as '*a new approach not only for protecting the biosphere, but also for improving profits and competitiveness'*. According to them '*some very simple changes to the way we run our businesses, built on advanced techniques for making resources more productive, can yield startling benefits both for today's shareholders and for future generations'*. Using numerous case studies and statistics, the authors describe the four major shifts in business practice that constitute the journey to natural capitalism: dramatically increasing the productivity of natural resources; shifting to biologically inspired production models; moving to a solutions-based business model and reinvesting in natural capital.

In their widely cited article in the *Harvard Business Review*, Michael Porter and Class van der Linde (1995) paint a picture of the firm very similar to that set out in the two previous chapters. They too argue that firms are not the all-knowing profit maximizers described by neoclassical economics and that numerous opportunities exist for firms to cost effectively improve their environmental performance. They go on to argue that, given the existence of such opportunities, strict environmental regulation will not necessarily impose a cost on companies – or, put another way, that legislating for *social* benefit will not necessarily impose a *private* cost. Instead they argue that strict environmental regulations, if properly designed, will stimulate firms to discover hitherto hidden win–win opportunities, thus enabling them to meet the tougher standards whilst keeping compliance costs to a minimum or even saving money. Indeed, Porter and van der Linde argue that strict regulation is necessary to bring about this process of discovery in most firms, pointing out the important role of outside pressure in overcoming such barriers as bounded rationality[2] and principal-agent problems:[3]

> *The belief that companies will pick up on profitable opportunities without a regulatory push makes a false assumption about competitive reality – namely that all profitable opportunities for innovation have already been discovered, that all managers have perfect information about them and that organizational incentives are aligned with innovation. In fact, in the real world, managers often have highly incomplete information and limited time and attention. Barriers to change are numerous* (p127).

What has become known as the 'Porter Hypothesis' has sparked a great deal of debate. For instance, in a letter to the *Harvard Business Review* responding to Porter and van der Linde, Paul Portney takes issue with what he sees as the two basic messages in Porter and van der Linde's article.[4]

> *… their take-away messages are two. First, business people are either not bright enough or too distracted by other concerns to recognize the many opportunities to reduce pollution, improve their productivity or production processes and make money all at the same time. Second, Porter and van der Linde suggest that the way to prod managers into taking advantage of these opportunities is a dose of good old fashioned regulation. Call me old fashioned but I don't believe either … It is important not to generalize from success stories. Indeed, the cases we are most likely to hear about are precisely those in which regulation turns out to cost much less than expected, for they are the exceptions. It is hardly news when compliance burdens are significant* (Portney, 1995, p204).

In the final chapter in this section Landis Gabel and Bernard Sinclair-Desagné offer some thoughts on the Porter Hypothesis. An important theme in their chapter is the role of economic models and they argue that to criticize the neoclassical model of the firm as not accurately reflecting reality (see, for example, Chapter 5) is to misunderstand the purpose of economic models.[5] The whole point about models, they argue, is that they are:

> built on simplifying assumptions that are necessarily 'wrong' because they are simplifications. Physical bodies do not move on frictionless surfaces in perfect vacuums, consumers do not always maximize utility and managers do not unfailingly maximize profit. The justification for creating simple models is that if well made, they can afford us insights we miss looking at the chaos of reality itself, they can be extremely powerful in predicting the behaviour of large numbers (of people or molecules) even if not the behaviour of a single unit and thus they can be very useful.

That said, the authors do acknowledge that the neoclassical model as it stands – 'a sole and rational decision-maker who maximizes the firm's value' – is unable to explain the substantial anecdotal evidence for the existence of 'low-hanging fruit' within companies – that is, opportunities to modify processes in such a way that they become both environmentally less damaging and cheaper.[6] In their chapter they therefore attempt to modify the neoclassical model in such a way that it can account for this low-hanging fruit. For them the virtue of this approach is that it avoids the two less palatable options which are *'either to rule such "phenomena" inadmissible to the domain of traditional economics and economists or to throw out their model with its incontrovertible power and value'*. They go on to note that *'the vitriol in the debate of Porter's Hypothesis is surely due in good part to the cost to one side or the other of a choice between these alternatives'*.

Like Porter, the authors recognize that in the real world managers suffer from bounded rationality and, drawing on the insights of behavioural economics, they describe how this bounded rationality results in the development within firms of what they refer to as systems, procedures and routines. The author's therefore modify the neoclassical model of the firm from that of the value-maximizing individual to one which consists of a principal (the head of the firm) and agents (employees) whose actions are governed by such systems, procedures and routines. They point out that:

> Although we might suppose that the firm's systems, procedures and routines are ideal when first devised, it should be clear that with the passage of time, they will become less and less so. Relative prices change, regulatory and other conditions change and the firm's competitive situation changes. If procedures could be changed frequently, marginally and at negligible cost, there should be no problem. Unfortunately, they cannot be. In the short run, they are essentially fixed.

The more out of step the firm's systems and procedures become with its business environment, the greater the constraint on profit maximization. Therefore the task for the principal is to restructure the firm's systems and procedures when the cost of doing so becomes less than the unrealized profit for which they are responsible.

The authors then use their model to investigate the Porter Hypothesis. They argue that to enable the firm to take advantage of cost-saving environmental initiatives, it is necessary for the principal to restructure its systems, procedures and routines in order to get the agents to look for them, noting that '*we are all surely aware from personal experience that we often fail to see what we are not looking for and the same is true of organizations*'. And in the author's model (which retains the feature of perfect knowledge) the principal is able to accurately assess whether such restructuring is cost effective – whether it will cost less than the low-hanging fruit it will reveal. The authors show that if restructuring is not profitable prior to the imposition of regulation, then it is not *logically* possible for win–win opportunities to arise after its imposition. Although available cost savings may exceed compliance costs after the imposition of the regulation, it is a mistake to suppose that this constitutes win–win. Why? Because not *all* costs have been taken into account. The restructuring costs necessary to exploit the cost-saving opportunities must also be accounted for and, if this is done, Gabel and Sinclair-Desagné show that the firm must *necessarily* be worse off than it was prior to the imposition of the regulation.

Although their model explains the existence of low-hanging fruit in a neoclassical firm, the authors acknowledge that it cannot recreate a true win–win situation, and they concede that this is problematic if such opportunities do in fact pervade the economy. The authors doubt that this is the case but argue that even if it is, existing case studies do not show that it is. '*We have seen no example that does an actual accounting for both the compliance costs and the costs of restructuring, including the cost of the managerial attention that it requires. The anecdotes, many though there may be, are simply too brief and unscientific.*'

References

Bannock, G, Baxter, R and Davis, E (1998) *The Penguin Dictionary of Economics*, Penguin Books, London

Golove, W and Eto, J (1996) *Market Barriers to Energy Efficiency; A Critical Reappraisal of the Rationale for Public Policies to Promote Energy Efficiency*, Lawrence Berkeley Laboratory, Berkeley, California

Porter, P and van der Linde, P (1995) 'Green and Competitive: Ending the Stalemate', *Harvard Business Review*, September–October

Portney, P (1995) 'Letter to the Editor', *Harvard Business Review*, November–December

Various authors (1994) 'The Challenge of Going Green', *Harvard Business Review*, July–August

Welford, R and Starkey, R (eds) (1996) *The Earthscan Reader in Business and the Environment*, Earthscan, London

Notes

1   This debate has a long history. According to Golove and Eto (1996) the debate began in the mid-70s and centred around the question of how to explain the so-called 'efficiency gap' in energy use

2   Bounded rationality is a term used to describe and explain the fact that managers operate on the basis of imperfect knowledge. Because there is a finite limit to the amount of information the human brain can deal with, managers, although they may intend to act optimally, in practice they may well not have the cognitive power to be able to do so and hence their rationality is bounded

3   Bannock et al (1998, p329) define this as '*the problem that arises in many spheres of economic activity, when one person, the principal, hires an agent to perform tasks on his behalf but cannot ensure that the agent performs them in exactly the way the principal would like. The efforts of the agent are impossible or expensive to monitor and the incentives of the agent differ from those of the principal.*'

4   See also Porter and van der Linde's response to this letter which follows directly after it. A more extensive exchange of views (which makes for interesting reading) appears in the Fall 1995 edition of the *Journal of Economic Perspectives*. Porter and van der Linde's piece makes a similar case to that of their *Harvard Business Review* article and Portney, along with colleagues Karen Palmer and Wallace Oates, set out in detail the opposing view summarized in Portney's letter

5   For Gabel and Sinclair-Desagné, the model's assumption of perfect knowledge is therefore not, as claimed in Chapter 5, '*an empirical proposition subject to experimental test*'

6   Note that for the authors 'low-hanging fruit' does not mean 'win–win'. Low-hanging fruit exists if a new process is cheaper than the one it replaces. However, although this new process may be cheaper in isolation, from the point of view of the Porter Hypothesis, it is 'win–win' only if the savings from the new process exceed the sum of compliance costs and restructuring costs

3

Bringing the Environment Down to Earth

Forest Reinhardt

The debate on business and the environment has been framed in simplistic yes-or-no terms: 'Does it pay to be green?'. Many business school academics and environmental leaders have answered yes. Yet business people are sceptical – and rightly so, since they instinctively reject such all-or-nothing thinking in other contexts: 'Does it pay to build your next plant in Singapore?' 'To increase your debt-to-equity ratio?' 'To sue your competitors for patent infringement?' The answer, of course, is 'It depends.'. And so it is with environmental questions: the right policy depends on the circumstances confronting the company and the strategy it has chosen.

Much of the writing about business and the environment ignores that basic point. The underlying assumption is that the earth is sick, and that therefore it *ought* to be profitable to find ways to help it return to good health. Promoting such causes and activities as recycling, solar energy and small-scale agriculture should rebound to business' benefit. But this is faulty reasoning. The truth is, environmental problems do not automatically create opportunities to make money. At the same time, the opposite stance – that it never pays for a company to invest in improving its environmental performance – is also incorrect.

That's why managers should look at environmental problems as business issues. They should make environmental investments for the same reasons they make other investments: because they expect them to deliver positive returns or to reduce risks. Managers need to go beyond the question 'Does it pay to be green?' and ask instead: 'Under what circumstances do particular kinds of environmental investments deliver benefits to shareholders?'.

I have identified five approaches that companies can take to integrate the environment into their business thinking. Some companies can distance themselves from their competitors by differentiating products and commanding higher prices for them. Others may be able to 'manage' their competitors by imposing a set of private regulations or by helping to shape the rules written by government officials. Still others may be able to cut costs and help the environment simultaneously. Almost all of them can learn to improve their management of risk and thus reduce the outlays associated with accidents, lawsuits and boycotts. And some companies may even be able to make systemic changes that will redefine competition in their markets.

The appeal of any of the five approaches will depend on the time horizon over which they are evaluated. As with other business problems, the environmental strategy that maximizes short-term cash flow is probably not the one that positions the company optimally for the long run. That's true of all business strategies in general, of course, but it applies especially to the environmental arena because benefits from environmental investments are often realized over long periods.

All of the approaches can help managers to bring the environment down to earth: to think systematically and realistically about the application of traditional business principles to environmental problems. They can enable some companies – those with the right industry structure, competitive position and managerial skills – to deliver increased value to shareholders while making improvements in their environmental performance.

Differentiating Products

The idea behind environmental product differentiation is straightforward: companies create products or employ processes that offer greater environmental benefits or impose smaller environmental costs than those of their competitors. Such efforts may raise the business' costs, but they may also enable it to command higher prices, to capture additional market share, or both.

Consider an example from the textile industry. When textile manufacturers dye cotton or rayon fabric, they immerse the material in a bath containing dyes dissolved in water and then add salt to push the dye out of the solution and into the cloth. Ciba Speciality Chemicals, a Swiss manufacturer of textile dyes, has introduced dyes that fix more readily to the fabric and therefore require less salt.

The new dyes help Ciba's customers in three ways. First, they lower the outlays for salt: textile companies using Ciba's new dyes can reduce their costs for salt by up to 2 per cent of revenues – a significant drop in an industry with razor-thin profit margins. Second, they reduce manufacturers' costs for water treatment. Used bathwater – full of salt and unfixed dye – must be treated before it is released into rivers or streams (even in low-income countries where environmental standards may be relatively lax). Less salt and less unfixed dye mean lower water-treatment costs. Third, the new dyes' higher fixation rates make quality control easier, thus lowering the costs of rework.

Ciba's dyes are the result of years of development in the laboratory. They are protected against imitation by patents and by the unpatentable but complicated chemistry that goes into making them. For those reasons, Ciba can charge more for its dyes and capture some of the value it is creating for customers.

If this sounds like any other story about industrial marketing – add value to your customers' activities and then capture some of that value yourself – it should. Lowering a customer's environmental costs adds value to its operations just as surely as a new machine that enhances labour productivity does.

Three conditions are required for success with environmental product differentiation and Ciba's approach satisfies all three. First, the company has identified customers who are willing to pay more for an environmentally friendly product.

Second, it has been able to communicate its product's environmental benefits credibly. And third, it has been able to protect itself from imitators for long enough to profit on its investment. If any of those three conditions break down, the product differentiation approach will not work. StarKist, the canned tuna subsidiary of H J Heinz, made the discovery when it decided to market dolphin-safe tuna.

Over the years, traditional techniques for catching tuna have caused the death of millions of dolphins. That's because the yellowfin tuna of the eastern tropical Pacific – the staple of tuna canners – often swim underneath schools of dolphin. A boat's crew would locate and chase a school of dolphins, drop a basketlike net under the school when the chase was over and then haul in the tuna and the dolphins, often killing the dolphins in the process. Criticism of this practice, dating from the 1970s, intensified dramatically in 1989, when an environmental activist group released gruesome video footage of dolphins dying in the course of tuna-fishing operations.

In April 1990, StarKist announced that it would sell only tuna from the western Pacific, where tuna do not swim beneath dolphins. But the company ran into problems with all three conditions for success.

First, contrary to the company's survey findings that people would pay significantly more for dolphin-safe tuna, consumers proved unwilling to pay a premium for a cheap source of protein. It didn't help that western Pacific tuna was not yellowfin but skipjack, which people found inferior in taste. Second, although StarKist made known its efforts to protect dolphins, it turned out that the fishing techniques practised in the western Pacific were no environmental bargain. For each dolphin saved in the eastern Pacific, thousands of immature tuna and dozens of sharks, turtles and other marine animals died in the western part of the ocean. Finally, the company had no protection from imitators. Its main competitors, Bumble Bee and Chicken of the Sea, matched StarKist's move almost at once.

It would be easy to take from this story a universally gloomy message about the prospects for environmental product differentiation in consumer markets. Environmental quality, after all, is a public good: everyone gets to enjoy it regardless of who pays for it. From the standpoint of economic self-interest, one might wonder why any individual would be willing to pay for a public good.

But that view is too narrow. People willingly pay for public goods all the time: sometimes in cash, when they contribute to charities and often in time, when they give blood, clean up litter from parks and highways, or rinse their soda bottles for recycling. The trick for companies is to find the right public good, or to offer an imaginative bundle of public and private goods, that will appeal to a targeted market.

For example, sellers of 'designer beef' – meat from cattle that have not been exposed to herbicides or hormones – offer consumers potential health benefits (a private good) in addition to a more environmentally friendly product (a public good). And Patagonia, a California maker of recreational clothing, has developed a loyal base of high-income customers partly because its brand identity includes a commitment to conservation. Patagonia and the beef marketers have not only cleared the willingness-to-pay hurdle but have also found ways to communicate credibly about their products and to protect themselves from imitators through branding.

BOX 3.1 BEWARE OF WHAT YOU KNOW

Treating environmental issues as business problems sounds straightforward, but it is not easy. The following assumptions, all of which are common in business thinking, make it difficult to reframe the issues:

Environmental problems are, first and foremost, matters of social responsibility. While considerations of social responsibility are important, executives who frame environmental problems solely in those terms may overlook the business opportunities and risk that come with such problems. Treating environmental issues like other business issues can lead to more creative problem solving as well as better bottom-line results.

Environmental questions are cause for pessimism. In most arenas, successful managers search for opportunity in adversity and find in complex problems a chance to separate their companies from competitors. So it's striking to hear how passive and pessimistic they sound when talking about environmental issues. They take that approach because they associate it not just with extra costs but also with a loss of control over their own operations. But, as the examples in this article show, it doesn't have to be that way.

Environmental management is a zero-sum game. For every winner in a zero-sum contest, there is a loser. Thus if the environment wins, the company loses and vice versa. That view is prevalent in part because it fits with the widespread perception that environmental problems are political or moral issues. Elections and crusades are win–lose by definition and by design, but businesses don't ordinarily operate that way. Instead, they look for chances to benefit themselves and others simultaneously. Some environmental problems are inevitably win–lose, but it's a mistake to think that none of them can be recast.

Government and environmental groups are the company's adversaries. At times, that view is justified; some regulators and advocates are indeed hostile to business. But government and non-profit organizations will always play a role in environmental management – the only question is what kind of role. Sometimes it makes sense to circle the wagons against an external threat. But sometimes it makes sense for a company to ally itself with regulators or advocates against the competitors.

While managers must remain on guard against undue pessimism and passivity in dealing with environmental problems, they also need to beware of wishful or insular thinking that can intensify their environmental problems and cost their shareholders unnecessary money. These are some of the common pitfalls:

Letting business interests sway your opinion of scientific and economic analysis. Managers shouldn't let the costs of solving an environmental problem affect their judgement of the scientific evidence that identifies the problem. Pulling the wool over your own eyes may convince you that you've averted disaster. In the long run, however, the fact that you can't see it does not mean you're hidden from danger.

Assuming that maintaining the status quo is an option. It is common to use the status quo as a baseline – to look at the way things are today and to think about how you can change things on your own. But some change is likely to occur in any case and managers need to be realistic about their ability to keep things as they are.

BOX 3.1 CONTINUED

Avoiding dissenting opinion. People find it comfortable to talk with those who share their views. Managers need to keep their minds open to the new perspectives and new facts that can come from regular conversations with government officials, environmentalists and others outside their usual circle.

Those problems can all be overcome. If executives bring to environmental decision making the same kind of optimism, opportunism, analytic thinking and openness that they instinctively bring to bear on other business problems, both their companies and the environment will benefit.

Managing Your Competitors

Not all companies will be able to increase their profits through environmental product differentiation. But some may be able to derive environmental and business benefits by working to change the rules of the game so that the playing field tilts in their favour. A company may need to incur higher costs to respond to environmental pressure, but it can still come out ahead if it forces competitors to raise their costs even more.

How can that be done? By joining with similarly positioned companies within an industry to set private standards, or by convincing government to create regulations that favour your product.

The first approach has been particularly successful in the chemical industry. In 1984, after toxic gas escaped from the plant of a Union Carbide subsidiary in Bhopal, India and killed more than 2000 people, the industry's image was tarnished and it faced the threat of punitive government regulation. The industry recognized that it had to act – to forestall government regulations and improve its safety record without incurring unreasonable costs. As a result, the leading companies in the Chemical Manufacturers Association (CMA) created an initiative called Responsible Care and developed a set of private regulations that the association's members adopted in 1988.

The US companies that make up the CMA must comply with six management codes that cover such areas as pollution prevention, process safety and emergency response. If they cannot show good-faith efforts to comply, their membership will be terminated. The initiative has enhanced the association's environmental reputation by producing results. Between 1988 and 1994, for example, US chemical companies reduced their environmental releases of toxic materials by almost 50 per cent. Although other industries were also achieving significant reductions during this period, the chemical industry's reductions were steeper than the national average.

Moreover, the big companies that organized Responsible Care have improved their competitive positions. They spend a lower percentage of their revenues to improve their safety record than smaller competitors in the CMA; similarly, they spend a lower percentage of revenues on the monitoring, reporting and administrative costs of the regulations. Finally, because the association's big companies do a great deal of business abroad, they have been able to persuade the CMA's foreign counterparts to initiate their own private regulatory programmes, even in developing countries where one might expect little enthusiasm for tough environmental policies.

The prerequisites for the success of private regulatory programmes like Responsible Care are the same as those for government regulatory programmes. The regulators must be able to set measurable performance standards, have access to information to verify compliance, and be in a position to enforce their rules. Private programmes also need at least the tacit approval of government; if they are incompatible with other rules such as antitrust laws, the private regulations won't hold up. And private regulations must cover all relevant competitors; it is no use for some companies to tie the hands of others if a third group has the potential to undercut them both.

The commodity chemicals business is better suited than most to private regulatory initiatives. Performance standards are comparatively easy to define because, for example, a perchloroethylene plant in Louisiana looks a lot like a perchloroethylene plant in New Jersey or Italy. Verifying compliance is not a problem either, because the companies constantly sell products to one another and thus can examine competitors' plants. Companies that violate the rules can be ousted from the association, even though it is illegal under antitrust law for the CMA to make compliance with Responsible Care a prerequisite for doing business with association members.

As an alternative to private regulation, companies that want to tie their competitors' hands can work with government regulators. Petrol marketers in California followed this strategy when they helped to design new state rules mandating reformulated petrol to reduce air pollution.

Despite aggressive regulation in California in the 1970s and 1980s, many urban areas in the late 1980s were still not close to meeting national standards for smog and regulators were threatening to require the use of methanol or ethanol fuels, or even to phase out petrol-powered cars altogether. Rather than watch their markets erode, California petrol refiners introduced reformulated petrols containing a compound called methyl tertiary butyl ether (MTBE) and then gained regulatory mandates effectively requiring the use of these fuels.

The California petrol refiners were in a strong position to use environmental regulation for strategic purposes. First, regulators were more than willing to act, given the state's ongoing smog problems. Second, the costs of the regulations would be spread among all of California's automobile drivers, so the chance of organized opposition was slight. Third, competitors from other states would have an even more difficult time selling in the California market. Outsiders already faced steep barriers to entry: pipeline capacity to California was limited and the costs of transporting petrol from, say, Texas were high. California's rules for reformulated petrol erected another barrier and increased the collective pricing power of the California refiners.

Although the overall strategy was sound, the reformulated-petrol policies have not been as effective as hoped. MTBE reduces air pollution, but leaks of the chemical have polluted groundwater. MTBE was found in municipal drinking-water wells in Santa Monica in 1977; it subsequently appeared in groundwater supplies elsewhere in the state. As a result, continued regulatory approval for MTBE use is now in jeopardy. Using environmental regulation strategically, as this example demonstrates, has both benefits and risks.

The approach of forcing rivals to match one's own behaviour is fundamentally different from that of environmental product differentiation. A manager thinking about the choice between the two approaches needs to ask: 'Am I better off if my competitors match my investment or if they don't?' If a company's customers are willing to reward it for improved environmental performance, the company will want to forestall imitation by competitors. But if its customers cannot be induced to pay a premium for an environmentally preferable good, then it may want its competitors to have to match its behaviour.

Saving Costs

A third approach to reconciling shareholder value with environmental management focuses not on competitors but on internal cost reductions. Some organizations are able to cut costs and improve environmental performance simultaneously. For instance, as many travellers know, major hotel chains over the past decade have tried to follow this approach. These companies' tactics include reducing their solid-waste generation and cutting their water and energy use. Many hotels have replaced small bottles of shampoo and lotion with bulk dispensers, saving money and reducing waste. One company saved nearly US$37,000 per year after installing dispensers at a cost of US$91,000. Others use recycled packaging amenities. Inter-Continental Hotels, for instance, reportedly saves US$300,000 per year in this way at its ten properties in the US and Canada. Industrial companies have cut costs and enhanced environmental performance at the same time by redesigning inflexible or wasteful routines. Consider Xerox's efforts. After nearly three decades of market dominance, the company found its traditional markets crowded in the late 1980s with well-funded new entrants. Xerox's market share declined and its margins eroded precipitously.

In 1990, the company's executives responded with a new management initiative – the Environmental Leadership Programme – that eventually included waste reduction efforts, product 'take-back' schemes and design-for-environment initiatives. By the mid-1990s, Xerox's large manufacturing complex in Webster, New York, was sending only 2 per cent of its hazardous waste to landfills. In the early 1990s, even before the programme had a chance to bear much fruit, Xerox's executives were already labelling the programme an unqualified success.

Xerox's story illustrates a common pattern: dramatic cost savings are often found when a company is under tremendous pressure. As long as Xerox was the unchallenged market leader, it could afford to be easy-going about cost savings – and it was. Yet when things got rough, it rose to the occasion with creative initiatives.

Observers of this pattern have wondered whether stringent environmental regulation could put the same kind of pressure on companies that competitive pressure does. They argue that 'free' opportunities to improve environmental performance, in which the direct benefits to the company exceed the costs, are ubiquitous and that stricter regulatory requirements or changes in the tax code could force companies to uncover them. Others disagree. They point out that managers are paid to minimize costs and wonder how adding new regulatory constraints could possibly reduce costs. Economists call this dispute the 'free lunch' debate. The underlying issue is the appropriate level of government regulation.

The free lunch advocates overstate their case. Even low-hanging fruit can only be gathered after an investment of management time and that resource is hardly free. Investment in environmental improvement, like all other investments, are worthwhile only if they deliver value after all the management costs have been included.

Fortunately, though, companies can remain agnostic on the question of whether free opportunities to improve environmental performance are widespread. From a business point of view, even if such opportunities are rare, managers should look for them as long as the search doesn't cost much in terms of their time or other resources.

Managing Environmental Risk

For many business people, environmental management means risk management. Their primary objective is to avoid the costs that are associated with an industrial accident, a consumer boycott or an environmental lawsuit. Fortunately, effective management of the business risk stemming from environmental problems can itself be a source of competitive advantage.

Alberta-Pacific Forest Industries, a Canadian venture of Japanese companies, has discovered that the voluntary provision of environmental goods can cost-effectively reduce long-term business risk. In 1993, the Japanese companies and their Canadian partners negotiated timber-harvesting rights on a vast tract of government-owned aspen and spruce forests in Northern Alberta. The venture planned to build a conventional pulp mill that would use chlorine bleaching. It also planned to run the forests as they had always been run in Western Canada where, as one forestry manager put it, *'There was never a plan for forest management and "forest planning" just meant "fibre extraction"'*.

But the project ran into a buzz saw of opposition from local farmers, the aboriginal residents of Northern Alberta and environmental activists from around the world. Alberta-Pacific went back to the drawing board. It returned with plans for a mill that would keep pollution levels far lower than the government required; it also developed forest management policies that would substantially reduce traditional clear-cutting. In addition, it promised to hold regular public meetings, to communicate explicitly about the environmental impact of the company's operations, to carry out collaborative research with biologists from outside the company and to provide recreational access to the woods.

The costs of the changes were modest and, in return, Alberta-Pacific improved its community relations and achieved more stable long-term costs. The changes are

Box 3.2 Integrating Risk Management

Thinking about environmental improvement as a risk-management strategy, as managers at Alberta-Pacific and Chevron do, leads to the question: 'Should companies try to manage environmental risk in the same ways they manage other business risks?'

In many companies, environmental risk is handled by the department that deals with environmental, health and safety issues, while the management of currency and other financial risk is centralized under the treasurer or the financial officers. Those different parts of the organization usually take widely varying approaches to risk management and may even be ignorant of each other's activities.

There are legitimate reasons for managing environmental risk differently from other risks. Environmental risk is exceedingly difficult to assess quantitatively: no one can really know the probability of an accident occurring at a particular factory. By contrast, it's easier, say, to assess the probability that the dollar will move up or down against the yen – and market instruments exist that allow companies to hedge against such a risk.

Although it makes sense to manage environmental risk differently from other business risks, companies commonly make a serious mistake in the process: they rely too heavily on command-and-control mechanisms – in the form of procedural manuals and rules – to govern line managers' behaviour. That approach impedes flexibility and fails to tap the expertise of individual line managers – the same problems that arise when government imposes command-and-control regulations.

Some reliance on command-and-control policies is probably necessary, but there are other ways to ensure effective risk management and the wise risk manager uses a variety of approaches. A manager's environmental performance can be made a factor in determining the incentive pay. Similarly, it can be considered in regular performance reviews and in the promotion process. And, as information about environmental risks and their effects on a company's finances improves, it will become increasingly possible to handle environmental risk like other risks within the organization. For example, companies often buy insurance against environmental liability at the corporate level but don't charge operating managers for their unit's portion of the premiums. If they did, the managers' incentives would be better aligned with those of the company.

But even the steps outlined here will not change the inherently muddy nature of investments in environmental risk management. You can never be sure, even long after the fact, that investments designed to prevent an accident or a lawsuit were the right ones. That's why even sensible investments in risk management are extremely vulnerable to cost-cutting pressure. At the same time, the inability to determine measurable results can lead to overspending on risk reduction as well as to empire building in the environmental office.

To avoid such problems, senior managers need to ensure that those responsible for environmental risk are clear about the potential benefits of their investments. Managers whose responsibilities include environmental risk should be pushed to articulate why the level and type of investments they have chosen are appropriate. Furthermore, they need to communicate with those responsible for other sorts

---

BOX 3.2 CONTINUED

of business risk so that the approaches are consistent. That doesn't mean the approaches should be identical. Until managers have the same information about environmental risk as they have about currency risk, it will not make sense to manage the two in the same way – and that day is a long way off. But environmental risk management should not be shoved off to one side of the organizational chart and managed as a special case. Integrating it into the company's overall risk-management approaches will yield better decisions in the long run.

---

an insurance policy against regulatory difficulties, sour community relations, business interruptions and related cost shocks. The leaders of Alberta-Pacific have realized that their ability to operate is contingent on society's approval, that the formal property rights they possess are necessary but not sufficient for them to cut timber and run mills and that environmental improvement can make sense as risk management devices.

If Alberta-Pacific had not heeded the concerns of local residents and environmentalists, it likely would have been prohibited from using the land at all. And the stakes were high – the costs of raw materials were on a level one might find in Indonesia or Brazil, but the political and exchange-rate risks were far lower. The venture's small initial investments in the environment allowed it to profit from use of the forest.

Indeed, any company can benefit from an audit of its environmental insurance policies and risk management systems. Is the company buying the right policies? Is it retaining risk when the coverage is overpriced? Is it rewarding managers who reduce risk in their own operations or subsidizing risky behaviour by failing to police it adequately?

Managers at Chevron are trying to answer those questions. They're analysing the relative value of investing more in sprinkler systems, rapid response teams, maintenance and other systems and activities that reduce environmental risk. They are also working to change employees' attitudes towards environmental and safety issues in order to reduce the risk of accidents. Chevron has found that environmental risk can be managed more effectively both by applying more rigorous quantitative analysis and by increasing its emphasis on training and cultural change programmes.

It is not easy to prove that investments in environmental risk management are bearing fruit. And the potential for overinvestment is a concern. But just as it is for more traditional business risks, some investment in environmental risk management is prudent. (For a comparison of environmental and traditional risk management, see Box 3.2.)

Redefining Markets

Some companies are following several approaches at once. In the process, they are rewriting the competitive rules in their markets.

As we've seen, Xerox has been a leader in searching for cost reductions. More dramatically, it has also attempted to redefine its business model. Rather than simply selling office equipment, it retains responsibility for the equipment's disposal and it takes back products from customers when they are superseded by new technology. The machines are then disassembled and remanufactured to incorporate new technology and resold at the same price as new machines. This practice enables Xerox to reduce its overall costs and also to make life difficult for competitors who lack similar capabilities. Customers benefit, too, because they no longer have to worry about the disposal of cumbersome machinery.

Rethinking traditional notions about property rights, as Xerox has done, is a useful way of discovering corporate opportunities to redefine markets based on environmental challenges. Instead of transferring all rights and responsibilities of ownership to their customers, Xerox and other manufacturers are retaining the obligation of disposal in return for control of the product at the end of its useful life.

Because of that initiative, Xerox reportedly saved US$50 million in 1990, its first year. A drop in raw-materials purchases was the most significant component of the cost savings – fewer natural resources were used to make new machines. By 1995, Xerox estimated that it was saving more than several hundred million dollars annually by taking back used machines. Other manufacturers of electronic equipment such as Kodak, IBM, Canon and Hewlett-Packard have undertaken similar initiatives.

Companies like Xerox that combine innovations in property rights and advances in technology may be able to create very strong competitive positions. Monsanto, DuPont, Novartis and others are using this approach to redefine the agricultural industry. Instead of making traditional insecticides for crop pests, the companies transfer genetic material from naturally occurring bacteria to seeds so that the plants themselves become inedible to insects. These new seeds are highly profitable; they avoid the financial and environmental costs of making, transporting and applying insecticides. But the path has not been free of rocks: environmental groups and consumers, especially in Europe, have protested the sale of genetically engineered products in their markets.

Like Xerox, Monsanto also redefined the property rights that go with its product. In order to recover its investment in seed technology Monsanto needs repeat customers every year. But farmers commonly engage in a practice known as 'brown bagging' – they save seeds left over from one year's crop to plant the following year. In return for the right to use the new type of seeds, Monsanto requires farmers to stop brown bagging and to submit to inspections to ensure compliance.

The ambitious strategies that Monsanto and Xerox are following have attracted a great deal of attention. But such strategies can entail significant market, regulatory and scientific risks; they're not for every company, or even for every industry.

The companies that appear to be succeeding are leaders in industries that face intensifying environmental pressure. Those companies have the research capabilities to develop new ways of delivering valuable services to their customers, the staying power to impose their vision of the future on their markets and the resources to manage the inevitable risks. Moreover, by creating an appealing vision of a more profitable and environmentally responsible future, they may be better able to attract and retain the managers, scientists and engineers who will enable them to build on their initial success.

Beyond All-or-Nothing

All-or-nothing arguments have dominated thinking about business and the environment, but it does not have to be that way. Consider how ideas about product quality have changed. At first, conventional wisdom held that improvements in quality had to be purchased at a cost of extra dollars and management attention. Then assertions were made that 'quality is free'; new savings would always pay for investments in improved quality. Now companies have arrived at a more nuanced view. They recognize that improving quality can sometimes lead to cost reductions, but they acknowledge that the right strategy depends on the company and its customers' requirements. It is time for business thinking on the environment to reach a similar middle ground.

As we've seen, environmental problems are best analysed as business problems. Whether companies are attempting to differentiate their products, tie their competitors' hands, reduce internal costs, manage risk or even reinvent their industry, the basic tasks do not change when the word 'environmental' is included in the proposition.

Does all this mean that questions of social responsibility can be safely ignored? Not at all – but they're only one part of the equation. Companies aren't in business to solve the world's problems, not should they be. After all, they have shareholders who want to see a return on their investments. That's why managers need to bring the environment back into the fold of business problems and determine when it *really* pays to be green.

Not all companies can profit from concern about the environment. Others will be able to do so by following one – and in some cases more than one – of the approaches described here. At any rate, a systematic look at environmental management opportunities is worth the time. Imaginative and capable managers who look at the environment as a business issue will find that the universe of possibilities is greater than they ever realized.

4

The Imperfect Market

Ernst Ulrich von Weizsäcker, Amory B Lovins and L Hunter Lovins

The fifty examples of resource efficiency shown in *Factor Four* show that in many cases saving resources could cost less than buying and using them.[1] This reduction in cost represents a theoretical profit opportunity. In an astonishing irony, one of the greatest obstacles to realizing this opportunity – of creating huge new industries in resource efficiency – has been the mind set of the free-market's staunchest proponents.

This is the naïve belief, particularly common among many free-market economists (and the ideologues they instruct), that existing markets are so close to perfection that any shortfall from the ideal is hardly worth examining, let alone taking much trouble over. In this view, if people live in draughty houses, it is because, after careful consideration, they have concluded that draughtproofing is not worthwhile. If a factory pollutes a river, it is because the factory's output benefits society more and abating the pollution would cost more than any harm from the pollution. Or, in short, as Alexander Pope put it, *'Whatever is, is right.'* After all, we live in a market economy driven by consumer preference as expressed through purchasing decisions; and if people wanted to buy something different from the society they've got, surely they'd already have done so.

This fatalistic dogma conveniently relieves us of the need to take any responsibility to change what's wrong, or even to acknowledge that anything is wrong. After all, saith the Market Doctrine, if a thing is worth doing, the market has already done it and conversely, if the market has not done it, then it must not be worth doing. (This is reminiscent of the impregnable circularity with which economists define 'utility': people buy things because those things have utility for them and the way we know the things have utility is that people buy them.) The assumption that the way things already are is indistinguishable from an economic optimum is an unexamined article of faith more than a reasoned conclusion. But it dominates public discourse and public policy and it has consequences. This simple and simply false belief causes more than a million million dollars' worth of resources to be wasted every year.

Economists – of the sort who lie awake at night worrying about whether what works in practice can possibly work in theory – place the burden of proof on others to show that existing arrangements are not optimal and that market failures do exist. After all, the preconditions for a perfect market – perfect information about the future, perfectly accurate price signals, perfect competition, no monopoly or monopsony, no unemployment or underemployment of any resource, no transaction cost, no subsidy and so forth – are so elegant in their glittering austerity that it must be painful to descend to a world less perfect. But gentle ways can be found to remind economists of the distance between their theoretical world and the actual world the rest of us inhabit – the best way being to remind them that they live here, too.

One way, for example, is to ask how much electricity and money it took to run the economist's refrigerator last year. (Correct, indeed any answers to this question are rare. The inability to provide an answer indicates market failure.) One can then ask if the economist knew that a model far (say, twofold) more efficient is on the market (generally a safe bet) with essentially the same price and features. It will often turn out that the economist, like most people, paid very little attention to energy efficiency when buying the refrigerator, or that someone else altogether (such as a landlord), who does not pay the bill to run the refrigerator, bought it. Usually, one will find that the economist's information about the refrigerator market is not merely imperfect, but virtually non-existent. At some point the economist will object, 'I'm too busy living to take the trouble to find out all that'. Precisely: perfect information about available options, available without charge and digestible without transaction cost, does not exist as market theory requires. The same game can then be repeated with lamps, cars, computers or practically any other device the economist uses. In every case, the economist will typically be found to be making economically inefficient decisions because of poor information, the transaction cost of changing, lack of fair access to capital or other well-known barriers.

Transaction cost will deserve special attention. In its broadest sense it embraces the cost of changing laws, standards and norms; the costs of redesigning mass products, their assembly lines and their distribution logistics; the cost of writing off sunk capital; the cost of changing infrastructures, civilized customs (including values), habits of thought and education; the cost of overcoming ignorance on the part of consumers, producers, maintenance staff; the cost of removing bureaucrats who define their jobs in terms of dinosaur procedures; the cost of creating new jobs for workers now employed in the mega-inefficiency machine, and so on.

At some point, even the most theoretically devout economist will usually start to get the idea that market failures do exist and are actually experienced, even by economists. The economist may ask, 'Why should I insulate my roof? I rent my house and although my heating bills would go down, the landlord would own the asset I was paying for. But I haven't been able to get the landlord to insulate the roof because I pay the energy bills'. Just so: the classic 'split incentive' between those who pay and those who benefit. Or the economist may admit that when she invests in saving energy in her own home or business, she wants, like most of the rest of us, to get her money back in just a year or two – about ten times faster than energy companies want to get their money back from the power plants they invest in. This 'payback gap', requiring about tenfold better financial performance from saving than from producing energy, is equivalent to about a tenfold distortion in the energy price – it makes us buy too much energy and too little efficiency.

The reality and importance of market failures boil down to a simple story. Once upon a time, an elderly economist was taking his mannerly little granddaughter for a walk when she spied a £20 note lying in the street. When she asked, 'Please, grandpa,

BOX 4.1 PROFITABLE ENERGY AND WASTE SAVINGS IN A LOUISIANA FACTORY

Ken Nelson is an engineer who formerly directed energy conservation for Dow USA and has long been helping Dow Chemical Company's 2400-worker Louisiana Division save energy and reduce waste. Dow is one of the world's largest and most sophisticated chemical companies – a leader in a cut-throat industry noted for penny-pinching. Dow's competitors would hardly say that Dow is stupid or lazy. Yet Dow has made the astounding discovery that there are US$10,000 and US$100,000 bills lying all over its factory floors, and that the more of them it picks up, the more it finds.

For each of the 12 years between 1981 and 1993, Ken Nelson organized a contest among the Louisiana Division's staff, never going higher than supervisor level, to elicit suggested projects that save energy or reduce waste, that can pay for themselves within a year and (initially) that cost under US$200,000. Submissions were peer-reviewed and the most promising and profitable ones were implemented. After more than a thousand projects, shown by subsequent audit to have saved, on average, within 1 per cent of the predicted amount, some startling findings have emerged:

- In one of the 12 years, the average return on investment for the implemented projects slipped down to only double digits, at 97 per cent per year. But the other 11 years yielded average triple-digit returns and for all 12 years, the confirmed return on the 575 projects that were subsequently audited averaged 204 per cent per year (vs 202 per cent predicted), with total savings of US$110 million per year (Nelson, 1993).
- In recent years, the energy savings being achieved became both larger and more profitable. Far from exhausting the cheapest opportunities, Nelson's contests were expanding the opportunities even faster through institutional learning and better technologies. It is as if each US$100,000 bill picked up exposed a couple of new ones underneath.
- In the first year, 27 projects costing a total of US$1.7 million had an average return on investment (ROI) of 173 per cent and 'many people felt there couldn't be others with such high returns'. They were wrong. The next year, 32 projects costing a total of US$2.2 million averaged a 340 per cent ROI. Learning quickly, Nelson changed the rules to eliminate the US$200,000 limit – with such lucrative opportunities, why stick to the small ones? – and to include projects that would raise manufacturing output. In 1989, 64 projects costing US$7.5 million saved the company US$37 million in the first year and every year thereafter, for a 470 per cent ROI (the best so far). Even in the tenth year of the contest, 1992, nearly 700 projects later, the 109 winning projects averaged a 305 per cent ROI and in 1993, 140 projects averaged a 298 per cent ROI.
- This manna from heaven was being picked up by ordinary workers, for no special reward except the recognition of their peers and not because of the CEO's intervention, but because the CEO didn't know about it and therefore couldn't get in the way. Though meticulously measured and documented, Nelson's additions to Dow's bottom line didn't come from fancy management

---

Box 4.1 Continued

theories, quality circles, empowerment processes, committees or other managerial rituals; rather, they came from a practical shop-floor process that
translated volunteer ingenuity into saved money. That is how markets really
work, when they really work – and yet there are so few Ken Nelsons to make
them work. How many market economists does it take to screw in a compact
fluorescent lightbulb? None (goes the joke) – the free market will do it. But
without a Ken Nelson and without the common sense and hard work of the
workers he organized, the lamp might never get from the shelf into the socket.

It is not easy to estimate the total percentage of energy and waste savings from
Ken Nelson's 12 years of devoted practice, or from similar efforts elsewhere that
offer dozens of examples of quadrupling productivity over the years. You might
expect such commercial success to be quickly emulated everywhere. Oddly, that
does not seem to be happening. Even Dow's own Texas Division was resisting
calls to imitate the adjacent Louisiana Division because it has its own ways of
doing things and, by some accounts, a classic 'not-invented-here' resistance to
innovation. Indeed, after Ken Nelson retired in 1993, his organizing committee
was disbanded in a restructuring, tracking of further progress ceased and it therefore became impossible to evaluate how much progress, if any, continued without
him. This illustrates the difference between demonstrated (let alone theoretical)
potential and actual realization.

---

may I pick that up?' he replied, 'Don't bother, my dear; if it were real, someone
would have picked it up already.'.

The economist's disbelief in windfalls is an empirical proposition subject to
experimental test. Theoretical economists usually suppose that large, well-informed
businesses have little opportunity left to save energy or other resources in a way
that also saves money; any such opportunities, they assume, would long ago have
been found and exploited by profit-maximizing managers. But is this how the world
really works? Scarcely. Consider the experience of Ken Nelson (see Box 4.1).

It is a pity so few market economists have ever met anyone like Ken Nelson. Most
economists will be hard pressed to believe the Dow example (or many more like it).
It is hardly conceivable to them that such huge and juicy savings would have lain
about untapped for all these decades, let alone that exploiting them should turn up
even bigger and juicier ones all the time. This faith that what's worth doing has already been largely done is unfortunately not just an intellectual error; it has the
disastrous practical consequence of preventing people from seeing what can be done.

During the Reagan/Bush era, a distinguished professor of economics at Yale
University, William Nordhaus (1990), published a famous calculation supposedly
proving that for the US to achieve the stabilization of CO_2 emissions set by an international negotiating group in Toronto and considered by most climatologists as
a modest first step on the path to stabilizing the earth's climate, would depress the
GDP (or, as national headlines trumpeted, would 'cost') about US$200 thousand

million per year. This astronomical 'cost' of even a preliminary climate-stabilizing action got stuck in the head of the president's chief of staff, John Sununu and paralysed policy on this issue for the rest of the Reagan and Bush administrations.

Dr Nordhaus' method of calculating the bill was simple:

- First he assumed that more efficient use of energy must not be cost effective at today's prices because if it were, people would have bought it already. Any market distortions were assumed to be immaterial and no £20 notes were presumed waiting to be found. The existence of a huge empirical literature from people who actually sell energy efficiency and who spend their days battling against a formidable array of all too real market failures, was ignored.
- Next, Nordhaus assumed that the only way to induce people to buy more energy efficiency would be to raise the price of energy and that this could be done only through taxation. Since market failures had been assumed not to exist to any material degree, correcting those failures while leaving energy prices the same obviously wasn't an option.
- Next, he assumed that the revenues raised from the energy taxation would be rebated to taxpayers, so they could buy whatever they wanted, rather than invested. (This assumption makes GDP go down; investing the revenue makes GDP go up.)
- Next, he looked up historic studies of how much less energy people buy when its price rises. (This so-called price elasticity of demand is a shorthand way of summarizing how people used to make millions of disparate decisions under conditions that no longer exist and that it is often a goal of energy policy to change as much as possible.)
- Finally, he turned the crank on a computer model to see how much energy taxes would have to be raised in order to depress energy use by an amount corresponding to the Toronto CO_2 targets and how much that level of taxation would decrease total economic activity. The result: about US$200,000 million a year.

Actually, he may have got the number about right but the sign wrong. Meeting the Toronto CO_2 target would not cost but could in principle save the US about US$200 thousand million a year, because saving fuel could cost less than burning it. Puzzled by this potential US$400,000 million-a-year discrepancy, one of us went to Nordhaus' presentation of his thesis at a major scientific conference and asked, in the discussion period, why he hadn't used the vast empirical literature on how much it actually costs to save energy, as measured and documented by thousands of utilities and industries that actually do it every day. His reply: '*I just used an assumption from economic theory. That is an interesting hypothesis you have, Mr Lovins, that a lot of energy-saving measures are cost effective at today's prices but are not being bought because of some sort of market failure. Of course, if you used that assumption instead of mine, then you'd get a very different answer.*' But he refused to take responsibility for how his theoretical assumption had stymied global efforts to approach climatic questions in a least-cost, best-buys-first sequence. In fact, he was so fond of theory that he didn't want to consider the facts and didn't seem to know the difference between the two.

References

Nordhaus, W (1990) 'Count Before You Leap: the Economics of Climate Change', *Economist*, July 1990

Nelson, K E (1993) 'Dow's Energy/WRAP Contest', lecture given at the 1993 Industrial Energy Technology Conference, Houston, 24–25 March

Notes

1   *Factor Four: Doubling Wealth, Halving Resource Use* (Earthscan, 1997) is the book from which this chapter is taken

5

A Road Map for Natural Capitalism

Amory B Lovins, L Hunter Lovins and Paul Hawken

On September 16 1991, a small group of scientists was sealed inside Biosphere II, a glittering 3.2-acre glass and metal dome in Oracle, Arizona. Two years later, when the radical attempt to replicate the earth's main ecosystems in miniature ended, the engineered environment was dying. The gaunt researchers had survived only because fresh air had been pumped in. Despite US$200 million worth of elaborate equipment, Biosphere II had failed to generate breathable air, drinkable water and adequate food for just eight people. Yet Biosphere I, the planet we all inhabit, effortlessly performs those tasks every day for six billion of us.

Disturbingly, Biosphere I is now itself at risk. The earth's ability to sustain life and therefore economic activity, is threatened by the way we extract, process, transport and dispose of a vast flow of resources – some 220 billion tons a year, or more than 20 times the average American's body weight every day. With dangerously narrow focus, our industries look only at the exploitable resources of the earth's ecosystems – its oceans, forests and plains – and not at the larger services that those systems provide for free. Resources and ecosystem services both come from the earth – even from the same biological systems – but they're two different things. Forests, for instance, not only produce the resource of wood fibre but also provide such ecosystem services as water storage, habitat and regulation of the atmosphere and climate. Yet companies that earn income from harvesting the wood fibre resource often do so in ways that damage the forest's ability to carry out its other vital tasks.

Unfortunately, the cost of destroying ecosystem services becomes apparent only when the services start to break down. In China's Yangtze basin in 1998, for example, deforestation triggered flooding that killed 3700 people, dislocated 223 million and inundated 60 million acres of cropland. That US$30 billion disaster forced a logging moratorium and a US$12 billion crash programme of reforestation.

The reason companies (and governments) are so prodigal with ecosystem services is that the value of those services doesn't appear on the business balance sheet. But that is a staggering omission. The economy, after all, is embedded in the environment. Recent calculations published in the journal *Nature* conservatively estimate the value of all the earth's ecosystem services to be at least US$33 trillion a year. That's close to the gross world product and it implies a capitalized book value in the order of half a quadrillion dollars. What's more, for most of these services, there is no known substitute at any price and we can't live without them.

This article puts forward a new approach not only for protecting the biosphere but also for improving profits and competitiveness. Some very simple changes to the way we run our businesses, built on advanced techniques for making resources more productive, can yield startling benefits both for today's shareholders and for future generations.

This approach is called 'natural capitalism' because it's what capitalism might become if its largest category of capital – the 'natural capital' of ecosystem services – were properly valued. The journey to natural capitalism involves four major shifts in business practices, all vitally interlinked:

- *Dramatically increase the productivity of natural resources.* Reducing the wasteful and destructive flow of resources from depletion to pollution represents a major business opportunity. Through fundamental changes in both production design and technology, farsighted companies are developing ways to make natural resources – energy, minerals, water, forests – stretch 5, 10, even 100 times further than they do today. These major resource savings often yield higher profits than small resource savings do – or even saving no resources at all would – and not only pay for themselves over time but in many cases reduce initial capital investments.
- *Shift to biologically inspired production models.* Natural capitalism seeks not merely to reduce waste but to eliminate the very concept of waste. In closed-loop production systems, modelled on nature's designs, every output either is returned harmlessly to the ecosystem as a nutrient, like compost, or becomes an input for manufacturing another product. Such systems can often be designed to eliminate the use of toxic materials, which can hamper nature's ability to reprocess materials.
- *Move to a solutions-based business model.* The business model of traditional manufacturing rests on the sale of goods. In the new model, value is instead delivered as a flow of services – providing illumination, for example, rather than selling light bulbs. This model entails a new perception of value, a move from the acquisition of goods as a measure of affluence to one where wellbeing is measured by the continuous satisfaction of changing expectations for quality, utility and performance. The new relationship aligns the interests of providers and customers in ways that reward them for implementing the first two innovations of natural capitalism – resource productivity and closed-loop manufacturing.
- *Reinvest in natural capital.* Ultimately, business must restore, sustain and expand the planet's ecosystems so that they can produce their vital services and biological resources even more abundantly. Pressures to do so are mounting as human needs expand, the costs engendered by deteriorating ecosystems rise and the environmental awareness of consumers increases. Fortunately, these pressures all create business value.

Natural capitalism is not motivated by a current scarcity of natural resources. Indeed, although many biological resources, like fish, are becoming scarce, most mined resources, such as copper and oil, seem ever more abundant. Indices of average commodity prices are at 28-year lows, thanks partly to powerful extractive technologies which are often subsidized and whose damage to natural capital remains unaccounted for. Yet even despite these artificially low prices, using resources manyfold more productively can now be so profitable that pioneering companies, large and small, have already embarked on the journey towards natural capitalism.[1]

Still the question arises: if large resource savings are available and profitable, why haven't they all been captured already? The answer is simple: scores of common practices in both the private and public sectors systematically reward companies for wasting natural resources and penalize them for boosting resource productivity. For example, most companies expense their consumption of raw materials through the income statement but pass resource-saving investment through the balance sheet. That distortion makes it more tax efficient to waste fuel than to invest in improving fuel efficiency. In short, even though the road seems clear, the compass that companies use to direct their journey is broken. Later we'll look in more detail at some of the obstacles to resource productivity, and at some of the important business opportunities they reveal. But first, let's map the route towards natural capitalism.

Dramatically Increase the Productivity of Natural Resources

In the first stage of a company's journey towards natural capitalism, it strives to wring out the waste of energy, water, materials and other resources throughout its production systems and other operations. There are two main ways companies can do this at a profit. First, they can adopt a fresh approach to design that considers industrial systems as a whole rather than part by part. Second, companies can replace old industrial technologies with new ones, particularly with those based on natural processes and materials.

Implementing whole-system design

Inventor Edwin Land once remarked that '*people who seem to have had a new idea have often simply stopped having an old idea*'. This is particularly true when designing for resource savings. The old idea is one of diminishing returns – the greater the resource saving, the higher the cost. But that old idea is giving way to the new idea that bigger savings can cost less – that saving a large fraction of resources can actually cost less than saving a small fraction of resources. This is the concept of expanding returns and it governs much of the revolutionary thinking behind whole-system design. Lean manufacturing is an example of whole-system thinking that has helped many companies dramatically reduce such forms of waste as lead times, defect rates and inventory. Applying whole-system thinking to the productivity of natural resources can achieve even more.

Consider Interface Corporation, a leading maker of materials for commercial interiors. In its new Shanghai carpet factory, a liquid had to be circulated through a standard pumping loop similar to those used in nearly all industries. A top European company designed the system to use pumps requiring a total of 95 horsepower. But before construction began, Interface's engineer, Jan Schilham, realized that two embarrassingly simple design changes would cut that power requirement to only 7 horsepower – a 92 per cent reduction. His redesigned system cost less to build, involved no new technology and worked better in all respects.

What two design changes achieved this 12-fold saving in pumping power? First, Schilham chose fatter than usual pipes, which create much less friction than thin pipes do and therefore need far less pumping energy. The original designer had chosen thin pipes because, according to the textbook method, the extra cost of fatter ones wouldn't be justified by the pumping energy that they would save. This standard design trade-off optimizes the pipes by themselves but 'pessimizes' the larger system. Schilham optimized the *whole* system by counting not only the higher capital cost of the fatter pipes, but also the *lower* capital cost of the smaller pumping equipment that would be needed. The pumps, motors, motor controls and electrical components could all be much smaller because there'd be less friction to overcome. Capital cost would fall far more for the smaller equipment than it would rise for the fatter pipe. Choosing big pipes and small pumps, rather than small pipes and big pumps, would therefore make the whole system cost less to build, even before counting its future energy savings.

Schilham's second innovation was to reduce the friction even more by making the pipes short and straight rather than long and crooked. He did this by laying out the pipes first, then positioning the various tanks, boilers and other equipment that they connected. Designers normally locate the production equipment in arbitrary positions and then have a pipe fitter connect everything. Awkward placement forces the pipes to make numerous bends that greatly increase friction. The pipe fitters don't mind: they're paid by the hour, they profit from the extra pipes and fittings and they don't pay for the oversized pumps or inflated electricity bills. In addition to reducing those four kinds of costs, Schilham's short, straight pipes were easier to insulate, saving an extra 70 kilowatts of heat loss and repaying the insulation's cost in three months.

This small example has big implications for two reasons. First, pumping is the largest application of motors and motors use three-quarters of all industrial electricity. Second, the lessons are very widely relevant. Interface's pumping loop shows how simple changes in design mentality can yield huge resource savings and returns on investment. This isn't rocket science; often it's just a rediscovery of good Victorian engineering principles that have been lost because of specialization.

Whole-system thinking can help managers find small changes that lead to big savings that are cheap, free or even better than free (because they make the whole system cheaper to build). They can do this because often the right investment in one part of the system can produce multiple benefits throughout the system. For example, companies would gain 18 distinct economic benefits – of which direct energy savings is only one – if they switched from ordinary motors to premium-efficiency motors or from ordinary lighting ballasts (the transformer-like boxes that control fluorescent lamps) to electronic ballasts that automatically dim the lamps to match available daylight. If everyone in the US integrated these and other selected technologies into all existing motor and lighting systems in an optimal way, the nation's US$220 billion-a-year electricity bill would be cut in half. The after-tax return on investing in these changes would in most cases exceed 100 per cent per year.

The profits from saving electricity could be increased even further if companies also incorporated the best off-the-shelf improvements into their building structure and their office, heating, cooling and other equipment. Overall, such changes could cut national electricity consumption by at least 75 per cent and product returns of around 100 per cent a year on the investments made. More important, because workers would be more comfortable, better able to see and less fatigued by noise, their productivity and the quality of their output would rise. Eight recent case studies of people working in well-designed, energy-efficient buildings measured labour productivity gains of 6–16 per cent. Since a typical office pays about 100 times as much for people as it does for energy, this increased productivity in people is worth about 6 to 16 times as much as eliminating the entire energy bill.

Energy-saving, productivity-enhancing improvements can often be achieved at even lower cost by piggybacking them on to the periodic renovations that all buildings and factories need. A recent proposal for reallocating the normal 20-year renovation budget for a standard 200,000 square foot glass-clad office tower near Chicago, Illinois, shows the potential of whole-system design. The proposal suggested replacing the ageing glazing system with a new kind of window that lets in nearly six times more daylight than the old sun-blocking glass units. The new windows would reduce the flow of heat and noise four times better than traditional windows do. So even though the glass costs slightly more, the overall cost of the renovation would be reduced because the windows would let in cool, glare-free daylight that, when combined with more efficient lighting and office equipment, would reduce the need for air-conditioning by 75 per cent. Installing a fourfold more efficient, but fourfold smaller air-conditioning system would cost US$200,000 less than giving the old system its normal 20-year renovation. The US$200,000 saved would pay, in turn, for the extra cost of the new windows and other improvements. This whole-system approach to renovation would not only save 75 per cent of the building's total energy use, it would also greatly improve the building's comfort and marketability. Yet it would cost essentially the same as the normal renovation. There are about 100,000 20-year-old glass office towers in the US that are ripe for such improvement.

Major gains in resource productivity require that the right steps be taken in the right order. Small changes made at the downstream end of a process often create far larger savings further upstream. In almost any industry that uses a pumping system, for example, saving one unit of liquid flow or friction in an exit pipe saves about ten units of fuel, cost and pollution at the power station.

Of course, the original reduction in flow itself can bring direct benefits, which are often the reason that changes are made in the first place. In the 1980s, while California's industry grew by 30 per cent, for example, its water use was cut by 30 per cent, largely to avoid increased waste-water fees. But the resulting reduction in pumping energy (and the roughly tenfold larger saving in power-plant fuel and pollution) delivered bonus savings that were at the time largely unanticipated.

To see how downstream cuts in resource consumption can create huge savings upstream, consider how reducing the use of wood fibre disproportionately reduces the pressure to cut down forests. In round numbers, half of all harvested wood fibre is used for such structural products as lumber; the other half is used for paper and cardboard. In both cases, the biggest leverage comes from reducing the amount of the retail product used. If it takes, for example, three pounds of harvested trees to produce one pound of product, then saving one pound of product will save three pounds of trees, plus all the environmental damage avoided by not having to cut them down in the first place.

The easiest savings come from not using paper that's unwanted or unneeded. In an experiment at its Swiss headquarters, for example, Dow Europe cut office paper flow by about 30 per cent in six weeks simply by discouraging unneeded information. For instance, mailing lists were eliminated and senders of memos got back receipts indicating whether each recipient had wanted the information. Taking those and other small steps, Dow was also able to increase labour productivity by a similar proportion because people could focus on what they really needed to read. Similarly, Danish hearing-aid maker Oticon saved upwards of 30 per cent of its paper as a by-product of redesigning its business processes to produce better decisions faster. Setting the default on office printers and copiers to double-sided mode reduced AT&T's paper costs by about 15 per cent. Recently developed copiers and printers can even strip off old toner and printer ink, permitting each sheet to be reused about ten times.

Further savings can come from using thinner but stronger and more opaque paper and from designing packaging more thoughtfully. In a 30-month effort at reducing such waste, Johnson & Johnson saved 2750 tons of packaging, 1600 tons of paper, US$2.8 million and at least 330 acres of forest annually. The downstream savings in paper use are multiplied by the savings further upstream, as less need for paper products (or less need for fibre to make each product) translates into less raw paper, less raw paper means less pulp and less pulp requires fewer trees to be harvested from the forest. Recycling paper and substituting alternative fibres such as wheat straw will save even more.

Comparable savings can be achieved for the wood fibre used in structural products. Pacific Gas and Electric, for example, sponsored an innovative design developed by Davis Energy Group that used engineered wood products to reduce the amount of wood needed in a stud wall for a typical tract house by more than 70 per cent. These walls were stronger, cheaper, more stable and insulated twice as well. Using them enabled the designers to eliminate heating and cooling equipment in a climate where temperatures range from freezing to 113°F. Eliminating the equipment made the whole house much less expensive both to build and to run while still maintaining high levels of comfort. Taken together, these and many other savings in the paper and construction industries could make our use of wood fibre so much more productive that, in principle, the entire world's present wood fibre needs could probably be met by an intensive tree farm about the size of Iowa.

Adopting innovative technologies

Implementing whole-system design goes hand in hand with introducing alternative, environmentally friendly technologies. Many of these are already available and profitable but not widely known. Some, like the 'designer catalysts' that are transforming the chemical industry, are already runaway successes. Others are still making their way to market, delayed by cultural rather than by economic or technical barriers.

The car industry is particularly ripe for technological change. After a century of development, motorcar technology is showing signs of age. Only 1 per cent of the energy consumed by today's cars is actually used to move the driver: only 15–20 per cent of the power generated by using petrol reaches the wheels (the rest is lost in the engine and drive-train) and 95 per cent of the resulting propulsion moves the car, not the driver. The industry's infrastructure is hugely expensive and inefficient. Its convergent products compete for narrow niches in saturated core markets at commodity-like prices. Car manufacture is capital intensive and product cycles are long. It is profitable in good years but subject to large losses in bad years. Like the typewriter industry just before the advent of personal computers, it is vulnerable to displacement by something completely different.

Enter the Hypercar. Since 1993, when Rocky Mountain Institute placed this vehicle concept in the public domain, several dozen current and potential car manufacturers have committed billions of dollars to its development and commercialization. The hypercar integrates the best existing technologies to reduce the consumption of fuel by as much as 85 per cent and the amount of materials used by up to 90 per cent by introducing four main innovations.

First, making the vehicle out of advanced polymer composites, chiefly carbon fibre, reduces its weight by two-thirds while maintaining crashworthiness. Second, aerodynamic design and better tyres reduce air resistance by as much as 70 per cent and rolling resistance by up to 80 per cent. Together, these innovations save about two-thirds of the fuel. Third, 30–50 per cent of the remaining fuel is saved by using a 'hybrid-electric' drive. In such a system, the wheels are turned by electric motors whose power is made on board by a small engine or turbine, or even more efficiently by a fuel cell. The fuel cell generates electricity directly by chemically combining stored hydrogen with oxygen, producing pure hot water as its only by-product. Interactions between the small, clean, efficient power source and the ultralight, low-drag car body then further reduce the weight, cost and complexity of both. Fourth, much of the traditional hardware – from transmissions and differentials to gauges and certain parts of the suspension – can be replaced by electronics controlled with highly integrated, customizable and upgradable software.

These technologies make it feasible to manufacture pollution-free, high-performance cars, sports utilities, pick-up trucks and vans that get 80–200 miles per gallon (or its energy equivalent in other fuels). These improvements will not require any compromise in quality or utility. Fuel savings will not come from making the vehicles small, sluggish, unsafe or unaffordable, nor will they depend on government fuel taxes, mandates or subsidies. Rather hypercars will succeed for the same reasons that people buy compact discs instead of phonograph records: the CD is a superior product that redefines market expectations. From the manufacturers' perspectives, hypercars will cut cycle times, capital needs, body part counts and assembly effort and space by as much as tenfold. Early adopters will have a huge competitive advantage, which is why dozens of corporations, including most car manufacturers, are now racing to bring hypercar-like products to markets.[2]

In the long term, the hypercar will transform industries other than cars. It will displace about an eighth of the steel market directly and most of the rest eventually, as carbon fibre becomes far cheaper. Hypercars and their cousins could ultimately save as much oil as OPEC now sells. Indeed, oil may well become uncompetitive as a fuel long before it becomes scarce and costly. Similar challenges face the coal and electricity industries because the development of the hypercar is likely to accelerate greatly the commercialization of inexpensive hydrogen fuel cells. These fuel cells will help shift power production from centralized coal-fired and nuclear power stations to networks of decentralized, small-scale generators. In fact, fuel cell-powered hypercars could themselves be part of these networks. They'd be, in effect, 20-kilowatt power plants on wheels. Given that cars are left parked – that is, unused – more than 95 per cent of the time, these hypercars could be plugged into a grid and could then sell back enough electricity to repay as much as half the predicted cost of leasing them. A national hypercar fleet could ultimately have five to ten times the generating capacity of the national electricity grid.

As radical as it sounds, the hypercar is not an isolated case. Similar ideas are emerging in such industries as chemicals, semiconductors, general manufacturing, transportation, water and waste-water treatment, agriculture, forestry, energy, real estate and urban design. For example, the amount of carbon dioxide released for each microchip manufactured can be reduced almost 100-fold through improvements that are now profitable or soon will be.

Some of the most striking developments come from emulating nature's techniques. In her book *Biomimicry*, Janine Benyus points out that spiders convert digested crickets and flies into silk that's as strong as Kevlar without the need for boiling sulphuric acid and high-temperature extruders. Using no furnaces, abalone can convert seawater into an inner shell twice as tough as our best ceramics. Trees turn sunlight, water, soil and air into cellulose, a sugar stronger than nylon but one-fourth as dense. They then bind it into wood, a natural composite with a higher bending strength than concrete, aluminium alloy or steel. We may never become as skilful as spiders, abalone or trees, but smart designers are already realizing that nature's environmentally benign chemistry offers attractive alternatives to industrial brute force.

Whether through better design or through new technologies, reducing waste represents a vast business opportunity. The US economy is not even 10 per cent as energy efficient as the laws of physics allow. Just the energy thrown off as waste heat by US power stations equals the total energy use of Japan. Materials efficiency is even worse: only about 1 per cent of all the materials mobilized to serve America is actually made into products and still in use six months after sale. In every sector, there are opportunities for reducing the amount of resources that go into a production process, the step required to run that process and the amount of pollution generated and the by-products discarded at the end. These all represent avoidable costs and hence profits to be won.

Redesign Production According to Biological Models

In the second stage on the journey to natural capitalism, companies use closed-loop manufacturing to create new products and processes that can totally prevent waste. This, plus more efficient production processes, could cut companies' long-term materials requirements by more than 90 per cent in most sectors.

The central principle of closed-loop manufacturing, as architect Paul Bierman-Lytle of the engineering firm CH2M Hill puts it, is *'waste equals food'*. Every output of manufacturing should be either composted into natural nutrients or remanufactured into technical nutrients – that is, it should be returned to the ecosystem or recycled for further production. Closed-loop productions systems are designed to eliminate any materials that incur disposal costs, especially toxic ones, because the alternative – isolating them to prevent harm to natural systems – tends to be costly and risky. Indeed, meeting Environmental Protection Agency (EPA) and US Occupational Safety and Health Administration (OSHA) standards by eliminating harmful materials often makes a manufacturing process cost less than the hazardous process it replaced. Motorola, for example, formerly used chlorofluorocarbons (CFCs) for cleaning printed circuit boards after soldering. When CFCs were outlawed because they destroy stratospheric ozone, Motorola at first explored such alternatives as orange-peel terpenes. But it turned out to be even cheaper, and to produce a better product, to redesign the whole soldering process so that it needed no cleaning operations or cleaning materials at all.

Closed-loop manufacturing is more than just a theory. The US remanufacturing industry in 1996 reported revenues of US$53 billion – more than consumer-durables manufacturing (appliances; furniture; audio, video, farm and garden equipment). Xerox, whose bottom line has swelled by US$700 million from remanufacturing, expects to save another US$1 billion just by remanufacturing its new, entirely reusable or recyclable line of 'green' photocopiers. What's more, policy-makers in some countries are already taking steps to encourage industry to think along these lines. German law, for example, makes many manufacturers responsible for their products forever and Japan is following suit.

Combining closed-loop manufacturing with resource efficiency is especially powerful. DuPont, for example, gets much of its polyester industrial film back from customers after they use it and recycles it into new film. DuPont also makes its polyester film ever stronger and thinner so it uses less material and costs less to make. Yet because the film performs better, customers are willing to pay more for it. As DuPont chairman Hack Krol noted in 1997, *'Our ability to continually improve the inherent properties* [of our films] *enables this process* [of developing more productive materials, at lower cost and higher profits] *to go on indefinitely.'*

Interface is leading the way to this next frontier of industrial ecology. While its competitors are 'down cycling' nylon-and-PVC-based carpet into less valuable carpet backing, Interface has invented a new floorcovering material called Solenium, which can be completely remanufactured into identical new product. This fundamental innovation emerged from a clean-sheet redesign. Executives at Interface

could sell more carpet of the familiar kind; they asked how
eam product that would best meet their customers' needs while
...hing natural capital.

...u lasts four times longer and uses 40 per cent less material than ordi-
, carpets – an 86 per cent reduction in materials intensity. What's more, Solenium
is free of chlorine and other toxic materials, is virtually stainproof, doesn't grow
mildew, can easily be cleaned with water and offers aesthetic advantages over traditional carpets. It's so superior in every respect that Interface does not market it
as an environmental product, just a better one.

Solenium is only one part of Interface's drive to eliminate every form of waste.
Chairman Ray C Anderson defines waste as '*any measurable input that does not
produce customer value*' and he considers all inputs to be waste until shown otherwise. Between 1994 and 1998, this zero-waste approach led to a systematic treasure
hunt that helped to keep resource inputs constant while revenues rose by US$200
million. Indeed, US$67 million of the revenue increase can be directly attributed
to the company's 60 per cent reduction in landfill waste.

Subsequently, president Charlie Eitel expanded the definition of waste to include all fossil fuel inputs and now many customers are eager to buy products from
the company's recently opened solar-powered carpet factory. Interface's green strategy
has not only won plaudits from environmentalists, it has also proved a remarkably
successful business strategy. Between 1993 and 1998, revenue has more than dou-
bled, profits have more than tripled and the number of employees has increased by
73 per cent.

Change the Business Model

In addition to its drive to eliminate waste, Interface has made a fundamental shift
in its business model – the third stage on the journey towards natural capitalism.
The company has realized that clients want to walk on and look at carpets, but not
necessarily to own them. Traditionally, broadloom carpets in office buildings are
replaced every decade because some portions look worn out. When that happens,
companies suffer the disruption of shutting down their offices and removing their
furniture. Billions of pounds of carpets are removed each year and sent to landfills,
where they will last up to 20,000 years. To escape this unproductive and wasteful
cycle, Interface is transforming itself from a company that sells and fits carpets into
one that provides floorcovering services.

Under the Evergreen Lease, Interface no longer sells carpets but rather leases a
floorcovering service for a monthly fee, accepting responsibility for keeping the
carpet fresh and clean. Monthly inspections detect and replace worn carpet tiles.
Since at most 20 per cent of an area typically shows at least 80 per cent of the wear,
replacing only the worn parts reduces the consumption of carpeting material by
about 80 per cent. It also minimizes the disruption that customers experience –
worn tiles are seldom found under furniture. Finally, for the customer, leasing carpets can provide a tax advantage by turning a capital expenditure into a tax-deductible

expense. The result: the customer gets cheaper and better services that cost the supplier far less to produce. Indeed, the energy saved from not producing a whole new carpet is in itself enough to produce all the carpeting that the new business model requires. Taken together, the 5-fold savings in carpeting material that Interface achieves through the Evergreen Lease and the 7-fold material savings achieved through the use of Solenium deliver a stunning 35-fold reduction in the flow of materials needed to sustain a superior floor-covering service. Remanufacturing and even making carpet initially from renewable materials, can then reduce the extraction of virgin resources essentially to the company's goal of zero.

Interface's shift to a service-leasing business reflects a fundamental change from the basic model of most manufacturing companies, which still look on their businesses as machines for producing and selling products. The more products sold, the better – at least for the company, if not always for the customer or the earth. But any model that wastes natural resources also wastes money. Ultimately, that model will be unable to compete with a service model that emphasizes solving problems and building long-term relationships with customers rather than making and selling products. The shift to what James Womack of the Lean Enterprise Institute calls a 'solutions economy' will almost improve customer value *and* provides bottom lines because it aligns both parties' interests, offering rewards for doing more and better with less.

Interface is not alone. Elevator giant Schindler, for example, prefers leasing vertical transportation services to selling because leasing lets it capture the savings from its lifts' lower energy and maintenance costs. Dow Chemical and Safety-Kleen prefer leasing dissolving services to selling solvents because they can reuse the same solvent scores of times, reducing costs. United Technologies' Carrier division, the world's largest manufacturer of air conditioners, is shifting its mission from selling air-conditioners to leasing comfort. Making its air conditioners more durable and efficient may compromise future equipment sales, but it provides what customers want and will pay for – better comfort at lower cost. But Carrier is going even further. It's starting to team up with other companies to make buildings more efficient so that they need less air-conditioning, or even none at all, to yield the same level of comfort. Carrier will get paid to provide the agreed-upon level of comfort, however it's delivered. Higher profits will come from providing better solutions rather than from selling more equipment. Since comfort with little or no air-conditioning (via better building design) works better and costs less than comfort with copious air-conditioning, Carrier is smart to capture this opportunity itself before its competitors do. As they say at 3M: '*We'd rather eat our* own *lunch, thank you.*'

The shift to a service business model promises benefits not just to participating businesses but to the entire economy as well. Womack points out that by helping customers reduce their need for capital goods such as carpets or lifts and by rewarding suppliers for extending and maximizing asset values rather than for churning them, adoption of the service model will reduce the volatility in the turnover of capital goods that lies at the heart of the business cycle. That would significantly reduce the overall volatility of the world's economy. At present, the producers of capital goods face feast or famine because the buying decisions of households and corporations are extremely sensitive to fluctuating income. But in a continuous flow-of-services economy, those swings would be greatly reduced, bringing a welcome stability to businesses. Excess capacity – another form of waste and source of risk – need no longer be retained for meeting peak demand. The result of adopting the new model would be an economy in which we grow and get richer by using less and become stronger by being leaner and more stable.

Reinvest in Natural Capital

The foundation of textbook capitalism is the prudent reinvestment of earnings in productive capital. Natural capitalists who have raised their resource productivity dramatically, closed their loops and shifted to a solutions-based business model have one key task remaining. They must reinvest in restoring, sustaining and expanding the most important form of capital – their own natural habitat and biological resource base.

This was not always so important. Until recently, business could ignore damage to the ecosystem because it didn't affect production and didn't increase costs. But that situation is changing. In 1998 alone, violent weather displaced 300 million people and caused upwards of US$90 billion worth of damage, representing more weather-related destruction than was reported through the entire decade of the 1980s. The increase in damage is strongly linked to deforestation and climate change, factors that accelerate the frequency and severity of natural disasters and are the consequences of inefficient industrialization. If the flow of services from industrial systems is to be sustained or increased in the future for a growing population, the vital flow of services from living systems will have to be maintained or increased as well. Without reinvestment in natural capital, shortages of ecosystem services are likely to become the limiting factor to prosperity in the next century. When a manufacturer realizes that a supplier of key components is overextended and running behind on deliveries, it takes immediate action lest its own production lines come to a halt. The ecosystem is a supplier of key components for the life of the planet and it is now falling behind on its orders.

Failure to protect and reinvest in natural capital can also hit a company's revenues indirectly. Many companies are discovering that public perceptions of environmental responsibility, or its lack thereof, affect sales. MacMillan Bloedel, targeted by environmental activists as an emblematic clear-cutter and chlorine user, lost 5 per cent of its sales almost overnight when dropped as a UK supplier by Scott Paper and Kimberly-Clark. Numerous case studies show that companies leading the way in implementing changes that help protect the environment tend to gain disproportionate advantage, while companies perceived as irresponsible lose their franchise, their legitimacy and their shirts. Even businesses that claim to be committed to the concept of sustainable development but whose strategy is seen as mistaken, like Monsanto, are encountering stiffening public resistance to their products. Not surprisingly, University of Oregon business professor Michael Russo, along with many other analysts, has found that a strong environmental rating is '*a consistent predictor of profitability*'.

The pioneering corporations that have made reinvestments in natural capital are starting to see some interesting paybacks. The independent power producer AES, for example, has long pursued a policy of planting trees to offset the carbon emissions of its power plants. That ethical stance, once thought quixotic, now looks like a smart investment because a dozen brokers are now starting to create markets in carbon reduction. Similarly, certification by the Forest Stewardship Council of certain sustainably grown and harvested products has given Collins Pine the extra profit margins that enabled its US manufacturing operations to survive brutal competition. Taking an even longer view, Swiss Re and other European reinsurers are seeking to cut their storm-damage losses by pressing for international public policy to protect the climate and by investing in climate-safe technologies that also promise good profits. Yet most companies still do not realize that a vibrant ecological web underpins their survival and their business success. Enriching natural capital is not just a public good – it is vital to every company's longevity.

It turns out that changing industrial processes so that they actually replenish and magnify the stock of natural capital can prove especially profitable because nature does the production; people need just step back and let life flourish. Industries that directly harvest living resources, such as forestry, farming and fishing, offer the most suggestive examples. Here are three:

- Allan Savory of the Center for Holistic Management in Albuquerque, New Mexico, has redesigned cattle ranching to raise the carrying capacity of rangelands which have often been degraded not by overgrazing but by undergrazing and grazing the wrong way. Savory's solution is to keep the cattle moving from place to place, grazing intensively but briefly at each site, so that they mimic the dense but constantly moving herds of native grazing animals that coevolved with grasslands. Thousands of ranchers are estimated to be applying this approach, improving both their range and their profits. This 'management-intensive rotational grazing' method, long standard in New Zealand, yields such clearly superior returns that over 1 per cent of Wisconsin's dairy farms have adopted it in the past few years.
- The California Rice Industry Association has discovered that letting nature's diversity flourish can be more profitable than forcing it to produce a single product. By flooding 150,000–200,000 acres of Sacramento valley rice fields – about 30 per cent of California's rice-growing area – after harvest, farmers are able to create seasonal wetlands that support millions of wildfowl, replenish groundwater, improve fertility and yield other valuable benefits. In addition, the farmers bale and sell the rice straw, whose high silica content – formerly an air-pollution hazard when the straw was burned – adds insect resistance and hence value as a construction material when it is resold instead.
- John Todd of Living Technologies in Burlington, Vermont, has used biological Living Machines – linked tanks of bacteria, algae, plants and other organisms – to turn sewage into clean water. That not only yields cleaner water at a reduced cost, with no toxicity or odour, but it also produces commercially valuable flowers and makes the plant compatible with its residential neighbourhood. A similar

plant at the Ethel M Chocolates factory in Las Vegas, Nevada, not only handles difficult industrial wastes effectively but is showcased in its public tours.

Although such practices are still evolving, the broad lessons they teach are clear. In almost all climates, soils and societies, working with nature is more productive than working against it. Reinvesting in nature allows farmers, fishermen and forest managers to match or exceed the high yields and profits sustained by traditional input-intensive, chemically driven practices. Although much of mainstream business is still headed the other way, the profitability of sustainable, nature-emulating practices is already being proven. In the future, many industries that don't now consider themselves dependent on a biological resource base will become more so as they shift their raw materials and production processes more to biological ones. There is evidence that many business leaders are starting to think this way. The consulting firm Arthur D Little surveyed a group of North American and European business leaders and found that 83 per cent of them already believe that they can derive '*real business value* [from implementing a] *sustainable-development approach to strategy and operations*'.

A Broken Compass?

If the road ahead is this clear, why are so many companies straying or falling by the wayside? We believe the reason is that the instruments companies use to set their targets, measure their performance and hand out rewards are faulty. In other words, the markets are full of distortions and perverse incentives. Of the more than 60 specific forms of misdirection that we have identified,[3] the most obvious involve the ways companies allocate capital and the way governments set policy and impose taxes. Merely correcting these defective practices would uncover huge opportunities for profit.

Consider how companies make purchasing decisions. Decisions to buy small items are typically based on their initial cost rather than their full life-cycle cost, a practice that can add up to major wastage. Distribution transformers that supply electricity to buildings and factories, for example, are a minor item at just US$320 apiece and most companies try to save a quick buck by buying the lowest-price models. Yet, nearly all the nation's electricity must flow through transformers and using the cheaper but less efficient models wastes US$1 billion a year. Such examples are legion. Equipping standard new office-lighting circuits with fatter wire that reduces electrical resistance could generate after-tax returns of 193 per cent a year. Instead, wire as thin as the National Electrical Code permits is usually selected because it costs less up-front. But the code is meant only to prevent fires from overheated wiring, not to save money. Ironically, an electrician who chooses fatter wire – thereby reducing long-term electricity bills – does not get the job. After paying for the extra copper, he's no longer the low bidder.

Some companies do consider more than just the initial price in their purchasing decisions but still don't go far enough. Most of them use a crude payback estimate rather than more accurate metrics like discounted cash flow. A few years ago, the median simple payback these companies were demanding from energy efficiency was 1.9 years. That's equivalent to requiring an after-tax return of around 71 per cent per year – about six times the marginal cost of capital.

Most companies also miss major opportunities by treating their facilities costs as an overhead to be minimized, typically by lashing off engineers, rather than as a profit centre to be optimized, by using those engineers to save resources. Deficient measurement and accounting practices also prevent companies from allocating costs, and waste, with any accuracy. For example, only a few semiconductor plants worldwide regularly and accurately measure how much energy they're using to produce a unit of chilled water or clean air for their clean-room production facilities. That makes it hard for them to improve efficiency. In fact, in an effort to save time, semiconductor makers frequently build new plants as exact copies of previous ones – a design method nicknamed 'infectious repetitis'.

Many executives pay too little attention to saving resources because they are often a small percentage of total costs (energy costs run to about 2 per cent in most industries). But those resource savings drop straight to the bottom line and so represent a far greater percentage of profits. Many executives also think they already 'did' efficiency in the 1970s, when the oil shock forced them to rethink old habits. They're forgetting that with today's far better technologies, it's profitable to start all over again. Malden Mills, the Massachusetts maker of such products as Polartec, was already using 'efficient' metal-halide lamps in the mid-1990s. But a recent warehouse retrofit reduced the energy used for lighting by another 93 per cent, improved visibility and paid for itself in 18 months.

The way people are rewarded often creates perverse incentives. Architects and engineers, for example, are traditionally compensated for what they spend, not for what they save. Even the striking economics of the retrofit design for the Chicago office tower described earlier wasn't incentive enough actually to implement it. The property was controlled by a leasing agent who earned a commission every time she leased space, so she didn't want to wait the few extra months needed to refit the building. Her decision to reject the efficiency-quadrupling renovation proved costly for both her and her client. The building was so uncomfortable and expensive to occupy that it didn't lease, so ultimately the owner had to unload it at a fire-sale price. Moreover, the new owner will for the next 20 years be deprived of the opportunity to save capital cost.

If corporate practices obscure the benefits of natural capitalism, government policy positively undermines it. In nearly every country on the planet, tax laws penalize what we want more of – jobs and income – while subsidizing what we want less of – resource depletion and pollution. In every state but Oregon, regulated utilities are rewarded for selling more energy, water and other resources and penalized for selling less, even if increased production would cost more than improved customer efficiency. In most of America's arid Western states, use-it-or-lose-it water laws encourage inefficient water consumption. Additionally, in many towns, inefficient use of land is enforced through outdated regulations, such as guidelines for ultrawide suburban streets recommended by 1950s civil-defence planners to accommodate the heavy equipment needed to clear up rubble after a nuclear attack.

The costs of these perverse incentives are staggering: US$300 billion in annual energy wasted in the US and US$1 trillion already misallocated to unnecessary air-conditioning equipment and the power supplies to run it (about 40 per cent of the nation's peak electricity load). Across the entire economy, unneeded expenditures to subsidize, encourage and try to remedy inefficiency and damage that should not have occurred in the first place probably account for most, if not all, of the GDP growth of the past two decades. Indeed, according to former World Bank economist Herman Daly and his colleague John Cobb (along with many other analysts), Americans are hardly better off than they were in 1980. But if the US government and private industry could redirect the dollars currently earmarked for remedial costs towards reinvestment in natural and human capital, they could bring about a genuine improvement in the nation's welfare. Companies, too, are finding that wasting resources also means wasting money and people. These intertwined forms of waste have equally intertwined solutions. Firing the unproductive tons, gallons and kilowatt-hours often makes it possible to keep the people, who will have more and better work to do.

Recognizing the Scarcity Shift

In the end, the real trouble with our economic compass is that it points in exactly the wrong direction. Most businesses are behaving as if people were still scarce and nature still abundant – the conditions that helped to fuel the first Industrial Revolution. At that time, people were relatively scarce compared with the present-day population. The rapid mechanization of the textile industries caused explosive economic growth that created labour shortages in the factory and the field. The Industrial Revolution, responding to those shortages and mechanizing one industry after another, made people a hundred times more productive than they had ever been.

The logic of economizing on the scarcest resource, because it limits progress, remains correct. But the pattern of scarcity is shifting: now people aren't scarce but nature is. This shows up first in industries that depend directly on ecological health. Here, production is increasingly constrained by fish rather than by boats and nets, by forests rather than by chain saws, by fertile topsoil rather than by ploughs. Moreover, unlike the traditional factors of industrial production – capital and labour – the biological limiting factors cannot be substituted for one other. In the industrial system, we can easily exchange machinery for labour. But no technology or amount of money can substitute for a stable climate and a productive biosphere. Even proper pricing can't replace the priceless.

Natural capitalism addresses those problems by reintegrating ecological with economic goals. Because it is both necessary and profitable, it will subsume traditional industrialism within a new economy and a new paradigm of production, just as industrialism previously subsumed agrarianism. The companies that first make the changes we have described will have a competitive edge. Those that don't make the effort won't be a problem because ultimately they won't be around. In making that choice, as Henry Ford said, '*Whether you believe you can, or whether you believe you cannot, you're absolutely right.*'

Notes

1   Our book, *Natural Capitalism*, provides hundreds of examples of how companies of almost every type and size, often through modest shifts in business logic and practice, have dramatically improved their bottom lines
2   Non-proprietary details are posted at http://www.hypercar.com
3   Summarized in the report 'Climate: Making Sense *and* Making Money' at http://www.rmi.org/catalog/climate.htm

6

The Firm, its Routines and the Environment

H Landis Gabel and Bernard Sinclair-Desgagné[1]

Introduction: The Neoclassical Paradigm and Environmental Economics

The firm in mainstream economic theory has often been described as a 'black box'. And so it is. This is very extraordinary given that most resources in a modern economic system are employed within firms, with how these resources are used dependent on administrative decisions and not directly on the operation of a market (Coase, 1992, p714).

Most production in modern economies occurs within organizations and this production is regulated only to a limited extent by prices ... These observations make it clear that if economists wish to understand how resources in modern economies are allocated, we must understand what goes on inside organizations (Stiglitz, 1991 p15).

It has been customary among environmental economists working in the neoclassical tradition to assume that the link between environmental regulatory policy and the allocation of environmental resources is very simple. It is a perfectly rational and efficient black box firm which maximizes profits given whatever technological, market and regulatory policy constraints are imposed on it. Because economists have been content to model its behaviour as such, they saw no reason to pierce the corporate veil to understand in microanalytic detail the management processes taking place within the firm.

This tradition has had several predictable results. One was that economists concerned with environmental problems focused their attention almost exclusively on market-based public policy instruments rather than on policies directly related to management systems or procedures. The assumption was that all would be well if the firm's managers just faced the right market signals. This was a natural assumption for the economists to make since their model provided little substance to the firm, per se. The model was more concerned with the web of market relationships between the firm and other economic agents, so economists naturally believed that environmental problems originated in the market. The assumed cause of the problems was reality's violation of some assumption critical to sustaining the efficiency of a perfect market. For example, the neoclassical model assumes that producers and consumers – the decision-makers in the model – bear all the costs of their decisions. If third parties bear some of these costs (called 'external costs'), as is typical with the environment, then the decision-makers' incentives are distorted and the market will fail to function efficiently. The consequence of market failure is typically that natural resources are overused (polluted, to use the pejorative term).

Since environmental problems had to originate in market relationships, it was natural to seek to solve them by fixing the market's flaws. Economists have for several generations proselytized for the cause of public policy instruments that do so. Marketable quotas which establish property rights to environmental resources, effluent taxes which increase inefficiently low prices and legal liability for compensating victims of third-party damage are favoured instruments.

A second predictable result of the neoclassical paradigm was that although managers of business firms foundered trying to cope with the rising tide of environmental pressures, of which public policy was only one, economists had little advice to offer. Proffered advice came from other academics and business consultants,[2] but it lacked the rigour characteristic of economic science. In particular, there has been little rigorous analysis of how a company's environmental strategy is operationalized in the management control systems, formal and informal, that would normally convert strategy into action.

None of this is said to criticize economic analysis of market failure or to detract from economists' well-founded enthusiasm for market-based policy instruments. Rather, it is to suggest that the logic that looks for failed assumptions to the neoclassical model of the market should be carried into the firm. It is inconsistent, albeit convenient, to assume that markets are flawed but that firms are perfect.

Firms are, of course, exceedingly complex institutions and profit maximization is far from trivially easy even in a context of relatively simple and stable market relationships. Instead of a sole and rational decision-maker who maximizes the firm's value, any reasonably large real firm has a titular principal, its chief executive officer, but it is actually 'run' by vast numbers of agents. Many of them have been granted a great deal of autonomy to manage their day-to-day activities. These activities are controlled and coordinated, however, by a set of interrelated management systems and a multitude of procedures for operationalizing the principal's objectives.

The point to emphasize is that the principal does not directly make the decisions that determine the firm's performance. Rather, the process is indirect. Profit maximization must be accomplished, or attempted, via this network of systems and procedures that link the principal's objectives to the agents' actions.[3] We use the term 'management systems' broadly to include formal systems (budgeting, accounting, compensation, etc), corporate policies, standard operating procedures and simpler work routines and habits, many of which may not be explicitly defined.[4] These systems are the grist of consulting firms and the management literature they hold centre stage in business school curricula and they preoccupy practising managers. To assume that the firm simply and perfectly maximizes profit is to assume away one of the main challenges facing its managers.[5]

Thus, the link between environmental regulatory policy and the allocation of environmental resources is complex, multistep and imperfect. Designing regulatory policy is only a first step. That policy may occasionally intervene in the management systems themselves,[6] but more commonly, it alters the external rules to which the corporate principal is subject. These altered rules must then pass through the firm's management systems which may have to change in reaction to the policy initiative. It is these management systems that play a crucial role motivating and controlling the actions of the agents. Finally, the agents must respond to the changed incentives, presumably in consort with the objectives of both the corporate principal and the regulatory policy-maker. Only at this last step is there an environmental impact.

In these steps, there are invariably slips that break the direct link traditionally assumed between the regulator and the environment. Managers have limited attention spans, information flows imperfectly between superiors and subordinates, systems and procedures are often poorly suited to the specifics of any given situation and employees work according to their own objectives. All these imperfections and more cause organizational failures within the firm. The term 'organizational failure' refers to a difference between the action of an agent in the firm we describe and what the traditional model's perfect profit maximizer would do. As we will argue in this paper, organizational failures are systematic; they are in many respects similar to the market failures long studied by environmental economists and there are instruments available to fix them analogous to the instruments available to fix markets.

Because our focus is within the firm, our analysis is not just relevant to the public policy-maker. It should be obvious that organizational failures are relevant to the firm's management as well, since their presence often means that the firm is failing to realize all its potential profits. To give an example which will reappear below, if a firm is systematically losing money by wasting environmental resources, the firm's management would like to know it as much as, and possibly more than, the environmental policy-maker.

The objective of the chapter is to show that organizational failure is pervasive and systematic; that it has important implications for environmental management; and thus that it is an interesting phenomenon for academics, business managers and public policy-makers to understand.

This chapter is organized as follows. In the next section, we will look at the evidence that justifies our interest in entering the firm's doors. The fact that the neoclassical model makes a simple assumption that the firm is just a profit-maximizing black box does not per se justify building a more realistic model of the firm. We must show that the insights to be gained justify the added complexity of the model. The evidence we examine is a claim that has attracted much attention: that strict environmental regulations might be 'win–win', simultaneously reducing the firm's private costs and the external costs it imposes on the environment. We discuss this claim and then present a non-technical model of the phenomenon. Sections follow on corporate and public policy implications. The chapter ends with some conclusions.

Low-hanging Fruit and Win–Win Environmental Regulations

Economists ... tend to regard energy efficiency like the man whose friend draws his attention to a £20 note lying on the pavement. 'It cannot be,' he says. 'If it were, somebody would have picked it up.'

Every scheme to encourage investment in energy efficiency finds plenty of what the industry calls 'low-hanging fruit' – projects with succulent returns. Robert Ayres, in a paper at a conference on energy and the environment in the 21st century at the Massachusetts Institute of Technology last year, drew attention to the 'energy contest' begun in 1981 by the Louisiana division of Dow Chemical, to find capital projects costing less than US$200,000 with payback times of less than a year. In 1982 the contest yielded 27 projects in which Dow invested US$1.7m: the return averaged 173 per cent (a payback period of about seven months). The contest continued, with more projects backed each year. In 1988–95 projects were picked, costing a total of US$21.9m – and yielding an average return of 190 per cent (The Economist, 1991, p15).

Dow's experience is not unique. The 3M company has eliminated 500,000 tons of waste and pollutants and saved US$482 million in so doing and another US$650 million by energy conservation since it started its 3P ('Pollution Prevention Pays') programme in 1975. An 18-month project run by the Centre for the Exploitation of Science and Technology in the UK to test the benefits of waste reduction and clean technologies saved more than £11 million a year for the 11 participating companies, mostly from simple changes in processes which reduced inputs of water, energy and raw materials. The US Environmental Protection Agency has estimated that if the entire country were to switch to energy-efficient lighting, its electricity bill would fall by 10 per cent and air pollution would be reduced by between 4 and 7 per cent. The Agency's Green Lights Program, initiated in 1991, has helped companies switch to energy-efficient lighting to save money and the environment.

There seems to be anecdotal evidence that low-hanging fruit is abundant; so abundant that Michael Porter, in an article published in *Scientific American*, claimed that, '*Strict environmental regulations do not inevitably hinder competitive advantage against foreign rivals, indeed, they often enhance it*' (Porter, 1991, p96). That is, environmental policies are potentially win–win policies. They may prompt firms to see and pick low-hanging fruit – a harvest for both the environment and those firms.

The significance of what has become known as the 'Porter Hypothesis' is that it apparently contradicts the conventional wisdom that environmental regulations shift formerly external costs back on to firms, burdening them relative to competing firms in countries with less strict regulations. Porter has subsequently elaborated on the hypothesis with many more examples (Porter and van der Linde, 1995) and others have taken up his argument, including senior officials in the US government (Gore, 1993).

The precise claim and meaning of the Porter Hypothesis are unclear because Porter's original examples mix several different ways by which the hypothesis could be true. The box that follows attempts to categorize these ways to show that most

Box 6.1 The Porter Hypothesis

'*Strict environmental regulations do not inevitably hinder competitive advantage against foreign rivals, indeed, they often enhance it*' (Porter, 1991, p96). A purposely provocative claim, but how truly provocative is it? What are the different ways in which the Porter Hypothesis might be true?

Enhanced competitiveness of producers of complementary products and services
Environmental regulations can obviously benefit firms that specialize in offering products and services that protect the environment. There is nothing controversial about this. For example, US and EU auto emission standards help their catalytic converter producers and the regulations could stimulate their exports and international competitiveness if other countries were to adopt the same technology later.

Porter has this variant in mind when he gives examples like German exports of air emission abatement equipment and technologies to the US (Germany is the more strict) and US exports of relatively benign pesticides (an industry in which it has strong regulations). The factual accuracy of these examples is questionable, however (Oates et al, 1994) and in any case, they are not really win–win. Private economic costs increase to those ultimately subject to the regulations – that is, US public utilities and farmers respectively in the examples above. There is no implication in these examples that firms are blind to low-hanging fruit.

Relatively enhanced competitiveness of the regulated firms
A second and considerably stronger variant of the Porter Hypothesis is that stringent regulations help the firms subject to them – the polluters themselves. What is the logic?

There are actually two different stories that can be told here. One is that strict domestic environmental regulations will *raise* the costs of domestic firms subject to them (and thus raise consumer prices), but they will raise the costs of foreign competitors subject to the regulations by even more.[23] Domestic firms, forced by strict regulations to be first-movers, may get a relative advantage developing the technology, achieving experience efficiencies, or by some other means.

Porter has this story in mind with his example of the Montreal Protocol ban on CFCs. The ban helped DuPont and ICI in the more profitable CFC-replacement business (Gabel, 1995). But the replacement HCFCs and HFCs are privately more costly to produce, so they sell at a higher price on the market. This is not win–win. The cost burden on the private sector rises even though some firms (and possibly countries) benefit at others' expense. Thus, rational firms would not unilaterally adopt the requirements of the regulation, yet they would benefit if the regulation were forced on all. And, of course, for this to work, it is necessary that analogous environmental regulations be later adopted in other countries. If those other countries were to ignore the environment or pass alternative regulations, then the first mover may be left at a competitive disadvantage.

BOX 6.1 CONTINUED

Absolutely cost reduction for the regulated firms
The final story that can be told is that strict regulations will prompt a firm to find so much low-hanging fruit that it will reduce its private costs at the same time as it will improve its environmental performance. This is the only variant of the Porter Hypothesis that is truly win–win. It is also the only variant that is controversial to economists because it assumes there is widespread organizational failure in the firm.

Another reason why this is controversial is that it seems to imply the paradox that firms should adopt environmental policies voluntarily and unilaterally since it is in their narrow self-interest to do so. Were it not for the stupidity of firms' managers, environmental policy would be self-enforcing. Porter (1991, p96) clearly has this in mind when he concludes that, '... *the "Chicken Little" mind-set that regulation inevitably leads to costs and an adversarial posture toward regulators must be discarded*'.

This is the variant of the Porter Hypothesis that is relevant to the analysis in this chapter.

---

are actually not controversial. The only one that is, at least to mainstream economists, is the case where regulations purportedly reduce the absolute costs of the firms subject to them. It is controversial because it requires the existence of abundant low-hanging fruit, and this in turn contradicts the neoclassical model of the firm in which there is never any low-hanging fruit. This is the case we will address in this paper.

If regulations are to lower the costs of firms subject to them, several conditions must occur. One is that firms are not productively efficient (they are not minimizing private costs), ex ante. They are operating inside a cost-efficiency frontier as diagrammed in Figure 6.1.[7] On the frontier, a policy such as an effluent tax that shifts formerly external costs on to the firm will reduce social costs as the firm reoptimizes to reduce its effluent emissions. This will raise social welfare. But the investment costs to reduce emissions and the amount of tax paid will also raise the firm's private costs and reduce its profit. The firm will move down and to the right along the trade-off curve. Only from a starting point inside the frontier – for example, at a point like 'a', above and to the right of the frontier – is it feasible to reduce simultaneously both social and private costs – that is, to move down and to the left.

Note that because social costs equal the sum of private and external costs, this is not just a cost transfer from society to the firm. If external costs were simply shifted to the firm, social costs would not change. Rather, the expectation is that when external costs are shifted to the firm, the firm will then reoptimize and in so doing reduce social costs.

Another way of illustrating this is via a marginal cost of effluent reduction curve of the sort often shown in basic economics texts.[8] Figure 6.2 illustrates this. The low-hanging fruit metaphor assumes that the firm is operating in the region where

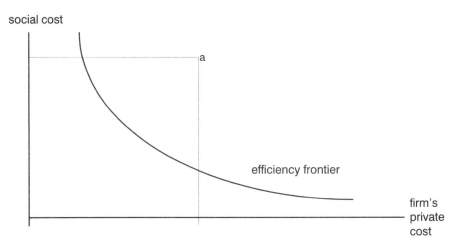

Figure 6.1 *Social and Private Cost Frontier*

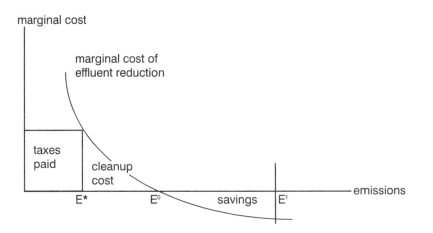

Figure 6.2 *Marginal Cost of Effluent Reduction*

clean-up *saves* it money – that is, to the right of E^0 at a point like E^1. The neoclassical firm, by contrast, would operate at point E^0.

All of this presupposes, in terms we have been using, that there is an organizational failure in the firm.

A second condition concerns the firm's behavioural response. Clearly, the existence of win–win opportunities is not the end of the story. Environmental regulations must prompt the firm to find and exploit opportunities valuable enough to it to offset the internalized costs. In diagrammatic terms, regulations must move the firm down and to the left from point 'a' in Figure 6.1. In Figure 6.2, if we were to take an effluent tax as our example, the savings from the clean-up from E^1 to E^0 must pay for both the costly clean-up from E^0 to the optimum level of effluent E^* and the tax liability incurred at E^*.[9] We can see from the figure that win–win is most likely in situations where the firm is far from the efficiency frontier, where the burden of the tax is light and where the shift to the frontier can be made cheaply.

A final condition that is required for the hypothesis to be interesting to academics and practitioners is that it is systematically true. One can always find some anecdotal examples to contradict the simplifying assumptions of abstract deductive models. Porter apparently believes that it is systematically and commonly true, even though he qualifies his statements with words like 'may', 'often' and 'in many cases'. Yet when he uses Japan and Germany as examples to argue that strict environmental policies have helped promote their productivity growth, he is clearly making a general statement.[10]

Porter's claim has spawned a number of papers, both pro and con, in business and academic journals. Most are anecdotal, some are theoretical and a few are empirical. As examples, Meyer (1992) claims to find some statistical evidence in the US of a positive impact of environmental regulations on economic performance. Palmer and Simpson (1993, p17), by contrast, find Porter's arguments *'based on unlikely assumptions and inconclusive anecdotal evidence'*. Similarly, Oates et al (1994, p21) conclude that *'Until such time as we acquire more compelling evidence on the Porter Hypothesis, it is our sense that it should not be given much credence'*. Walley and Whitehead (1994) believe that win–win opportunities exist but are rare. Jaffe et al (1995, p159) conclude their survey paper saying, *'there is ... little or no evidence supporting the revisionist hypothesis that environmental regulation stimulates innovation and improved international competitiveness'*.

Procedures and Routines in Companies

'People are, at best, rational in terms of what they are aware of and they can be aware of only tiny, disjointed facets of reality' (Simon, 1985, p302).

'The lengthy and crucial processes of generating alternatives, which include all the processes that we ordinarily designate by the word 'design', are left out of the [traditional] account of economic choice' (Simon, 1987, p267).

'The way in which the organization searches for alternatives is substantially a function of the operating rule it has ... The organization uses standard operating procedures and rules of thumb to make and implement choices. In the short run these procedures dominate the decisions made' (Cyert and March, 1992, pp133–134).

We have already argued that the firm can be imagined as a principal who is linked to his or her agents by a network of systems, procedures and routines. These systems, procedures and routines are key features of any organization. Cyert and March (1992) identified several types of procedures: task performing, record keeping, information handling and planning. A critical function these procedures perform is to economize on our time and attention span, the limits to which are assumed away in traditional neoclassical modelling.

Because neoclassical economists assumed away these limits, company systems and procedures never had any significance to them. It was left to behavioural economists to examine rational choice by decision-makers with limited knowledge and computational abilities; decision-makers suffering from 'bounded rationality' (see Simon, 1987).[11] This rendered management systems and procedures important to them, and, as the reader will see, our approach follows their lead.

Let us imagine a decision-maker in a firm facing a flow of questions, problems or demands for decisions, each of which must be resolved not only in isolation but in relation to other parts of the organization. Perhaps initially, in the process of learning a new job, he or she regards each event as unique and fashions a unique and novel resolution for each. After some time, however, patterns emerge which make it possible to categorize incoming events according to standard types and to devise standard operating procedures (SOPs) appropriate for resolving each type. These SOPs allow work to proceed much more quickly and efficiently, but there will be errors introduced into the work from the inevitable mismatches between the unique actual events and their standardized types. By refining its SOPs or by creating new ones, a firm can reduce these mismatches, but this will raise administrative costs. An optimally constructed set of SOPs will balance administrative costs with the costs of mismatches.

Thus, for example, the image of a firm setting each product's price by some idiosyncratic calculus of marginal costs and revenues is descriptively inaccurate. In reality, pricing decisions are standardized. They might be done, for example, by applying a fixed profit margin to standardized cost figures generated by a highly standardized cost accounting system. As Cyert and March (1992, p124) observed, pricing decisions are *'almost as routinized as production line decisions'*.

When one imagines a firm as a collection of systems, procedures and routines, one can introduce a concept of productive efficiency which is similar but not identical to that of neoclassical economics. The firm devises its systems in order to minimize operating costs. Those systems are rigid, however, so that once they are installed, they can act as a constraint on the firm's objective of profit maximization. If the costs of that constraint are great enough, the firm can invest in changing the systems. Although the system constraint on profit maximization is novel, the logic of cost minimization and thus productive efficiency should be familiar to those schooled in neoclassical economics.

Less familiar is the fact that the firm constrained by its routines can make 'mistakes' – that is, the organizational constraint may prevent the firm from seeing and reacting to opportunities or threats which would be evident to the neoclassical firm with its single perfectly rational decision-maker.[12] This is what we call organizational failure. The failure may be either an unwitting violation of the environmental laws and regulations or a missed opportunity to make a profit – that is, low-hanging fruit left unpicked. We will be concerned exclusively with the latter mistake here.[13] It should be clear, however, that the term 'organizational failure' does not connote that the firm is inefficient given its need for systems and procedures to economize on managerial time and attention.

Although we might suppose that the firm's systems, procedures and routines are ideal when first devised, it should be clear that with the passage of time, they will become less and less so. Relative prices change, regulatory and other environmental conditions change and the firm's competitive situation changes. If the procedures could be changed frequently, marginally and at negligible cost, there should be no problem. Unfortunately, they cannot be. In the short run, they are essentially fixed. Paradoxically, the procedures that increase an organization's efficiency also reduce its adaptability to changing circumstances.

The model of the insides of a firm that we have presented may be unfamiliar to traditional economists, but it is alive in the literature of organizational theory. Readers of that literature will encounter firms comprised of sets of systems, the elements of which must be congruent with each other and with the external environment (Nadler and Tushman, 1997; Tushman and O'Reilly, 1996). Expressed by Kogut and Zander (1992, p384), '... *the capabilities of the firm ... rest in the organizing principles by which relationships among individuals, within and between groups and among organizations are structured*'. It will be explained to readers that these systems coalesce in '*quantum states*' (Miller and Friesen, 1984). Tushman and O'Reilly (1996) call these '*punctuated equilibria*'.

This organizational literature does not bequeath to us formal mathematical models of systems and procedures, quantum states or punctuated equilibria. However, in economics there are mathematical models of analogous phenomena: technical compatibility standards and the processes of shifting from one to another.[14] (For a survey of that literature, see David and Greenstein, 1990.) Explaining the analogies might help make the organizational literature comprehensible to those unfamiliar with it.

One analogy between technical standards and organizational systems is that both are a means of assuring compatibility between different elements of a system. Technical standards assure compatibility between software and hardware; organizational standards assure compatibility between design, production and marketing, or between the accounting system and the compensation system. Each possible outcome of the application of a set of procedures in one part of an organization – that is, each standard solution to a routine problem – must be matched with procedures in many other parts. There is a related analogy: a change in one technical standard requires coordinated changes in others and so does a change in one element of an organizational system. Otherwise, behaviour will not be controlled. Miller and Friesen (1984) implicitly recognize the analogy when they explain that movement between organizational quantum states cannot be made by changing each element of the system piecemeal but only by changing all simultaneously in a quantum leap.

This implies a third analogy. Major conversions of technical standards – for example, from black and white to colour television – are usually complex operations. Similarly, a change in organizational systems will be complex, revolutionary, disruptive and costly. It is like a miniature paradigm revolution in science about which Kuhn (1962) wrote. It is revolutionary in that the old systems are not pushed to evolve further but are destroyed to be replaced new ones. It is disruptive because agents must abandon traditional patterns of behaviour in which they have specific competencies and thus value to the firm and they must learn new routines in their place. Clearly, agents may have a personal motive to resist this: the benefits of the change may be external to them. And it is costly. Apparent resistance to change may be more than just selfishness. Experimental evidence indicates that learning new routines is more difficult and costly when old routines must first be unlearned (Shiffrin and Schneider, 1977).

Inertia to change is a final analogy between technical standards and organizations. Inertia appears in models of conversion from an old technical standard to a new (Farrell and Saloner, 1985, 1986) and organizational inertia is the dominant theme of organization ecology and evolutionary economics.[15] Some sources of organizational inertia arise from human traits like myopia, hubris and denial (Rumelt, 1995). Others (closer to the focus of this chapter) are *'rooted in the size, complexity and interdependence in the organization's structures, systems, procedures and processes'* (Tushman and O'Reilly, 1996, p18).

Take the example of manufacturing systems. We are all familiar with the way that modern manufacturing systems with lean inventories, paced production, high quality standards at each production stage and extremely high coordination, differ from their mass-production antecedent. The difference is not one of degree; it is radical. Any single department or work group could not have done the change from the old to the new unilaterally. It would have lacked both information on what was needed and the authority to coordinate the related moves. There was a crucial role for the principal to make the organizational design decisions. Some American firms in the car industry had to set up greenfield plants in order to introduce the revolution. It could not succeed in any established plant. And with relevance for what will be discussed, the new systems spread from firm to firm as information on 'best practice' spread.

One may bemoan companies' reluctance to change manufacturing systems, environmental management systems or many others. But one should note that this rigidity could be the penalty of success. Companies are often successful because they have imbedded their routines so deeply into their employees' consciousness and subconsciousness that they become part of the company culture. To Nelson and Winter (1982), the skills and capabilities of an organization are bound up in its routines. Indeed, one could argue that some companies amount to little more than their routines and the associated brand identity. McDonald's is one obvious example: it is essentially the company's routines and the brand identity they have created that are franchised. IBM and Apple differ by much more than their product lines. Both firms succeeded for a long time in great part due to their routines, different though they were and each eventually fell victim to the rigidity of its routines when a changing situation necessitated restructuring. General Motors is a widely cited example of a once-successful organization nearly destroyed by its inertia. In the environmental domain, The Body Shop is best known not for its products but for a set of practices that support a philosophy embodying environmental virtue.

The rigidity they introduce into a firm is not the only — and possibly not the worst — curse of systems and procedures. They may also blind the firm to the changes that make those same systems and procedures obsolete. As Cyert and March observed regarding procedures for record keeping: '*The records that are kept determine in large part what aspects of the environment will be observed and what alternatives of action will be considered by the firm*' (Cyert and March, 1992, p126).

Modelling the Phenomenon

In this section, we present a non-technical model of low-hanging fruit and win–win environmental regulation. The reader should appreciate that this model, like all models of complex social or physical phenomena, is not intended to reproduce reality faithfully and completely. Rather, models are built on simplifying assumptions that are necessarily 'wrong' precisely because they are simplifications. Physical bodies do not move on frictionless surfaces in perfect vacuums, consumers do not always maximize utility and managers do not unfailingly maximize profit.[16] The justification for creating simple models is that, if well made, they can afford us insights we miss looking at the chaos of reality itself, they can be extremely powerful in predicting the behaviours of large numbers (of people or molecules) even if not the behaviour of a single unit and thus they can be very useful.

The objective of this model is to show that some sense can be made of low-hanging fruit and win–win environmental regulation within the spirit of neoclassical economics. The virtue of this effort is that the alternative is either to rule such phenomena inadmissible to the domain of traditional economics and economists, or to throw out their model with its incontrovertible power and value. The vitriol in the debate over Porter's Hypothesis is surely due in good part to the cost to one side or the other of a choice between these alternatives.

The model we present accepts that stories of low-hanging fruit may be more than isolated and inconvenient anecdotes of the sort inevitable with any simple model. It attempts to explain how even ubiquitous low-hanging fruit can exist in the presence of competitive market and shareholder pressure so intense that chief executives must push profits to the limit. With an insight regarding the possible source of low-hanging fruit in such an environment, we can then take the next step of thinking about corporate and public policy implication, which is done later in the paper.

A crucial issue for any model is what to assume of the actors it includes. In this model, there is a corporate principal who is assumed to maximize profits and who is assumed to be responsible for the company's policies and procedures. These policies and procedures govern the actions of the agents and their actions in turn have an impact on the world outside the firm. The agents either have or can acquire knowledge of micro-level technologies of which the principal is ignorant. But the principal does understand at an aggregate and macro level the relationship between technology and the firm's profitability.

We start the model with Figure 6.3. The variables x and y are two activities of the firm, related, as Cyert and March say in the quotation leading the previous section, by '*the operating rule it has*'. They could represent, for example, pricing and promotion, inventory management and logistics, or similar paired activities (in this

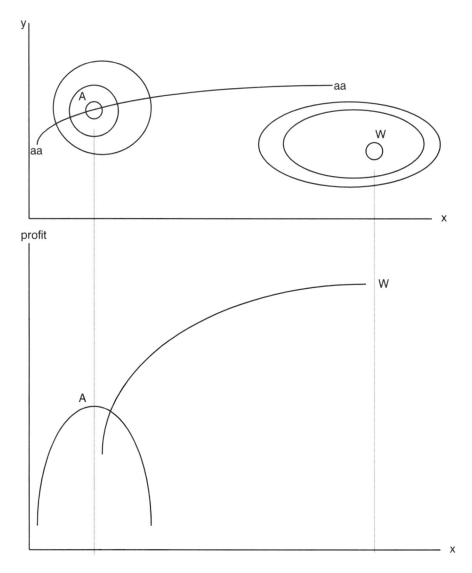

Figure 6.3 *Optimal Procedures Locus and Value*

two-dimensional diagram). These internal activities indirectly create the products and services that generate profit for the firm and both costs and benefits for society, as will be discussed. The concentric rings in the figure, resembling contour lines around a hill projecting from the page, are lines of equal profit. Thus, the level at which activities x and y are conducted will determine the firm's profit. The firm's maximum profit is at point A, the top of the profit hill.

The levels of activities x and y can be independently chosen only once when the firm sets up its organizational systems and procedures. Once that is done, x and

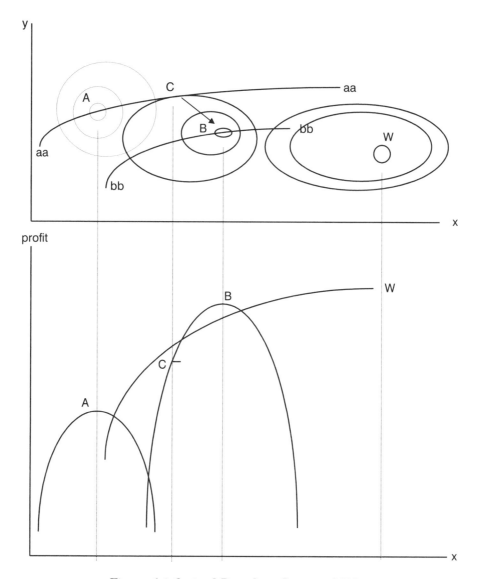

Figure 6.4 *Optimal Procedures Locus and Value*

y are linked by the need for compatibility among the management system elements that govern those activities. That is, if the original systems and procedures were designed and implemented to achieve point 'A', further changes in x and y are still possible, but they are constrained to the line 'aa'. To move off that line, the firm would have to completely scrap and rebuild its systems and procedures.

In the ideal world that Adam Smith described more than 200 years ago (Smith, 1776), the firm that maximized profits simultaneously maximized its contribution to social welfare and so in the figure the private profit peak 'A' and a related social welfare peak 'W' would coincide. They do not in the figure, let us assume, because the firm imposes an external environmental cost on society. The difference in what the firm could contribute to society, 'W' and what it actually does (as defined by the height of point 'A' on the hill with its top at 'W') is the value of the environmental cost. This is the traditional perspective taken in environmental economics.

Initially, the firm's procedures match its situation perfectly as shown in Figure 6.3. Over time, however, its situation changes, but let us assume that the systems and procedures do not. For example, the prices of materials and labour change, product prices change, new technology appears, regulatory and other environmental conditions change and the firm's competitive situation changes. All these changes create a new profit maximizing x and y and a new profit hill with its peak at 'B' in Figure 6.4. We see that the firm, still at point A, is well below B and is thus no longer doing as well as it could. Without a radical restructuring, the firm can only partially reoptimize by moving along aa from point A to C, the highest point of aa on the new profit hill.

In short, the firm's systems and procedures are no longer a perfect match to its situation and a performance gap develops between the firm's profit and the maximum profit available to the firm if its systems and procedures were optimized for the new situation.

We will assume that the principal knows this. He or she knows that the firm's systems and procedures have begun to drag the firm's performance down and that a radical restructuring and reoptimization would improve it. This would entail defining some new line like 'bb' which goes over the top of the new profit hill. Such a reoptimization, which would allow the firm to move from 'C' to 'B', would make economic sense only if in present value terms the cost of the performance gap exceeded the cost of restructuring and reoptimization.

In the model, we assume that the principal can make this macro cost comparison even though he or she does not have perfect information about each piece of low-hanging fruit that reorganization may reveal. This is the domain of the agents.

Let us now use this model to see if we can make sense of win–win environmental regulations. Can we imagine, in the context of the model, that new and stricter environmental regulations could improve the state of the environment and simultaneously earn the firm higher profits? Along the way, we will want to address the paradox that troubles neoclassical economists: if profits go up with the new and stricter regulations, why did the firm not move unilaterally to impose higher environmental standards on itself? Why were new regulations necessary?

We start by assuming that the firm is initially located at point 'C'. It has chosen not to go through the reoptimization of systems and procedures necessary to move from 'C' to 'B' because costs exceed benefits as discussed above. That is, there is surely low-hanging fruit around and the principal knows this, but he or she also knows that the cost of the changes that would have to be made to surmount organizational inertia, ignorance, shortsightedness and resistance to change, are too great to be worthwhile.

Now let us imagine that new environmental regulations are imposed on it. To determine whether this can be win–win, we have to examine the firm's reaction to the new regulations. First, the firm finds it faces new and higher costs of regulatory

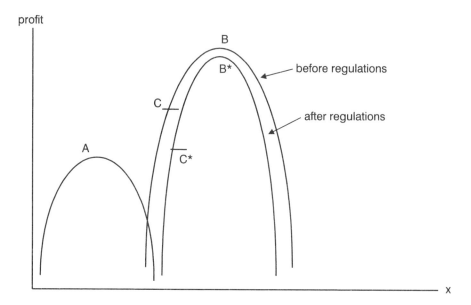

Figure 6.5 *Optimal Procedures Locus and Value*

compliance. For example, a new tax on carbon emissions will result in expenses for energy-saving devices and tax payments for the continuing, albeit diminished, emissions. New legal liability will result in expenditures to reduce risk, plus penalties for the occasional, albeit less likely, accident.

We can model this compliance cost simply by depressing the new profit hill vertically by the amount of the cost. This is shown in Figure 6.5 where 'C*' and 'B*' are analogous to 'C' and 'B' but are on the lowered profit hill.[17] What will the firm do in this situation?

One possibility is that it 'goes green' – that is, it goes through the radical restructuring that takes it off the constraint aa and on to the constraint 'bb'. This will be profitable if the gain in altitude from 'C*' to 'B*' due to harvesting low-hanging fruit is great enough to overcome the cost of the restructuring. Let us assume it is and thus that the firm does the restructuring.

We can now go part way to answer the paradox that troubles the neoclassical economists. We can see why the firm would voluntarily and profitably restructure after the new regulations even though it was not profitable to do so before. The difference from 'C*' to 'B*' may exceed that from 'C' to 'B' (as is actually drawn). If the cost of restructuring lies between the two differences, it is rational for the firm to restructure after the new regulations but not before.

If this move to 'B*' is a move in the direction of 'W', as the environmental policymaker surely intended, then we have the environmental 'win'. In addition, new environmental regulations provoked a radical restructuring and reorganization in the firm that revealed formerly overlooked profitable opportunities.

But can the firm really be more profitable after the new regulations, the restructuring and the harvested low-hanging fruit than it was before the new regulations? Expressed in other terms, can the profit B* minus the restructuring cost exceed the profit C? The answer is 'no' and it is proven in the Appendix on p110.

The result we reach is that although we see apparent evidence in support of the Porter Hypothesis, there is a critical failing, at least as our model interprets the phenomenon. There is no second 'win'. The firm would be better off had the strict regulations never appeared.

How is it, then, that there are so many claims apparently supporting Porter? We believe that the explanation is that those who believe they see examples of win–win are neglecting to account for all the costs. Some just assume that harvested fruit validates Porter per se. For example, the experience of 3M noted above is often cited as support, but it is a non sequitur to draw any conclusions without considering restructuring costs – both explicit restructuring costs and the implicit cost of management attention drawn away from other important business matters. Others may argue that the value of the harvest does cover costs. This would seem to be true in a case appearing in the next section of the substitution of soap and water for costly CFCs when the latter were banned. But again, this does not account for the massive investments that companies made in response to environmental regulations, one minor consequence of which was discovering the low-hanging fruit of soap and water. In fact, we have seen no example that does an actual accounting for both the compliance costs and the costs of the restructuring, including the cost of the managerial attention that it requires. The anecdotes, many though there may be, are simply too brief and unscientific.

The Model and the Story of CFCs

To give the model some life, we can retell it in the language of a particular case: that of CFCs in the last decades.[18] This story is offered with the same caveat that started the last section. The reader should not expect a perfect match between simple abstract model and historical incident. A better test of the model and the value of this section is whether the case helps the reader understand the model and whether the model offers insight into what is going on in the case.

We start the story with a firm in the early 1970s, using CFCs for a variety of applications with no awareness of their environmental impact.[19] Assume it is at point 'A'. Management practices and routines ('aa') ignore all but obvious legal issues concerning the environment and this is optimal in the '70s.

By the late 1980s, CFCs have been convincingly implicated for ozone destruction and the 1987 Montreal Protocol has introduced a number of restrictions on their use. That and many other changes in the environmental arena and in the firm's markets have moved the profit peak to 'B'. The firm has adapted to the changes to some extent (moving to 'C'). For example, CFCs were removed from aerosols when mandated by the US EPA in 1978. But CFCs are still used in other applications where they are legal and where the firm feels that it can easily pass the cost on to customers. Using CFCs to clean electronic circuitry is a good example. The technology is standard and the cost is trivial compared to the total cost of the final product.

It is important for the reader to appreciate what we are *not* saying at this point. We are not saying that there are no cost-effective alternatives for CFCs available to the firm. As history later showed, cheaper alternatives – low-hanging fruit – are there. What we are saying is that management does not feel that it is worthwhile to pay the cost (the cost of shifting from 'aa' to 'bb') to make the changes in systems, procedures and even culture that are necessary to look for those alternatives. In short, no one is paying any attention to the matter because it is not worth concern. There are better things to do.

To express this in terms we used earlier, there is organizational failure evident here. Low-hanging fruit is left on the tree. The neoclassical firm would see this, but our firm does not because it faces a constraint that the neoclassical firm does not face: the organizational constraint. Because of that constraint, our firm does not find it worthwhile to 'go green' – to go through the organizational trauma of changing systems and procedures. Thus, it is blind to an opportunity.

One might object and argue that no significant systems or procedural changes should be needed to see and pick low-hanging fruit: to discover, for example, that soap and water are as effective as the much more expensive CFCs in cleaning electronic circuitry. So it might seem. But we are all surely aware from personal experience that we often fail to see what we are not looking for and the same is true of organizations. Many of the anecdotes of win–win environmental regulations can be interpreted as cases where regulations forced firms to focus on environmental matters more closely than before and in so doing revealed hitherto unnoticed opportunities.

When environmental regulatory costs were lower, companies commonly dealt with them with a 'regulatory compliance' mentality (Epstein, 1996c) rather than with a cost-effectiveness mentality. It was sufficient then for managers to ask company experts what was necessary to ensure regulatory compliance and then the necessary actions were taken without question. They were not questioned because the logic driving the actions derived from a legalistic as opposed to an economic or a strategic perspective. A natural result was that company staff with environmental, health and safety responsibility rarely initiated cost-saving ideas since it was neither their charge nor were they held accountable for cost.

The situation changes for our firm in 1990 when the Montreal Protocol is revised to ban CFCs completely by the year 2000. Suddenly the firm has to contemplate the absence of CFCs at *any* price. In other words, the cost of the status quo approach to the CFC issue has become prohibitive. This is the shock that finally provokes a radical change in perspective and its specific manifestation, a serious and thorough campaign of CFC replacement. Once the campaign is launched, the firm discovers, incidental to its objective of CFC replacement, that in some applications there had been alternatives available that were cheaper than CFCs.

Because strict environmental regulations indirectly reveals some CFC replacements that are actually cheaper than the CFCs, this looks superficially like a story of win–win regulations. But as we noted in the previous section, to draw this conclusion is to ignore the cost of the replacements that are more expensive than CFCs and all the changes the company has to make that are necessary to provoke the search. In short, from its own selfish perspective, the firm would be better off in a world in which it cleaned circuit boards with expensive CFCs rather than in a world with cheap soap and water and the whole of the ozone depletion issue bearing down on it.[20]

The story recounted above could be paralleled by stories of campaigns for energy savings, waste reduction and others. These campaigns may be provoked by environmental regulations and they often generate production cost savings. But as a generalization, we doubt that these savings repay the full costs of the corporate response to the environmental movement of the last decades.

Corporate Policy Implications

What can a company do to retard the slow obsolescence of its procedures and routines? What can it do to provoke a revolution when it becomes necessary, rather than let decay proceed? What can be done to minimize the costs of that revolution? What is the state of the art in companies' policies and procedures to deal with environmental issues?

Answers to the first couple of questions take one into the enormous literature on change management and it is not our intention to go there in this chapter. It will have to suffice to offer a few remarks that come directly from the analysis above.

We have seen that agents may have little incentive or ability to provoke a radical revolution in the SOPs they have learned. Having said that, the environmental field is one where a company may be able to harness agents' own values of respect for the environment in a way that may not be possible in other, less morally laden fields.

Beyond that, if the revolution will not start at the bottom of the organization, it will have to be led by the principal at the top. This necessitates that the principal be as aware as possible of circumstances lower in the organization. This is invariably difficult. Simon notes the problem: '*The insulation of the higher levels of the administrative hierarchy from the world of fact known at first hand by the lower levels is a familiar administrative phenomenon*' (Simon, 1945, p238). Furthermore, the principal must be prepared to provoke the instability that every transition brings. This may be an unattractive prospect for even the most proactive manager, even though the periodic need to upset outdated habits is familiar to most individuals and to management theory. The alternative may be to await the instability of a crisis.

There are aids available to managers to surmount these obvious problems. One is benchmarking to industry best practice. Referring again to the analogy of the hill, managers can always draw inferences of their position by reference to their immediate surroundings and in this way they may learn of the marginal changes their organizations need to make to improve performance. But it is harder for a manager to see a completely new peak in the far distance. By the practice of benchmarking, managers make an explicit point of looking in detail at the practices that other firms, in particular effective ones, are using to solve some problem. This gives managers vision they too often lack looking only inward.

Both business process re-engineering and total quality management programmes are two other methods by which principals can force a re-evaluation of procedures prior to a crisis and with only a presumption that a re-evaluation is cost effective.

What constitute state-of-the-art environmental SOPs? 'Green accounting' is one.[21] When environmental liabilities and regulatory costs were insignificant for most firms, they developed accounting procedures that hid those costs in general, administrative or other overhead accounts. Environmental costs and threats have increased, but few firms have changed their accounting procedures. This has effectively hidden low-hanging fruit. Epstein, commenting on his survey of more than 100 companies' activities in this area, says that: '... *not only do companies not know the total of their environmental costs, they do not know what causes those costs. To improve the management of these costs, managers must understand the cost drivers*' (Epstein, 1996c, p12). Modifications of activity-based costing procedures assign current environmental costs to the specific activities that cause them, allowing companies to focus on cost reduction.

Accounting properly for current environmental costs is not difficult once companies make the necessary adjustments. Accounting for future liabilities associated with actions taken today is a much harder challenge and few companies have begun to wrestle with it. Today's heavy and unplanned burden for clean-up under Superfund legislation resulted from undercosting and underpricing products years ago. Costs that were assumed to be external to the firms ended up as internal. Wise managers now see product take-back legislation on the horizon. But unless current accounting and incentive systems impose expected future liabilities on today's decision-makers, the experience of Superfund will be repeated years from now. Not only will today's undercosted and underpriced products fail to provide reserves for the liabilities, but design and production decisions that would lessen future liabilities will go unnoticed. Tomorrow's low-hanging fruit is being planted.

One can see in green accounting some of the rigidities and barriers to the implementation of procedural changes discussed earlier. To account explicitly for speculative but potentially huge future liabilities is alien to traditional accounting practice. Line managers to whom they are an unwanted burden must meet data requirements for green accounts. Once environmental costs are isolated and then allocated to specific products and processes, there will be an impact on profit and loss centres and change must then extend to pricing procedures, to expectations of return on net assets, to budgeting and investment processes and to compensation and promotion procedures.

Public Policy Implications

Porter (1991) had little to say regarding the kind of public policy tools he espoused, but his criticism of command and control standards and end-of-pipe technologies, and his praise of flexibility and policies that stimulate investment and innovation, all suggest that market-based instruments win his favour. In this, of course, he keeps company with the fraternity of economists whose model he rejects. But this is not the only seeming irony. It seems ironic as well that Porter would favour market-based incentives for firms that do not appear to respond efficiently to market incentives in the first place.

We see less conventional policy messages in our analysis. One is that policy that seeks to push companies through the revolution in procedures that we have spoken of must entail an attention-getting shock. Irrespective of the particular instrument – whether command and control or market incentive – it is better to hit the firm with a stunning blow rather than slowly to ratchet up the regulatory burden. The case of CFCs discussed previously illustrates this and Porter and van der Linde (1995) make the same point. Lax regulations allow firms to adapt incrementally, without any fundamental change in thinking. Strict regulations, they say, '*promote real innovation*' (p124).[22] Generally, crisis is a powerful motivator.

Another message is that public policy can play an important role by setting performance standards, encouraging voluntary codes of practice (whether originating in the public or private sector) and disseminating information on best practice. Management practices and standards are public goods for which the exclusion of non-payers is difficult. If a firm invests to develop industry best practice, other firms may observe and adopt those practices without the cost of developing them. This can undermine a principal's incentive to develop wholly new systems and procedures. Public investment gets around the problem.

Examples of such initiatives include the International Organization for Standardization's ISO 14001, environmental accounting and auditing standards like the European Commission's EMAS, consulting help like the US EPA's 'Green Lights' and many countries' eco-labelling schemes for products. Encouraging private industry codes of conduct like the Valdez Principles and Responsible Care fits here as well.

Although none of these voluntary policies is easily explicable by traditional economic analysis, all make sense in our framework. All of these examples provide information to companies about best practices which the companies' own procedures might obscure. Each provides the companies with means to operationalize integrated sets of procedures by reference to the experiences of others. The fact that none of the examples is obligatory does not lessen policy effectiveness; it simply means that firms will not bear the administrative cost unless they see a return in it.

Notwithstanding what was just said, there is an element of compulsion to these 'voluntary' agreements. Courts in the US and Canada are coming to regard failure to meet best practice as a signal of negligence. So practices like Responsible Care and ISO 14001 may de facto entail a legal obligation not only for those firms agreeing to them but for others as well (Webb and Morrison, 1996). In parallel fashion, adoption of best practice is a defence against negligence. So there is a quasi-regulatory incentive for firms to adopt these standards.

Finally, we see a new argument in favour of market-based environmental policies: they are economical in terms of their consequences for a firm's organizational systems. This is because in the limit, they entail no special burden on those systems.

Imagine that all external environmental costs were internalized into market prices. In this idealized situation, environmental issues would disappear completely as explicit concerns for the firm and they would reappear imbedded inseparably in new prices of inputs and outputs. As far as the environment is concerned, the firm becomes the traditional neoclassical firm in the sense that the environment does not exacerbate the burden of the organizational constraint. There is no more risk of 'regulatory mentality' since that mentality was the result of legalistic regulations. Market-based policies allow the firm to think with only a commercial mentality. Thus, in an ironic sense, strict and pervasive market-based policies allow a firm to be less, not more, conscious of the environment.

Conclusion

We have argued that low-hanging fruit may be ubiquitous in companies. Its likely causes are inertia or static friction in SOPs which both blind firms to changing conditions and thus emerging opportunities and also make adjustment to new conditions slow, difficult and costly even when the need becomes apparent.

If low-hanging fruit is commonplace, then it is feasible that an environmental regulation could break the inertia and be win–win in a limited sense. Companies' reactionary changes in SOPs may reveal pre-existing opportunities to save money sufficient to pay compliance costs. This is how we interpret the anecdotes used as evidence for the Porter Hypothesis. We call this 'win–win in a limited sense' because the anecdotes do not suggest that the savings, real though they may be, repay both the compliance costs and the cost of the requisite changes in the SOPs.

Taking the case of CFCs as an example, tightening regulatory controls on the chemicals eventually forced companies to launch intensive campaigns of CFC replacement. When executed, these campaigns revealed some low-hanging fruit, the best known being soap and water for cleaning electronic assemblies. This example has appeared often as evidence in the debate Porter started. But before accepting it as compelling evidence of the accuracy of the Porter Hypothesis, one must also weigh in the balance the cost of all those difficult CFC replacements – in air conditioning, for example, which were not low-hanging fruit – and the cost the companies bore in terms of management attention to launch and manage the campaign.

The model in this chapter shows how it is possible to have low-hanging fruit in a neoclassical firm, albeit one with an organizational constraint. Furthermore, it shows how strict environmental regulations can reveal that fruit and see it harvested. So, it has generated the observable phenomenon that has fed much of the debate. However, the model cannot re-create a true win–win result – one in which the firm and the environment end up with lower costs.

This may, of course, be the fault of the model. Perhaps it is still too narrowly constructed to capture an aspect of reality. True win–win regulatory changes may exist, at least as isolated oddities and perhaps they are systematic. However, it is also possible that the Porter Hypothesis, taken as a generalization, is false. As this paper has argued, regulatory changes can impose significant organizational cost on firms. Out of the often long and difficult process of organizational change may emerge some low-hanging fruit to harvest, but selectively chosen anecdotes and examples of this are clearly biased in favour of the Porter Hypothesis. To take an example from the chapter, the gain from discovering that soap and water can easily and profitably replace CFCs must be matched against all the difficult and costly CFC replacements.

We close this chapter with a reminder that the justification for environmental regulations does not, and never did, rest on increasing private profit. It rests on increasing social welfare. Our presumption throughout this chapter is that environmental regulations are in the public interest. If they are not simultaneously in the interest of companies subject to them, so be it. Admittedly, from a political viewpoint, it might be advantageous if there were no potential losers and thus no opponents to a policy. But in our view, it is not credible for environmental policy-makers to argue that businessmen should welcome their visits. Rather, policy-makers should focus on the public interest and consider any low-hanging fruit that firms might pick an unintended but welcome bonus.

Appendix

We want to demonstrate the argument presented on p104 that the firm cannot be more profitable after the new regulations and consequent restructuring than before the new regulations.

The profit after regulations and restructuring is B*. From that we must subtract the restructuring cost which must be at least (B – C) or the firm would have reorganized without the new regulations. The profit with no regulations and no restructuring is C.

If we subtract the smallest possible restructuring cost from B*, we get: $B* - (B - C) = (B* - B) + C$. Since B* – B is negative, it follows that this expression is less than C.

References

Anderson, P and Tushman, M (1990) 'Technological Discontinuities and Dominant Designs: A Cyclical Model of Technological Change', *Administrative Science Quarterly*, vol 35, pp604–33

Beckenstein, A and Gabel, L (1986) 'The Economics of Antitrust Compliance', *Southern Economic Journal*, vol 52, no 3, pp673–92

Coase, R (1992) 'The Institutional Structure of Production', *American Economic Review*, vol 82, no 4, pp713–9

Commission of the European Communities (1993) 'EC Council: Regulation Setting up an EC Eco-Management and Audit Scheme', European Union, Brussels

Cyert, R and March, J (1992) *A Behavioral Theory of the Firm*, 2nd ed, Blackwell, Cambridge

David, P and Greenstein, S (1990) 'The Economics of Compatibility Standards: An Introduction to Recent Research', *Economics of Innovation and New Technology*, vol 1, no 1, pp3–42

The Economist (1991), 31 August, p15

Epstein, M (1996a) *Measuring Corporate Environmental Performance*, Burr Ridge, Irwin, Illinois

Epstein, M (1996b) 'You've Got a Great Environmental Strategy – Now What?', *Business Horizons*, September–October, pp53–9

Epstein, M (1996c) 'Improving Environmental Management with Full Environmental Cost Accounting', *Environmental Quality Management*, autumn, pp11–22

Farrell, J and Saloner, G (1985) 'Standardization, Compatibility and Innovation', *Rand Journal of Economics*, vol 16, no 1, pp70–83

Farrell, J and Saloner, G (1986) 'Installed Base and Compatibility: Innovation, Preannouncements and Predation', *American Economic Review*, vol 76, no 5, pp940–55

Gabel, H L (1995) 'Environmental Management as a Competitive Strategy: The Case of CFCs', in H Folmer, H L Gabel and J B Opschoor (eds) *Principles of Environmental and Resource Economics: A Guide for Students and Decision-Makers*, Edward Elgar, Aldershot, pp328–46

Gabel, H L and Sinclair-Desgagné, B (1995) 'Corporate Responses to Environmental Concerns', in H Folmer, H L Gabel and J B Opschoor (eds) *Principles of Environmental and Resource Economics: A Guide for Students and Decision-Makers*, Edward Elgar, Aldershot, pp347–61

Gore, A (1992) *Earth in the Balance: Forging a New Common Purpose*, Earthscan, London

Jaffe, A, Peterson, S, Portney, P and Stavens, R (1995) 'Environmental Regulations and the Competitiveness of US Manufacturing', *Journal of Economic Literature*, vol XXXIII, no 1, pp132–63

Kogut, B and Zander, U (1992) 'Knowledge of the Firm, Combinative Capabilities and the Replication of Technology', *Organization Science*, vol 3, no 3, pp383–97

Kuhn, T (1962), *The Structure of Scientific Revolutions*, University of Chicago Press, Chicago

Mansfield, E (1974) *Economics: Principles, Problems, Decisions*, Norton, New York

Meyer, S (1992) 'Environmentalism and Economic Prosperity: Testing the Environmental Impact Hypothesis', unpublished manuscript, MIT

Milgrom, P and Roberts, J (1992) *Economics, Organization and Management*, Prentice-Hall: Englewood Cliffs

Miller, D and Friesen, P (1984) *Organizations: A Quantum View*, Prentice-Hall: Englewood Cliffs

Molina, M and Roland, S (1974) 'Stratospheric Sink for Chlorofluoromethanes: Chlorine Atom Catalyzed Destruction on Ozone', *Nature*, vol 249, no 5460, pp10–12

Nadler, D and Tushman, M (1997) *Competing by Design*, Oxford University Press, New York

Nelson, R and Winter, S (1982) *An Evolutionary Theory of Economic Change*, Harvard University Press, Cambridge MA

Oates, W, Palmer, K and Portney, P (1994) 'Environmental Regulation and International Competitiveness: Thinking about the Porter Hypothesis', unpublished manuscript, University of Maryland and Resources for the Future

Palmer, K and Simpson, D (1993), 'Environmental Policy as Industrial Policy', *Resources*, Summer, pp17–21.

Porter, M (1991) 'America's Green Strategy', *Scientific American*, April, p96

Porter, M and van der Linde, C (1995) 'Green and Competitive: Ending the Stalemate', *Harvard Business Review*, September–October, pp120–34

Postrel, S and Rumelt, R (1992) 'Incentives, Routines and Self-Command', *Industrial and Corporate Change*, vol 1, no 3, pp397–425

Rumelt, R (1995) 'Inertia and Transformation', in C Montgomery (ed) *Resource-Based and Evolutionary Theories of the Firm*, Kluwer, Boston, pp101–32

Segerson, K and Tietenberg, T (1992) 'The Structure of Penalties in Environmental Enforcement', *Journal of Environmental Economics and Management*, vol 23, pp179–200

Shiffrin, R and Schneider, W (1977) 'Controlled and Automatic Human Information Processing: II. Perceptual Learning, Automatic Attending and a General Theory', *Psychological Review*, vol 84, pp127–90

Simon, H A (1945) *Administrative Behavior*, 3rd ed, Free Press, New York

Simon, H A (1985) 'Human Nature in Politics: The Dialogue of Psychology with Political Science', *The American Political Science Review*, vol 79, no 2, pp293–304

Simon, H A (1987) 'Bounded Rationality', in J Eatwell, M Milgate and P Newman (eds) *The New Palgrave Dictionary of Economics*, Macmillan, London, vol 1, p267

Smith, A (1776) *An Inquiry into the Nature and Causes of the Wealth of Nations*, Collier, New York

Stiglitz, J (1991) 'Symposium on Organizations and Economics', *Journal of Economic Perspectives*, vol 5, no 2, pp15–24

Tushman, M and O'Reilly, C (1996) 'Ambidextrous Organizations', *California Management Review*, vol 38, no 4, pp8–30

Walley, N and Whitehead, B (1994) 'It's Not Easy Being Green', *Harvard Business Review*, May–June, pp46–52

Webb, K and Morrison, A (1996) 'Voluntary Approaches, the Environment and the Law', unpublished manuscript, Office of Consumer Affairs and Carlton University, Canada

Notes

1. We would like to express our sincere appreciation for the many helpful suggestions from the editor, Richard Starkey, which in our view have significantly improved the initial version of the chapter
2. Good examples of work in this genre are Epstein (1996a, 1996b, 1996c)
3. For an elaboration of some of this, see Milgrom and Roberts (1992, Chapter 4)
4. The notion of routines is developed in Nelson and Winter (1982) and Postrel and Rumelt (1992)
5. To keep the paper focused, we will maintain the traditional assumption that the firm's principal desires are to maximize profits. Our point of departure from neoclassical economics is to reject its assumption that the firm can be represented as a single perfectly rational decision-maker
6. For example, in a Canadian case over illegal sulphur emissions, a court ordered the company, Prospec, to obtain ISO 14001 certification
7. The reader should note that this static curve implies a given state of technological knowledge. The discovery of new technology that simultaneously allows less environmental damage and lower private cost is not evidence in favour of the Porter Hypothesis, nor does it contradict the neoclassical assumption that the firm maximizes profit. Many technological improvements economize on material intensity and this is generally good for both the firm and the environment. One only needs to compare a steel mill in Britain in the second half of the 1800s with one a century later to realize that the newer is both cleaner and lower in cost. Most of the difference has nothing to do with environmental regulations. Porter implies in part that strict environmental regulations will induce more of this kind of innovation than would otherwise appear. This is difficult to validate, however and the anecdotes (see text) are not really new technology
8. See, for example, Mansfield (1974, p380)
9. An example will make this point clear. The US EPA's Green Lights Program, noted in the text, helped companies save money and the environment by switching

to energy-efficient lighting. Had this been a tax on energy rather than a voluntary programme, the energy cost saving would have had to offset the taxes paid for continuing energy use

10 The obvious alternative hypothesis is that the causality is reversed; that those countries' productivity levels and wealth caused their strict environmental regulations

11 The behaviouralists justified their assumption with empirical observations of human behaviour and the cognitive limitations that influence it

12 In a mathematical maximization model, this simply represents the reduced objective function value that the new constraint causes

13 Beckenstein and Gabel (1986) formally model a firm able to make both error types and they apply it to antitrust

14 Compatibility standards are the technological or dimensional standards that allow different products to work together. Examples are standards for computer hardware and software, standards for audio or video hardware and software, automobile wheels and tyres, etc

15 Organization ecology posits that firms cannot change in any significant way; evolutionary economics accepts that they can, albeit with great difficulty

16 In the limit, a truly 'realistic' model would not be a model at all. It would have to be reality itself

17 The regulations would certainly shift the horizontal position of the hill as well, since it would be coincidental if the same combination of x and y were equally suited before and after the regulations. For the sake of simplicity in the figure, however, we assume that the horizontal location of the hill is unchanged; only its height changes

18 CFCs are chlorofluorocarbons which deplete the ozone layer in the stratosphere. The ozone layer protects humans, animals and plants from the damaging effects of ultraviolet radiation from the sun. See Gabel (1995) for a development of this case

19 For reference, this impact was first suggested as a theoretical possibility in 1974 (Molina and Roland, 1974)

20 This chapter does not offer empirical evidence that CFC regulations were *not* win–win, of course. To the best of the author's knowledge, no one has done an adequate study of the firm-level costs and benefits of the regulations. Yet because the Porter Hypothesis is so provocative, both to environmental economists and to the managers on whom the costs and benefits of regulations actually fall, it seems to us that the burden of proof should fall on those who espouse that hypothesis

21 'Green accounting' is an imprecise term which typically implies identifying and assigning all environmental costs to specific products and processes. Whereas truly 'external costs' may be neglected for decision-making, they are commonly identified and often regarded as relevant to decisions on the grounds that they will likely be internalized by future regulations. Life-cycle assessment and costing legacy costing and full environmental cost accounting are related tools or synonyms for green accounting

22 There are physical science analogies with this. The coefficient of static friction is greater than the coefficient of kinetic friction. Put into layman's words, when a system stops moving, it starts growing roots

23 Foreign firms can be subject to the same regulations either if the regulations are product- rather than production-based, or if the foreign country is pressured into adopting the same production-based regulations

Section 3

Environmental and Social Accounting

Introduction

In Chapter 2, John Elkington emphasized the importance of social and environmental accounting, showing how sustainable development will require companies to account against their environmental and social bottom lines. Given their importance and the considerable activity and development that occurred in both fields during the 1990s, we felt that it would be useful to include a section covering these forms of accounting. The four chapters in this section have therefore been selected as they cover the 'what?', 'why?' and 'how?' of social and environmental accounting – what are they, why do them and how exactly should they be done?

In Chapter 7, Rob Gray, Dave Owen and Carol Adams answer the first of these questions and their description of the main features of environmental and social accounting provides a helpful conceptual framework for the rest of the section. The authors point out that financial accounting, the form of accounting with which business is most familiar, covers only one aspect of business activity – the financial/economic aspect. However, business activity also has environmental and social aspects and environmental and social accounting enable business to account for the consequences of its activities in these spheres. The authors conclude by noting that addressing the 'what?' question is not enough and pose the question: '*Why do organizations report at all and, more importantly, why do they not report and why should they report?*' These are issues addressed in the next three chapters.

As Martin Bennett and Peter James point out in Chapter 8, understood in its broadest sense firm-level environmental accounting has both financial and non-financial aspects. The non-financial aspect involves accounting for the stocks and flows of energy and materials within a firm or product life-cycle, and for the environmental impacts associated with these stocks and flows. And the generation, analysis and use of relevant financial information relating to these stocks, flows and impacts constitutes the financial aspect. The non-financial aspect of environmental accounting is often referred to as 'environmental management' and during the 1990s a large number of tools have been developed to assist in this activity (see Box 3.1). However, it is on the financial aspect of environmental accounting that this chapter focuses.

So why do firms carry out financial evironmental accounting? Bennett and James point out that the accounting literature '*initially focused – and to a considerable extent, still does – on external accountability to stakeholders outside the company, rather than on serving the needs of management*'. This, say the authors, reflects the fact that a number of companies have recognized the concerns of various stakeholder groups about their environmental impact. These companies regard themselves as having a duty to account to their stakeholders and understand that by discharging

---

BOX I3.1 TOOLS FOR ENVIRONMENTAL MANAGEMENT

The 1990s saw the rapid development of environmental management tools with academics, consultants, government bodies and the business community itself all contributing to this development. There now exists a plethora of tools which include environmental management systems, environmental audits, environmental labelling, environmental indicators, life-cycle assessment, environmental reporting, ecobalances, design for the environment, cleaner production and environmental risk assessment.

In an effort to standardize practice in the environmental management field, the International Organization for Standardization (ISO) is in the process of publishing a series of standards on the first five tools listed above. ISO 14001, the specification standard on environmental management systems published in 1996, is the most well known and widely used of these, with over 10,000 certifications to the standard having taken place by the end of 1999 and 30,000 expected by the end of 2000 (anon, 1999a).

Environmental reporting among large firms has increased in the 1990s. A recent survey of the top 100 firms in 11 countries (anon, 1999b) found that 24 per cent of these firms had prepared environmental reports in 1999, compared with 19 per cent in 1996 and 13 per cent in 1993. The survey also noted that although not issuing a dedicated stand-alone environmental report, another 23 per cent of firms disclose information on their environmental activities in financial or other reports. The Global Reporting Initiative (GRI) formed by the Coalition for Environmentally Responsible Economies (CERES) in 1997 aims to standardize practice in the field of environmental reporting. According to CERES (1999) the GRI's mission is:

> To establish, through a global, voluntary and multi-stakeholder process, the foundation for standardized (or uniform) corporate sustainability reporting worldwide. We plan to accomplish this mission by developing three tools: a set of core metrics applicable to all business enterprises; sets of sector-specific metrics customized to specific types of enterprises; and a uniform format for reporting these metrics and related information integral to a company's sustainability performance. In addition, GRI seeks to identify, or help create, a permanent institutional 'home' to monitor, advocate and continually upgrade the practice of standardized reporting worldwide.

---

this duty they help to preserve what the authors refer to as their societal '*licence to operate*'. And in addition, it reflects a concern amongst the accountancy profession and certain financial regulators that financial reports to shareholders accurately reflect the effect that environmental issues have on business.

However, the authors go on to note the growing literature that adopts a genuine management accounting approach, focusing on providing information to support internal decision-making. This approach the authors refer to as environment-related management accounting, which they define as: '*the generation, analysis and use of financial and non-financial information in order to optimise corporate environmental and economic performance and achieve sustainable business.*' The primary objective of environment-related management accounting '*is to better inform and otherwise support decision-making processes that are influenced by environmental factors*', and achieving this requires the generation of relevant non-financial and financial data which is then processed into relevant information using various accounting techniques. The authors describe the various types of data and techniques involved and how the resulting information can be used to aid decision-making relating to objectives such as identifying cost reduction and other improvement opportunities, guiding product pricing, mixing and development and supporting sustainable business.

Chapter 9 by Rob Gray, Colin Dey, Dave Owen, Richard Evans and Simon Zadek, engages with both the theory and practice of social accounting. In a detailed and stimulating discussion, the authors set out to do three things: '*to theorize a social accounting, to deduce lessons of best practice and to begin to derive standards for social accounting practice.*' The first of these involves synthesizing what the authors regard as the three dominant theoretical perspectives on the relationship between an accounting entity and the rest of the world. These are the stakeholder, the accountability and the polyvocal citizen perspectives – perspectives which give a voice to the accounting organization, society at large and the organization's stakeholders. Although the stakeholder perspective is useful in defining clearly the organization's stakeholders, from this perspective the accounting organization will only engage in the accounting process if it is in its interest to do so. However, the second perspective brings in the notion of accountability: that organizations have a duty to account to society for, and that society has a concomitant right to this account of their activities. The polyvocal perspective completes the picture by giving stakeholders a real voice in the process of accounting, enabling them to express their views on what the nature of the accounting relationship between the organization, its stakeholders and society should be, and to contribute to the preparation of the social accounts themselves.

Having synthesized these perspectives to build up '*a rich conception of the organization-society interaction*' and having examined what can be learned from the experiences of Traidcraft plc and Traidcraft Exchange in developing their own social accounts, the authors address the 'how?' question, briefly setting out the key elements they believe should constitute '*the backbone of a systematic social accounting practice and might, thus, form a basis for the emergence of social accounting standards*'.

Chapter 10 by Simon Zadek continues the discussion of the theory and practice of social accounting. In the first part of the chapter, Zadek discusses why a company should consider social accounting – or, as he calls it, social and ethical accounting, auditing and reporting (SEAAR) – and in the second part he goes on to look at how it should be done. There are essentially two reasons that a company will voluntarily undertake SEAAR: self-regarding (instrumental) reasons and other-regarding (moral) reasons. For Zadek, the first of these has two components: the managerialist and public interest rationales. The managerialist rationale is the firm's wish to manage its stakeholders effectively in order to optimize its business performance, and this requires, amongst other things, a knowledge of their views and opinions on social issues relating to the firm. The public interest rationale, on the

---

BOX 13.2 DEVELOPMENTS IN THE FIELD OF SOCIAL ACCOUNTING

Not only did the 1990s see considerable activity and development within the field of environmental accounting but also within the field of social accounting. One aspect of this development has been the formation of the Institute of Social and Ethical AcountAbility – AccountAbility for short – in 1996. AccountAbility (1999) describes itself as '*a professional body committed to strengthening social responsibility and ethical behaviour of the business community and non-profit organizations*', something it aims to achieve by '*promoting best practice social and ethical accounting and auditing and the development of standards and accreditation procedures for professionals in the field*'. AccountAbility (2000) has recently launched AA 1000, a standard that '*provides both a framework that organizations can use to understand and improve their ethical performance and a means for others to judge the validity of ethical claims made*'.

Another development in the field has been the publication of *Social Account-Ability 8000* (SA8000), a standard for the protection of workers' rights. The standard was written by an advisory group convened by the Council of Economic Priorities Accreditation Agency (CEPAA). (CEPAA is an affiliate of the Council of Economic Priorities (CEP), a corporate social responsibility research institute founded in 1969.) Based on the conventions of the International Labour Organization (ILO) and related international human rights instruments (including the Universal Declaration of Human Rights and the UN Convention on the Rights of the Child), SA8000 has nine core areas: child labour, forced labour, health and safety, compensation, working hours, discipline, fee association and collective bargaining and management systems. As of January 2000, 26 organizations were certified to the standard.

---

other hand, is linked to the growth of civil action in relation to corporate social performance. As Zadek puts it: '*businesses are not merely* choosing *to undertake some form of social and ethical accounting, auditing and reporting as a means of understanding and manipulating their social environment, but are rather being* forced *to respond to the demands from the actors that make up the environment.*' (For a further discussion of civil action, see Chapter 16.) Zadek's final rationale is moral in nature and he refers to it as the value-shift rationale. Here SEAAR is carried out not with a view to enhancing competitiveness but because it is the right thing to do. As Zadek notes: '*Anyone working with the business community will have been impressed by the commitment of many people working within this community to improving the social and environmental footprint of the companies in which they work.*'

Turning from 'why?' to 'how?', Zadek notes that there are definite signs of a convergence of standards taking place in the practice of SEAAR. This emerging consensus has been driven mainly by the Institute of Social and Ethical AccountAbility (see Box 13.2) which has formulated a set of eight 'quality principles' on which its members believe that SEAAR should be based. These principles have been broken down into various elements and a methodology for scoring an organization's SEAAR against these elements has been developed, along with a five-stage developmental model for SEAAR similar to that developed by UNEP and the consultancy SustainAbility for environmental reporting.

Another initiative to promote standardization in the field of social accounting has been the publication of the standard Social Accountability 8000 (SA8000) on workers' rights (see also Box I3.2).

References

AccountAbility (1999) http://www.accountability.org.uk [2/12/1999]

AccountAbility (2000) http:www.accountability.org.uk/B1.htm, [3/8/00]

Anon (1999) 'ISO 14001 Certificates Predicted to Reach 30,000 Next Year', *The ENDS Report*, no 293, June 1999, Environmental Data Services, London

Anon (1999) 'Environmental Reporting Grows Amid Wide Variation in Quality', *The ENDS Report*, no 297, October 1999, Environmental Data Services, London

7

What is Social Accounting?

Rob Gray, Dave Owen and Carol Adams

Gray et al (1987) defined corporate social reporting (CSR) as:

> *... the process of communicating the social and environmental effects of organisations' economic actions to particular interest groups within society at large. As such, it involves extending the accountability of organisations (particularly companies), beyond the traditional role of providing a financial account to the owners of capital, in particular, shareholders. Such an extension is predicted upon the assumption that companies do have wider responsibilities than simply to make money for their shareholders (pix).*

Some idea of the relationship between conventional accounting and CSR and of the extent and potential limits of CSR may be useful to begin with. At its most basic there are four necessary (although not sufficient) defining characteristics which enable the derivation of conventional Western accounting practice (see Laughlin and Gray, 1988). These four characteristics are: that the world which the accountant recognizes be restricted to:

1   the financial description;
2   specified (priced) economic events;
3   defined organizations or accounting entities; and
4   provide information for specified users of that information.

This profoundly narrow image of all possible interactions between the 'world' and the organization is created by the conventional accounting system. Conventional accounting thus stands as a political and social process that creates it own social reality (Cooper and Sherer, 1984; Gambling, 1977a, b; Hines, 1989, 1991). In broad terms the social accounting literature has sought to challenge the propriety of the four characteristics of conventional accounting. More specifically, social accounting is about some combination of:

1   accounting for different things – that is, other than accounting strictly for economic events;
2   accounting in different media – that is, other than accounting in strictly financial terms;
3   accounting to different individuals or groups – that is, not necessarily only accounting to the providers of finance; and

> • Animal testing.
> • Armaments.
> • Environment.
> • Irresponsible marketing.
> • Land rights.
> • Nuclear power.
> • Oppressive regimes.
> • South Africa.
> • Trade union relations.
> • Wages and conditions.

Figure 7.1 *The Ethical Consumer Criteria for the Evaluation of Products and Companies*

4 accounting for different purposes – that is, not necessarily accounting only to enable the making of decisions whose success would be judged in financial or even only cash flow terms.

Thus we might consider traditional financial accounting as a significantly and artificially constrained set of all accountings – that is, traditional accounting is one particular form of the broader, richer 'social accounting', or social accounting is what you get when the artificial restrictions of conventional accounting are removed. However, while we might wish to encompass all possible 'accountings' (which would include everything from descriptions of one's time at university to novels, from journalism to advertising, from prayer to excuses) this will be somewhat impractical. As a result, CRS tends to restrict itself, first to formal (as opposed to informal) accounts, and second to formal accounts that are prepared by organizations either for themselves or which are (less commonly) disclosed to others. The social accounting literature tends to assume that the reports are prepared about certain areas of activities – typically those that affect:

- the natural environment;
- employees;

and wider 'ethical issues which typically concentrate upon:

- consumers and products;
- local and international communities.

An indication of the potential range of issues that CSR might need to address is given in Figure 7.1, taken from the *Ethical Consumer* criteria for the evaluation of products and companies.

Social accounting also tends to assume that in addition to reporting to shareholders and other owners and finance providers, organizations should report to their 'stakeholders' – the other internal and external participants in the organization. These are normally assumed to be:

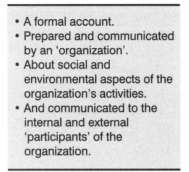

- A formal account.
- Prepared and communicated by an 'organization'.
- About social and environmental aspects of the organization's activities.
- And communicated to the internal and external 'participants' of the organization.

Figure 7.2 *The Basic Elements of the Conventional Corporate Social Accounting Model*

- members of local communities;
- employees and trade unions;
- consumers; and
- society at large.

These, then, are the basic elements of the social accounting/CSR framework – the basic (but often implicit) assumptions that the CSR literature adopts. They are summarized in Figure 7.2. These basic characteristics are, however, underspecified in that they do not tell us, for example, why an organization might self-report, or why it might, or should, report on particular aspects and to particular groups of individuals. Clearly, international companies do not, for example, communicate to everybody the detail of their environmental impacts, their impacts on communities in lesser developed countries or their attempts to persuade governments not to pass legislation that might restrict their commercial activities. So why do organizations report at all and, more importantly, why do they *not* report and why should they report?

These questions raise ethical, social and political – as well as economic – issues. In fact, all of accounting and as a result all of CSR, implicitly begs a whole range of fundamental questions about the structure of, and power in, society, the role of economic as opposed to social and political considerations, the proper ethical response to issues, and so on. Sadly, these matters are rarely made explicit in accounting and finance education and training, so, as a result, we as accountants tend to be ill-equipped to consider these issues.

References

Cooper, D J and Sherer, M J (1984) 'The Value of Corporate Accounting Reports: Arguments for a Political Economy of Accounting', *Accounting Organizations and Society*, vol 9, no 3–4, pp207–232

Gambling, T (1977) 'Magic, Accounting and Morale', *Accounting, Organizations and Society*, vol 2, no 2, pp141–151

Gambling, T (1977) 'Accounting to Society', in B V Carsberg and A J B Hope (eds) *Current Issues in Accounting*, Philip Allen, Oxford

Gray, R H, Owen, D L and Maunders, K T (1987) *Corporate Social Reporting: Accounting and Accountability*, Prentice-Hall, Hemel Hempstead

Hines, R D (1988) 'Financial Accounting: in Communicating Reality, We Construct Reality', *Accounting, Organizations and Society*, vol 13, no 3, pp251–261

Hines, R D (1989) 'The Sociopolitical Paradigm in Financial Accounting and the Maintenance of the Social World', *Accounting, Organization and Society*, vol 2, no 1, pp52–76

Hines, R D (1991) 'The FASB's Conceptual Framework, Financial Accounting and the Maintenance of the Social World', *Accounting, Organization and Society*, vol 16, no 4, pp313–332

Laughlin, R C and Gray, R H (1998) *Financial Accounting: Method and Meaning*, Van Nostrand Reinhold, London

8

The Green Bottom Line

Martin Bennett and Peter James

This chapter begins by addressing three questions:

1 What is environment-related management accounting?
2 Why should it be undertaken?
3 Who should do it?

It then identifies relevant sources of financial and non-financial information and discusses the ways in which existing management accounting techniques can be modified to take account of environmental issues. A final section then draws conclusions.

What is Environment-related Management Accounting?

The term 'environmental accounting' has been used to cover both national and firm-level accounting activities, the processing of both financial and non-financial information and the calculation and use of monetized external damage costs as well as those that are internal to the firm (see US EPA, 1998a). For clarity, Figure 8.1 distinguishes six different domains of environmental accounting that are relevant to the firm level, based on their boundaries of attention – an individual organization, the supply chain of which it forms part and the whole of society – and the extent to which they focus on financial and/or non-financial information.

The six domains that emerge can be defined in this way (the two life-cycle definitions are based on the discussion in US EPA, 1998a):

1 *Energy and materials accounting:* the tracking and analysis of all flows of energy and substances into, through and out of an organization.
2 *Environment-related financial management:* the generation, analysis and use of monetized information to improve corporate environmental and economic performance.
3 *Life-cycle assessment:* a holistic approach to identifying the environmental consequences of a product or service through its entire life-cycle and identifying opportunities for achieving environmental improvements.

Reproduced in full from M Bennet and P James (eds) (1998) *The Green Bottom Line: Environmental Accounting for Management*, pp30–60, by kind permission of Greenleaf Publishing, Sheffield, UK

	Organization	Supply chain	Society
Financial focus	Environment-related financial management	Life-cycle cost assessment	Environmental externalities costing
Non-financial focus	Energy and materials accounting	Life-cycle assessment	Environmental impact assessment

Figure 8.1 *The Domains of Firm-level Environmental Accounting*

4   *Life-cycle cost assessment:* a systematic process for evaluating the life-cycle costs of a product or service by identifying environmental consequences and assigning measures of monetary value to those consequences.
5   *Environmental impact assessment:* a systematic process for identifying all the environmental consequences of the activities of an organization, site or project.
6   *Environmental externalities costing:* the generation, analysis and use of monetized estimates of environmental damage (and benefits) created by the activities of an organization, site or project.

Firm-level environmental accounting can potentially encompass all the six domains, but in practice is centred in the first two as the areas where accountants' experience and accounting techniques (as opposed to those of, say, environmental managers and environmental management techniques) have the most to contribute.

The literature on firm-level environmental accounting initially focused – and, to a considerable extent, still does – on external accountability to stakeholders outside the company, rather than on serving the needs of management. There are two distinct aspects to this:

1   A broad concept of accountability to all of a company's stakeholders.
2   The traditional financial accounting focus of providing accurate and reliable information on the financial position of companies to their shareholders.

In both cases, the emphasis is on collecting, verifying and reporting information to audiences outside the organization, as opposed to the internal audience of the organization's own management.

The broad accountability approach is founded on the premise that the responsibility of companies should not be seen – as in the traditional micro-economic theory that still largely shapes company law – as limited to maximizing profits or value for the benefit of their owners (shareholders) alone. On the contrary, the activities of companies have wider impacts on society and the environment and an enlightened company will recognize this and ensure that it maintains good relationships with all its stakeholder groups in order to preserve its implicit 'licence to operate' (RSA, 1994). This was the main theme in much of the early literature on environmental accounting (Bebbington and Thompson, 1996; CICA, 1992; Grayson, Woolston and Tanega, 1993; Müller et al, 1994; Gray, Bebbington and Walters, 1993; Gray, Owen and Adams, 1996; Owen, 1992; Zadek, Pruzan and Evans, 1997) and has been largely responsible for prompting many companies to publish corporate environmental reports (KPMG, 1997; Lober et al, 1997; Owen, Gray and Adams, 1997; SustainAbility/UNEP, 1997). Even some authors who have seen themselves as following a management accounting approach – ie one that focuses on the provision of information for internal decision-making – have, in practice, placed considerable emphasis on its role in generating information for external stakeholders (Birkin and Woodward, 1997a–f).

There has also been a narrower concern, particularly within the accountancy profession and among financial regulators such as the US Securities and Exchange Commission (SEC), that regular financial reports by companies to their shareholders may be significantly inaccurate. It is said that these do not adequately reflect the effect on the business of environmental issues, particularly in the US where 'Superfund' liabilities can be substantial (Ethridge and Rogers, 1997; Schoemaker and Schoemaker, 1995). The accounting profession in Europe and internationally has also considered this and has provided guidance to its members (ASB, 1997; FEE, 1996; IASC, 1997; ICAEW, 1996), although the prevailing consensus seems to be that existing financial accounting practices, so long as they are properly applied, are adequate to deal with environmental effects on business and do not require change.

Both these bodies of work can be seen as adopting a 'financial accounting' approach – that is, with a focus on reporting to external stakeholders. However, there is now a growing literature that adopts a genuine 'management accounting' approach that does focus on providing information to support internal decision-making (although, of course, much of this data may be of value to external stakeholders also). The starting point for this was probably the well-known '3P' (Pollution Prevention Pays) initiative introduced by 3M during the 1970s. This was expanded during the 1980s and early 1990s by further pollution prevention initiatives introduced by companies and/or government-sponsored programmes in The Netherlands, the US and other countries. These required more precise data on the costs and benefits of environmental action and therefore spawned new methodologies such as the 'total cost assessment' technique developed by the Tellus Institute for the US Environmental Protection Agency (EPA) (White, Becker and Goldstein, 1991; see also Reiskin et al, 1998). The EPA has since sponsored a number of studies and publications on the topic and the Tellus Institute has continued with its applied research and application. Other important US contributions have been made by Bailey and Soyka (1996), Ditz, Ranganathan and Banks (1995), Epstein (1996a, 1996b), IMA (1995) and Rubenstein (1994). In Europe, the topic has been addressed by, inter alia, IIIEE and VTT (1997), Schaltegger, Müller and Hindrichsen (1996), Tuppen (1996) and Wolters and Bouman (1995).

This book is positioned within this management accounting approach and contains contributions from most of the authors and organizations cited. We see this focus as being complementary, rather than an alternative, to a financial accounting approach. It addresses different needs and is also necessary in order to provide many of the data that are of interest to external stakeholders.

Our working definition of environment-related management accounting is therefore: '*The generation, analysis and use of financial and non-financial information in order to optimize corporate environmental and economic performance and achieve sustainable business.*' The term 'environmental' precedes 'economic' in order to indicate an environmental bias. As we discuss below, the main aim at present must be to overcome the barriers to environmental action that can be created by current management accounting practices. However, there will be occasions when even modified practices reveal trade-offs between environmental and economic parameters which will result in the latter being given priority over the former. For this reason, we use the term 'environment-related management accounting' in our following discussions to signal that the activity is focused on meeting corporate as well as societal objectives.[1]

We include the term 'sustainable business' to indicate that, although much of the practical action generated by environment-related management accounting involves the adaptation of existing activities, such as management accounting and environmental management, part of its objective is to support the goals of sustainable development (see below).

A final point is that environment-related management accounting relies heavily on non-financial information, particularly regarding inputs, outputs and flows of energy, materials and water (see below). Some would see the development of this information as a primary objective – for example, Birkin and Woodward (1997a–f). However, we would argue that, at present, such information is a means rather than an end for environment-related management accounting. Its ultimate objective is to provide information to support environment-related decision-making by mainstream business managers. While this may sometimes require 'raw' physical data, we believe that the need is more often for either productivity measures – for example, materials consumption or waste generation per unit of production – or information expressed in financial units. This is because:

- For profit-seeking firms, the ultimate objective (maximizing shareholder value or profitability) is expressible in monetary form and information that can be expressed in the same or related – for example, productivity – terms is always likely to attract more immediate attention.
- The financial side of management is relevant to all functions, including environmental management. Not only do environmental budgets need to be managed, but proposals for action that can be justified in terms of conventional methods of financial investment appraisal and product costing, for example, are more likely to be successful.

A supporting point is that environmental and operational managers are fully capable of developing and using such data and are often doing so in practice. Hence, there is no need to invent a new discipline or activity to accomplish this. Indeed, to do so could be counterproductive because it may foster resentment and defensiveness among line staff about territorial aggrandizement by accountants.

More pragmatically, there is little evidence that the accountancy and finance functions are greatly involved in energy and materials accounting activities in most companies or have the interest and expertise to do so in the near future. A case study at Zeneca (Bennett and James, 1998a), for example, found that the substantial savings that followed such an exercise at the company's Huddersfield site were almost entirely driven by operational staff and had only a marginal accounting involvement.

At first sight, this argument may appear to be in conflict with advocates such as Kaplan and Norton (1992, 1993, 1996a, 1996b), Simmonds (1991) and Wilson (1997) who have argued for the development of strategic management accounting and, as part of this, for greater use of non-financial data and indicators. However, we would argue that their views are less relevant to an area that usually has a relative abundance of non-financial data and a shortage of financial data. Moreover, their arguments have had – at least as yet – only a limited impact on management accounting practice. While there is certainly more attention being paid to the strategic use of non-financial data and indicators through 'balanced scorecards', anecdotal evidence suggests that it is more often strategic planning, business excellence and other functions that are implementing it, rather than accountancy and finance. Research in other areas of management accounting has also found that practice can be slow to adapt (Drury et al, 1993) and that initiatives in new or developing areas such as non-financial performance measurement are often taken by functions other than accounting.

For all these reasons, we would suggest that the immediate priorities for environment-related management accounting are the generation, analysis and use of financial or neo-financial – for example, indicators of resource productivity – information and modifying and adapting the established techniques of management accounting and financial management to take account of environmental issues.

Why Undertake Environment-related Management Accounting?

The primary aim of environment-related management accounting is to better inform and otherwise support decision-making processes that are influenced by environmental factors – which are primarily those of accounting and financial management, environmental management and operational management.[2] Some of the specific objectives that this creates can be summarized as:

- Demonstrating the impact on the income statement (profit and loss account) and/or balance sheet of environment-related activities.
- Identifying cost reduction and other improvement opportunities.
- Prioritizing environmental actions.
- Guiding product pricing, mix and development decisions.
- Enhancing customer value.
- Future-proofing investment and other decisions with long-term consequences.
- Supporting sustainable business.

Income statement and balance sheet impact

There is growing evidence that the environment can have significant impacts on expenses, revenues, assets and liabilities and that these impacts are often underestimated.

Making such financial impacts apparent can make it easier to take and win support for further environmental initiatives.

In the US, most attention has focused on the balance sheet issue of environment-related liabilities. This is a consequence of the high levels of damage claims and fines and of specific legislation such as that requiring the clean-up of contaminated land. It has been estimated that American industry may be under-provided for 'Superfund'-related clean-up liabilities by up to a trillion dollars (Schoemaker and Schoemaker, 1995). Liabilities are less in the UK and other European countries, but still significant for some companies. They may become more significant if proposed legislation on the topic comes into force.

Investment in environment-related assets can also be significant: the chemical industry has estimated that up to 20 per cent of its new capital investment in recent years has been to deal with environmental problems. This is financially significant because these assets have to be financed but, to the extent that the need for them is driven by compliance rather than by commercial business criteria, they do not generate any direct return.

European attention has been focused more on opportunities to reduce or avoid expenses than on liabilities and this topic is increasing in importance in the US too. Initiatives are usually taken on a one-off basis (see below), but an aggregate measure of savings can be a useful means of demonstrating that environmental management can be a profit contributor rather than merely an additional cost burden on business and of building bridges between environmental staff and mainstream management. 3M calculates the accumulated first year's savings from initiatives carried out under its Pollution Prevention Pays (3P) programme, while Baxter International (Bennett and James, 1998b), produces an annual environmental financial statement with details of expenses and savings. So far, less attention has been paid to the revenue opportunities arising from environmental action, but these too may be significant in future.

Cost reduction and improvement

A number of corporate programmes, practical demonstration projects and research studies have shown that waste minimization and similar initiatives can create savings and cost avoidance. In the first phase of the Aire and Calder Valley study (Johnston, 1994), for example, potential improvements worth £2 million per annum were identified across the 11 industrial sites studied, with more longer term possibilities in prospect when the project had run longer. Of the proposals stimulated by the project, 72 per cent had payback periods of either zero or less than 12 months. Similarly impressive results have been reported by other waste minimization and energy efficiency projects (see, for example, Schroeder, 1998, Bennett and James, 1998b, 1998c). In addition, these and other initiatives, such as product redesign, can sometimes increase product quality and therefore sales revenues.

Of course, once the low-hanging fruit has been gathered, there may be a point at which further cost reductions are not available (Walley and Whitehead, 1994). However, if regulatory and social demands continue to increase and to create new potential costs for business, this point may be delayed for some time. Even after many years of waste minimization initiatives, Dow, for example, continues to expect to find a large number of waste minimization and similar projects that can provide annual returns on capital of at least 30–40 per cent over the coming decade (McLean and Shopley, 1996).

Prioritize environmental actions

If they are fortunate, companies will need to prioritize between a number of win-win improvement opportunities. If not, they may need to prioritize between environmental improvements that do not create any net economic benefit but which may, nonetheless, have differing rates of (negative) return. DuPont, for example, calculates the costs of different means of meeting given emission reduction targets as a means of achieving this.

Guide product pricing/mix/development decisions

To maximize product profitability, it is vital that accurate product cost information is available and taken into account when setting prices. This information also allows poorly performing products to be changed or dropped from the product range. A study by the World Resources Institute (Ditz, Ranganathan and Banks, 1998) found, at several of the companies they examined, that, although environmental costs were significant, they were not being fully identified and allocated to products, so that pricing was not reflective of real costs (Ditz, Ranganathan and Banks, 1995). As previously noted, the environment can also influence the lifetime costs of products – for example, by requiring end-of-life disposal routes. Gaining a better understanding of these costs – as with the Philips model for considering end-of-life disposal costs (Brouwers and Stevels, 1997) – allows timely action to be taken to minimize or avoid them through redesign and/or to put more cost-effective disposal routes in place.

In the long run, too, many markets are likely to be shaped by environmental factors – including the changing cost structures resulting from eco-taxes and other developments. Although this threatens some existing products and services, it also creates opportunities for others (Fussler with James, 1996; Porter and van der Linde, 1995). Gaining a better understanding of medium- to long-term environmental costs and benefits can help to neutralize threats and ensure that opportunities are taken.

Enhance customer value

Environmental actions taken within discrete portions of product chains can sometimes be economically and/or environmentally suboptimal, so coordinated action can provide higher returns for all the chain members involved. One example from our research was a company providing a chemical in a small disposable container. The containers were expensive to buy and incurred waste-disposal costs for the customer. Changing to reusable containers reduced procurement costs for the supplier and eliminated the customer's waste costs. Demonstrating a detailed business case for such actions can spur improvement and also provide opportunities to develop closer relationships with customers.

Future-proofing decisions

Many investment and product development decisions are determined by levels of costs and benefits arising some years in the future. Unanticipated environmental factors can often affect these costs and benefits, sometimes to the point where returns become negative. Bennett and James (1998d) discuss how the risks of this can be reduced through better analysis of environment-related costs and benefits (see also below).

Supporting sustainable business

There is increasing discussion of the implications of sustainable development for business, which are clearly considerable (DeSimone and Popoff, 1997). They include:

- radical improvements in environmental performance: a minimum 'factor-four' reduction in environmental impact is needed for the delivery of final goods and services to consumers, according to some estimates (von Weizsäcker, Lovins and Lovins, 1997);
- 'eco-innovation' – that is, development of new products and processes that are capable of meeting these objectives (Fussler with James, 1996);
- a long-term perspective in decision-making, with greater emphasis on the impacts of decisions on future generations; and
- a greater degree of internalization of the external environmental costs to business.

This implies the need for environmental and management accounting systems to collect new types of data, such as those relating to environmental effects throughout the entire product chain. It also suggests that more attention needs to be paid by accountants and others to identifying and raising internal awareness of long-term cost trends.

The section on environmental value analysis towards the end of the chapter discusses one way in which environment-related management accounting can operationalize these ideas.

Who Are the Environment-related Management Accountants?

Our answer is: anyone who is involved in generating financial and neo-financial information about the business impacts of environmental issues. Hence, many environmental and operational managers and some management accountants are already practising environment-related management accounting. In this respect, environment-related management accounting is largely a 'virtual' activity enhancing what already exists rather than creating something completely new. This is primarily:

1 Making better use of, or modifying, existing sources of data and generating new ones.
2 Making better use of, or modifying, existing management accounting techniques.

One additional task is to foster the longer term perspective that allows the challenge of sustainable development to be addressed by the business (see above). A second is the need to create processes that bring together the accounting, environmental and other functions to achieve both specific objectives and a more general awareness of each other's concerns and activities. An obvious example is to include environmental managers in both regular investment appraisal and other business case procedures and also irregular accounting change activities such as activity-based costing (ABC) or business process re-engineering. Conversely, accountants and accounting data need to be included within environmental management systems (McLaughlin and Elwood, 1996).

Researchers have found that the benefits from such processes can be as important as any specific outcomes. That is also the conclusion of many practical initiatives, such as the environmental financial statement developed by Baxter (Bennett and James, 1998b).

This combined requirement to change the conduct of existing tasks, to establish a longer term view of the business implications of sustainable development and to initiate and maintain new processes, suggests that there is a need for a concrete manifestation of environment-related management accounting in the form of an organizational 'champion'. To be effective, he or she will require a combination of personal dynamism and vision and accounting, business and environmental know-how. In principle, this could be found and therefore located in any business function, but the critical need at present to change the attitudes and actions of accountants and the accounting function suggests that the champion will have maximum impact if located there.

The seeds of such a development have been sown by professional management accountancy institutes who have called for more involvement in environmental management by their members. The UK Chartered Institute of Management Accountants (1997) has commented that:

> *the forward-thinking management accountant should be taking an active role in environmental management … as he or she has key skills to apply to the process, including the provision of advice relating to strategy formation and the effective use of resources.*

Parker, commenting for the US Institute of Management Accountants' Foundation for Applied Research on the Tellus Institute's study of environmental cost accounting for capital budgeting (White et al, 1995; White and Savage, 1995), has also observed that:

> *corporate accountants and financial managers are not necessarily in the best position to recognize and understand the trend toward transforming internal costs. In many cases, recognition of what is at stake comes from non-financial professionals. But management accountants, aware of the strategic value of environmental accounting and aided*

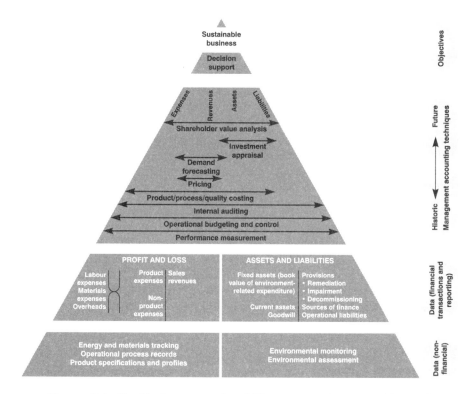

Figure 8.2 *The Environment-related Management Accounting Pyramid*

by decision support tools, can wake up senior management to the necessity for analyzing environmental costs. This leadership can change senior management's perception that management accountants are simply corporate scorekeepers (Parker, 1995, p53).

There is less evidence to date of individual companies taking the initiative, but this is likely to change in future.

The Practice of Environment-related Management Accounting

Figure 8.2 provides a graphical representation of what this involves in practice. It is divided into three vertical levels to indicate a progression from the foundation of non-financial and financial data, through the techniques that process this into information – that is, outputs that are useful for managers and stakeholders – to the highest level objectives (see discussion above). The next section discusses the base of the triangle – that is, relevant data – in more detail, while the subsequent section considers the techniques that convert this into information.

Key Data for Environment-related Management Accounting

This section discusses the existing data sources and systems that can provide inputs to environment-related management accounting, the extent to which they take the environment into account (or conceal its importance) at present and possible ways in which they can be modified or supplemented to reflect environmental considerations in future.

Non-financial data

As Kaplan and Norton (1992, 1993, 1996a, 1996b) and others have stressed, non-financial data is an important element in all areas of management accounting. This is particularly true of environment-related management accounting whose ultimate 'raw material' is data on physical and energy flows and stocks, and their impacts on the environment. This is collected in operational process records, material resource planning systems, resource planning, emissions monitoring and other systems which are managed by production, environmental and other non-accounting functions. Moreover, Shields, Beloff and Heller's study of five oil and chemical companies in the US and Mexico (1998) found that such non-financial information was more useful for day-to-day environmental decision-making than was financial data. We believe that the generation of non-financial data should not be seen as a central objective of environment-related management accounting, on the grounds that it is either already being provided – or could more easily be provided in future – by functions such as environmental management or production. However, this is not to say that accounting techniques or accounting professionals cannot play a role in this area. The potential for this has been explored in detail by the ECOMAC project (Bartolomeo, Bennett and James, 1998). One of the key opportunities that has emerged from this and other studies is to obtain a better understanding of the extent and financial implications of energy, materials and water flows through organizations (see Bartolomeo, 1998; Haveman and Foecke, 1998, Bierma et al, 1998 and Schroeder, 1998). This is important for many reasons, but especially because the full costs of wasted materials – that is, including their purchase price and the costs of processing them to the point where they become waste – are often the single most significant environmental cost (see Bennett and James, 1998a). Except for specific industry sectors, such as chemicals and pharmaceuticals which have always been concerned with the yields and detailed characteristics of their processes, few organizations in the UK and US appear to have a full picture of their energy and material flows; indeed, obtaining such a picture is usually the first step in successful waste minimization programmes and often creates non-environmental business benefits.

As yet, there are no American or British equivalents (at least in the public domain) of the Germanic 'eco-balancing' approach practised by Kunert and other companies, which builds a picture of all energy and material flows on a periodic basis (Bennett and James, 1998e; Birkin and Woodward, 1997d; James, Prehn and Steger, 1997). This is then used as the basis for day-to-day 'eco-controlling' in order to reduce environmental impacts (Hallay and Pfriem, 1992; Hopfenbeck and Jasch, 1993; Schulz and Schulz, 1994). One potential task for environment-related management accounting in the US and the UK is therefore to apply these ideas and associated techniques there.

Financial data

The accounting function in business (and non-business organizations) has, potentially, three distinct objectives:

- The day-to-day operational needs of initiating and recording transactions and of managing assets and liabilities such as, respectively, working capital and bank loans.
- Supplying regular external financial reports to shareholders, to provide them with reassurance that their assets are being safeguarded and their interests are being met. This is a legal obligation for companies in all advanced economies.
- Providing management within the organization with information that is relevant to its function of making decisions and ensuring that the organization's activities and outputs are kept under proper control.

The first objective is essential for day-to-day operations. The second is a legal obligation. The third objective is optional and the extent to which financial information and techniques are used in management is discretionary and will reflect the particular management style adopted. However, some internal financial processes are near-universal in organizations of any significant size, such as budget-setting and budgetary control and tracking costs through the organization to the responsible department and manager.

To support these three objectives in large organizations, an integrated system of accounting data capture and collection is needed – ledgers, registers, cash books, etc. Although the principal factors in the design of these systems are likely to be determined by the needs of the first two objectives, they also represent a financial database that is available for use by management.

This subsection reviews the breadth of the financial data that are usually available, based for convenience on the classification of the legally required published financial reports. These are centred on two core financial statements. The first is the income statement, which aggregates expenses and revenues throughout a given financial period (usually a year). The second is the balance sheet which summarizes a company's assets and liabilities at a particular point in time (usually at the end of the same financial period). These four basic categories of expenses, revenues, assets and liabilities are reflected in Figure 8.2.

Expenses and Revenues

The basic accounting systems within organizations (the bookkeeping systems and ledgers) will generally capture and collate expenses in terms of a combination of two parameters:

1   The type of resource being acquired and consumed: materials, labour, services, depreciation, etc.
2   The functional area of the business in which the expenses are incurred: production, selling and distribution, general and administrative, etc.

These classifications reflect the sources of the data in the various subsystems of a normal business accounting system. Labour costs will be available from payroll systems; materials costs from materials management systems which draw their data from invoices and bills of materials; the depreciation charge from a register of fixed assets; etc.

Traditionally in management accounting (including here its junior sibling, cost accounting), there has been more emphasis on dealing with costs than with revenues. This reflects the origins of cost accounting in the production function, due in large part to the financial requirement to report in published financial reports the historic cost of stocks (inventories). This requires detailed analyses of production costs.

There is no equivalent external compulsion to carry out detailed analyses of revenues. Only relatively recently in most organizations, in terms of the historic development of accounting, has the marketing function achieved the importance that it has in modern business. Hence, the traditional emphasis has been on production and costs rather than on marketing and revenues.

The accounting systems will need to capture and collect data on revenues as they arise through transactions, as evidenced by shipping documentation and invoices and will need to analyse these in sufficient detail to support management – as a minimum, by type of product, customer, market sector and distribution channel.

Reclassifying accounting data after its initial entry is sometimes impossible and almost always time-consuming and costly. Hence, the secret of success in all areas of management accounting – including that related to environmental issues – is to capture any data necessary for analysis (such as the purpose of expenses) – when the data are entered. However, modifying existing systems can also be costly. The lowest-cost option is to build in environmental considerations when systems are being changed for other reasons: for example, because of the introduction of an activity-based costing system (see below). A key task for environment-related management accounting is therefore to ensure that the needs of environmental management are considered when changes are being made. The opportunity is to obtain better-quality data, but almost as important is to avoid a deterioration in the quality of existing data. In one company that we researched, a re-engineering exercise resulted in previously separate categories for energy purchases – electricity, gas, etc. – being collapsed into a single energy category. As a result, it lost the ability to calculate easily its energy-related carbon dioxide emissions.

Assets

Accountants identify three broad categories of asset: fixed (or long-term) assets, current assets and goodwill (a particular type of long-term asset). Fixed assets are those with a useful life beyond a single accounting year and are (with some exceptions) stated in the balance sheet at their original historic cost, reduced by depreciation provided to date in respect of the portion of their useful life that, to date, has expired. The high cost and long life of assets such as pollution control equipment and landfill sites means that these can be significant fixed assets and the depreciation on them can also be significant, although this is often excluded in calculations of environmental costs.

An alternative method of valuing fixed assets is at their replacement cost. This is of potential environmental significance because rising environmental standards often mean that the cost of building new environment-related facilities is much higher than those that are being replaced (see below). This is the case with landfill at Zeneca's Huddersfield site (Bennett and James, 1998a). The company has a long-standing site which is fully depreciated. Hence, only operating expenses are charged back to product and process cost centres. As the site has many years' life, this can be practically justified but, at current rates of waste generation, a replacement landfill facility will have to be built at some point. This is likely to be very expensive and will therefore result in an immediate increase in recharged costs as depreciation is included in the figures. However, the conventional method of basing these recharges on historic costs means that managers who take decisions that affect the volume of wastes generated, through process control and product design, are not encouraged by the system to take into account also the opportunity cost that is indirectly incurred as landfill capacity is consumed.

The main current assets for most companies are cash balances, debtors (accounts receivable) and stocks and work in progress. Although the environment has some tangential relevance to these – changes in environmental legislation could result in stocks becoming more difficult or impossible to sell – this is not for most a major area of concern.

Goodwill is an asset with whose treatment the accounting profession has been struggling, with only limited success, for some time. Conventional accounting practice recognizes and includes goodwill in company balance sheets only when money is directly outlaid to acquire it, when one company is purchased by another. The goodwill then arising is the amount by which the purchase consideration exceeds the value of the tangible net assets acquired and represents what the acquirer is prepared to pay for the present value of the amount by which the acquirer's future profits are expected to exceed a normal rate of return. However, the true value of goodwill in any company should also include what it has built up within the business as a result of operating over time and building up a reputation among customers, even though this is not represented by any specific outlays and is therefore not captured by the accounting system. Several authors have suggested that the environment is an important determinant of company reputation, although the precise extent of this is difficult to quantify (DeSimone and Popoff, 1997; Charter, 1992).

Liabilities

Liabilities can be distinguished by type into three broad categories: sources of finance; liabilities arising from normal operations; and provisions.

In most major corporations, the raising of finance and the balancing of debt and equity is handled within the finance function by a treasury management function which is separate from the financial controlling activities of then allocating, managing and accounting for this finance within the business. Environmental performance is increasingly significant for treasury management since the extent of risks being borne by a company, including those that are environment-related, can affect access to, and the cost of, raising new capital. Several studies – for example, Butler, 1997 – have shown that funds that invest in companies with good environmental records have matched and sometimes outperformed the market average, thereby lowering the cost of raising equity, and, conversely, that those investing in companies that have experienced major environmental incidents have been depressed, making new equity more expensive (Blumberg, Korsvold and Blum, 1997). Kvaerner, for example, has paid slightly lower interest rates on loans because of its good environmental record and consequently greater creditworthiness. Some analysts and insurers are coming to see evidence of good environmental management by a company as indicative of the quality of its management generally.

Liabilities arising from normal operations include trade and most sundry creditors, corporation tax due and tax collected but not yet paid over in connection with PAYE (pay as you earn) and VAT (value added tax), etc. These may be affected by any events occurring within the business, including environment-related events, but are unlikely to be particularly significantly affected by environmental management.

Provisions are amounts allocated to cover any likely future liabilities or losses that have arisen but have not yet been settled (provisions included under 'liabilities' will exclude any provisions made in connection with the impairment in value of assets, such as those arising from the depreciation of fixed assets or from the obsolescence of inventories, which will be reflected in the balance sheet as a reduction in the value of the related assets). There is considerable concern that significant liabilities could exist in respect of, for example, remediation or future decommissioning costs, which are frequently not fully provided for in company financial reports. The US Environmental Protection Agency (1998b) provides an overview of how potential remediation liabilities can be assessed as an aid to both internal decision-making and external reporting. Barth and McNichols (1994) and Schoemaker and Schoemaker (1995) also provide good overviews.

Until now, the emphasis has been on quantifying liabilities arising from past events but, while this remains important, Brent Spar and other developments have focused attention on potential future liabilities. In order to be proactive and to ensure that environmental liabilities are not underprovided, Chevron has introduced a systematic cross-functional process to identify, evaluate, measure and disclose its environmental liabilities and then monitor their remediation (Lawrence and Cerf, 1995).

Techniques

The second tier of the pyramid in Figure 8.2 identifies the main management accounting techniques that are used to process the data arising from the financial and non-financial systems into information for management's benefit: performance measurement, operational budgeting and control, internal auditing, costing, pricing, demand forecasting, investment appraisal and shareholder value analysis. All of these are actually or potentially relevant to the environment. One important distinction is between those that are concerned with current data and those (broadly, demand forecasting, investment appraisal and shareholder value analysis) that make projections into the future. Subsequent sections discuss the environmental relevance of each of these techniques.

Performance Measurement

Performance measurement is a growing field in all areas of business. Traditional performance measurement in the UK and the US, particularly at higher levels of management, has focused on meeting financial targets. However, over the last decade, the quality movement and other drivers have focused attention on the importance of non-financial performance measures and schemes such as the European Quality Award, and Kaplan and Norton's 'balanced scorecard' now provide templates for this (Kaplan and Norton, 1992, 1993, 1996a, 1996b). To date, environment-related performance management has been developed largely by environmental managers and has limited interaction with management or others involved in strategic performance measurement (Bennett and James, 1998e). However, as other authors – for example, Epstein (1996b) – have noted, the environment should be an important part of a balanced scorecard for many companies and more interaction is needed in future. Many of the practical challenges of developing and implementing environment-related performance measurement are also generic to all areas of performance measurement and greater interaction would facilitate mutual sharing of experience and learning. Finally, the dependence of environment-related management accounting on the non-financial data that is generated by environmental, operational and other functions makes it important that its needs are considered during each of their own performance measurement processes.

Operational Budgeting and Control

The setting of budgets is an important means of implementing strategic objectives, while tracking budgetary outcomes can be a valuable means of monitoring how well objectives are being achieved. Budgeting is relevant to environmental management for three reasons. First, environmental actions will require resources that need to be specified within budgets. Second, budgetary outcomes can be a useful means of checking whether environmental goals are being achieved – for example, over-budget expenditures on energy provide an early warning that energy efficiency targets are unlikely to be achieved. Finally, as has been previously noted, identifying and allocating environmental costs to specific budgets provides a powerful incentive for action to be taken.

Internal Auditing

An external audit to verify the published financial report is required of companies by law. In addition, most companies of a significant size also operate an internal audit function. This is optional and its responsibilities, activities and position in the organization are at the discretion of each company, although professional guidance on internal auditing generally is available from bodies such as the Institute of Internal Auditors.

Traditionally, an internal audit has been a part of the finance function, reporting to the finance director and primarily concerned with internal checks and controls on financial data and activities. One motive in many organizations was to minimize the costs of external auditors by using internal audit as a more cost-effective means of providing assurance on the quality of internal controls and thereby to reduce the quantity of detailed checking work that the external auditors needed to do directly themselves. More recently, the role of internal audit has expanded to include the audits of (in particular) computer systems, operations and the quality of management. An internal audit has become central to risk assessment and management in many companies and its importance has been enhanced by recent concerns over corporate governance. One effect of this has been that internal audit now reports within the organization, increasingly frequently, not within the finance function but at chief executive level, often with a further reporting line to an audit committee at board level.

Internal audit is potentially relevant to environmental management in several ways, especially for companies for whom environmental issues may represent potentially significant risk factors to their businesses. One area of apparent potential overlap or cooperation is the environmental audit, although this will depend on the objectives of the particular environmental audit and how far the competences that it requires may be outside the scope of the other activities of internal audit. In most organizations, most environmental audits are handled by a specialist corporate environmental management function, although some environment-related checks may be included in regular internal audit programmes.

Internal audit can also be relevant through its original purpose of checking and confirming the accuracy and integrity of information – the information that is used internally by management, as well as what is published externally. This function includes both the integrity of the data that are captured and collected through the organization and how these are then converted into usable information and disseminated in reports to management and/or published externally. For example, the Environmental Issues Unit of British Telecom enlists the support of their colleagues in the company's internal audit function to help to assure the integrity of the information that they plan to publish in their annual environmental report, prior to its further verification by an external party.

Costing

Costing is perhaps the area of greatest activity within environment-related management accounting (Ditz, Ranganathan and Banks, 1995; Epstein, 1996a, 1996b; Russell, Skalak and Miller, 1995). This section discusses six main issues associated with costing:

1   Activity-based costing
2   Quality costing
3   Product costing
4   Life-cycle costing
5   Cost projection
6   Strategic costing

Activity-based costing (ABC)

Traditional costing techniques have been based on specific categories of direct cost such as labour and materials, plus a residual overhead. The latter is then frequently either allocated to products or processes on a more or less arbitrary basis – for example, the EPA's study of the electroplating industry (Haveman and Foecke, 1998) found that square footage of product was the easiest way to do this for environment-related costs – or written off as a period cost and therefore not tracked through to products or processes at all. Indeed, in many companies, the main part of environment-related costs such as energy, water, waste disposal and the salaries of environmental staff are likely to be included in overheads (White et al, 1995; White and Savage, 1995). These practices mean that, where products or processes have high environmental costs, the figures can be hidden from decision-makers. This decreases the motivation to reduce the costs and can also create a bias against pollution prevention projects (Hamner and Stinson, 1993).

One potential solution to this problem – which is common to other areas of management accounting – is cost system redesign (Drury and Tayles, 1998). As Schaltegger and Müller (1998) discuss, an approach that is of particular relevance to the environment is activity-based costing. This tries to create more meaningful cost information by tracking costs to products and processes on the basis of the underlying 'drivers' that cause those costs to be created in the first place. The amount of cost lost in overheads is thereby greatly reduced. As a result, product prices can be set more accurately and significant cost drivers can be targeted for cost-reduction measures. Where the environment is a significant cost driver, it will be highlighted naturally by ABC activities. However, there is usually considerable scope for more proactive environmental concern, either by building a more detailed picture of environmental cost drivers and categories where these have already emerged as important, or by highlighting them when this is not the case (Kreuze and Newell, 1994). Schaltegger and Müller (1998) explore this issue at a conceptual level, while Bierma, Waterstraat and Ostrosky (1998) show the close relationship between ABC and environment-related management accounting at Chrysler's Belvidere plant. However, Shields, Beloff and Heller (1998) found that ABC was not widely used by the North American companies that they studied. The ECOMAC survey (Bouma and Wolters, 1998) reached similar conclusions for Europe. Hence, supplementary routes will be needed to introduce environment-related management accounting for the foreseeable future.

Quality costing

Several authorities have identified the links between total quality management programmes and good environmental management (Roth and Keller, 1997; Davies, 1997). Quality costing aims to measure in financial terms the benefits of good quality management and is complementary to ABC. The rationale of quality costing is to highlight the costs of non-quality in order to stimulate motivation to reduce these and to prioritize possible actions. Conventional quality costing distinguishes three types of cost:

1   *Failure:* the costs of putting right or otherwise dealing with defects, arising through either internal failure or external failure – that is, those defects that occur in use by customers).

2   *Monitoring:* inspection and other costs to ensure that defects are eliminated or detected.
3   *Prevention:* costs of avoiding defects.

The finding from cost-of-quality studies is frequently that, in the long run, total costs are minimized when the emphasis is placed on prevention rather than on either monitoring or the toleration of failures. However, without these studies, this might not be apparent since failure costs include several that are intangible and/or at some distance in the organization from the point in the operational process at which the loss in quality occurred.

Quality costing techniques can be applied easily to the environmental area (Hughes and Willis, 1995). A Dutch study that used this model to calculate the 'costs of non-environment' found that, on a narrow definition of environment as the costs of dealing with pollution and wastes, they amounted to around 2 per cent of total operating costs (Diependaal and de Walle, 1994). To be valuable in the environmental field, 'failure costs' probably need to be defined more broadly so that they include what might be called 'indirect failure costs' or the 'costs of inefficiency' – that is, the costs of purchasing and processing materials and energy that end up as waste.

Product costing
Producers need accurate information about the cost make-up of their products in order to determine price and to identify cost-reduction opportunities. Users need data about the total costs of products that they are buying in order to compare alternatives that have different proportions of acquisition and operating costs. Designers need both types of information in order to create products that have reasonable purchase and running costs. Environmental costs are important in all these cases and there can be detrimental consequences if they are not properly identified and allocated.

As several case studies demonstrate (Ditz, Ranganathan and Banks, 1995), it is not uncommon for a small number of products to generate a disproportionately large share of total emissions and wastes. If these costs are not allocated to individual products but instead are treated as a general overhead, then 'clean' products will appear to have higher costs than is actually the case, while 'dirty' products will appear to be cheaper to produce than they really are.

Life-cycle costing
Environmental costs are increasing at every stage of the product life cycle. Green taxes are being introduced on many types of raw materials, emissions, wastes and products at the end of their lives. Certain disposal routes for materials and products are being banned or are subject to stringent regulation which makes them very expensive. As the nuclear and oil industries have discovered, it can also be much more costly to decommission equipment than was originally anticipated. Producers can incur potentially liabilities as a result of environmental problems related to their products.

These changes, to some extent, can be incorporated within the emerging management accounting concept of life-cycle costing (Bailey, 1991). This means extending horizons beyond the purchase costs of products to consider all the costs that will be incurred over their operating lifetime – including, in principle, the environmental costs involved in buying, using and disposing of the product. However, the dispersal of responsibility between and within suppliers and their customers can often obscure this. Bierma, Waterstraat and Ostrosky (1998), for example, demonstrate that this is a serious problem with regard to the whole-life costs of chemicals. It can be sensible therefore, for the various parties to work together to identify and calculate these at the time of purchase. Two particular areas that a number of organizations have already started to examine are the costs of dealing with emissions or wastes from the operation of equipment, or of disposing of products at the end of their lives. Bartolomeo (1998) provides examples of this from Italy.

Of course, this interpretation of life-cycle costing is a narrow one which ignores all environmental costs incurred before equipment is acquired, or downstream costs for which an organization has no responsibility. A broader definition is therefore required if environment-related management accounting is to be useful in the area of product development, which must consider these areas.

Some authors have seen the ultimate goal of life-cycle costing as being the monetization of all impacts identified by life-cycle assessment (LCA). However, the difficulties of achieving consensus about even the relatively simple issue of the most appropriate means of undertaking LCAs, quite apart from the contentious issue of reaching agreement on appropriate conversions from physical to monetary units, make this unrealistic for the foreseeable future.

More limited work has taken place on calculating financial costs and benefits as an input to design for the environment (DFE) initiatives. These aim to reduce life-cycle impacts by taking action in the design stage – for example, making recycling easier by making equipment easier to disassemble. Brouwers and Stevels (1997) have described an end-of-life costing model developed for this purpose at Philips. Kainz, Prokopyshen and Yester (1996) also describe an exercise at Chrysler to calculate the whole-life costs of two designs. This found that, although a design that contained mercury was cheaper to purchase, its whole-life costs were greater as the wastes generated in its production then had to be treated as special wastes.

The former leader of AT&T's green accounting team, has noted the opportunities to extend these initiatives into a more strategic approach which she terms 'environmental life-cycle costing' (Wood, 1998). Monsanto provides one example of this by giving its salespeople a checklist to identify opportunities to reduce its own and/or customers' environment-related costs to their mutual benefit (Tuppen, 1996). The Xerox case (Bennett and James, 1998c) demonstrates the potential for cross-chain initiatives to change completely perceptions of key business activities and consequently to reveal major environment-related savings opportunities.

Cost projection

Projecting future costs is an important part of investment appraisal and is also valuable for other purposes. The environment can be an important determinant of these future costs. This is highly visible with new legislative or regulatory demands. However, forward-looking companies will be considering also the potential costs of possible future legislation or other environmental action. One indication that this may happen is when costs in one country are much lower than in others. Another is when there are large external damage costs created by environmental impacts that are not yet reflected in the company's internal financial calculations, but which could be in future as a result of governmental or social action. There is a growing amount of research that suggests that these externalities are considerable for energy production (Cookson, 1997; EC, 1995; Oak Ridge National Laboratory and Resources for the Future, 1992–1996; Office of Technology Assessment, 1994), transport and other economic activities. However, there is considerable controversy about the results of such research and the methodology employed so that, from a business perspective, the figures are best regarded as indicative rather than exact (Hongisto, 1997).

Even so, Epstein (1998) and other researchers (CICA, 1997; Tuppen, 1996) have argued that companies making capital investment and other decisions with long-term financial consequences might be wise at least to consider the implications of these. Several business leaders and companies, notably Ontario Hydro (US EPA, 1998c) and two senior Dow executives (Popoff and Buzzelli, 1993), have also advocated the use of 'full-cost accounting' (including external costs) by companies, although little has happened in practice as a result.

Strategic costing
As Burritt (1998) notes, costing is not always about creating an accurate reflection of real costs. It can also be a strategic tool to encourage or discourage certain inputs, activities and outputs by influencing relative prices – for example, by putting a high overhead on labour to encourage moves towards automated production (Bromwich and Bhimani, 1994). In principle, it is easy to apply this approach to the environment – for example, by introducing internal taxes on energy consumption or on waste disposal. The level of these taxes, and their trajectory over time, could be based on long-term cost projections. In practice, it is difficult to do this because of fears about competitive disadvantage if other companies do not follow suit. None the less, more use is likely to be made of this approach in future.

Pricing
Pricing requires consideration of customers and competitors as well as costs, so accounting techniques are only one aspect. However, adequate cost analysis is an essential part of pricing decisions which may be distorted by any inaccuracies in costing systems.

Life-cycle costing provides the framework to consider costs not only within the organization itself, but also along the product chain by including both internal costs and also those costs incurred upstream (by suppliers) and downstream (by customers and consumers). This can help to identify opportunities where modest extra spending by the company may increase value for the customer disproportionately, which can be reflected in an increased selling price and/or increased sales volume. As Bennett and James' study (1998b) demonstrates, Baxter International has generated substantial savings in materials costs for itself through packaging redesign. As well as this benefit, reducing the quantity of packaging that the final user has to dispose of is becoming an increasingly significant selling point in countries such as Germany which have strict legislative controls.

Demand Forecasting

Environmental factors are already shaping many markets and will influence more in future. This influence takes two forms: the volume of a product or a service that can be sold and the price at which it is sold. Sales volumes of a number of products – for example, CFCs – have already been largely or completely curtailed by law as a result of environmental considerations and the likelihood is that more will be withdrawn from the market (or 'sunsetted') in future. Customers may also discriminate against products with poor environmental performance, especially if better performing ones offer similar value. Sunsetting and other environmental developments also create opportunities for new products. Indeed, it may be that the revenue streams from future eco-efficient products – that is, those that offer greater customer value and better environmental performance – will have far greater impact than any of the other areas discussed in this chapter. Of course, it is not usually possible to do more than guess at the amounts of potential future revenues from hypothetical new products and consequently less attention has been paid to this area in the environment-related management accounting literature than to methods of cost analysis. However, it is important that it should receive more attention in future.

Investment Appraisal

Environmental factors can be significant in determining the ultimate returns from new investments. It is therefore important that they are identified and considered during the early stages of investment decision-making (Kite, 1995; Rückle, 1989). This not only allows major problems to be avoided, but also provides an opportunity for remedial action at a stage when the costs of doing so can be relatively low.

Many companies are currently bringing the environment into capital budgeting by requiring qualitative assessments of impacts arising from major investments. This can be done in two main ways: by widening the range of costs and benefits that are taken into account, and by adapting appraisal techniques. A 1995 Tellus Institute survey of US companies, for example, found that over 60 per cent of respondents are now considering the costs of emissions and waste monitoring, treatment and disposal in project evaluations (White et al, 1995; White and Savage, 1995). However, many costs are still excluded from most evaluations, as Haveman and Foecke (1998) confirm for the US electroplating sector.

Research suggests that most investments in US and UK companies, including those related to the environment, are appraised on the basis of relatively high discount rates (Bouma and Wolters, 1998). This means that the long-term benefits that often result from environmental action frequently have a low, or even zero, net present value. Many observers also believe that conventional techniques do not properly consider the issue of risk (Busby and Pitts, 1997). Hence, new or modified appraisal techniques might be required. Appraisal techniques can be adapted to take account of the long-term benefits of environmental actions and/or the potential risks of investments with serious environmental impacts. This can be done, for example, by applying lower or higher discount rates to environmentally significant investments, or for long-life projects by extending the period for which future benefits are considered beyond the usual truncation point.

Shareholder Value Analysis

In recent years, there has been an increasing interest in measuring shareholder value (Rappaport, 1986; Stewart, 1991, 1994). This has in part been in recognition of the principle that, at least in the UK and the US, in law (and so far as capital markets are concerned) corporations exist primarily for the benefit of equity investors. It is also a correction for the generally perceived deficiencies of conventional measures of accounting profitability as the main indicator of business performance.

The term is often used only loosely but, when used more precisely, defines shareholder value as the present value of the company's future cash flows, discounted at an appropriate rate that reflects the risks involved. As the environment can affect all the main parameters in this equation – future expenses, revenues and cost of capital – it is therefore an important element to be considered in any calculations.

The ultimate aim of shareholder value analysis is to influence equity valuations, both directly by influencing capital market perceptions and indirectly by making it a priority issue for internal managers. Several studies have suggested that financial analysts and fund managers are either ignorant of, or unconcerned about, the environmental performance of the companies in whom they invest (Business in the Environment, 1994; UNDP, 1997). However, other more recent studies have established a strong case for trying to establish a link between the environment and shareholder value and/or have provided evidence that such a link already exists (Barber, Daley and Sherwood, 1997; Blumberg, Korsvold and Blum, 1997; Cohen, Fenn and Naimon, 1995; *EAAR*, 1997; Müller et al, 1994; Müller et al, 1996; Schaltegger and Figge, 1997; Schmidheiny and Zorraquin, 1996; Verschoor, 1997). Schaltegger and Figge (1997) have also developed a detailed framework, with examples, to analyse the linkages. An important element in their analysis is the importance of environment-related financial risk, which has also been addressed by the Centre for the Study of Financial Innovation. It has developed an environmental equivalent to the well-established financial risk-rating processes of Moodys and Standard & Poor (CSFI, 1995).

Establishing the existence of links between the environment and shareholder value is not sufficient to influence market perceptions. Companies also need to communicate effectively, in terms relevant to the financial markets, the significance of environmental issues to their long-term business success and the adequacy of the efforts that they are taking to manage them (ACBE, 1996; Kreuze, Newell and Newell, 1996).

Environmental Value Analysis

This is the relationship between an organization's economic value added and its environmental impacts. Although there have been few attempts to measure this to date, it is an important issue which in principle can be evaluated in two ways. The first is by developing relational measures. The output measure can take a variety of forms – for example, turnover or profits – but, as value added is a more direct measure of the net economic contribution made by a company, it is widely considered to be the most appropriate. Calculations can then be made of value added per tonne of emission or per unit of environmental impact or, alternatively, tonnes emitted or units of environmental impact per £ of value added. These give a crude measure of how efficiently organizations – or, in aggregate, industries – are using environmental resources.

However, knowing that an organization is using resources efficiently says little about whether its use is sustainable. Sustainability implies limited 'eco-capacity' – that is, a finite availability of physical resources such as fossil fuels and biological materials and of environmental 'sinks' such as the atmosphere. The costs of exceeding this eco-capacity can, in principle, be calculated and then disaggregated to the level of an individual business via taxes – for example, a carbon tax – or other means. The relationship between these 'costs of unsustainability' and value added can therefore serve as a crude measure of an enterprise's sustainability.

Of course, in a world where all such costs are internalized through taxes and other measures, sustainable value added would be equal to economic value added, but this is far from being the case at present. Hence, approximations to sustainable value added can be produced by taking estimates of damage costs. In the case of environmental damage costs, figures are available for many impacts, although there is limited consensus about the best basis of calculation or their accuracy. In the case of social damage costs, few figures are available and this situation seems unlikely to change for the foreseeable future.

Only one organization has so far made even a crude attempt to calculate its sustainable value added. This is the Dutch computer services company BSO Origin, which, in its 1992 environmental report, calculated its main environmental impacts and then converted these into financial amounts to represent the imputed costs of those impacts. The data for this were based on calculations of long-term costs of control in the Dutch National Environmental Protection Plan. This gives a net cost of each environmental impact individually and of all its environmental impacts in aggregate, which can be compared with the value added as calculated through its conventional business accounting processes.

The methodology of this can easily be criticized, both for the bases on which costs per unit of impact are calculated and on how far upstream and downstream costs should legitimately be included. At the present level of understanding of business (and other) impacts on the environment, it is difficult to assess what meaning, if any, can be attributed to the values generated; BSO recognizes this and claims only that its system indicates orders of magnitude rather than precise values. However, the BSO exercise is best seen as a first experiment in devising a comprehensive system that recognizes and quantifies all the environmental impacts of a business, irrespective of the quality of current legislation and regulation in the country of operation.

Conclusions and Future Trends

As the previous discussion demonstrates, there is now a growing and rich theoretical and practical body of work on the topic of environment-related management accounting. There is also a trend towards integration of the work and practices being carried out within individual countries. US practice and research is becoming well known in Europe and practitioners and researchers in individual European countries are also interacting to a greater degree.

This interaction has demonstrated that the relevance and form of environment-related management accounting is influenced by many contingent variables, such as organizational structure and strategic objectives. These are often related to national circumstances which also have a direct influence – for example, by requiring the collection of detailed environmental expenditure statistics.

One broad difference is between the two sides of the Atlantic Ocean. In general, the US has a tougher environmental liabilities regime and higher regulatory penalties, but somewhat lower resource costs, than Europe. Hence, much of the focus of environment-related management accounting in the former has been on recognizing and avoiding liabilities and penalties. In Europe, there has been relatively greater attention paid to the systematic analysis of energy, materials and waste flows to identify opportunities for reduction and also to the consideration of further internalization of the externalities created by resource consumption and transport use.

Within Europe, there is also a divide between the UK, on the one hand, and, on the other, Germany and several other countries in continental Europe. British companies, like those of the US, are generally strongly influenced by capital markets, tend to have shorter decision-making horizons and are more likely to consider the creation of shareholder value as their principal corporate objective. By contrast, German and many other European companies are less dependent for finance on capital markets, usually have longer decision-making horizons and place greater relative weight on the interests of other stakeholders such as employees and communities. All of these have a considerable influence on environment-related management accounting in practice – for example, with regard to the introduction of systematic eco-balancing approaches (see above and James, Prehn and Steger, 1997). However, there is currently a great deal of convergence both within Europe and between Europe and America and it may be that some of these differences will become less important in future.

Despite these variations, it is clear that there can be considerable business benefits from the application of environment-related management accounting and the development of 'green bottom-line' frameworks. In most cases at present, these applications will be relatively simple ones, such as adjustments to investment appraisal procedures or ad hoc 'costs of waste' initiatives. However, as the Baxter, Xerox and other case studies indicate, there is also the opportunity for more advanced initiatives in organizations with substantial environmental costs and/or potential environment-related financial benefits. Although the numbers of these may be relatively low at present, they are likely to increase in future.

Environment-related management accounting can also reach beyond these utilitarian financial goals by helping to implement the goals of sustainable development within the business community. Of course, sustainability is about far more than economics, just as business encompasses many elements other than income statements and balance sheets. Nonetheless, environment-related management accounting can be a significant driver of action through demonstrating the long-term financial implications of sustainability and creating a vision of the most appropriate responses.

In this respect, it has what McAuley, Russell and Sims (1997) have termed a 'narrative' role of making sense of a complex world, as well as a 'logico-scientific' one of developing an accurate representation of reality. One practical implication of this is the introduction of internal taxes, as advocated by Burritt (1998). Even when this is impractical, such a role can at least reduce any danger that environment-related management accounting could introduce a systematic bias towards environmental inaction. This could occur if immediate financial drivers are limited and net financial benefit is seen as the only justification for action.

However, it is important to avoid exaggerating the speed at which environment-related management accounting is likely to be adopted by business. There remain many internal barriers, of which the most significant is the difficulty of considering issues of risk and long-term benefit within high discount-rate investment appraisal models. The strength and durability of these barriers will be determined primarily by the extent to which regulation and other political and social drivers increase the costs to business of poor environmental performance and enhance the financial incentives for environmental improvement. To date, these are much slower in developing than we and most environmentally concerned observers would like. As a result, the development of environment-related management accounting is likely to be discontinuous in nature. Most organizations will probably experience occasional bursts of activity as, on the one hand, external events, such as the introduction of new taxes, raise actual costs and/or business' awareness of them, or, on the other hand, internal changes, such as the introduction of ABC, provide opportunities.

This is consistent with the findings of a recent study to which the present authors made a contribution (Tuppen, 1996). This concluded that most actions being taken at present are mainly relatively simple ones, such as the identification and allocation of energy and waste-disposal costs that either did arise, or could well have arisen for non-environmental reasons. However, it noted eight practical environment-related management accounting options that could be introduced by the report's sponsors, BT and, by extension, other European companies.

One interpretation of these conclusions could be that environment-related management accounting is merely an instance of empire-building by academics and that the simple tasks identified can easily be handled by existing accounting and environmental management accounting activities and staff. A similar criticism might be that the concept is merely a form of aggrandizement by the accounting profession and that the tasks identified are already, and can in future be accomplished successfully by environmental and operational managers. In either case, environment-related management accounting would be merely creating a new bottle for old wine which is already maturing nicely.

We have some sympathy for these points and generally believe that the long-term aim of those interested in the field should be to make the environment a part of everyday management accounting. However, we also note the evidence from many of the following chapters that a number of environment-related costs are often not identified by normal procedures, and that it therefore requires a systematic environment-related management accounting exercise to identify them and to drive action to reduce them. Equally, while we would certainly argue that the role of environment-related management accounting is, like management accounting generally, to support decision-makers in other functions, our experience also suggests that environmental and other operational managers often lack sufficient understanding of accounting concepts and techniques to utilize fully the information that these can provide. A final point is that some of the longer term issues, such as the progressive internalization of externalities or the broader requirements of sustainable development, can be difficult to integrate into management activities that normally focus on day-to-day operational issues. Hence, for the foreseeable future, the adoption of environment-related management accounting is likely to be an extraordinary rather than an ordinary activity and one that will require unusual champions, such as financially astute environmental managers or environmentally aware accountants, to drive it. We hope that this chapter will encourage the development of more such individuals within business.

References

Accounting Standards Board (ASB) (1997) *Provisions and Contingencies*, Financial Reporting Exposure Draft, no 14, ASB Publications, Milton Keynes

Advisory Council on Business and the Environment (ACBE) (1996) *Environmental Reporting and the Financial Sector: An Approach to Good Practice*, Department of the Environment, London

Bailey, P (1991) 'Full Cost Accounting for Life-Cycle Costs: A Guide for Engineers and Financial Analysts', *Environmental Finance*, spring, pp13–29

Bailey, P and Soyka, P (1996) 'Environmental Accounting: Making it Work for Your Company', *Total Quality Environmental Management*, summer, pp13–30

Barber, J, Daley, F and Sherwood, M (1997) 'Rating Environmental Risk', *Certified Accountant*, March, pp42–43

Barth, M and McNichols, M (1994) 'Estimation and Market Valuation of Environmental Liabilities Relating to Superfund Sites', *Journal of Accounting Research*, no 32 (supplement) pp177–209

Bartolomeo, M (1998) 'The Italian Method of Environmental Auditing' in M Bennett and P James (eds) *The Green Bottom Line*, Greenleaf Publishing, Sheffield

Bartolomeo, M, Bennett, M and James, P (1998) *Eco-Management Accounting: A Framework for Analysis and Action*, Wolverhampton Business School Environmental Management Accounting Group, Wolverhampton, UK

Bebbington, J and Thompson, I (1996) *Business Concepts of Sustainability and the Implications for Accountancy*, Association of Chartered Certified Accountants, London

Bennett, M and James, P (1998a) 'The Cost of Waste at Zeneca', in M Bennett and P James (eds) *The Green Bottom Line*, Greenleaf Publishing, Sheffield

Bennett, M and James, P (1998b) 'Making Environment Management Count', Baxter International's Environmental Financial Statement, in M Bennett and P James (eds) *The Green Bottom Line*, Greenleaf Publishing, Sheffield

Bennett, M and James, P (1998c) 'Life-Cycle Costing and Packaging at Xerox Ltd', in M Bennett and P James (eds) *The Green Bottom Line*, Greenleaf Publishing, Sheffield

Bennett, M and James, P (eds) (1998d) *The Green Bottom Line*, Greenleaf Publishing, Sheffield

Bennett, M and James, P (1998e) *Environment-Related Performance Measurement*, Association of Chartered Certified Accountants, London

Bierma, T, Waterstraat, F and Ostrosky, J (1998) 'Shared Savings and Environmental Management Accounting: Innovative Chemical supply Strategies', in M Bennett and P James (eds) *The Green Bottom Line*, Greenleaf Publishing, Sheffield

Birkin, F and Woodward, D (1997a) 'Introduction', *Management Accounting* (UK) Management Accounting for Sustainable Development Series, June, pp24–26

Birkin, F and Woodward, D (1997b) 'From Economic to Ecological Efficiency', *Management Accounting* (UK), Management Accounting for Sustainable Development Series, July–August, pp42–45

Birkin, F and Woodward, D (1997c) 'Stakeholder Analysis', *Management Accounting* (UK), Management Accounting for Sustainable Development Series, September, pp58–60

Birkin, F and Woodward, D (1997d) 'The Eco-Balance Account', *Management Accounting* (UK), Management Accounting for Sustainable Development Series, October, pp50–52

Birkin, F and Woodward, D (1997e) 'Accounting for Sustainable Development', *Management Accounting* (UK), Management Accounting for Sustainable Development Series, November, pp52–54

Birkin, F and Woodward, D (1997f) 'A Zero-Base Approach to Accounting for Sustainable Development', *Management Accounting* (UK), Management Accounting for Sustainable Development Series, December, pp40–42

Blumberg, J, Korsvold, A and Blum, G (1997) *Environmental Performance and Shareholder Value*, World Business Council for Sustainable Development, Geneva

Bouma, J and Wolters, T (1998) *Management Accounting and Environmental Management: A Survey Among 84 European Companies*, EIM, Zoetermeer, The Netherlands

Bromwich, M and Bhimani, A (1994) *Management Accounting: Pathways to Progress*, Chartered Institute of Management Accountants, London

Brouwers, W and Stevels, A (1997) 'A Cost Model for the End-of-Life Stage of Electronic Consumer Goods', *Greener Management International*, no 17, spring, pp129–39

Burritt, R (1998) 'Cost Allocation: An Active Tool for Environmental Management Accounting?' in M Bennett and P James (eds) *The Green Bottom Line*, Greenleaf Publishing, Sheffield

Busby, J and Pitts, C (1997) 'Real Options and Capital Investment Decisions', *Management Accounting* (US), November, pp38–39

Business in the Environment and Extel Financial (1994) *City Analysts and the Environment*, Business in the Environment, London

Butler, D (1997) 'I'm Green, Buy Me', *Accountancy*, March, pp36–38

Canadian Institute of Chartered Accountants (CICA) (1992) *Environmental Accounting and The Role of the Accounting Profession*, CICA, Toronto

Canadian Institute of Chartered Accountants (CICA) (1997) *Full Cost Accounting from an Environmental Perspective*, CICA, Toronto

Centre for the Study of Financial Innovation (CSFI) (1995) *An Environmental Risk Rating for Scottish Nuclear*, CSFI, London

Charter, M (ed) (1992) *Green Marketing: A Responsible Approach to Business*, Greenleaf Publishing, Sheffield, UK

Chartered Institute of Management Accountants (CIMA) (UK) (1997) *Environmental Management: The Role of the Management Accountant*, CIMA, London

Cohen, M, Fenn, S and Naimon, J (1995) *Environmental and Financial Performance: Are They Related?*, Investor Responsibility Research Center, Washington, DC

Cookson, C (1997) 'World Must Look to Nature's Free Services', *Financial Times*, 17 February

Davies, A J (1997) 'The Environment and Business Today', *Certified Accountant*, 20–23 June

DeSimone, L and Popoff, F (1997) *Eco-Efficiency: The Business Path to Sustainable Development*, MIT Press, Cambridge, MA

Ditz, D, Ranganathan, J and Banks, R D (eds) (1995) *Green Ledgers: Case Studies in Corporate Environmental Accounting*, World Resources Institute, Washington, DC

Ditz, D, Ranganathan, J and Banks, D (1998) 'Green Ledgers: An Overview', in M Bennett and P James (eds) *The Green Bottom Line*, Greenleaf Publishing, Sheffield

Drury, C, Braund, S, Osborne, P and Tayles, M (1993) *A Survey of Management Accounting Practice in UK Manufacturing Companies*, Chartered Association of Certified Accountants, London

Drury, C and Tayles, M (1998) 'Cost System Design for Enhancing Profitability', *Management Accounting* (UK), January, pp40–42

Environmental Accounting and Auditing Reporter (EAAR) (1997) 'Are Financial and Environments Performance Interlinked?', *EAAR*, May, pp4–8

Epstein, M J (1996a) 'Improving Environmental Management with Full Environmental Cost Accounting', *Environmental Quality Management*, autumn, pp11–22

Epstein, M J (1996b) *Measuring Corporate Environmental Performance: Best Practices for Costing and Managing an Effective Environmental Strategy*, Institute of Management Accountants, Irwin, Chicago

Epstein, M (1998) 'Integrating Environmental Impacts into Capital Investment Decisions', in M Bennett and P James (eds) *The Green Bottom Line*, Greenleaf Publishing, Sheffield

Ethridge, J and Rogers, V (1997) 'Transactions that may Prompt Environmental Reporting Problems', *Management Accounting* (US), July, pp57–58

European Commission (EC) (1995) *JOULE ExternE: Externalities of Energy*, 6 vols, DG XII, European Commission, Luxembourg

Fédération des experts comptables européens (FEE) (1996) *Expert Statements on Environmental Reports*, research paper, FEE, Brussels

Fussler, C with James, P (1996) *Driving Eco-Innovation: A Breakthrough Discipline for Innovation and Sustainability*, Pitman Publishing, London

Gray, R H, Bebbington, J and Walters, D (1993) *Accounting for the Environment*, Paul Chapman and Association of Chartered Certified Accountants, London

Gray, R H, Owen, D and Adams, C (1996) *Accounting and Accountability: Changes and Challenges in Corporate Social and Environmental Reporting*, Prentice-Hall, Hemel Hempstead

Grayson, L, Woolston, H and Tanega, I (1993) *Business and Environmental Accountability: An Overview and Guide to the Literature*, Technical Communications, London

Greene, T (1998) 'The Road Not Taken: Acting on "Beyond Environmental Compliance" in Managerial Decision-Making', in M Bennett and P James (eds) *The Green Bottom Line*, Greenleaf Publishing, Sheffield

Hallay, H and Pfriem, R (1992) *Öko-Controlling. Umweltschutz in mittelständischen Unternehmen*, Campus, Frankfurt

Hamner, B and Stinson, C (1993) *Managerial Accounting and Compliance Costs*, University of Washington discussion paper, Washington, DC; reprinted in *Journal of Cost Management*, summer 1995, pp4–10

Haveman, M and Foecke, T (1998) 'Applying Environmental Accounting to Electroplating Operations: An In-Depth Analysis', in M Bennett and P James (eds) *The Green Bottom Line*, Greenleaf Publishing, Sheffield

Hongisto, M (1997) 'Assessment of External Costs of Power Production', paper presented to IIIEE and VTT Seminar on Total Cost Assessment, Nagu, June, IVO, Helsinki

Hopfenbeck, W and Jasch, C (1993) *Öko-Controlling: Umdenken zahlt sich aus! Audits, Umweltberichte und Ökobilanzen als betriebliche Führungsinstrumente (Eco-Controlling: New Philosophy Pays! Audits, Environmental Reports and LCA as Management Tools)*, Verlag Moderne Industrie, Lansberg

Hughes, S and Willis, D (1995) 'How Quality Control Concepts can Reduce Environmental Expenditures', *Journal of Cost Management*, summer 1995, pp15–19

Institute of Chartered Accountants in England and Wales (1996) *Environmental Issues in Financial Reporting*, ICAEW, London

Institute of Management Accountants (US) (1995) *Practices and Techniques: Implementing Corporate Environmental Strategies*, IMA, Montvale, NJ

International Accounting Standards Committee (1997) *Provisions, Contingent Liabilities and Contingent Assets*, exposure draft, 58, IASC, London

International Institute for Industrial Environmental Economics and VTT Non-Waste Technology (1997) *Challenges and Approaches to Incorporating the Environment into Business Decisions: International Expert Seminar*, Lund, IIIEP, Sweden, VTT, Helsinki

James, P, Prehn, M and Steger, U (1997) *Corporate Environmental Management in Britain and Germany*, Anglo-German Foundation, London

Johnston, N (1994) *Waste Minimisation: A Route to Profit and Cleaner Production*, Centre for Exploitation of Science and Technology, London

Kainz, R, Prokopyshen, M and Yester, S (1996) 'Life Cycle Management at Chrysler', *Pollution Prevention Review*, spring, pp71–83

Kaplan, R and Norton, D (1992) 'The Balanced Scorecard: Measures that Drive Performance', *Harvard Business Review*, January–February, pp71–79 (reprint 92105)

Kaplan, R and Norton, D (1993) 'Putting the Balanced Scorecard to Work', *Harvard Business Review*, September–October, pp134–42 (reprint 93505)

Kaplan, R and Norton, D (1996a) 'Using the Balanced Scorecard as a Strategic Management System', *Harvard Business Review*, January–February, pp75–85 (reprint 96107)

Kaplan, R and Norton, D (1996b) *The Balanced Scorecard*, Harvard Business School Press, Cambridge, MA

Kite, D (1995) 'Capital Budgeting: Integrating Environmental Impact', *Journal of Cost Management*, summer 1995, pp11–19

KPMG, *Survey of Environmental Reporting 1997*, KPMG, London

Kreuze, J G and Newell, G E (1994) 'ABC and Life-Cycle Costing for Environmental Expenditures', *Management Accounting* (US), February, pp38–42

Kreuze, J G, Newell, G E and Newell, S J (1996) 'Environmental Disclosures: What Companies are Reporting', *Management Accounting* (US), July, pp37–43

Lawrence, J E and Cerf, D (1995) 'Management and Reporting of Environmental Liabilities', *Management Accounting* (US), August, pp48–54

Lober, D, Bynum, D, Campbell, E and Jacques, M (1997) 'The 100 Plus Corporate Environmental Report Study', *Business Strategy and the Environment*, May, pp1–12

McAuley, L, Russell, G and Sims, J (1997) 'How Do Financial Directors Make Decisions?', *Management Accounting*, November, pp32–34

McLaughlin, S and Elwood, H (1996) 'Environmental Accounting and EMSs', *Pollution Prevention Review*, spring, pp13–21

McLean, R and Shopley, J (1996) 'Green Light Shows for Corporate Gains', *Financial Times*, 3 July

Müller, K, de Frutos, J, Schüssler, K and Haarbosch, H (1994) *Environmental Reporting and Disclosures: The Financial Analyst's View*, Working Group on Environmental Issues of the Accounting Commission of the European Federation of Financial Analysts' Societies, London

Müller, K, de Frutos, J, Schüssler, K, Haarbosch, H and Randel, M (1996) *Eco-Efficiency and Financial Analysis*, European Federation of Financial Analysts' Societies, Basel

Oak Ridge National Laboratory and Resources for the Future (1992–1996) *External Costs and Benefits of Fuel Cycles*, 8 vols, US Department of Energy, Washington, DC

Office of Technology Assessment (1994) *Studies of the Environmental Costs of Electricity*, US Government Printing Office, Washington, DC

Owen, D (ed) (1992) *Green Reporting: Accountancy and the Challenge of the Nineties*, Chapman & Hall, London

Owen, D, Gray, R and Adams, R (1997) *Corporate Environmental Disclosure: Encouraging Trends*, Association of Chartered Certified Accountants, London

Parker, J N (1995) 'Profits and Ethics in Environmental Investments', *Management Accounting* (US), October, pp52–53

Popoff, F and Buzzelli, D (1993) 'Full Cost Accounting', *Chemical Engineering News*, 11 January, pp8–10

Porter, M E and van der Linde, C (1995b) 'Green *and* Competitive: Ending the Stalemate', *Harvard Business Review*, September–October, pp120–34

Rappaport, A (1986) *Creating Shareholder Value: The New Standards for Business Performance*, Free Press, New York

Reiskin, E, Savage, D and Miller, D (1998) 'Making Environmental Management Count: Baxter International's Environmental Financial Statement', in M Bennett and P James (eds) *The Green Bottom Line*, Greenleaf Publishing, Sheffield

Roth, H P and Keller, C E (1997) 'Quality, Profits and the Environment: Diverse Goals or Common Objectives?', *Management Accounting* (US), July, pp50–55

Royal Society of Arts (1994) *Tomorrow's Company*, RSA, London

Rubenstein, D B (1994) *Environmental Accounting for the Sustainable Corporation*, Quorum Books, Westport, CT

Rückle, D (1989) 'Investitionskalküle für Umweltschutzinvestitionen' ('Investment Appraisal for Environmental Investments'), *Betriebswirtschaftliche Forschung und Praxis (BFuP)*, vol 41, no 1, pp51–65

Russell, W, Skalak, S and Miller, G (1995) 'Environmental Cost Accounting: The Bottom Line for Environmental Quality Management', in J Willig (ed), *Auditing for Environmental Quality Leadership*, John Wiley, Chichester

Schaltegger, S and Figge, F (1997) *Environmental Shareholder Value*, Centre of Economics and Business Administration, University of Basel, Basel

Schaltegger, S with Müller, K and Hindrichsen, H (1996) *Corporate Environmental Accounting*, John Wiley, Chichester

Schaltegger, S and Müller, K (1998) 'Calculating the True Profitability of Pollution Protection', in M Bennett and P James (eds) *The Green Bottom Line*, Greenleaf Publishing, Sheffield

Schmidheiny, S and Zorraquin, F (1996) *Financing Change: The Financial Community, Eco-Efficiency and Sustainable Development*, MIT Press with the World Business Council for Sustainable Development, Cambridge, MA

Schoemaker, P J H and Schoemaker, J A (1995) 'Estimating Environmental Liability: Quantifying the Unknown', *California Management Review*, vol 37, no 3, spring, pp29–61

Schroeder, G (1998) 'Environmental Accounting at Sulzer Technology Corporation', in M Bennett and P James (eds) *The Green Bottom Line*, Greenleaf Publishing, Sheffield

Schulz, E and Schulz, W (1994) *Umweltcontrolling in der Praxis (Environmental Controlling in Practice)*, Vahlen, Munich

Shields, D, Beloff, B and Heller, M (1998) 'Environmental Cost Accounting for Chemical and Oil Companies: A Benchmarking Study', in M Bennett and P James (eds) *The Green Bottom Line*, Greenleaf Publishing, Sheffield

Simmonds, K (1991) 'Strategic Management Accounting', *Management Accounting* (UK), April, pp26–29

Stewart, G B (1991) *The Quest for Value*, Harper Business, New York

Stewart, G B (1994) 'EVA: Fact and Fantasy', *Journal of Applied Corporate Finance*, summer, pp71–84

SustainAbility/United Nations Environment Programme (1997) *Engaging Stakeholders: The Third International Progress Report on Company Environmental Reporting*, SustainAbility, London; UNEP, Paris

Tuppen, C (ed) (1996) *Environmental Accounting in Industry: A Practical Review*, British Telecom, London

United Nations Development Programme (1997) *Valuing the Environment: How Fortune 500 CFOs and Analysts Measure Corporate Performance*, ODS working paper, United Nations Office of Development Studies, New York

US Environmental Protection Agency (US EPA) (1998a) 'An Introduction to Environmental Accounting as Business Management Tool: Key Concepts and Terms', in M Bennett and P James (eds) *The Green Bottom Line*, Greenleaf Publishing, Sheffield

US Environmental Protection Agency (US EPA) (1998b) 'Valuing Potential Environmental Liabilities for Managerial Decision-Making: A Review of Available Techniques', in M Bennett and P James (eds) *The Green Bottom Line*, Greenleaf Publishing, Sheffield

US Environmental Protection Agency (US EPA) (1998c) 'Full-Cost Accounting for Decision-Making at Ontario Hydro', in M Bennett and P James (eds) *The Green Bottom Line*, Greenleaf Publishing, Sheffield

Verschoor, C C (1997) 'Principles Build Profits', *Management Accounting* (US), October, pp42–46

von Weizsäcker, E U, Lovins, A B and Lovins, L H (1997) *Factor Four: Doubling Wealth, Halving Resource Use*, Earthscan, London

Walley, N and Whitehead, B (1994) 'It's Not Easy Being Green', *Harvard Business Review*, May–June, pp46–52; see also follow-up letters: 'The Challenge of Going Green', *Harvard Business Review*, July–August, pp37–50

White, A and Savage, D (1995) 'Budgeting for Environmental Projects: A Survey', *Management Accounting* (US), October, pp48–54

White, A, Becker, M and Goldstein, J (1991) *Total Cost Assessment: Accelerating Industrial Pollution Prevention through Innovation Project Financial Analysis*, Tellus Institute; sponsored by the US Environmental Protection Agency; Boston, MA

White, A, Savage, D, Brody, J, Cavanader, D and Lach, L (1995) *Environmental Cost Accounting for Capital Budgeting: A Benchmark Survey of Management Accountants*, Tellus Institute; sponsored by the US Environmental Protection Agency; Boston, MA

Wilson, R (ed) (1997) *Strategic Cost Management*, Ashgate, Aldershot

Wolters, T and Bouman, M (eds) (1995) *Milieu-investeringen in Bedrijfseconomisch Perspectief*, Sansom Bedrijsinformatie, Alphen aan den Rijn/Zaventem, The Netherlands

Wood, J (1998) 'Environmental Life Cycle Costing', mimeo available from Life Cycle Dimensions, 30 Cambridge Road, Bedminster, MJ 07921, USA

Zadek, S, Pruzan, P and Evans, R (eds) (1997) *Building Corporate Accountability: The Emerging Practices in Social and Ethical Accounting, Auditing and Reporting*, Earthscan, London

Notes

1 Note that these are the authors' opinions and terminology and would not necessarily be accepted and used by all the other contributors to the book
2 See Bartolomeo, Bennett and James (1998) for a more detailed discussion of objectives, based on research conducted for the ECOMAC project

9

Struggling with the Praxis of Social Accounting: Stakeholders, Accountability, Audits and Procedures

Rob Gray, Colin Dey, Dave Owen, Richard Evans and Simon Zadek

Introduction

Social accounting, after its brief heyday in the early to mid-1970s (see, for example, AICPA, 1977; Estes, 1976; Gray et al, 1987; Grayet al, 1996b), had disappeared almost entirely from both the language of practice and the orthodoxy of conventional accounting by the late 1970s. It returned to its previous obscurity even in accounting academe (see, for example, Gray et al, 1987, 1991; Parker, 1986). The re-emergence of environmental accounting in the late 1980s and early 1990s (in so far as environmental accounting can, perhaps, be conceived of as one part of the social accounting concern), appears to have been at least one of the reasons behind a current resurgence of interest in social accounting. By the mid-1990s, not only was there an increase in the academic attention given to the area but, more importantly for this chapter, there was a notable re-emergence of practice in the field. Indeed, social accounting is attracting an almost unprecedented level of interest at the present time. Recent social accounts issued by Traidcraft plc, Shared Earth, The New Economics Foundation and The Body Shop in the UK and the SbN Bank in Denmark and Ben and Jerry's in the US, for example, have all attracted widespread publicity. The Royal Society of Arts in the UK has published *An Inquiry into Tomorrow's Company* which recommends the development, use and disclosure of social performance indicators. These and related developments, together with the recent formation of the Institute of Social and Ethical Accountability (ISEA), have made the technical problems of social accounting a matter of some urgency if social accounting now is to develop in any systematic way and neither fizzle out through lack of direction nor be captured and trivialized by powerful organizations.

This emergence of practice has brought both an increase in the examples from which researchers could learn about social accounting practice as well as an urgency to the question: 'How does one do social accounting?' How to do social accounting

Reproduced by kind permission of MCB University Press Limited, from *Accounting, Auditing and Accountability Journal*, vol 10, no 3, 1997 should not be a trivial question. If organizations are permitted to develop methods of social accounting without any critical assessment of their activities, then any emerging 'best practice' can be expected to be partial, ad hoc, immanent and legitimizing, thereby falling foul of the Marxian, deep green and feminist critiques of social accounting (see, for example, Cooper, 1992; Maunders and Burritt, 1991; Puxty, 1991; Tinker et al, 1991). Therefore, what might a 'good' or even an 'ideal type' of social accounting look like? Once we have an idea what it might look like, we must consider how it might be developed as an applied practice. Such questions, in turn, raise two fundamental problems:

1 What is social accounting?
2 What is the theoretical, political and ethical framework within which one's answers are to be framed?

Not only is there the tautological concern that assessing 'good' social accounting needs a yardstick against which it might be judged, but the justification for deriving a practice must lie in the values and emancipatory moment which underpin the suggestions for practice.

Social accounting academics have long found themselves in this difficult and relatively underpopulated area, lying between sophisticated critiques of current practice, imagining new (and 'ideal') accounting systems and actively engaging with (hopefully emancipatory) practice. The need to resolve the tensions that result from this separation of the 'academic' and the 'practical' is an increasingly important theme in the accounting literature (see, for example, Gray, 1992; Gray et al, 1988, 1991, 1996b; Mitchell et al, 1991; Sikka, 1987; Sikka et al, 1989, 1991; Tinker et al, 1991). It is for this reason that we use the term praxis in the title of this chapter. While the theoretical critiques of accounting and new accountings in the interests of scholarship, must be fully engaged with, this is not enough. Practice must be encouraged and we must find ways to encourage that practice to develop in a manner which is potentially emancipatory, not repressive.

It is these tensions that this chapter seeks to address. The chapter is, therefore, very, perhaps overly ambitious. To theorize a social accounting, to deduce lessons of best practice and to begin to derive standards for social accounting practice, while remaining cognizant of the radical critiques of social accounting, are clearly more than a single chapter could hope to achieve. At the same time, the practice of social accounting is developing rapidly. New methods of accounting are being derived, new institutional arrangements are being developed and practitioners are meeting new difficulties. The chapter is therefore explicitly exploratory and excuses its thinness in places in its attempts to bring some system to developing practice as a matter of some urgency. If the chapter, then, can act as a catalyst, research agenda and starting-point for further refinement, it will have been more than successful.

This chapter belongs to a continuing series in which we seek to develop our understanding of the theoretical and practical issues of social accounting (see, for example, Dey et al, 1995; Evans, 1991; Gray et al, 1988, 1996b; Harte and Owen, 1987; Raynard, 1995; Zadek and Evans, 1993; Zadek and Raynard, 1995). In line with those other papers, the present discussion is based on a belief in the primacy of democracy, the importance and power of accountability in the development and discharge of democracy, and is empirically grounded in the experience arising from the production of the social accounts mentioned above.

The chapter itself seeks a synthesis of the different approaches to social accounting and then explores how the resulting theoretical structure can be employed in the systematic production of 'auditable' social accounts. This exploration is undertaken through an illustration of two cases based on the UK Traidcraft experience. This process, we believe, takes us towards a 'portable' social accounting methodology that allows us (to use conventional accounting terminology) to begin a process of iteration towards a conceptual framework for social accounting and the derivation of generally accepted social accounting principles and basic social accounting standards.

The chapter is structured as follows. The second section introduces some of the underlying themes on which this chapter draws. Rather than analysing these themes, this section simply attempts to locate the discussion in the wider theoretical literature. The third section then looks at terminology and outlines some different approaches to social accounting. The fourth and fifth sections examine three of the theoretical perspectives which can be taken on the organization–society relationships and which, thus, can be employed to guide the form of any subsequent social account. A broad synthesis of these three perspectives is offered in the sixth section. Sections seven and eight report the experiences of, respectively, Traidcraft plc and Traidcraft Exchange in their development of their own social accounts. Lessons about constructing the (social) accounting entity are drawn from the first case. The second case is used to illustrate how 'three layers of information' can bring us towards a more complete social account. This case also flags up the role of auditing. Section nine is a short report of the key elements that our experiences have led us to believe are the backbone of a systematic social accounting practice and might, thus, form a basis for the emergence of social accounting standards.

Locating the Discussion:
Some Initial Theoretical Reflections

It would be inappropriate – if only for reasons of space – to attempt to revisit all aspects of the social accounting debate here (but see Gray et al, 1996b, for an introduction to some of the issues). This section will, therefore, seek to identify in very general terms, the principal theoretical themes which will underpin the later analysis and discussion.

In the first place, social accounting is conceived of as the universe of all possible accountings. From a conventional accounting perspective, it is what happens if the constraining principles of conventional accounting – that is, an accounting entity, a focus on economic events, financial description of those events and an assumption of (predominantly financial) users; see Gray et al (1996a) – are relaxed. This universe is, probably, infinite and, consequently, beyond our scope here. So initially we restrict our discussion to formal accounts from accounting entities. (These issues are discussed in more detail below.) We thus exclude, most obviously, informal (verbal and non-verbal accounts) between individuals and groups.

Similarly we restrict ourselves to a concern with the production of single periodic accounts. We should, however, stress that such single accounts do not assume a single point of view – that is, the social accounts are assumed to be, at least potentially, both polyvocal and multiple (see, for example, Zadek and Evans, 1993). This restriction to a single, formal account may well open the resulting social accounting to criticisms from feminist, and perhaps post-modern, critiques – that is, our approach to the social account may be masculine-gendered and modern. We have not addressed this formally, but the later discussion does, we suggest, acknowledge these charges and may go some way towards meeting the criticisms.

Furthermore, there are both political and social issues embedded in the social accounting which we have not explicitly explored. For example, almost any system of social accounting of which one can conceive will involve transfers of power, either through the democratization of organizations and of capital, or through the capture and manipulation of social issues by organizations and by capital. Similarly, there is a wide range of concerns over such matters as the role of accounts in reifying, constructing, reinforcing and trivializing organizations and relationships, both within and between those organizations (see, for example, Francis, 1990; Hines, 1988, 1989, 1991, 1992; Lavoie, 1987; Meyer, 1986). How successfully such critiques can be levelled at this project, and perhaps undermine it, are matters dealt with only tangentially in this chapter.

Next, social accounting is conceived of here as being both hermeneutic and emancipatory. It is hermeneutic in the sense of a *'hermeneutic dialectic process'* (Laughlin and Broadbent, 1996) which seeks out a means that might lead us towards reflexive mutual understanding between the organization and its stakeholders. These understandings will relate to both organizational activity and the accountability(ies) (see below) attaching to those activities. In this sense, the social accounting practice must be continuing and evolving. It is emancipatory in that its aim is to redress power asymmetries between organizations and their stakeholders through the reporting of information. This emancipatory moment lies beyond the accountability itself and, rather, underpins the project and provides its motivation. The project seeks to enhance the democratic virtues of transparency and accountability. It seeks this through (admittedly underspecified) assumptions that an informed demos is thereby empowered in its decision-making and action to seek more benign organizational activity. Similarly, the production of social accounts is assumed to have an information inductance effect on the part of organizational managers that will encourage more ethically desirable forms of activity.

However, the specific focus employed here is rather less dependent on the optimism (and utility) which would justify a social accounting by reference to outcomes flowing from that accounting information, but is rather more concerned with deontological and intrinsic motivations – that is, the fulcrum of social accounting employed here is the discharge of organizational accountability. Accountability is conceived of as relating to the rights to information of a participatory democratic society which, for the sake of this project, is conceived of as neo-pluralist in structure. Such choices have two implications: first, the choice of a neo-pluralist democratic accountability defines a 'problem space' within which all parties can debate. It is reminiscent of, though in no sense synonymous with, Habermas' ideal speech situation – that is, Western practice and Western critique can all engage in this space because the conception does not necessarily deny the legitimacy of organizational practice, but brings to it critiques drawn from pristine liberal economic democracy, Marxism, deep green and feminist positions. While social accounting exists in a space critiqued by each of these positions – whether the critique from practice or the radical critique from academe, there remains a hermeneutic engagement which a priori we find valuable, even essential. The second implication of our choice is that, in a strict interpretation of accountability, action and decisions as a consequence of the discharged accountability are not necessarily part of the story. A participatory demos may well have rights to information, but once informed may choose not to act on that information. The assumptions of action and decision lie prior to the concern with accountability itself.

With this outline of the prior concerns which attempt to link this project with the wider theoretical literature, we can turn now to the body of the chapter and explore the issue of terminology and definition, before moving into an exploration of the conceptual frameworks for an applied social accounting.

Social? Ethical? Accounting? Auditing?

A wide variety of terms have been employed in social accounting. Historically, the terms 'social audit', 'social responsibility accounting' and 'corporate social reporting' have, from time to time, been popular (see, for example, Mathews, 1993), while more recently social accounts have appeared under the titles, inter alia, 'social audits' (the early Traidcraft reports, for example), 'ethical statements' (SbN Bank), 'values report' and 'social statement' (The Body Shop). Further analogues can be found – 'ethical audits' is a term favoured by some individuals. The confusion generated by the diversity of terms is partly illusory, but also partly real. All the discussion and the practice hold a number of central ideas in common but, through the use of a diverse terminology, feature these central ideas with different degrees of exactitude. Indeed, the different conceptions permit undefined terms to encourage agreement and also, perhaps, to avoid historical baggage attached to terms which some parties may prefer to avoid.

Nevertheless, we stay with social accounting as the generic term because it is the longest established and the simplest term (and construct) with which to work. Furthermore, as we shall see, we find its resonances of conventional accounting especially useful when defining the elements of a social accounting process.

All social accounting (regardless of its actual title) relates to the presentation of information about organizational activity. The resulting account (whatever the form it takes) is presented to someone, even if it is only the organization itself (see below). The social account, as with any other account, presupposes some defined accounting entity (there has to be something about which to account), although, as we shall see, the relationship is reflexive. Equally, there is an implication of complexity and size in the relationship between the accounting entity and those to whom the account is presented. This last point arises because we tend to find that formal

Report for the consumption of ...	Report compiled by ...	
	Internal participants	*External participants*

Internal participants	• Social accounts
	• Programme evaluation
	• Attitudes audit
	• Performance indicators
	• Compliance audit
	• Environmental audit and accounting
		• Quango reports ed:
		  – Health and safety
		  – Equal opportunities
		  – EPA
		• Environmental consultants
		• Waste and energy audits

External participants	• Social accounts
	• Social reports
	  – narrative
	  – quantitative
	  – qualitative
	  – financial
	• Compliance audit
	• Mission statements
	• Environmental report
	• Employee reports
		• Social Audit Ltd
		• Counter Information Services
		• New Consumer
		• Consumers' Association
		• Friends of the Earth
		• Greenpeace
		• Journalists
		• Ethical investment/EIRIS
		• External 'social audits'

Source: adapted from Gray, 1991, p3

Figure 9.1 *Examples of Different Approaches to Social Accounting*

accounts are only necessary in complex situations in which personal communication, trust and intimacy (what Rawls calls 'closeness') are threatened or have disappeared. (For more detail see, for example, Lehman, 1995.) In personal and usually relatively simple situations involving only a small number of parties and/or activities, an informal account will suffice. The precise point at which an informal accounting in or by, for example, families breaks down and leads to the need for a formal account in or by, for example, multinational companies is quite unclear but deserving of further research. Finally, implicit in the notion of an account there is some intended or actual recipient to whom the account is (informally, perhaps) addressed. In the neo-pluralist accountability framework employed here, the stakeholders are those with rights to the account and it is for them that the account is prepared. Whether or not they use it and if so for what and whether or not other parties see and/or use the account, are largely irrelevant. So, beyond the identification, prioritization and needs of stakeholders (see below), it is possible to leave any conception of the recipient's decision-making about, or choice of action, implicit in the discussion.

These three elements – the accounting entity, the account and the intended recipient (or group of recipients) of the account – are not sufficient in themselves to define social accounting. Figure 9.1 provides a collection of possible accounting processes which involve these three elements. The possible groupings of social accounts are initially defined by reference to who prepares and who receives the account.

We are going to restrict ourselves to the formal account and, furthermore, to the formal account which is prepared by (or on behalf of – see below) the accounting entity and (externally) reported or disclosed to parties other than the directors/ controllers of the reporting organization (although this does not preclude such parties from receiving – and, indeed, from using – such an account). (This restriction places us in the shaded box in Figure 9.1.) The reasons for these restrictions, we believe, are not trivial. The restriction to the formal account arises from the complexity of the organizations about which the questions of social accounting most obviously arise. The restriction to externally disclosed reports is driven by the commitment to accountability – of which more later (see, for example, Medawar, 1976). The matter of who prepares the report is really a matter of pragmatic and economic concern. For example, while the first Traidcraft report (social audit 1992–1993) was prepared with considerable external input from the New Economics Foundation (NEF), it was ultimately published by, and thus 'owned by', the reporting entity. This ownership is important because the organization must thus stand by the contents of the report – it was, after all, the duty of the organization to be accountable that had driven the account in the first place. But there are other pragmatic reasons, most especially that:

- externally prepared reports typically experience problems in gaining access to the appropriate levels of data; and
- the economics of the regular production of social accounts will effectively preclude any systematic mechanism other than self-reporting by the organization involved (see, for example, Gray et al, 1987, 1996b; Medawar, 1976). Furthermore, the analogue of relating social accounting to conventional financial accounting naturally leads us to assume the preparation of the report by the accounting entity.

These restrictions, while placing us in the shaded box in Figure 9.1, still do not, of themselves, produce a full definition of the social account. As Figure 9.1 might suggest, a wide range of fairly basic examples, as well as the more developed examples to which we have already referred, would still be encompassed by our terms. Indeed, most large companies produce a range of social and environmental information which, if collated, might pass as a social account (see, for example, Gray, 1997).

Consequently, it might be helpful if a further schema, refining slightly the elements of Figure 9.1 were to be presented at this point. The following provides a classification of approaches to social accounting based on the complexity and system of the approaches and, more pertinently, their likely desirability to a conventional business organization:

1 Company preferred:
    - existing corporate reporting of both voluntary and mandatory data;
    - existing corporate public relations and advertising/education data;
    - collation of the above into a single 'social accounting' document – the 'silent account';
    - 'one-off' experiments with approaches to social accounting.

2   Systematic corporate social accounts:
    –   stakeholder reporting;
    –   describing the characteristics of the stakeholder relationship(s);
    –   accountability reporting;
    –   reporting of the voices of the stakeholders.

3   External 'social audits':
    –   single issue reporting – for example, consumers, environmentalists etc;
    –   systematic social audits;
    –   one-off reporting – for example, investigative journalism.

The terms will be discussed and developed as the chapter progresses. It is the second group – the systematic social accounts – that is of concern to us in this chapter.

To refine our definition further we need to address the matter of theory and, in particular, the place and interpretation of accountability in the derivation of a social account.

Accountability and Stakeholder Perspectives

Our experience with social accounting plus our reading of the literature lead us to conclude that there are three dominant ways of theorizing the (accountability) relationship between an accounting entity and its 'outside world'. We want to conceive of these theoretical perspectives as a series of (overlapping) layers which can be synthesized and built up into a rich conception of the organization–society interaction. These three perspectives are a stakeholder perspective, an accountability perspective and what we shall call a polyvocal citizenship perspective (PCP). These three conceptions build up from the 'harder', more functional organization-centred stakeholder perspective, through the slightly 'softer', society-centred accountability perspective to (perhaps) the 'softest', stakeholder-centred polyvocal citizenship perspective. (We will discuss the first two below and then examine PCP in more detail in the next section.)

Stakeholder perspective

The stakeholder approach to analysis is well-established in the management (and accounting) literature (see, for example, Donaldson, 1988; Nasi, 1995; Roberts, 1992; Ullmann, 1985). Its essence is the definition of all those groups or parties who are influenced by and/or who influence the organization (or accounting entity). From this point on, stakeholder theory struggles to maintain anything other than an organization-centred legitimacy because, while the groups may be defined with a fair degree of objectivity, who (other than the organization) is left to define the priorities among the stakeholders and the information that should be disclosed to each one? Stakeholder theory, therefore, is concerned typically with how the organization manages its stakeholders. Thus, information disclosed to the stakeholders may be assumed more properly by the organization to be part of a legitimacy and/or social construction process. Stakeholder theory is relatively silent on how the organization does, if at all, monitor and respond to the needs of the stakeholders. It will do so, generally speaking, when it is in the organization's traditional interests – profit-seeking, for example – to do so. Therefore a social account based on the stakeholder perspective has social value only if we assume the beneficence of the organization and further assume that the stakeholders' needs can be subsumed morally with those of the organization. If we assume this, then 'market forces' will generally produce the sort of social accounting that is in the organization's best interests. We might reasonably assume that it is this thinking that produces the sort of voluntary social and environmental disclosure we currently see.

Despite its serious limitations, stakeholder theory does help us. It defines the influencing/influenced groups for us and explicitly defines what accountability the organization itself is willing to recognize and discharge. To deny the organization any role in a definition of a social account seems inappropriate and largely indefensible. This, therefore, provides our first layer – the stakeholder analysis in which the organization defines the accountability. To this we now add the accountability perspective – society's views.

Accountability perspective

Accountability and its role in social accounting has been discussed widely. It is concerned with the relationships between groups, individuals, organizations and the rights to information that such relationships entail. Simply stated, accountability is the duty to provide an account of the actions for which one is held responsible. (For more detail see, for example, Gray et al, 1986, 1987, 1988, 1991, 1996b.) The nature of the relationships, and the attendant rights to information, are contextually determined by the society in which the relationship occurs.

It is definitionally true that some sort of relationship will exist between an organization and each of its stakeholders. As we saw above with stakeholder theory, part of these relationships may be economic in nature and the terms determined by the parties, reflecting their relative power in the relationships. The information flowing through the relationship will be determined by the power of the parties to demand it (a power which, where it exists, could arise from either the intrinsic abilities and power of the groups concerned or from the legislative processes of the society) and/or the willingness/desire of the organization to provide it. Society as a whole reflects (what might be thought of as) a concern that all such relationships and their attendant information rights should not be left entirely to the parties. The most obvious manifestation of this is statute law – for example, companies' acts, equal opportunities legislation – and standards established by statutory bodies, for example, an environmental protection agency, health and safety at work inspectorate. Additionally, other mechanisms, such as voluntary codes of practice, will from time to time enter the public domain as an agreed or, at least, negotiated part of the stakeholder relationship. These 'empirical, beyond-law' determinants of accountability have been referred to as 'quasi-law', (see, for example, Gray et al, 1987, 1988, 1991, 1996b). The extant law plus this 'quasi-law' will therefore represent the first (and major) element in the construction of society's views on the accountability of organizations (see, for example, Stone, 1975).

It is, of course, naïve to assume a simple one-to-one mapping of a 'society's' beliefs about the nature of relationships and the attendant information rights and extant law, even with the addition of 'quasi-law'. On the one hand, rights to information must reflect asymmetries of power and essential lags between a society's views and the enactment of law (see especially Dowling and Pfeffer, 1975; Epstein and Votaw, 1978; Stone, 1975). On the other hand, such rights to information can be argued to comprise both 'positive' (legal) and 'normative' (moral) rights (see, for example, Likierman, 1986; Likierman and Creasey, 1985). Empirical determination of the moral rights is clearly contestable. These moral rights must, in some manner, be added to the positive rights to reflect current views of accountability. Some of these rights will be accepted by organizations – through, for example, mission and/or ethical statements – and, to this extent at least, there will be a convenient overlap between the information rights determined by stakeholder theory and those determined by accountability theory. But there are moral rights that will not be so accepted. Here one must resort, within an accountability framework, to other expressions of society's values. Malachowski (1990), for example, argues for a recognition of media concern as an approximation of new emerging issues of society's concern. Broadly, this may be a plausible basis. For illustration, health and safety concern over accidents rose as a major issue in the UK in the 1980s, while environmental issues clearly claimed a place in society's conception of the organization–society relationship in the early 1990s (see, for example, Gray et al, 1995). Less obvious issues that are not governed by extant law – for example, fair trade and impact on developing countries – are more clearly a matter for negotiation.

The second strand of social disclosure would derive therefore from the established accountability relationships and seek to provide information to which the stakeholders have a right.

There is a danger, however, that a social accounting founded on a combination of stakeholder and accountability perspectives would be too inert and only slowly responsive to changing stakeholder needs. More particularly, the modern basis of these perspectives leave them open to challenge from perspectives arising out of critiques informed by more fluid and, perhaps, more 'post-modern' conceptions. It is concerns such as these that have encouraged many of the newer social accounts to adopt the polyvocal citizenship perspective. It is to this that we now turn.

New Conceptions of the Organization–Society Dialogue: a Challenge

Many of the more recent social accounts, especially those influenced by NEF and Traidcraft plc, have adopted an approach to social accounting which has not previously been discussed in the social mainstream accounting literature (but see, for example, Raynard, 1995; Zadek and Evans, 1993; Zadek and Raynard, 1995). This polyvocal citizenship perspective draws broadly on Habermasian discourse ethics and directly from Guba and Lincoln's (1989) *Fourth Generation Evaluation* and then applies the ideas in a social accounting setting. In its novelty, its explicitly hermeneutic concern and its emphasis on privileging the voices of stakeholders, the PCP offers an alternative conception of social accounting.

The approach is built around stakeholder dialogue and its essence lies in providing each of the stakeholders with a 'voice' in the organization. Focus groups are held with each stakeholder group, from which key issues are identified and a wider constituency of the stakeholder group is consulted to collate their views on these and other issues. The social account comprises predominantly (but not exclusively) a reporting of the voices of the stakeholders. PCP thereby constitutes a different way of seeing the organization. Thus, if we were to take this to extremes (and thus attempt to typify the PCP approach as a post-modern 'straw man'), the terms of the organization–society/group relationship are established, not by the organization or the society, but by the stakeholders themselves. More precisely, though, PCP is a form of symbolic interactionism (Guba and Lincoln, 1989) in which (to borrow the words of Innes, Nixon and Tagoe, 1996, p6), '*the organizational stakeholders are seen as constituting and sustaining their own reality – and that of the organization – both socially and symbolically*'. The PCP social account aims to give voice to these actors so that their systems of interpretation and meanings, and processes of structuring and organizing, are revealed.

The PCP, in drawing from Guba and Lincoln, is clearly working at the boundary of the modern and the post-modern. The most important element of this is the way in which the organization is conceived. Again, taking this to extremes, the PCP might be typified assuming that the organization has no existence prior to or independent of the stakeholders – that is, the stakeholders in a social constructivist sense create the organization. Such a view is central to Guba and Lincoln's analysis which ontologically denies the existence of an objective reality and assumes that epistemologically understanding (in this case represented by the social account) emerges from the interaction between observer and observed (Guba and Lincoln, 1989, p44). Therefore, while the stakeholders are privileged in the construction of the organization and the social account, the approach is hermeneutic and iterative with refined and developed understandings emerging over several cycles of the social accounting process.

The NEF/Traidcraft approach does not stop here, though. First, at least in the early attempts at (what were referred to as) 'social audits', the 'social auditor' was cast in the role of Guba and Lincoln's evaluator whose job it is to encourage and engage with the dialogue process towards a responsive constructivist evaluation (in our case, a social account rather than an 'evaluation' as such). Thus, there is no role for an external objective audit or attestation because, quite simply, such 'externality' and 'objectivity' cannot exist in the model. Second, the NEF/Traidcraft approach placed the 'core values' of the organization at the heart of the dialogue (and thus at the heart of the account). These core values – which may emerge from the social accounting process or may be enshrined in mission statements or statements of ethics or principles – become that thing which the social accounting process is 'evaluating' and negotiating and, hopefully, changing as a consequence of the stakeholder dialogue. Consequently, the resulting social account will contain data reflective of the 'core values' of the organization and which, inevitably, must overlap with the information we would expect to flow into a social account from the stakeholder and accountability perspectives itemized above.

Hopefully it is apparent from the brief outline above that the NEF/Traidcraft version of PCP (more usually called the 'stakeholder dialogue' approach) is concerned with praxis. In its concern to evolve an active practice, it has clearly moved away from the solipsism (see, for example, Laughlin and Broadbent, 1996) of the 'pure' Guba and Lincoln approach and similarly edged away from the post-modern conceptions of organizational interactions, towards something which begins to look more like a Habermas 'ideal speech situation' (Habermas, 1978).

Thus, in the context of social accounting, it seems that in the PCP 'social auditing' process three things are happening simultaneously:

1   The stakeholders are being encouraged to voice the terms of the accountability relationship, both as they see it currently and how they would wish it to be – that is, the stakeholders are defining the terms of accountability.
2   The stakeholders are active in defining the accounting entity itself.
3   The voices of the stakeholders provide an essential element of the basis for the social account of the organization.

Each of these matters needs to be further explored.

Synthesizing the Perspectives?

The first of the above points – that the stakeholders define their own terms of accountability – fits well with the discussion so far. Allowing through the voices of the stakeholders provides a systematic solution to the hitherto unaddressed problem of how to deal with the inevitable limits that an empirical accountability imposes on the social account. So, in terms of this chapter, PCP provides our third (and final) 'layer' of the accountability relationships which comprise the social account: organization-, society- and stakeholder-determined terms of accountability.

The second point – how one is to conceive of, and practically determine, the definition of the accounting entity – is a subtle and important matter that is all too easily ignored in the stakeholder and accountability perspectives. We will examine this point more fully in a later section.

The third point – that it is the stakeholders who (in effect) provide the social account – produces both a significant synergy and a significant conflict with other forms of social accounting (as restricted above). The synergy arises from the type of information that PCP generates. This information includes such matters as employees' levels of satisfaction and motivation, customers' levels of satisfaction and environmentalists' anxieties about the organization. This sort of information, while it might be thought of loosely as accountability information, is, indeed, both an expression of the stakeholders' voices and management information of the sort that any organization needs if it is to manage its stakeholders, as suggested by stakeholder theory. In this way, information generated by PCP is both an important addition to the potential discharge of accountability and information which management can use under the stakeholder perspective.

On the other hand, the conflict arises between PCP and more conventional approaches for several reasons:

1   Under 'conventional' forms of social accounting, the organization provides the social account, whereas in PCP the stakeholders provide it (although the account is actually published and distributed by the organization itself). This latter point places the PCP within the more conventional interpretations of social accounting (see, for example, Gray et al, 1996b) as a hybrid of self-reporting (the shaded quadrant in Figure 9.1) and the independent social reporting pioneered by units such as Social Audit Ltd (see the bottom right-hand quadrant of the figure.

2   Under the extreme version of PCP the account exists only as a social construction of the organization – the organization and its relationships do not exist without that construction. The stakeholder-accountability approaches assume an underlying reality which is reconstructed by the social account – that is, the latter suggests that the relationships and rights exist prior to the social accounting. Under PCP the relationships and rights do not so exist and are constructed through the account.

3   While the conventional forms of social accounting have been accused of being conservative (see, for example, Tinker et al, 1991), they do have potential for change and evolution (see, for example, Gallhofer and Haslam, 1995; Gray et al, 1996a; Lehman, 1995; Power, 1994). They offer this potential by reference to a wider set of societal values that, it is normally assumed, will challenge the organization's existence. On the face of it, PCP appears to do the same but may well have more conservative, albeit democratic, tendencies – that is, as a consequence of its genesis in the work of Guba and Lincoln, it *may* – we emphasize may – be less likely to assume, seek out and expose conflict between organizational legitimacy and stakeholder views. This is, however, a practical rather than a theoretical problem and relates to the final potential source of conflict with more conventional versions of social accounting.

4   There is a potential difficulty in that stakeholders, while their right to a voice is not, to our mind, contestable, may not be informed in a manner which permits the expression of their voice to challenge the essential problems of organizational legitimacy. Unlike the 'external social audits' which raise and extend the boundaries of accountability (see, for example, Gray et al, 1988; Harte and Owen, 1987), the voices may be heard only internally and offer comment only in the terms already set for them by the organizational hegemony.

But these are problems only of degree – all forms of social accounting are susceptible to these problems (see, for example, Puxty, 1986, 1991). Rather, PCP may, in offering greater synergy with other forms of social accounting, go some way towards muting the criticisms of the social accounting project.

Can the 'conventional' stewardship-accountability approaches to social accounting be synthesized with the PCP approach? The answer is probably that they cannot be fully synthesized, but only because they draw from a fundamentally different ontology. While all three approaches to social accounting can be thought of as essentially social constructionist, it is the way in which PCP constructs the organization that raises the essential conflict. Yet it is apparent that both are motivated by similar principal concerns – that is, to develop social accounting and thereby extend accountability and democracy. The two approaches, although ontologically incompatible, are not necessarily mutually exclusive, but rather it seems to us that they represent alternative perspectives on the organization and are, therefore, mutually reinforcing. There is little question in our minds that the PCP brings an important additional dimension to the processes of social accounting. It adds the (hitherto silent) voices of the stakeholders to the specification and construction of accountability and, as we will see in the next section, helps to crystallize the way in which the accounting entity is conceptualized. These, in our judgement, are important developments in the conceptualization and application of accountability. But for predominantly practical (even pragmatic) reasons, we believe the systematic development of social accounting requires that the organization be the reporting body. As such, it is the business of the reporting organization to construct the social account; and such a social account, to be complete, must, we infer, recognize the voices of the stakeholders. Under the continuing assumption that the organization constructs the account, then the organization needs to report:

1   that the stakeholders have (or have not) been given a voice; and
2   what those voices had to say about the terms of the organization's accountability.

This does not require that the organization reports the full detail of those voices (as we see in, for example, The Body Shop *Values Report*, 1996). Should the organization choose to report the detailed findings from the consultations with stakeholders, that then goes beyond the essential requirements of an accountability report. In this way, although we stay grounded in the somewhat more realist ontology of the stakeholder-accountability perspective, we open up that perspective in a way that can recognize challenges to that ontology.

Whatever the remaining theoretical conflicts, for reasons of practicability and political expedience, some synthesis needs to be found. The further issues that arise in this reconciliation will become clearer, we suggest, when we examine first, the construction of the accounting entity and second, the information which must be contained in the channels of accountability. These follow in subsequent sections.

To try to ground the discussion thus far, we turn now to two examples of social accounting produced by Traidcraft plc and Traidcraft Exchange. We will discuss the Traidcraft plc case to illustrate the issues arising when we seek to define the accounting entity and their implications for the accountability information produced. We then discuss Traidcraft Exchange as an illustration of how the three layers of social accounting information can be used to work together.

The Traidcraft plc Case

This section provides a very brief outline of one experience of identifying the organizational stakeholders and defining–negotiating the accounting entity. More detail on the Traidcraft plc experience can be found in Dey et al (1995); Evans (1991); Zadek and Evans (1993), and the published social accounts from the company.

Traidcraft plc (sometimes referred to as 'the plc', hereafter), a small 'values-based' UK company working with the NEF, produced its first comprehensive 'social audit' in the UK in 1993. This was the first example of a systematic self-generated and reported social account by a UK company and was a remarkable phenomenon for that alone. But the plc went further, publishing a booklet explaining their underlying thinking (Zadek and Evans, 1993) and committed the company to developing regular systematic social accounts of the company in future years.

Traidcraft plc has a called-up share capital of £1.8 million and an annual turnover of nearly £7 million. The company's share capital consists of widely held, but non-voting, 'B' shares, a single 'guardian share' which prevents the takeover or control of the company against the principles of the company and a body of voting 'A' shares which are held by the Traidcraft Foundation Trustees.

The company has about 150 employees and has reported modest profits in most of the last few years. While the company operates in a financial climate and must be economically viable, the relationships it has with its employees and directors (all of whom accept relatively low salaries), its representatives, agents and shareholders all ensure that the company is not subject to the full blast of the rigours of the late 20th-century market economy.

The company exists to encourage 'fair trade' between the so-called developed and developing countries. Most especially, profit and cash-flow are means to that end and not, as in conventional economic and accounting theory, vice versa. It was not inappropriate, therefore, that the company should examine the extent to which it was living by its principles, especially as the company has always prided itself on its sensitivity to criticism from constituents.

The 1993 social audit was a joint effort by Traidcraft and NEF, with a member of NEF working in the company on the development of the principles of the audit and the collation of the appropriate data (see Zadek and Evans, 1993). The audit was subject to a degree of independent attestation from an advisory board established by NEF and the report was published in late 1993. The 1993 experience had highlighted two major factors:

1   There was confusion of roles over accounting and auditing.
2   It was apparent that producing a systematic and transparent account of the company's activities was more difficult, technically and spiritually, than had been anticipated.

The 1994 and 1995 social audits were conducted with less involvement from NEF but were still subject to the audit process from the audit advisory board.

In the development of the 1995 social account (as it is now called), the plc and the audit advisory board met a real practical difficulty in conceiving of the organization and its social audit. A systematic heuristic was needed to allow an explicit specification of the elements of the organization–society constituents relationship that was practical enough to be applicable to a functioning company and which could be articulated in a way that recognizes the societal and political assumptions of the approach in a way sufficiently specific to resonate with the theoretical literature on organizations and accountability.

Defining the accounting entity

Prior to the inception of the project of which this chapter is a part, there was no established method for defining a social accounting system. Equally, there is little likelihood that it is possible to derive any one, unique, social account of any organization. One of the many characteristics that makes Traidcraft's social accounting unique is its 'semiotic nature', in the sense that the whole process is designed to elicit a shared meaning or expression of the entity known as 'Traidcraft'. While power assymetries are inevitable, all parties who are active in the Traidcraft plc enterprise are given a voice. By this means, a shared account of the organization begins to emerge. This is not to deny that other interpretations of the account are possible (or even desirable), but rather to suggest that the widely shared expression of the account is essentially an expression of communitarian accountability (see, for example, Pallot, 1987, 1991). The process is one in which all active parties, including the widely drawn social audit advisory board, the researcher-advisers of the NEF and the present researchers construct the organization.

The organization and its accountability

Traidcraft is conceived of as an organization with a transparent permeable membrane, the organizational boundary of which is constantly negotiated (Llewellyn, 1994). It is then conceived of as lying at the centre of a nexus of social relationships which are articulated in a manner akin to a stakeholder model located in a neo-pluralist conception of society. The key here is the notion of relationship. The 'best' social accounts are those which, presumably, seem best to express the essence of those relationships. This conceptual model is illustrated, with a significant degree of simplification, in Figure 9.2.

The relationships are, inevitably, of unequal importance and strength. They are prioritized, to a large degree, by Traidcraft's own mission statement. The strength – or, indeed, the closeness (Gray, 1992) – of the relationships is also part of the defined organization. The 'closer relationships' – with employees, the producer communities and even the representatives/agents – are negotiated so that these groups actually become part of 'Traidcraft' – that is, the organizational boundary membrane is especially thin at these points and is managed to accommodate all, or part of, these additional parties. This could be shown in a development of Figure 9.2 (see Figure 9.3 which is a basic attempt at a move towards this) in which, for example, the dominance of the relationship could be shown by the thickness of the line

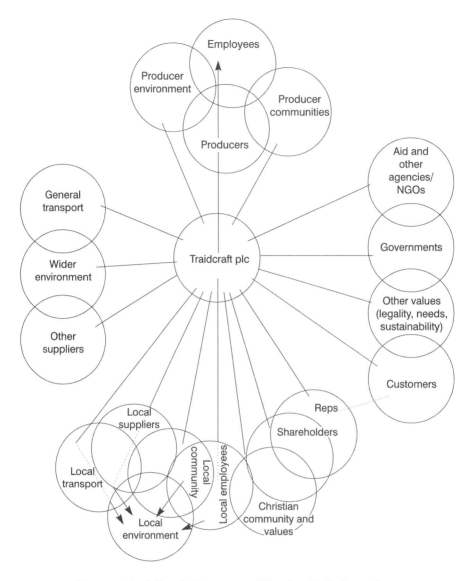

Figure 9.2 *A Simple Depiction of Traidcraft's Relationships*

suggesting that relationship and a new 'fuzzy' Traidcraft organizational boundary shown by the shaded area (some of this is shown in Figure 9.3).

The accountability of Traidcraft is an imposed accountability only in the case of any government reporting, any especial demands from the voting shareholders and the existing financial accountability of all UK companies. All other account-ability is assumed because of the moral rights of the accountee parties and/or because of the value-based nature of the organization and its desire to be accountable (Zadek and Evans, 1993). This principle is then extended via consultation with the stakeholders

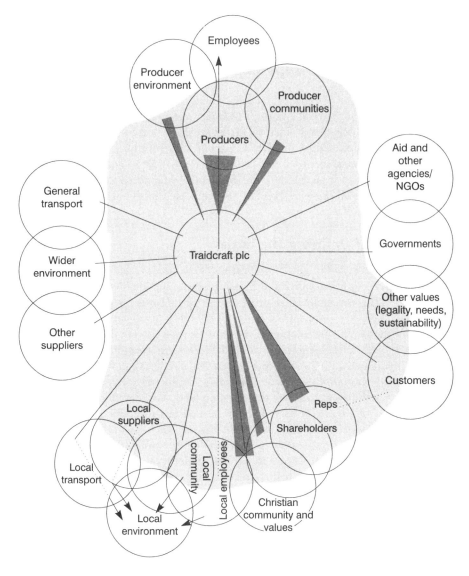

Figure 9.3 *Prioritizing the Stakeholder Relationships*

to give them an explicit voice, one element of which tells the organization (and the auditors) whether their initial perception of the relative strengths and 'closeness' of the organizational relationships are adequately represented in the conception of the organizational boundary.

The organizational boundary – the 'accounting entity' – is thus defined by the organization's, society's and the stakeholders' negotiations of closeness. Those stakeholders who come into the 'entity' are then part of the entity and consequently need to be included in the account. In this way, what the account is of and who the account is *to* are clarified. Additionally, some initial prioritization of stakeholder relationships is explicitly undertaken.

Traidcraft's relationships and the definition of the accounting entity

The 19 broadly prioritized relationships (shown in Figures 9.2 and 9.3) now have to be defined in somewhat greater detail. To provide a full social account, each of the 19 social relationships need to be accounted for: for completeness, the stakeholder, accountability and PCP information needs to be collated, synthesized and reported. However, at the time the Traidcraft social accounts were being prepared these were still unclear. This issue is explicated in the Traidcraft Exchange case below.

Discussion of defining the entity

The foregoing has tried to give an indication of the process that was used to begin to define the accounting entity and to prioritize its stakeholders. Hopefully, it is apparent that this was an iterative process driven by a convergence between a conventional stakeholder conception, the accountability perspective and the 'softer' PCP conceptions. The articulation of the entity is then used to determine the relationships and the consequent information that the social account should attempt to convey. Undoubtedly, the process was a great deal simpler than it would have been for a more explicitly profit-centred organization. Traidcraft plc is explicitly 'values-centred', is by nature a transparent organization (with considerable interactions and shared values with many of its stakeholders) and has formally articulated these principles in very extensive mission statements.

Furthermore, ideally, the conception of the entity would be explicitly discussed with all the stakeholders to ensure that it has semiotic validity. It seems inevitable, however, that such organizational conceptions will be (often implicitly) negotiated and the organization itself, as the dominant stakeholder, is likely to have a disproportionate influence on the final determination of the entity and, consequently, on the terms of reference offered to the stakeholders in which to express their voices. It is difficult to know at this stage how serious a limitation on social accounting this will prove to be.

The Traidcraft Exchange Case

This section reports a later experiment with the plc's sister organization, the Traidcraft Exchange, in which a systematic social account was sought employing the three layers of accountability information discussed above. The results of this have been published in the Exchange's social accounts for 1995–1996.

Traidcraft Exchange (referred to as TX hereafter) is a small charitable company (limited by guarantee) involved in a range of activities concerned primarily with encouraging fair trade. TX has an annual income of a little under £1 million (derived through fundraising, grants and contracts) and a staff of 15–20 people, some of whom are 'shared' with the plc. It is, thus, a very small organization. In 1995, TX decided to try to produce its own social account. This would be novel in a number of ways:

1   The organization is so small that while data therefore would be easier to capture, it would not be practicable to try to systematize the process through a social bookkeeping system.
2   The definition of the accounting entity would be even more problematic in that the edges of TX and the plc blur at times and, while this did not seem to be material for the plc, the relative size made it more important for TX; and voluntary organizations frequently have much less formal organizational interactions, and the 'membrane' was therefore likely to be thinner, fuzzier and more likely to float back and forth.
3   The experience of the plc showed that, despite the dominance of the PCP approach, the final social accounts had to contain other data which did not emerge from the voices. These, it seemed in discussions, increased the importance of 'completeness' that is central to constructing the social account.
4   It was judged to be a good time to try to discover whether it was possible to derive a 'portable' social accounting process. To this end it was decided that the social accounting process should not rely on NEF, should be undertaken by a member of TX with no previous experience of social accounting (although consultancy advice was available from the authors) and, perhaps most dramatically, the statutory financial auditors would be requested to publish an audit opinion on the social accounts.

This final point – the statutory financial auditors expressing an opinion – became the touchstone for much else that followed. From discussions with the auditors it became clear that the whole process would have to be documented, social accounting principles derived and stated, and the accounting standards of information disclosure would have to be applied. A version of the standard long-form audit report, possibly with heavy qualifications, would be appended to the social accounts. Convincing the firm of accountants to take on this responsibility was not simple and they required a great deal of 'comfort' from TX. This, in turn, had a remarkable 'tightening-up' effect on the whole process and certainly introduced a higher degree of independence into the process.

The auditors had to be convinced by the definition of the stakeholders. This was achieved by following the same procedure described above for the plc. TX used its (very detailed) mission statement to categorize and prioritize its stakeholders to the satisfaction of the auditors. Then three levels of information were collected about each relationship with each stakeholder. The stakeholder information – in the sense of an organization seeking to manage its stakeholders – was not strictly appropriate because of TX's highly transparent culture and the existence of the detailed mission statement which acts as an effective contract between the organization and its constituents. Information descriptive of the relationships was, however, essential and this was referred to as the 'stakeholder data'. The legal (identified by reference to statute law) and moral rights (as expressed in the TX mission statement) were then identified, and information designed to discharge the resultant accountability was collated for each. Finally, arrangements were made, where possible through (relatively independent) third parties to seek out and collect the voices of the stakeholders. Throughout the process an audit trail was maintained whenever possible and specific notes were kept of all decisions, value judgements and missing information that (inevitably) arose during the process.

The resultant social account then comprised: a section outlining the process used; the auditors' report; and the social account itself, covering the six groups of stakeholders, which was finally agreed as covering most of the material stakeholders. Each stakeholder section provided the three layers of information: the descriptions of the relationship, the accountability information and the 'voices' of the stakeholders. Although not all information was collected for all aspects of each of the stakeholder groups – completeness, it seems, will always be a problem – the result was a relatively transparent and replicable account. It seriously engaged the auditors and it looks highly likely that the method could be applied to any organization.

The TX social accounting process, then, has two distinctive elements:

1　The relatively programmed approach to the collection and reporting of information.
2　The 'true and fair' report from the statutory financial auditors.

The relatively programmed approach has clearly forced the active participants in the social accounting process towards a more specific explication of the processes and judgements made – that is, although the TX experience, drawing heavily from the plc experience, was an explicitly programmed process, it was not simply mechanical. Too many of the data and relationships were 'soft' and required judgement by the social accountant. Such judgement was equally required by the auditors. The auditors' involvement forced a much more explicit process on the accounting process and threw into relief the absence of any accounting standards or generally accepted accounting principles (GAAP) for social accounting. While generally accepted auditing principles were found to be helpful in the attestation process, it was an absence of anything with which to define the account that caused problems. (This is a subject for the final section of the chapter.) We could usefully express the view that, in our opinions, there never could be – nor, indeed, should be – a completely unqualified audit report on a social account. As a process designed primarily to enhance transparency and accountability, judgement will be essential and one should not expect an independent view to reach, or even agree with, such social judgements. As long as this is clear, the qualification of a 'true and fair' report seems a desirable attribute, although it is less easy to be prescriptive about the form that a PCP/evaluator's audit report should take.

In the next section we attempt to synthesize the present experience in order to move towards some social accounting standards.

Towards Social Accounting Standards

It is clear that Traidcraft plc and Exchange are very unusual organizations – in their orientation, values-based transparent cultures and in their size. It would be inappropriate, therefore, to generalize their experience as applicable to all organizations. However, subsequent experience with different organizations (many of which are less willing to allow themselves and their inner secrets to be discussed with the same openness and freedom as Traidcraft has permitted) suggests that the basic experience derived from the Traidcraft cases provides an especially useful basis on which to move towards identification of some key elements in the social accounting process. That is what this (final) section will attempt to do – but succinctly, leaving more detailed discussion of the theoretical coherence of key social accounting principles to future papers.

There is not, nor is there ever likely to be, a single type of social account. The range of approaches and experiments increases all the time. We consider this healthy and desirable, not least because many different organizations in different social contexts will have different conceptions of the elements discussed here. (The range discussed in Zadek and Raynard (1995) and the emerging non-governmental organization (NGO) community-based social accounts with their own special concerns speak eloquently of this.) Furthermore, as Tinker et al (1991) have shown, no account of organization–society interactions can be static through time – issues, concerns and accountabilities change. This is inevitable.

However, an alternative approach which responds to the increasing requests for guidance on 'how to do a social account' with a statement like 'any way you want' is not helpful and does not necessarily advance the cause of accountability reporting in any productive way. The recent formation of the ISEA was predicated on the need to guide organizations seeking to develop social accounting and to try to deduce best practice in the field where this is possible. This is not a simple task, nor one which can be accomplished quickly. This chapter is an early attempt to begin the process of articulating some of the key matters which bodies such as ISEA will need to address.

What, then, do we believe are the key elements in an approach to an 'ideal type' of social account that seem to have emerged from the experiences discussed above?

The following is an attempt to synthesize the messages that appear to emerge from the foregoing discussion and from the experiences of social accounting to date:

1   Conceptual prerequisites for an accounting:
    –   an accounting entity;
    –   an accounting/account.

2   Definitions derived for:
    –   social accounting;
    –   the recognition and boundaries of the accounting entity, via stakeholder analysis;
    –   the nature of the account and its completeness.

3   Assumed:
  - a neo-pluralist context;
  - that a stakeholder relationship conception of an organization reflects a neo-pluralist assumption;
  - desirability of democracy;
  - accountability as a democratic mechanism;
  - organizational self-reporting (as opposed to 'social audits');
  - information should possess the characteristics of completeness, reliability, verifiability, consistency, comparability;
  - understandability;
  - the account socially reconstructs an organization which pre-exists the account;
  - the reconstruction should be a reflexive and complex series of views from all stakeholders.

4   Deduced:
  - groups and individuals have rights to information;
  - these are resolved informally in smaller non-complex situations;
  - formal accounts are needed for accountability in complex situations;
  - organizations need to produce accountability accounts;
  - rights to information determined by the organization, society, the stakeholders;
  - the three layers of information, plus the descriptors of the relationships, must be a 'complete' account of information provided to assess the extent of the incompleteness;
  - independent judgement – preferably without experience in social accounting – is essential to assess completeness and reliability.

5   Asserted
  - social accounting is a dynamic and developing process: nothing here should limit further development and experimentation;
  - the social accounting is a continuous process of iteration and negotiation.

In time, each of these elements will either prove to be sound, and be expanded on, or will be rejected and replaced. At the present time, they appear to be key useful factors that social accounting needs to consider.

The conceptual framework above accommodates a fairly high degree of synthesis between the TX 'accounting-style' approach, which incorporates the stakeholder dialogue voices, and the NEF–Traidcraft approach, in which the voices are paramount and the stakeholder and accountability information are incorporated; nevertheless, there still remains a tension about the emphasis given to these two sides of the story.

This tension is perhaps best expressed in the role attributed to the auditor or even the 'social auditor'. Two alternative approaches have been mentioned above. The first was the use of a completely independent auditor (in the case of TX, the statutory financial auditor) who has no involvement with the construction of the account and simply expresses a (perhaps detailed) opinion on the account's 'truth and fairness'. The second approach to 'auditing' was the far more active involvement of an organization like the NEF which helps to construct the social account, oversees the collection of data and responses from stakeholders and relies, in its turn, on an 'audit advisory body' to suggest some degree of impartiality in the assessment of the account. We remain split on this issue, but hope – indeed anticipate – some further synthesis of thinking on this matter as experience develops. Our current thinking suggests that we may, indeed, have two – probably similar and complementary – constructs. The first such construct – that with which this chapter is primarily concerned – is a formal 'social account' whose primary purpose is to construct a social image of the organization. The second construct is the 'social audit' (which may or may not produce a social account) whose principal purpose is to encourage a negotiation for change between the organization and its stakeholders. The precise dividing line, if indeed there is one, needs further definition.

A final matter which still needs detailed specification is the way in which the stakeholder's voices are 'heard' and collated. These voices are not making a single statement. They are making statements about:

- things about which the accounting organization wishes to know;
- information which each stakeholder would like to receive; and
- their views – for example, complaints – on the organization and its activities, plus the activities and issues the stakeholders would like the organization to address.

The first of these seems to relate to the stakeholder perspective and be useful for organizational management. The second seems to relate to accountability and the stakeholders determining the terms of accountability that they would wish. In both of these cases, it seems likely that the data could be collected by, inter alia, questionnaires. Confidentiality does not appear to be so important here. The third type of information, however, does require to be collected and collated – and reported? – by an entirely independent unit which the stakeholder can trust. (Otherwise are, for example, employees going to say things which might incur the wrath of management?) This is an emerging issue on which more work is required.

The social accounting agenda has opened out as never before. Certainly, for the first time in more than 20 years there is an active and dynamic process with which researchers and teachers need to engage. Academic engagement with the environmental accounting and reporting process has been fairly successful. Drawing from that, academe now needs to help bodies like ISEA to set a new foundation for the formal accountability of organizations. It is an important, exciting and very urgent challenge.

References

AICPA (1977) *The Measurement of Corporate Social Performance*, American Institute of Certified Public Accountants, New York, NY

Cooper, C (1992) 'The Non and Nom of Accounting for (M)other Nature', *Accounting, Auditing & Accountability Journal*, vol 5, no 3, pp16–39

Dey, C, Evans, R and Gray, R H (1995) 'Towards Social Information Systems and Bookkeeping: a Note on Developing the Mechanisms for Social Accounting and Audit', *Journal of Applied Accounting Research*, vol 2, no 3

Donaldson, J (1988) *Key Issues in Business Ethics*, Academic Press, London

Dowling, J and Pfeffer, J (1975) 'Organizational Legitimacy: Social Values and Organizational Behaviour', *Pacific Sociological Review*, January, pp122–136

Epstein, E M N and Votaw, D (1978) (ed) *Nationality, Legitimacy, Responsibility: Search for New Directions in Business and Society*, Goodyear, California

Estes, R W (1976) *Corporate Social Accounting*, Wiley, New York, NY

Evans, R (1991) 'Business Ethics and Changes in Society', *Journal of Business Ethics*, vol 10, pp871–976

Francis, J (1990) 'After Virtue? Accounting as a Moral and Discursive Practice', *Accounting, Auditing & Accountability Journal*, vol 3, no 3, pp5–17

Gallhofer, S and Haslam, J (1995) 'Worrying about Environmental Auditing', *Accounting Forum*, vol 19, nos 2/3, pp205–18

Gray, R H (1991) *Trends in Corporate Social and Environmental Accounting*, British Institute of Management, London

Gray, R H (1992) 'Accounting and Environmentalism: an Exploration of the Challenge of Gently Accounting for Accountability, Transparency and Sustainability', *Accounting, Organizations and Society*, vol 17, no 5, July, pp399–426

Gray, R H (1997) 'The Practice of Silent Accounting', in S Zadek, P Pruzan and R Evans (eds) *Building Corporate Accountability: Emerging Practices in Social and Ethical Accounting and Reporting*, Earthscan, London

Gray, R H, Owen, D L and Maunders, K T (1986) 'Corporate Social Reporting: the Way Forward?', *Accountancy*, December, pp6–8

Gray, R H, Owen, D L and Maunders, K T (1987) *Corporate Social Reporting: Accounting and Accountability*, Prentice-Hall, Hemel Hempstead

Gray, R H, Owen, D L and Maunders, K T (1988) 'Corporate Social Reporting: Emerging Trends in Accountability and the Social Contract', *Accounting, Auditing & Accountability Journal*, vol 1, no 1, pp6–20

Gray, R H, Owen, D L and Maunders, K T (1991) 'Accountability, Corporate Social Reporting and the External Social Audits', *Advances in Public Interest Accounting*, vol 4, pp1–21

Gray, R H, Bebbington, K J, Walters, D and Thomson, I (1995) 'The Greening of Enterprise: an Exploration of the (Non) Role of Environmental Accounting and Environmental Accountants in Organizational Change', *Critical Perspectives on Accounting*, vol 6, no 3, pp211–39

Gray, R H, Laughlin, R C and Bebbington, K J (1996a) *Financial Accounting: Method and Meaning*, International Thomson Publishing Company, London

Gray, R H, Owen, D L and Adams, C (1996b) *Accounting and Accountability: Changes and Challenges in Corporate Social and Environmental Reporting*, Prentice-Hall, London

Guba, E S and Lincoln, Y S (1989) *Fourth Generation Evaluation*, Sage Publications, Newbury Park, CA

Habermas, J (1978) *Knowledge and Human Interests*, Heinemann, London

Harte, G and Owen, D L (1987) 'Fighting De-industrialisation: the Role of Local Government Social Audits', *Accounting, Organizations and Society*, vol 12, no 2, pp123–142

Held, D (1987) *Models of Democracy*, Polity Press, Oxford

Hines, R D (1988) 'Financial Accounting: in Communicating Reality, We Construct Reality', *Accounting, Organizations and Society*, vol 13, no 3, pp251–261

Hines, R D (1989) 'The Sociopolitical Paradigm in Financial Accounting Research', *Accounting, Auditing & Accountability Journal*, vol 2, no 1, pp52–76

Hines, R D (1991) 'The FASB's Conceptual Framework, Financial Accounting and the Maintenance of the Social World', *Accounting, Organizations & Society*, vol 16, no 4, pp313–332

Hines, R D (1992) 'Accounting: Filling the Negative Space', *Accounting, Organizations and Society*, vol 17, nos 3/4, pp313–342

Innes, J, Nixon, W A and Tagoe, N (1996) 'Accounting and Strategic Processes – a Case Study', University of Dundee Discussion Paper ACC/9601

Laughlin, R C and Broadbent, J (1996) 'Redesigning Fourth Generation Evaluation: an Evaluation Model for the Public Sector Reforms in the UK?', *Evaluation*, vol 2, no 4, pp431–451

Lavoie, D (1987) 'The Accounting of Interpretations and the Integration of Accounts: the Communication Function of the Language of Business', *Accounting, Organizations and Society*, vol 12, no 6, pp579–604

Lehman, G (1995) 'A Legitimate Concern for Environmental Accounting', *Critical Perspectives on Accounting*, vol 6, no 6, pp393–412

Likierman, A (1986) *Rights and Obligations in Public Information*, University College Cardiff Press, Cardiff

Likierman, A and Creasey, P (1985) 'Objectives and Entitlements to Rights in Government Financial Information', *Financial Accountability and Management*, vol 1, no 1, summer, pp33–50

Llewellyn, S (1994) 'Managing the Boundary: How Accounting is Implicated in Maintaining the Organization', *Accounting, Auditing and Accountability Journal*, vol 7, no 4, pp4–23

Malachowski, A (1990) 'Business Ethics 1980–2000: an Interim Forecast', *Managerial Auditing Journal*, vol 5, no 2, pp22–27

Mathews, M R (1993) *Socially Responsible Accounting*, Chapman Hall, London

Maunders, K T and Burritt, R (1991) 'Accounting and Ecological Crisis', *Accounting, Auditing & Accountability Journal*, vol 4, no 3, pp9–26

Medawar, C (1976) 'The Social Audit: a Political View', *Accounting, Organizations and Society*, vol 1, no 4, pp389–394

Meyer, J W (1986) 'Social Environments and Organizational Accounting', *Accounting, Organizations and Society*, vol 11, nos 4/5, pp345–356

Mitchell A, Puxty, A, Sikka, P and Willmott, H (1991) *Accounting for Change: Proposals for Reform of Audit and Accounting*, Fabian Society, London

Nasi, J (ed) (1995) *Understanding Stakeholder Thinking*, LSR Publications, Helsinki

Pallot, J (1987) 'Infrastructure Assets as a Concept in Governmental Accounting', paper given to AAANZ, Canberra

Pallot, J (1991) 'The Legitimate Concern with Fairness: a Comment', *Accounting, Organizations and Society*, vol 16, no 2, pp201–208

Parker, L D (1986) 'Polemical Themes in Social Accounting: a Scenario for Standard Setting', *Advances in Public Interest Accounting*, vol 1, pp67–93

Power, M (1994) 'Constructing the Responsible Organization: Accounting and Environmental Representation', in G Teubner, L Farmer and D Murphy (eds) *Environmental Law and Ecological Responsibility: The Concept and Practice of Ecological Self-organization*, John Wiley, London, pp370–392

Puxty, A G (1986) 'Social Accounting as Immanent Legitimation: a Critique of a Technist Ideology', *Advances in Public Interest Accounting*, vol 1, pp95–112

Puxty, A G (1991) 'Social Accountability and Universal Pragmatics', *Advances in Public Interest Accounting*, vol 4, pp35–46

Raynard, P (1995) 'The New Economics Foundation's Social Audit: Auditing the Auditors?', *Social and Environmental Accounting*, vol 15, no 1, pp7–10

Roberts, R W (1992) 'Determinants of Corporate Social Responsibility Disclosure', *Accounting, Organizations and Society*, vol 17, no 6, pp595–612

Sikka, P (1987) 'Professional Education and Auditing Books: a Review Article', *British Accounting Review*, vol 19, no 3, December, pp291–304

Sikka, P, Willmott, H C and Lowe, E A (1989) 'Guardians of Knowledge and the Public Interest: Evidence and Issues of Accountability in the UK Accountancy Profession', *Accounting, Auditing & Accountability Journal*, vol 2, no 2, pp47–71

Sikka P, Willmott, H C and Lowe, E A (1991) 'Guardians of Knowledge and the Public Interest: a Reply to Our Critics', *Accounting, Auditing & Accountability Journal*, vol 4, no 4, pp14–22

Stone, C D (1975) *Where the Law Ends*, Harper & Row, New York, NY

The Body Shop (1996) *The Values Report*, The Body Shop, Littlehampton

Tinker, A M, Lehman, C and Neimark, M (1991) 'Corporate Social Reporting: Falling Down the Hole in the Middle of the Road', *Accounting, Auditing & Accountability Journal*, vol 4, no 1, pp28–54

Ullmann, A E (1985) 'Data in Search of a Theory: a Critical Examination of the Relationships Among Social Performance, Social Disclosure and Economic Performance of US Firms', *Academy of Management Review*, vol 10, no 3, pp540–57

Zadek, S and Evans, R (1993) *Auditing the Market: A Practical Approach to Social Accounting*, New Economics Foundation, London

Zadek, S and Raynard, P (1995) 'Social Auditing, Transparency and Accountability', *Accounting Forum*, vol 19, nos 2/3, September–December

10

Balancing Performance, Ethics and Accountability

Simon Zadek

Why Ethics?

The inclusive company

The emergence of social and ethical accounting, auditing and reporting as a common practice within the corporate community is likely to have a major influence on the competencies, direction and basis of viability of companies as we move into the next century. It may also enhance the corporate sector's positive social, ethical and indeed environmental impact – but, then again, it may not.

To understand the emerging pattern of social and ethical accounting, auditing and reporting (SEAAR) and its possible range of substantive effects, requires first that one appreciates *why* there is a burgeoning interest in the field and from that gain some understanding of *what* approaches to SEAAR are emerging as best practice today and how this experience is likely to shape up in the future.

It is useful to start with the age-old question, 'Why ethics?'. What may be expensive procedures and processes to understand social and ethical performance are not taken on lightly by any organization. Most companies faced with the pressure to show healthy financial returns will want to see new activities contributing to, or at least not significantly detracting from, financial profitability.

One answer to the question of 'Why ethics?' is that the business community is recognizing the value of, and is responding to, increasing concern about its ethical performance. The Royal Society for the Arts study, *Tomorrow's Company*, examined what kind of companies are likely to be successful in tomorrow's business climate.[1] In the study report, a number of Chief Executives set out a vision of their own companies. Typical of these visions is that of the Group Chief Executive of Grand Metropolitan, George Bull:

> *Increasingly, business people are recognising that their prosperity is directly linked to the prosperity of the whole community. The community is the source of their customers, employees, their suppliers and, with the wider spread of share ownership, their investors.*[2]

Reproduced with kind permission from Kluwer Academic Publishers from the *Journal of Business Ethics*, vol 17, no 13, pp1421–1442, 1998

The study concluded that tomorrow's company will be 'inclusive' in forming deeper relationships with key stakeholders as a means of achieving financial success. Here, then, is the 'stakeholder economy' espoused by such contemporary figures as the British journalist and economist, Will Hutton and the prime minister of the UK, Tony Blair.[3] This view is then that the company which ignores its stakeholders does so at its peril and that similarly those who take them into account will form the bedrock of an inclusive society.

Professor Henk van Luijk and others from the European Institute of Business Ethics (EIBE) reinforces this perspective in summing up the business case by drawing a link between inclusivity and reputation:

> *High ethics companies such as Texas Instruments, IBM, or Marks and Spencer ... know that behaving ethically is integral to their success. They know that their reputation – a reputation for fair dealing, which gains them the trust of their customers, suppliers and the community at large – is crucial to their bottom line.*[4]

This view conforms with an increasing number of studies into the foundations for successful business, whether for the multinational or the corner shop: reputation counts.[5] Relationships matter in seeking business success. Values-in-action that result in trust, integrity and commitment are integral to making long-term relationships work and hence also profitable.

When do people care?

The argument underlying the simple 'inclusive company' approach is that: '*Deepening relationships is good for business; deepening relationships means being good to each other. Good business is therefore about being good to each other.*' This argument is, to say the least, problematic. This is not because it cannot be right and is certainly not because it should not be right. It is a problem because often it is not right in practice in the short run and the short run (as John Maynard Keynes pointed out) can last a hell of a long time.

Companies can and do seek to profit from doing things that are deemed negative by society, such as making people unemployed, damaging the environment, behaving in corrupt or underhand ways and selling products which harm people. The case of tobacco companies making profits by producing products which kill some of their customers and undermine the health of the rest, is an extreme, but poignant, demonstration of this fact. Less melodramatic but equally significant is the simple fact of companies increasing profitability through making people unemployed (as opposed to companies having to shed labour to survive, which is not at all the same situation, although it is often presented as such). As the Institute for Policy Studies reports, whilst annual worker layoffs across the US corporate sector increased by 39 per cent between 1990 and 1995, corporate profits over the same period increased by 75 per cent.[6] As the editors of the magazine *Business Week* concluded: '*It does not take a brain surgeon to see why millions of people who worked hard to make their companies competitive feel shafted.*'[7] Behaving in ways that in most situations to most people would seem 'unethical' *can* pay, at least in the short run, if stakeholders do not penalize the company through, for example, lower staff productivity, lower consumer interest or investment realignments.

It is therefore problematic to argue the view that the 'inclusive' company is *necessarily* a more profitable business model. It is certainly true in some cases. For example, the Centre for Tomorrow's Company together with the merchant bank Kleinwort Benson have argued that what they deem to be 'inclusive' companies from the FTSE 100 tend to perform better financially. However, to argue on this basis either that inclusive companies are 'good to people' or that only inclusive companies will survive, is clearly either wrong or in some sense tautological.

What we can say, however, is that the ethics of a company influences its business performance when stakeholders who count say that they should. 'Business ethics' can only become a reality if stakeholders that do or potentially have leverage over a company's business performance – which might include managers, directors and shareholders, as well as – the 'political consumer' – decide that their views need to be heard and taken into account. The fascinating and central questions then become: 'When do people choose to care, why and what do they do about it?'

There is growing evidence that the failure to behave ethically in the eyes of key stakeholders can and in cases does pose a threat to the financial health of some companies.[8] This is particularly the case with retail companies who are potentially vulnerable to direct consumer action. A recent study commissioned by the Co-operative Wholesale Society in the UK highlighted the rise in 'ethical' or 'vigilante' consumerism.[9] The survey of a sample of 30,000 of their food retail customers found that:

- 35 per cent answered 'yes' to the question: 'Have you boycotted any product because you are concerned about animal rights, the environment, or human rights?'
- 60 per cent answered 'yes' to the question: 'In the future, would you boycott a shop or product because you are concerned with these issues?'

Now clearly the results of 'quicky street surveys' should be treated with care – it is a little like asking someone whether they think that ethics is good. However, substantive practice seems to back up the view that these figures, if not quantitatively correct, are broadly accurate in identifying the basic pattern of response. There is growing evidence that people respond positively to a more ethical stance being adopted by companies, as witnessed by the success of companies such as the Co-operative Bank and The Body Shop in the UK to attract customers and high quality staff on this basis. Similarly, the willingness of very mainstream companies to respond to 'consumer ethics' suggests that their own, highly sophisticated research suggest that the 'ethical effect' is not to be taken lightly.

Attempts by companies to 'keep their heads down' have more recently met with plummeting returns, as corporate responsibility initiatives and the sophistication of the organizations managing such processes, has increased. As Shell discovered to its cost over first the Brent Spar fiasco and then through the disclosures over its approach to business in the Ogoni region of Nigeria, the views either that social and ethical performance can remain private or that the public do not care about what happens beyond their backyards, are both very wrong. Furthermore, companies are finding themselves victims to the excesses of their competitors. Shell's revealed performance in Nigeria led quickly to a far higher profile of the campaigns against the activities, for example, of the French oil company Total in Burma and of British Petroleum's operations in Colombia. The consumer campaigns launched at particular textiles and toys companies regarding labour standards of their suppliers in the 'South' (the 'third world') has now cascaded across key sectors that sell retail products produced in the South – textiles, sportswear, toys, food and flowers.

The consuming public is clearly an important, but by no means only, stakeholder group whose ethical views may encourage companies to rethink their approach to doing business. In a recent seminar held for a major oil company, a senior staff representative offered the following view:

The company has downsized in recent years with massive redundancies. You have to understand that people are disillusioned and frustrated. They cannot be driven to work harder through fear alone – they need to know that the company does care and does hear what they are saying, even although we all know all about business imperatives. The view that staff are disposable will eventually make for a disposable company.

The British standards organization, Investors in People (IIP), have for long argued that high productivity requires committed staff, which in turn requires a company that can earn that commitment. In offering evidence to support this assertion, IIP has sought to show that companies which have gone through the IIP process of staff consultation, staff-related systems and procedures development, improved staff training, etc, simply perform better in financial terms, whether measured in terms of return on capital or pre-tax profit.

So the corporate sector has good reason to show concern for its social, ethical and environmental performance. Beyond any possible personal views of managers and investors that companies do indeed have a social and ethical responsibility, there is the more hard-bitten view that social and ethical responsibility is good for business. It consolidates market positions, or at least protects the business from public interest campaigning and it can also strengthen the solidarity, commitment and productivity of a company's staff (and also, by extension, the productivity and quality of its suppliers and advisers).

Globalization and technological drivers

The argument that 'relationships' count is, of course, not new. What is new, however, are the economic and social conditions under which this most recent cycle of thinking and practice is happening. Most important are the organizational and market changes associated with contemporary developments in technology and the process of globalization.

With respect to the former, we are seeing the most radical shift in the manner in which commerce is organized since Taylorian mechanics entered our organizational vocabulary. The downsizing and flattening of the main rump of most organizations and the dispersal of many of their core functions into market networks through, for example, franchising and outsourcing, all raise new demands with regard to quality at every level. The combination of technological developments in the area of computing and communications – and increasingly their relationship – has vastly reinforced the tendencies towards 'functional dispersal', while at the same time tightening market and cost-based competition in such a manner as to place enormous pressure on the need to make these dispersed operations work at their peak of possible performance.

Globalization has both enabled and driven these tendencies further. Opportunities for cost reduction and accessing new markets through physical and cultural extensions of the business process has placed further pressures on the traditional business unit. For example, this has focused the source of value-added and profit on supply rather than on production, and brand rather than product leadership. Globalization, however, has not been only the prerogative of the corporations. Civil groups previously focused on narrow local or perhaps national agendas have increasingly found voice at international levels through taking advantage of the same rack of technological and organizational shifts and by seeing how to challenge the globalized brands by 'ethical intermediation' – for example, by showing people in Europe what a company is doing in Latin America.[10]

A 'stakeholder-based company' that is able to build trust and integrity into its key relationships thereby lowers the cost of establishing and maintaining increasingly complex networks of suppliers, franchisees and agents, physically dispersed staff and indeed multiple levels of actual and potential regulators from the local town council to the World Trade Organization. A stakeholder-based company is one that in many respects is most fit to take advantage of the technological and regulatory changes that underpin and enable the globalization of trade, production and marketing. A stakeholder-based company, however, is also one that has come to grips with their changing civil environment.

Non-instrumental values

It would be unfortunate to attribute all interest in 'ethics' to the instrumental reasoning of profit-oriented managers operating in increasingly complex and competitive markets. Anyone working with the business community will have been impressed by the commitment of many people working within this community to improving the social and environmental footprint of the companies in which they work. The announcement by BT in December 1996 that it intended to undertake a comprehensive 'ethical audit' was welcomed with some astonishment by those campaigning for greater corporate accountability. BT is certainly not a much-loved company, but was under no particular pressure at the time to take this step. The more cynical commentators pointed to BT's interest in gaining from its regulator, OFTEL, increased room for new commercial initiatives and also the possible link between this commitment and the subsequent move by BT to form a global alliance with MCI. The commitment to an ethical audit may indeed have improved BT's relationship with both the government at the time and the in-coming Labour government. However, there is little doubt that a major factor behind the decision was the personal interest and commitment of BT's leadership. Ethical leadership is not the prerogative of the public and private non-profit sectors.

At the same time, such leadership tends to flounder unless it can anchor its arguments to and practice within, a sound business model. As David Korten argues,

Box 10.1 The 'Rationale Triangle'

The managerialist rationale: that to survive and prosper in society, business needs to know what is happening, what people think about them and how best to influence those perspectives. At the simplest level, this speaks to the need for good market research and public relations. At the more sophisticated level, this highlights the need for managers to have a broader understanding and appreciation of stakeholder needs and views and the patterns of demands on business that are likely to arise in the future.

The public interest rationale at the second end of the triangular spectrum concerns the ability of society to make business respond to changing interests and needs. This public interest perspective emerged particularly in the 1970s, but has become institutionalized more recently in the growing ethical consumer and investment movements. Here, businesses are not merely choosing to undertake some form of social and ethical accounting, auditing and reporting as a means of understanding and manipulating their social environment, but are rather being forced to respond to demands from the actors that make up that environment.

The third corner of the triangle is the most contentious, since it refers more to a value-shift in business than to a compliance or managerialist-based response to new pressures. Here lies the view that business can evolve and take on a different historic role in society, at the same time as the roles traditionally taken on by the state are increasingly under threat. Leaders are tending to question the raison d'être of their company's and their own activities and are searching for an expanded repertoire of explanations and measures of success that are provided by the bottom line.

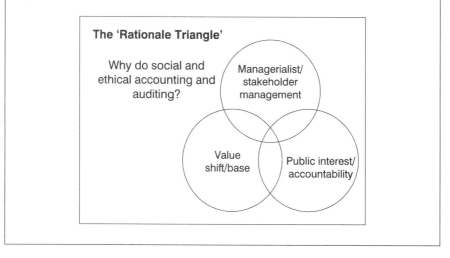

The 'Rationale Triangle'

Why do social and ethical accounting and auditing?

Managerialist/ stakeholder management

Value shift/base

Public interest/ accountability

any company that seeks to behave ethically against the flow of competitive pressures and sources of profitability will tend to be penalized by the market, either through a loss of market share arising from reduced competitiveness, or through the financial markets, or, most probably, both.[11]

Ethical leadership can, of course, change the terms on which profitability is secured throughout the market and thereby offset the dangers of reduced competitiveness through 'ethical innovation'. For example, it is unlikely in today's climate that a clothing retailer could improve its market position by cutting costs through the exploitative use of child labour. On the other hand, companies are increasingly pointing out to their customers, staff and other stakeholders where they have chosen to invest in the education or health and safety of people working for them. Similarly, most mass-consumer body and hair-care products are now explicitly not tested on animals. These developments are a tribute in part to the decision by particular companies such as Levi Strauss and The Body Shop International to lead the way in introducing a new ethos in a particular aspect of the way business is done. This is true irrespective of why these companies made such decisions. There are therefore a range of reasons why companies choose to respond to social, ethical and environmental challenges (see Box 10.1).

Why Measure It?

Companies need to know the social, ethical and environmental views of stakeholders who do count. They also need to know how these views are changing over time and how they are likely to determine attitudes and actions by stakeholders, whether individual or collective, towards the company. Thus, companies seek to measure and disclose their social and ethical performance in order:

- to understand what they are trying to achieve and how best to measure performance against their aims;
- to know what they are doing;
- to understand the implications of what they are doing;
- to understand in what ways, if any, they can explain their actions to increasingly sceptical and aggressive stakeholders; and
- to understand whether there are practical options for improving their social performance in ways that will not harm their business performance and may in many cases improve it.

The recent reports on corporate governance published in the UK as a follow-up to the *Cadbury Report* – the *Hempel Report* – made absolutely clear the need to count non-financial dimensions of business activities: '*Directors should maintain and review controls relating to all relevant control objectives* and not merely financial controls.'[12] Surely, you might argue, senior managers at least *know* what they are doing? The worrying answer to this is: not always and often not in critical areas where 'soft' information is required. In one recent internal seminar run for a major multinational, an overhead was shown of an article about people demonstrating against the employment of child labour. The seminar's facilitator laughingly said, '*Of course, you don't do this sort of thing*'. A nervous silence was followed by one of the more outspoken participants blurting out:

But that is the whole point. We don't know. This whole downsizing and decentralisation has meant that we no longer get information about these sorts of things. And even if we did, we would never get a chance to look at it, or do anything about it.

This proved a prescient statement. Just a few months later, the company was subjected to an aggressive challenge in the national press over its social, ethical and environmental record in and around one of its major facilities in the South, a facility that had the reputation *within* the company of having 'best practice' community relations and environmental programmes.

Managers need to understand the factors which influence their company's performance. These include an increasingly complex matrix of non-technical, non-financial factors – exactly the kinds of factors which they and their companies are ill-equipped to find out about, and even less equipped to understand. Hence the *Tomorrow's Company* initiative concluded: '... *tomorrow's company is able to develop a framework of measurement that ... will include financial components but will also feedback on the valued (and) the health of key relationships.*'

Understanding climate rather than weather conditions

This is not just a question of more market surveys covering a wider range of issues. Shell has been supporting environmental issues for several decades and, until the Brent Spar fiasco, was seen as a reasonably 'green company'. No amount of traditional market research would have been likely to predict the public response to Greenpeace's call not to sink the Brent Spar. Similarly, it is very unlikely that the managers of toys, sportswear and textiles companies in the late 1980s would have believed that the consuming public would respond as they have in the last couple of years to concerns about labour conditions in suppliers in the South. After all, they would have argued, it has always been this way and consumers benefit from poor labour conditions in terms of cheaper products. The evolution of people's ethical positions are, perhaps thankfully, not purely guided by such thoughtless logic.

Companies are increasingly realizing that merely asking people their opinion about things does not reveal the dynamic process of how and in what directions people develop their thinking on the basis of deeply rooted values. 'Counting' in the traditional sense of polling people's views may work in choosing between different flavours of ice-cream, but it rarely helps in understanding how people develop a sense of moral concern and how this concern is voiced. Understanding stakeholder's views requires much more than simple survey work. Some deeper social contract is needed to go beyond inaccurate counting to a point where stakeholders begin to feel that their views count.

Companies understand now that they need to understand the 'climatic conditions' that underpin people's values if they want to be able to predict how they will respond to any particular situation. This has dramatic implications. In moving away from the conventions of traditional market surveying that do little more than observe the 'weather' at any point in time, companies are faced with a far more complex dynamic that can only really be understood if they actually engaged and gain people's trust.

So companies understand now the need to 'count ethics'. Most importantly this is to understand things that are going on that were not previously considered important to the daily life of a busy manager. What follows from this acceptance of the need to measure is the realization that conventional approaches do not always work. Measuring turns out to be far more than a purely 'subject–object' phenomena, a 'we measure it' situation. It turns out that in so far as measuring is about understanding the deeper patterns that inform people's attitudes and actions, alternative approaches to measurement are needed.

But Why Disclosure?

Companies are finding in a growing number of cases that they need to respond to stakeholder concerns not only by changing their practices, but by being more open in reporting how they have performed against key social, ethical and environmental criteria.

For stakeholders to be willing to offer insights into their own deeper interests and concerns, they need an environment of trust and honesty. This in turn means that managers have to think quite differently about what they need to reveal about their own operations and practices. It is not possible to demand commitment from employees where the future of their own jobs is shrouded in secrecy. Suppliers are less likely to comply with codes of conduct imposed by their prime clients where they sense that these companies are less than concerned and even less open about their own behaviour. Consumers will simply not believe anymore the claims of companies without a more systematic, rigorous approach to disclosure.

Companies seek to influence public perceptions as to their social, ethical and environmental performance. Whilst this is a task that all companies take to with considerable relish and vigour, the ways in which they have done this has generated considerable scepticism and indeed cynicism towards corporate claims of good behaviour. Despite a veritable outpouring of information from companies about their social, ethical and environmental performance, there is ample evidence to suggest that stakeholders rarely believe what they are told by companies, certainly not beyond basic technical product-related information.

The clothing retail chain The Gap understood this when it agreed to adopt a code of conduct covering the factories in the South from which it purchases the products it sells. It understood that its customer base was open to being influenced by the growing number of non-profit organizations campaigning around labour conditions in these factories, particularly those focused on the emotive issue of child labour. The Gap, furthermore, along with an increasing number of companies throughout the clothing, sportswear and toys industries, have also come to accept that those stakeholders who are willing to penalize them for not behaving according to norms that they consider acceptable want 'proof' that they are keeping their promises. The fig leaves of codes of conduct are in themselves not enough. What is in addition demanded are reports of performance against these codes, externally verified by organizations in which stakeholders believe.[13, 14]

Reporting on social and ethical performance is not, therefore, only a matter of disclosure. It is an integral element of the process of communication between the company and key stakeholders. In this sense, reporting is a way in which stakeholders can see if the company 'listened' to their concerns and over time whether they have responded in practical terms. Further, reporting is an essential element of the process of deepening the understanding of managers as to what is going on and how people view it. Reporting, seen in this sense as a link in the chain of events that secures high quality feedback, is an obvious requirement. In conclusion, therefore, reporting is essentially an element of the communication, dialogue, learning and decision-making process, rather than the endpoint in a retrospective analysis.

A Side Note on Silent Reporting

Companies are, of course, accustomed to adopting an extensive array of procedures, including a range of forms of 'accounting and auditing'. Financial accounting, for example, started originally because of the need for managers to have some basic records of cash flows, to provide a means whereby shareholders could hold the stewards of their investments to account and as a means of working out how to divide the profits at the end of the day. It was only subsequently that the requirement to audit accounts became enshrined in law, principally as a means of protecting shareholders against unscrupulous managers and directors of the companies that they have bankrolled.[15]

Financial accounting was (and is still) therefore seen as a tool for seeing how the organization was doing, for being accountable to one particular stakeholder group – the shareholders – and for working out who should get what share of the financial surpluses generated by the company. Auditing was similarly seen as a means of ensuring that the financial accounts reported to shareholders (and subsequently the government for regulatory and tax purposes) were accurate.

Environmental assessment was extremely rare only a decade ago, but now is common practice by increasing numbers of companies. A recent survey carried out by the International Institute for Industrial Environmental Economics at Lund University, Sweden, concluded that 23 per cent of Europe's largest companies in 1995 produced some sort of environmental report, compared to 15 per cent in 1993.[16]

The reasons that companies are willing to undergo such exercises varies to a considerable degree, as does therefore the content and form of environmental assessment. One reason concerned the acquisition of knowledge to enable the avoidance of legal liability and in some cases to avoid confrontation with increasingly assertive and effective environmental campaigning organizations. Over time, the more positive business case for environmental auditing, as distinct from simply environmental reporting, has for many industries and contexts been proven many times over, particularly the 'win–win' arguments for cost-savings through eco-efficiency measures.[17]

Unlike in the financial sphere, statutory regulations guiding environmental accounting and auditing are not yet common. In Europe, for example, the Eco-Management and Audit Scheme (EMAS) is set out in non-mandatory legislation and has been adopted and advocated as a 'best practice' standard by the European Commission. As such, it is gradually being taken up by an increasing number of companies operating in Europe.[18]

A range of quality assurance systems has been developed over the last two decades to meet the needs of large organizations to organize and rationalize their change processes to achieve the maximum possible quality throughout their operations. Possibly the most well-known of these has been Total Quality Management (TQM), arguably (as its name suggests) the most comprehensive approach developed to date. What matters here is not so much the details of how or whether TQM works in practice, but that it is an entirely voluntary process completely devoid of any external pressure, such as campaigning organizations in the case of environmental performance.

The widespread adoption of TQM and other system-level quality assurance systems, such as ISO 9000 and BS 5750, by parts of the corporate sector illustrates the fact that companies *will* commit considerable resources to securing the information required to know what is going on in a systematized manner. It is worth noting, furthermore, that approaches such as TQM include not only quantitative 'output' data, such as the technical failure rate of a particular product or process, but also subjective 'outcome' data, such as the views of staff or indeed of the wider public of the organization.

So it turns out that companies invest heavily in procedures and processes that yield complex sets of quantitative and qualitative and objective and subjective, data covering issues both within and outside the organization. From this perspective, social and ethical accounting, auditing and reporting is not a 'future proposition', but a reality today. Professor Rob Gray from the Centre for Environmental and Social Accountancy Research at the University of Dundee alludes to the existing although dispersed forms of existing social and ethical accounting, auditing and reporting as 'silent accounting' (see Figure 10.1).[19] All companies today, he argues, *particularly* the larger corporations, are already offering ever-increasing volumes of information about their social, ethical and environmental performance, albeit in a fragmented form, of varying quality and often with quite inadequate or at least unclear levels of external verification.

This should, of course, hardly be surprising since it is precisely these combinations of views and facts that make or break a company at the end of the day. Indeed, it turns out that a major reason for a mainstream company's increased interest in social and ethical accounting, auditing and reporting is exactly to cope with the increasing complexity of their situation and associated management processes. As one senior manager of a major oil company said during an internal seminar introducing the topic:

> *We are having to cope with so many different quality issues at the same time, some technical, but many of them dealing with 'soft' issues. If social auditing helps us to deal with them more rationally, then we really could use it.*

So whilst companies love to hate procedures because of their time and financial costs, the most sophisticated and widespread systems have been developed for use

Voluntary	Required Mandatory
Environmental protection	Charitable donations
Energy saving	Employment data
Consumer protection	Pension fund adequacy
Product safety	Consultation with employees
Community involvement	Employee share ownership schemes
Value-added statement	Employment of the disabled
Health and safety	Health and safety or environmental remediation
Racial and sexual equality	
Redundancies	
Employee training	
Mission statement/statement of social responsibility	

Source: adapted from Gray, R H, 1991, *Trends in Corporate Social and Environmental Accounting*, British Institute of Management, London, p3

Figure 10.1 *Silent Reporting by Companies in UK Company Annual Reports*

principally by the business community, particularly larger scale corporations. So the key issue becomes more than a question of 'how to do it' in a cost-effective way.

The Need for Standards?

Language variations

There is a growing body of experiences in corporate social and ethical accounting, auditing and reporting, particularly across Europe and North America.[20] Associated with this development has been the emergence of varied terminology and differing approaches. There are 'ethical accounts', 'social audits', 'human accounting', 'intellectual capital', 'ethical audits', 'social performance reports', 'social balances', 'ethical budgets' and 'social reviews', just to name a few. As with any new or re-emerged field of work, we are faced with a veritable outpouring of new terminology. The question is whether this is helpful. How can we tell when terminological differences are a cover-up for sameness, imprecise thinking or a deliberate muddying of the waters; or when, on the other hand, it signifies real diversity and indeed productive innovation?

In some cases, different words seem to describe methodologies that appear on closer inspection to be very similar. The 'ethical audit' advocated by the European Institute for Business Ethics and the Mijenrode Business School,[21] for example, is similar in many respects to the method developed, adopted and applied by Traidcraft plc and the New Economics Foundation, which the former calls 'social accounts' and the latter organization calls 'social auditing'.[22] The Body Shop's 'ethical audit', on the other hand, seems quite different from that of the 'ethical auditing' of Nijenrode University, since it represents a combination of social, environmental and animal testing audits.[23] The 'ethical audit' of The Body Shop, on the other hand, is only in very particular areas comparable to the 'ethical accounting' developed at the Copenhagen Business School, and adopted by Sbn Bank and other companies and public sector organizations across Scandinavia.[24]

What some are calling social accounting or auditing is increasingly incorporating financial and environmental data and is slipping headlong towards what might be called 'sustainability auditing'.[25] These dimensions of sustainability in turn look quite similar in principle to what The Co-operative Bank has called the 'Partnership Approach'. British Telecom variously refers to its commitment as a social or an ethical audit without being entirely clear (at least to others) as to whether they are seen as equivalent. Grand Metropolitan has announced that it is piloting 'social audits', but as yet has not clarified what is and what is not included in their approach. Recently, we have seen the drafting of an audit model by the audit firm SGS in collaboration with the US corporate responsibility non-profit organization, the Council on Economic Priorities (CEP) – for dealing only with suppliers – that has been called a 'social accountability' audit. Then there are approaches that use entirely different language, but in some respects are quite similar to the mainstream of what is emerging, such as the Intellectual Capital model developed at Skanida in Sweden.[26]

Finally, there is intense work going on inside the closed portals of many of the larger 'blue-chips', particularly, but not exclusively, those subjected to public criticism over recent months and years. Shell International has formed a Social Accountability Group, including senior managers and are exploring how best to enhance its social reporting. Shell UK has already announced that it will publish a 'Shell in Society' report during 1998. The Danish pharmaceutical company Novo Nordisk has recently embarked on a three-year enquiry into what it calls 'human and social accounting' with the support of the Danish Ministry of Social Affairs. In many of these cases, the principles of social and ethical accounting, auditing and reporting are being taken on board in the methods deployed, although the companies are taking great care to avoid the use of such language that still seems to them to be associated with too extensive a public commitment to on-going and verified disclosure.

Acceptable variations

Much of the diversity in practice can be attributed to at least four significant differences in:

1   interests on the part of those initiating the process;
2   types of organizations;
3   contexts; and
4   theoretical and philosophical roots.

Many of these differences are entirely acceptable in that they reflect varied needs for which different methods are required. For example, organizations like Sbn Bank in Denmark and Woyen Molle in Norway start with an emphasis on the evolution of 'shared values' through ethical accounting.[27] Not surprisingly, they therefore focus on dialogue with key stakeholders, rather than third-party verification. On the other hand, a company with a concern that it meets the challenge of public accountability may well place far greater emphasis on securing adequate comparison with other companies or accepted social norms and benchmarks. For example, the move by companies in the textiles, sportswear and toys sectors to adopt and comply with labour codes of conduct in their production in and purchases from, the South, will focus on external verification precisely because the pressure comes from public consumer campaigns.[28]

Similarly, a company principally concerned with public accountability may focus exclusively on the production of a report for external publication, whereas a company with an interest in social and ethical accounting and auditing as a tool to facilitate internal change may have little or no interest in the published document, but may instead focus on the process of accounting and the reports generated for internal use.

Identifying the 'right' approach to social and ethical accounting, auditing and reporting is therefore intimately related to *why* the particular organization is engaging in the exercise. This implies that there is no single approach that is correct for all situations – that there is some strength in diversity for diverse needs.

Unacceptable variations

At the same time, there are variations between methods and practice that are not justified by any objective difference in circumstance and need. These are variations that are rooted in one or both of two reasons for poor practices:

- an under-specification of the accounting, auditing and reporting process because of insufficient knowledge, skills, experience and/or resources applied to the process; and/or
- a deliberate attempt to under-specify the accounts and the verification process in order to report in a less-than-accurate, incomplete or unintelligible manner.

For example, a company may forgo a dialogue with staff to determine key issues of concern to them because of inadequate resources and as a result develop a survey that omits a range of critical issues that would profile the company in a negative light. It would not be appropriate, for example, for a 'fair trade' organization – for example, one seeking to offer a better deal to community suppliers in the South by offering a better deal than in the fully commercial market – to carry out a social and ethical accounting, auditing and reporting exercise without adequate consultation with Southern suppliers.[29]

Similarly, a company may seek to undertake an externally verified exploration of the social impact of one area of their operations knowing full well that there is a critical problem associated with an area of their work that they have chosen to omit from the assessment. A social and ethical accounting or auditing exercise undertaken by a bank that did not deal with the nature of its investment portfolio, or an exercise by an advertising company that did not consider with care the nature of the images they were promoting and their effect, could not really be seen as being of adequate quality.

The challenge is to be able to distinguish between acceptable and unacceptable reasons for methodological (and terminological) differences. The failure to meet this challenge effectively will allow the 'bad to chase out the good' as companies and consultants alike find good reason to cut corners to save costs and to omit difficult areas from accounting, auditing and reporting. The ability to distinguish good from bad practice therefore provides a foundation on which standards can be set.

Many things can undermine what we understand as quality in social and ethical accounting, auditing and reporting. Economic downturn, for example, places pressure on resources and might also lessen the interest of some key stakeholders in the non-financial dimensions of corporate behaviour. Consumer's interest in 'green' products and services declined sharply, for example, after the onset of the economic recession of the late-1980s. Bad practice can also chase out the good. If some companies 'get away' with producing superficial or indeed deceptive social and ethical reports and statements, others will tend to turn away from the more costly quality processes. This will be all the more so if bad practice gives the whole field a bad name. It would only take a few demonstrably poor audits and accounting processes that had not been picked up on by external verifiers to undermine the credibility of the process.

It is not adequate for corporate social and ethical accounting, auditing and reporting to be only a 'fair weather' practice. For it to be meaningful, it needs to be a practice in which a company engages as automatically as it would with a financial audit, irrespective of their level of profits. Neither is the practice going to give any reliable indication of corporate social performance if a company or their consultants can design the process entirely to their needs and interests and name it and the results in any way they choose. For it to be meaningful requires that the quality of a company's practice of social and ethical accounting, auditing and reporting is as clear to all interested parties as is the technical quality of the goods and services they produce.

The consolidation of the practice of social and ethical accounting, auditing and reporting in a way that improves corporate social performance requires a mechanism for protecting the practice from such undermining conditions. There is, therefore, a need for agreed standards of corporate social and ethical accounting, auditing and reporting. Whilst experimentation has and can in some areas continue to yield a wealth of experiences, there is equally a need to limit the danger of a fragmentation of efforts and directions leading to considerable confusion as to what different methods are being used and to what effect. As Rob Gray explains, '*The long history of social and ethical accounting has been characterised by a* disturbing *variety of approaches and standards …*'.[30]

Although there are clearly dangers in seeking to determine standards for social and ethical accounting, auditing and reporting, there are also clear potential gains. First, divergent terminology and method can be a sign of flourishing creativity in the early stages of the life cycle of an innovation of any kind. For the innovation to mature in terms of more widespread use or take-up, however, requires that it becomes less dynamic, more stable and more recognizable. There is already evidence of resistance to take-up associated with a confusion as to which approach is more effective or, more generally, which will 'win-out' in the end.

Second, one of the reasons for organizations undertaking some kind of social and ethical accounting and auditing is that it allows them to make claims about their openness and hopefully about their sound social practice. Such claims can only be made, of course, where their basis is seen to be legitimate in the eyes of the intended audience. It is interesting to note that there appears to be little or no challenge of those organizations preparing ethical accounting statements, possibly in part because of the more open culture of Scandinavian countries, or the (perhaps associated) lower level of social conflict. In the UK and the US, on the other hand, organizations have invested heavily in securing some form of explicit legitimizing process in the form of an external audit or verification.

There is ample evidence that a strong 'assurance label' aids take-up where it is underpinned by robust standards that are widely acceptable, such as in the area of financial and environmental auditing, or product labels for organic, safety or 'fair trade' qualities. As the CEO of one major commercial bank stated quite bluntly: '*Come back to talk to me about social auditing when you have a quality label that is recognizable in the market that I can put on all of our literature.*' Rightly or wrongly, the value of social and ethical accounting and auditing in building an organization's public profile is an important factor in determining take-up and an agreed set of standards is an essential element of making this factor count.

By far the most important reason for standards, however, is to ensure quality in the process of accounting, auditing and reporting to support improved corporate social responsibility. This is not merely a question of what gives a method respectability, or what gives an organization some market gain from adopting such a method. This is about what methods seem to work best in achieving the underlying aim of assisting organizations in achieving continual improvement against agreed social and ethical aims and indeed of challenging and raising the aspirations of those aims themselves.

Routes to standards

Standards can be achieved in a number of different ways (see Figure 10.2). At one extreme is the benchmark of practice, where leadership in quality is established that others must follow if they want their attempts to be taken seriously. Leadership benchmarking has a critical role to play in the take-up of any innovation, itself a major reason for adopting the sort of five-stage corporate social reporting model outlined in Figure 10.3.[31]

There are many good examples of leadership benchmarking in this field. Sbn Bank's annual ethical accounting statement has certainly come to be seen as a benchmark against which corporate social reporting in Denmark and elsewhere in Scandinavia is judged. Traidcraft's social accounts have set a standard in the British context, as evidenced by the companies that have sought to draw from and be measured against Traidcraft's standards of quality. The latter case is interesting in the way that it has precipitated an escalation of standards. The Body Shop has drawn

- Mandatory legislation
- Non-mandatory legislation
- Private external screening
- Voluntary codes
- Leadership benchmarking

Figure 10.2 *The Standards Spectrum*

from both Traidcraft's and Sbn Bank's example, but has also sought to set new and higher standards. Ben & Jerry's Homemade is a further case in point, having undertaken some kind of social reporting for seven years. As the United States Trust Corporation, a socially responsive investment firm, stated in the August 1995 edition of its newsletter *Values*, '*Ben & Jerry's, which publishes unedited conclusions of its independent social auditor, remains the "gold standard" in open self-critical evaluation …*'.

Skandia, with its focus on 'intellectual capital', has established a very different kind of leadership in carving out a very different language and approach that is likely to prove a critical new element in the next round of evolution of social and ethical accounting and auditing more generally. Most recently, the position taken by British Telecom has provided a new form of leadership, if only at this stage by virtue of the fact that BT is the first 'blue-chip' which has committed itself to following in the emerging tradition of social and ethical accounting, auditing and reporting. It is clear that now BP and other companies are similarly seeking for ways to take a leadership role in their social accounting, auditing and reporting.

Leadership benchmarking does, however, have its limitations. A proliferation of different approaches, for example, can undermine the quality push of leadership benchmarking. It is possible, furthermore, for a concerted effort on the part of 'followers' who do not wish to follow to marginalize the example set by the leader. Representatives of large, mainstream corporations attending seminars on social and ethical accounting and auditing, for example, have argued that it is only relevant for '*weird companies that try to mix ethics with business*'.

The more radical the innovation in question, the more likely is it that a serious attempt to marginalize it will occur. So leadership benchmarking is important at the early stages in the life of an innovation, but can be of less use at the critical stage where serious mainstream adoption is being sought.

At the other extreme are standards established through the force of legislation. Clearly the advantage of legislation is that the standards cannot be simply ignored. This is most obviously the case with financial accounting and auditing, where extensive legislation exists. Over recent years, this has increasingly been the basis for standards in environmental auditing, although still to a far lesser extent than financial auditing and with far greater variation between countries. Some countries have legislation covering some aspects of social and ethical accounting and auditing. In the UK, for example, corporations over a particular size are obliged to report on their charitable giving, as well as having to provide certain information regarding staff conditions and employment practices, such as the proportion of staff who are registered disabled.

There are, however, also disadvantages to relying on the law to secure standards. First and foremost is the sheer time involved in getting to the point of legislation. Clearly a part of this process is very productive, involving an iterative process of distilling the required standards into a form that can be reasonably expected to hold across many different organizations in different situations. Much of the process, however, is decidedly unproductive time spent in endless, bureaucratic and extremely costly debates. Underlying this is a potentially far more serious objection to seeking legislation to secure standards. This is the danger of downgrading under pressure from strong vested interests. There is little doubt, for example, that any attempt to enshrine key principles of social and ethical accounting and auditing in law would elicit serious objection from many parts of the corporate sector. It is very likely, furthermore, that any legislation that was agreed upon would represent a watered-down compromise compared to the original vision. It is this weak legislation that would then become the basis for standards. The question is then whether weak legislation is better or worse than no legislation.

Between the extremes of leadership benchmarking and legislation are a range of other means through which standards can be set, including, for example, voluntary codes and private external screening. Those options that tend towards voluntarism and self-policing have the dangers of becoming confused over time and also of degrading in the face of pressure from the main body of organizations which do not wish to follow the examples set.

The most productive approach to standards is to see the various options as complementary rather than exclusive. It is necessary to set quality standards through leadership 'in practice'. These standards then need to form the basis for negotiation on voluntary codes and ultimately for legislation of some kind. Leadership standards create pressure for codes and legislation, and can help in resisting any watering down of what those standards might be. Voluntary codes and legislation ultimately help to prevent a gradual erosion of standards through the abuse of method and its use for crude public relations exercises.

The development of standards must therefore be skilfully managed by those who wish them to count. There is no reason to assume a priori that formal standards are better than no standards, whether set through voluntary codes or embedded in legislation. A key determining factor of whether the formalization of standards helps or hinders in building real quality (and in this case, real accountability) is who is 'at the negotiating table' and their relative strengths. The more open and public the debate, the more likely it is that the watering-down process can be avoided or at least minimized. At the same time, negotiation-by-confrontation is an inadequate route to agreeing standards that need to be both relevant and feasible, particularly in the business context.

Developing Standards

There are clear signs of a convergence of standards taking place in the practice of social and ethical accounting, auditing and reporting. The relevance of both external benchmarks and stakeholder dialogue is confirmed in most current practice, albeit to differing degrees in each case. Even those approaches which have focused exclusively on one or other element are now moving towards some combination. The originators of the Ethical Accounting Statement, for example, are actively exploring how external benchmarks as well as verification might be used where the approach has to date focused exclusively on stakeholder dialogue. Companies such as British Telecom which are known for their environmental reporting and activities related to the European Total Quality Management, are now actively exploring how best to integrate these experiences with the emerging standards in social and ethical accounting and auditing. Within the public[32] and private, non-profit communities,[33] increasingly attention is also being given to this emerging body of experience.

A similar convergence is taking place in the understanding of the need for and roles of the external agent, although again with different emphases. Ben & Jerry's, for example, has in its recent history of social performance reports seen the external agent essentially as an 'evaluator', asked to pass personal judgement on the company's social performance. More recently, however, they have been experimenting with a move away from this personalized judgement process more towards a view of the external agent as 'auditor', charged with the duty of ensuring that the published statement is a correct description of what happened over the period, rather than his or her view of those events.

There is a gradual consensus emerging as to what constitutes some of the key principles of 'good practice' that need to be reflected in any sound approach. This understanding is focused on three key areas. First, to ensure that social and ethical accounting, auditing and reporting becomes an increasingly bounded and hence defined set of activities; it needs to become less and less possible for anyone to describe anything as being the practice of social and ethical accounting and auditing. Second, that not only the activity and outcomes, but their quality, become subject to assessment as a part of the 'professionalization' process. Third, there is a need to ensure that what skills and experiences are required to support the process of social and ethical accounting, auditing and reporting becomes more and more precisely specified and testable.

This emerging consensus is being driven in the main by the Institute of Social and Ethical AccountAbility and the individuals and organizations which have come together around AccountAbility's networks of activity. Far from closing the door to further experimentation, this emerging consensus allows for a more systematic assessment of different approaches, a clearer dialogue between them and their users and a deeper appreciation of what skills and experience are required to make any process effective in achieving the understanding, transparency and accountability.

Principles of 'quality'

There are therefore good reasons for establishing ways to compare different approaches with a view to judging quality relative to the needs of the particular situation. There is a need to ask the question: 'In short, how can one tell if a specific exercise in social and ethical accounting, auditing and reporting is worth the candle?'

Below is offered a simple framework for exploring the quality of initiatives in social and ethical accounting, auditing and reporting. Given the sheer scale of experimentation in this area and its increasing quality across many different contexts, this framework should be seen as a first stab at what needs to be further developed over the coming period. The framework offers a means of categorizing experiences or initiatives by:

- the principles of quality social and ethical accounting, auditing and reporting;
- the elements into which the principles can be subdivided to enable more detailed analysis through an assessment of the disclosed documentation.

The key objectives against which quality needs to be assessed have been drawn together to take account of a number of factors:

- The need to secure appropriate levels and forms of stakeholders' dialogue to ensure good quality information and an 'inclusive' approach based on method rather than the discretionary interests of the organizations involved.
- The interests of key stakeholders in comparing the organization's performance over time and with other organizations.
- The pragmatic need to establish a method that is technically and financially feasible.
- The need to ensure that the method helps the organization and its stakeholders to learn and change for the better.
- The need to secure legitimacy of the overall process.

With these criteria in mind, a grouping of eight 'quality principles' have been evolved and tested:[34] inclusivity; comparability; completeness; regularity and evolution; embeddedness; externally verified; communication and continuous improvement.

1 *Inclusivity* The principle of inclusivity means that the social and ethical accounting and auditing must reflect the views and accounts of all stakeholders, not only the particular stakeholders who have historically had the most influence over the evolution of the organization's formal mission statement. What this means, furthermore, is that the assessment cannot be based on a single set of values or a single set of objectives. Whilst over time the various stakeholder groups *may* come to agree on many things, the assessment process cannot assume this to be the case and must therefore be able to accommodate such diversity.[35] It is important to distinguish 'consultation' in the form of one-way surveying – that is, essentially market research and 'dialogue' which can be understood as a two-way process that brings the views and interests of all parties to the table.[36]

Inclusivity does not only refer to the need for people to be included in the dialogue and broader process. Also of importance are other dimensions of what may concern people, such as the indirect and direct treatment of animals and of course the environment. These aspects of an integrated audit are reflected in the assessment of reporting discussed below.

2   *Comparability* The principle of comparability is quite simply that social and ethical accounting, auditing and reporting enables the performance of the organization to be compared as a basis of assessment. Comparison may be of the performance of the same organization in different periods, or with external benchmarks drawn from the experience of other organizations, statutory regulations or non-statutory norms.[37] It is important that external benchmarks are selected for their relevance and legitimacy, not only for their accuracy. For example, comparisons of wage rates with outside organizations need to select the appropriate types of organizations and also need to draw the comparative data from sources that would be considered to be legitimate, such as government statistics, or labour research bodies.[38]

3   *Completeness* The principle of completeness means that no area of the company's activities can be deliberately and systematically excluded from the assessment. This principle is important to ensure that the company is not 'cherry-picking' the areas of its activities that on inspection will show the most positive social and ethical performance. Comprehensiveness in combination with the principle of inclusivity raises major practical problems given the potential magnitude of the assessment process. A typical supermarket chain, for example, may have 10–20 million different individual customers and 5000 or so suppliers. What this means in practice is that not everything can be covered at once, or more specifically during any one cycle. The essence of this principle is therefore that no area of the organization's activities are necessarily excluded from any particular cycle because of any unwillingness on the part of the organization – that is, no 'malicious exclusion'. Over several cycles, furthermore, all the principle stakeholder groups would be covered through an exploration of all the effects of all the organization's activities.[39]

4   *Regularity and evolutionary* Not only may it not be possible to cover an entire company's 'social footprint' at the same time, but it is likely that this footprint will vary over time. Furthermore, the impact and meaning given to its footprint will also vary, as the composition and expectations of key stakeholder groups change over time. The implications of this is that one-off accounting exercises are not adequate to the needs of either management in seeking to understand what is happening, or in terms of the company's accountability to the wider public. A key principle against which the practice of social and ethical accounting, auditing and reporting needs to be judged is therefore whether the exercise is repeated in a manner that demonstrates 'learning' and continual challenge – that is, the process must follow an evolutionary path over time.

5   *Embeddedness* As with both financial and environmental auditing, it is not enough for an organization to get a snapshot of its performance to secure its learning processes in these areas. It is essential for any systematic process that the organization develops clear policies covering each accounting area. In addition it

needs procedures that allow accounting to be regularized and the organization's awareness and operationalization of policies and commitment to be assessed through an audit.

6   *Communication* The question of whether the social and ethical accounting and auditing processes are intended primarily for an internal audience – that is, as a management tool, or whether it is a means of strengthening public account-ability, is a tension that has figured in both the reasons why companies engage in the process and the means by which the accounting is undertaken. Clearly the focus on an internal audience obviates any need to disclose the results to the public, or even perhaps within the organization beyond the management and board. At the same time, an interest in strengthening the company's legiti-macy in the public domain would require some sort of disclosure. Where a disclosure route is chosen, the matter of quality concerns, then, the extent to which disclosure is a formality or an active means of communication with key stakeholders and the wider public. Merely publishing a document, however comprehensive, does not constitute 'good practice' if the document is difficult to obtain, costly or unintelligible to key stakeholders. Disclosure is essentially about communication, which in turn must be rooted in meaningful dialogue for it to be effective.

7   *Externally verified* The need for external verification concerns again the rela-tive emphasis between social and ethical accounting as a management tool and a means of strengthening accountability and legitimacy. Clearly an emphasis towards the latter implies the need for external verification of some kind. The challenge is, of course, what kind of 'external verification' process will be of a sufficiently high professional quality and independence for it to have its de-sired effect of validating the published material. In broad terms there appear to be three dimensions of external verification that need to be taken into account:

1   The professional competence that we would normally identify with audi-tors and verifiers.
2   The professional competence associated with management consultants who can understand process, risk assessment and strategic management.
3   The quality associated with it being awarded a sense of civil legitimacy, which is normally a role taken on by non-commercial organizations with a recognized public interest mandate.

8   *Continuous improvement* The aim of any social and ethical accounting, audit-ing and reporting system must be to assess and contribute to substantive progress, rather than only deal with retrospective performance, or focus exclu-sively on process achievements in terms of monitoring, measuring, auditing and reporting – that is, any relevant system must be able to identify whether the organization's performance has improved over time in relation to the values, missions and objectives set by the organization, its stakeholders and established as broader social norms. Moreover, beyond the measurement of progress is the need for a method that itself supports the improvement of social and ethical performance.

These eight principles seem to represent the most basic dimensions of quality against which any social and ethical accounting, auditing and reporting process can and should be judged. That does not mean to say that a case where several principles are not being adhered to is necessarily 'poor' in quality. For example, the Scandinavian applications of 'ethical accounting' reported on do not include external verification (principle 7), yet this may well be because it is not required given the social context or the particular applications. So the principles cannot in isolation be a basis for intercase judgement, although they *can* provide a checklist of things to look for in any assessment or selection process.

Scoring quality

The eight principles are relevant in offering an initial basis for assessing the quality of any exercise in social and ethical accounting, auditing and reporting. They are, however, too general to be of use in anything but the most basic assessment process. For example, how can one distinguish between stakeholder 'consultation' (essentially limited, one-way) and an approach to stakeholder 'dialogue' that it intended to be more deeply participative? When is a questionnaire-based survey acceptable as a form of dialogue and when is it an imposition, or simply an inappropriate means of collecting good quality information? There are clearly many possible ways in which 'external verification', 'comprehensiveness' and 'disclosure' can be interpreted. Similarly, there is a need to be able to distinguish between a basic treatment of the environment, such as the application of ISO 14001 and more sophisticated 'total system' approaches such as the Natural Step.

The approach taken in recent times has been to consider in more depth the possible elements that define the quality of each principle set out above. Specifically, work undertaken by the Institute of Social and Ethical AccountAbility and the New Economics Foundation has broken down the eight principles into elements against which any particular social and ethical accounting and auditing process can be judged.

The elements and methods for scoring have been based around the view that it must be possible to score the quality of an accounting, auditing and reporting process based only on the published – that is, disclosed – information. Drawing inspiration and method from work on environmental reporting undertaken by the United Nations Environment Programme and the environmental consultancy SustainAbility Ltd, we have therefore constructed a five-stage developmental model for social and ethical reporting (see Figure 10.3).[40]

This five-stage model clearly does take the step of defining to a large degree what principles and elements are more important than others. Whilst caution is needed in seeking to rank the initiatives of different organizations in often quite different contexts, the model does illustrate how necessary it is for the whole assessment of the quality of social and ethical accounting, auditing and reporting to develop in the future.

The Institute of Social and Ethical AccountAbility, in association with the New Economics Foundation, has more recently taken this scoring system one further stage in defining a more specific method for a quantitative scoring of any particular social

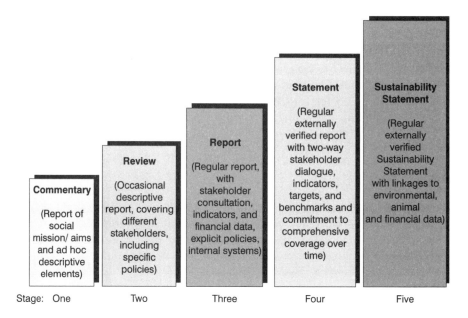

Figure 10.3 *Assessing Progress*

and ethical accounting, auditing and reporting exercise. Building on the five-stage model, the approach has involved the development of a comprehensive set of questions that need to be answered in assessing the accounting, auditing and reporting process through an examination of the disclosed documents. Scores are associated with the answer to each question, which, taken together, give an overall score that allows a rating along the five stages. This approach, currently being trialed, will form the basis for an award for the best social and ethical accounting, auditing and reporting to be launched during 1998 by the Institute.

Accountable Futures

There are and always have been, fine examples of organizations that go beyond the norm in seeking to demonstrate social and environmental responsibility in their practices. These organizations, with their driving mission statements and visionary leaders, show that it is possible to be socially responsible as well as financially viable and indeed profitable. These organizations, particularly those that are commercial businesses, find the spaces in the pipeline between investors and consumers where some choice in behaviour is possible. Furthermore, they take on the far more ambitious agenda of shifting the basic boundaries by raising public awareness towards social and environmental agendas and supporting the emergence of new forms of investors that take non-financial criteria into account.

These organizations, be they companies, charities or non-profit organizations, are the experimental laboratories of the future. Just as Nissan or Ford invest billions in the search for the most marketable car for the millennium, some companies choose to invest in the design of ethical aspects of 'tomorrow's company'. Social and ethical accounting, auditing and reporting has been nurtured and developed in these business laboratories in recognition of the need for conscious, mindful action to ensure that the corporation sector plays a positive role in securing our future. Measurement is not a passive, neutral activity. If we want social and environmental dimensions of business activity to be taken more seriously in decision-making, we must work out how to count them as one part of a complex and often difficult process of making them count.

Notes

1   Royal Society for the Encouragement of Arts Manufacture and Commerce (1996) *Tomorrow's Company: The Role of Business in a Changing World*, RSA, London
2   ibid
3   Will Hutton (1995) *The State We Are In*, Jonathan Cape, London
4   van Luikj, H J L, Carmichael, S M, Hummels, G J A and ten Klooster, A C (1995) *The Technology of Ethical Auditing*, Nijenrode University, The Netherlands Business School and the European Institute of Business Ethics, Breukelen, p1
5   See, for example, a discussion of this in the Royal Society for the Encouragement of Arts Manufacture and Commerce (1996) *Tomorrow's Company: The Role of Business in a Changing World*, RSA, London
6   Anderson, S and Cavanagh, J (1996) *Top 200: A Profile of Global Corporate Power*, Institute for Policy Studies, Washington, DC
7   *Business Week*, 22 April 1996
8   A good summary of this argument can be found in D Wheeler and M Sillanpää (1997) *The Stakeholder Corporation: A Blueprint for Maximising Stakeholder Value*, Pitman, London
9   Co-operative Wholesale Society (1995) *Responsible Retailing*, CWS, Manchester
10 Zadek, S, Lingah, S and Murphy, S (1997) *Consumer Works! Consumption, Civil Action and Human Development*, paper prepared for the UN Human Development Office
11 Korten, D (1996) *When Corporations Rule the World*, Earthscan, London
12 Reported in the *Financial Times*, Thursday 28 August, p10
13 Research was being undertaken at the time of writing this book into which monitoring and verification systems would be relevant and practical in these sorts of contexts. See, for example, Burns, M, Forstater, M, Osgood, D and Zadek, S (1996) *Open Trading: Monitoring Corporate Codes of Conduct*, New Economics Foundation and the Catholic Institute of International Relations, London
14 Similarly, the *Ethical Trading Initiative* in the UK involves a group of major retail companies working together with campaigning and specialist NGOs in formulating supplier-related codes of conduct and suitable approaches to external verification. See *AccountAbility Quarterly*, issue 4, for a description of this initiative

15 Thanks to Professor Rob Gray for this simplified but cogent summary of the origins of financial accounting

16 'International Survey of Environmental Reporting Results', presented at press conference, September 10th 1996, International Institute for Industrial Environmental Economics

17 Cairncross, F (1996) *Green Inc: A Guide to Business and the Environment*, Earthscan, London

18 Hilliary, R (1996)

19 See Gray, R (1997) 'The Silent Practice of Corporate Social Reporting in Companies Reconstructing the Silent Account', in S Zadek, P Pruzan and R Evans (eds) *Building Corporate AccountAbility: Emerging Practices of Social and Ethical Accounting, Auditing and Reporting*, Earthscan, London

20 Published information on corporate social and ethical accounting and auditing almost exclusively covers Western Europe and the US Research has revealed, however, that other experiences exist. One of the most important of these is probably the ground-breaking work of the Indian industrial conglomerate Tata Industries, which is covered in C Gonella and R Evans (eds) (1997) *The Windsor Business Roundtable on Social and Ethical Accounting and Auditing: Summary of Proceedings*, Institute of Social and Ethical AccountAbility, London

21 Nijenrode University, The Netherlands Business School/European Institute for Business Ethics (1995) *The Technology of Ethical Auditing: An Outline*, Nijenrode University, Breukelen

22 Zadek, S and Evans, R (1993) *Auditing the Market: the Practice of Social Auditing*, Traidcraft/New Economics Foundation, Gateshead

23 *The Body Shop Approach to Ethical Auditing* (1996) The Body Shop International, Littlehampton. See also the entire *Values Report* (1996) which contains all three audits

24 Pruzan, P (1995) 'The Ethical Accounting Statement', *World Business Academy Perspectives*, vol 9, no 2, pp35–46

25 See, for example, Zadek, S (1997) 'Sustainability Auditing', in *AccountAbility Quarterly*, winter, issue 5

26 Edvinsson, L and Malone, M (1997) *Intellectual Capital*, HarperCollins, London

27 See Pruzan, P (1997) *Ethical Accounting and Dialogue Culture: Worker Rehabilitation In Norway*, in S Zadek, P Pruzan and R Evans (ed)

28 See, for example, the paper prepared on this subject by a group of Northern NGOs (1996) 'New Economics Foundation and the Catholic Institute for International Relations'

29 See for some discussion of this, Zadek, S and Tiffen, P (1996) 'Fair Trade: Business or Campaign', in *Development*, autumn, no 3, pp48–53

30 *AccountAbility Quarterly*, no 1, summer, 1996, p5 (emphasis added)

31 The first volume of the UNEP/SustainAbility report *Engaging Stakeholders* offers a benchmark survey that seeks to set out who the leaders are in environmental reporting and in this manner to encourage others to follow

32 There has been a relatively weak link to date between the quality standards approaches within the public sector and social and ethical accounting, auditing and reporting. With the commitment of, for example, the Department for

International Development of the British government to explore the possibilities of undertaking a social audit, however, this may change in the future. Also, a significant number of cases of ethical accounting in Denmark have been applications within the public sector.

33 This chapter has not really explored the practice of social and ethical accounting, auditing and reporting in the private, non-profit sector. There is a great deal of work going on in this area, some of which is described in Mayo, E (1996) *Social Auditing in the Voluntary Sector*, City University, London

34 The first version of these principles was established in 1993 in a paper written by myself and Richard Evans in our preparations for the first social audit of Traidcraft plc. Zadek, S and Evans, R (1993) *Auditing the Market: Practical Approaches to Social Auditing*, Traidcraft/New Economics Foundation, Gateshead

35 The principle of inclusivity can also be understood as being the equivalent of the standard accounting principle of materiality – that is, the rights of stakeholders to choose performance indicators associated with their interests, in conjunction with the right of the organization to measure its performance also against its own mission statement, is part of what secures information that is not only accurate but relevant or 'material'.

There is an interesting connection with Fourth Generation Evaluation here, which suffers from the methodological defect of requiring balanced power conditions from the outset of the evaluation process. See Zadek, S (1995) 'Beyond Fourth Generation Evaluation', unpublished paper, New Economics Foundation, London

36 There have been enormous strides forward in the last decade in developing more participative approaches to dialogue between institutions and their stakeholders. Much of the most interesting work has been in the 'development' field, where 'participative learning' methods have been developed to cope with gross imbalances of power between the dialoguing partners, such as, for example, that existing between development agencies and village communities in the South. See, for example, Pretty, Jules, Guijt, Irene, Thompson, John and Scoones, Ian (1995) *Participatory Learning and Action: A Trainer's Guide*, International Institute for Environment and Development, London

37 As for the principle of inclusivity, this principle can be understood in the context of the accounting principle of *materiality*

38 There has been intense activity in the area of social indicator development over the last decade, particularly since the Rio Summit under Local Agenda 21. A good review of some of this material is provided by MacGillivray, Alex and Zadek, Simon (1995) *Accounting for Change: Indicators for Sustainable Development*, New Economics Foundation, London

39 Note too that this may mean that it may be more realistic and relevant for a large, diversified company to develop different social and ethical accounts amongst other things, for different subunits instead of trying to develop one single accounting, auditing and reporting system for the whole organization

40 See in particular United Nations Environment Programme (1994) *Company Environmental Reporting: a Measure of the Progress of Business and Industry*

Towards Sustainable Development, Technical Report 24, UNEP, Paris and UNEP/ SustainAbility (1996) *The Benchmark Survey: the Second International Progress Report on Company Environmental Reporting*, UNEP, Paris

Section 4

Critical Perspectives

Introduction

In the introduction to this Reader we argued strongly that business has a moral duty to play its part in bringing about the transition to a sustainable society. The problem, according to a number of commentators, is that business is not committed to the pursuit of sustainable development: it is not fulfilling its duty. This would not be a serious problem if business could be regulated effectively by goverment, but in the second half of the 20th century, business, so it is argued, has become the most powerful institution on the planet and is able to escape effective regulation by the state. In fact, a number of commentators have argued that business has used and is continuing to use, its position of power to obstruct environmental and social improvement – improvement which it perceives as imposing a high financial cost on its operations.[1] The aim of this section is to introduce some of these critical perspectives.

The section begins with a short chapter by Titus Moser and Damian Miller which provides a useful overview of the debate as to whether multinational corporations (MNCs) can contribute to sustainable development in less developed countries. On one side are *'those that question whether MNCs can ever serve as agents of sustainable development'* whilst on the other are those who argue that *'MNC's international expertise in project implementation, access to the latest technologies and considerable financial resources provide them with a unique capacity to behave in an environmentally and socially responsible manner'*. Moser and Miller discuss various themes within this debate and conclude with some recommendations to *'advance the responsiveness of MNCs to their social and environmental impacts'*.

David Korten argues that *'historically, exercise of the regulatory powers of the state was the primary restraint on the expansion of corporate power. Together, the processes of deregulation and globalization have effectively relieved that constraint by placing the power of global corporations and finance beyond the reach of the state'*. Business has now become the dominant institution and, argues Korten, in a healthy democratic society the dominant institution should be both responsible for and accountable to, the whole. However, business is neither responsible nor accountable, a state of affairs that, among other things, has resulted in the destruction of the natural environment and the marginalization of people, communities and cultures. For Korten, corporations have both a positive and a negative side, and the question for him is how to *'exorcize the dark side without destroying the essential and beneficial wealth creation face of the business sector'*. Once again we see the issues of accounting and accountability emphasized, for his solution is the introduction of social accounting as a legal requirement. Korten stresses that this accounting should be grounded in a coherent theory of the market and the corporation – something, he argues, that is not true of most social accounting initiatives. The system of accounting that he proposes, he calls a market efficiency audit (MEA), which would be a clear and specific measure of a corporation's externalized costs. This, he argues, is something that the public has the right to know and needs to know if it is to be able to make properly informed decisions.

In Chapter 13 Sharon Beder examines '*the way that corporations have used their financial resources and power to counter gains made by environmentalists, to reshape public opinion and to persuade politicians against increased environmental regulation*'. In the first part of the chapter she gives a fascinating history of this corporate activism from its beginning in the 1970s up to the present day, focusing in the main on developments in the US but also commenting on developments in the UK and Australia. In the second part of the chapter, Beder argues that this corporate activism has led to a failure of democracy, with government action on the environment consistently failing to live up to what the majority of the people want. Having described the various dimensions of corporate political influence – everything from making political donations and funding lobbyists to setting up think-tanks and threatening to withdraw investment from a particular country – Beder concludes by advocating the course of action she believes the environmental movement needs to take to counter effectively the power of the corporation.

Carl Frankel (Chapter 14) sees corporations as '*complex, multifaceted entities*' which give off '*mixed messages*'. A company can make positive environmental commitments and carry out positive environmental initiatives whilst at the same time acting in ways that can be environmentally questionable or downright obstructive of environmental progress. As Frankel puts it:

> *Far from being integrated entities, corporations contain what amount to multiple, parallel and often unaligned universes, with each responding to different – and often contradictory – rules of engagement. As a result, it is the rule, not the exception for environmental management and lobbying to occupy entirely separate tracks within a corporation … companies can be green inside their factories and in their environmental management and brown inside the beltway.*

There are two types of mixed message, says Frankel. The first is '*good old corporate duplicity*' where corporations proclaim their environmental commitment in public whilst feverishly lobbying to weaken environmental legislation in private. The second type – where a company's actions appear favourable from one standpoint but less so from another – is more subtle and Frankel gives some interesting examples. With regard to corporate environmental activity, he believes that the cons definitely outweigh the pros, concluding, '*We are clearly getting something less from the corporate community than the wholehearted engagement that the global problematique requires*', and he finishes with a number of suggestions as to how this situation might be remedied.

The final chapter in this section looks at the relationship between business and non-governmental organizations, specifically at the influence that NGOs exert on corporate behaviour. Jem Bendell and David Murphy suggest that we are seeing the emergence of what they refer to as 'civil regulation' – the ability of civil society to set standards for business behaviour by acting on markets. They argue that the rise of consumerism in the latter part of the 20th century saw the emergence of consumers as political actors, and they see NGOs as an organizational expression of this 'consumer politics'. Consumer politics is a form of politics that gains its power through controlling access to customers: as the authors put it, '*corporate boycotts and direct action protests are the confrontational outcomes of consumer politics and ... business–NGO partnerships are the cooperative tools of consumer politics*'. Whilst acknowledging the limitations of civil regulation and the decreased ability of national governments to regulate corporations effectively, they argue that civil regulation, in combination with regulation by intergovernmental bodies and national governments, can provide an increasingly effective means of controlling business behaviour and '*tip the market in favour of responsible business*'.

Notes

1   Whether this perception is accurate, of course, depends on how pervasive undiscovered win–win opportunities are within the economy – see Section 2

11

Multinational Corporations' Impacts on the Environment and Communities in the Developing World: a Synthesis of the Contemporary Debate

Titus Moser and Damian Miller

Introduction

Growing concern about the social and environmental impacts of multinational corporations' operations in less developed countries (LDCs) has generated considerable debate about the role of MNCs in sustainable development. This emotionally charged and often acerbic debate tends to be driven by, and concentrate on, sensational and high-profile cases, with limited analysis of common themes and possible solutions. In an attempt to move beyond the existing debate, this chapter provides a thematic framework for understanding the recurring issues at stake, supported by a range of case studies and concludes with a number of recommendations for promoting sustainable business practice in LDCs. The contents of this chapter derive primarily from the exchanges between non-governmental organizations and MNCs. A forum for such exchange was provided by a workshop held at Cambridge University under the title of 'Managing Sustainability Dilemmas' on 19 February 1997.[1] The views contained within are those of the major stakeholders as expressed at this workshop[2], with case study material and analysis provided by the authors.

Background

MNCs play an increasingly important role in LDC economies. LDC governments have retreated from direct intervention in the management of their economies to adopt more market-based policies that emphasize private-sector investment and free trade (see Fairbanks and Lindsay, 1997). Simultaneously, MNCs are increasingly attracted to LDCs, based on the size of potential markets, access to natural resources

Reproduced in full from W Wehrmeyer and Y Mulugetta (eds) (1999) *Growing Pains: Environmental Management in Developing Countries*, pp232–242, by kind permission of Greenleaf Publishing, Sheffield, UK and lower production costs. These concurrent trends have resulted in record high foreign direct investment (FDI) to LDCs.

Between 1981 and 1996, private sources of investment to LDCs grew from US$13 to US$244 billion, increasing fivefold between 1986 and 1993 and growing at over 30 per cent per annum in the first half of the 1990s (see IIF, 1997; UNCTAD, 1995). Of this total investment, the most important is FDI by corporations which in 1996 accounted for 40 per cent of total private flows, increasing from US$24 billion in 1990 to US$129 billion in 1997 (see French, 1997). Moreover, the World Bank estimates that FDI to LDCs will grow between 7 per cent and 10 per cent per annum over the next decade.

This increase in FDI by MNCs comes at a time when there is growing concern about how economic growth in LDCs can be achieved in a more sustainable manner – specifically how economic growth can be combined with environmental protection and greater social equity (see Cairncross,1992; Daly and Cobb, 1994; Redclift, 1987; WCED, 1987). This has prompted considerable discussion about whether MNCs can contribute to the sustainable development of LDCs.

There are those who question whether MNCs can ever serve as agents of sustainable development. Some view the prevailing global economic system – characterised by free trade and deregulation of local markets – as being the main cause of unsustainable business practice in LDCs (see Costanza et al, 1995; Daly and Cobb, 1994). Others point more to the intrinsic characteristics of MNCs and question whether their overriding pursuit of growth and profit enables them to behave in a sustainable manner (see Korten, 1995).

Those less critical argue that MNCs' international expertise in project implementation, access to the latest technologies and considerable financial resources provide them with a unique capacity to behave in an environmentally and socially responsible manner (see Hadlock, 1994; Harrison, 1994; Schmidheiny, 1992; Tahija, 1993; Wescott, 1992). In light of these considerable resources, MNCs are viewed as not only being capable of behaving sustainably, but of shaping more sustainable policy frameworks (see Choucri, 1993).

Given the growing expansion of MNC operations in LDC economies, much of the contemporary debate tends to focus less on whether MNCs have the potential to advance sustainable development and more on how they might do so. It accepts MNCs' presence in LDC society as a fait accompli and concentrates on the necessary changes, both external and internal to the MNC, for the latter to fulfil its potential as an agent of sustainable development.

Today, MNCs face criticism regarding where they choose to invest and how they operate once located in an LDC. Those MNCs facing the greatest pressure are high-profile companies involved in extractive industries, often operating in pristine environments and potentially inhabited by indigenous populations. MNCs involved in more downstream activities, such as chemical manufacturers, have also faced criticism over their impact on the broader environment. Finally, global consumer MNCs have more recently been criticized over their social policies, in particular their exploitative work practices in LDCs (see Jackson, 1997).

Four 'Rs' in the Current Debate

MNCs recognize that, as global players in a world of instantaneous communication, they must respond to these concerns. However, MNCs and their critics differ on how they and other stakeholders should respond. Four central themes (or 'four Rs') within the contemporary debate on MNC activities in LDCs are:

1 Responsibility for sustainable development.
2 Repositories of power for sustainable development.
3 Representation for sustainable development.
4 Reorganization for sustainable development.

1 – Responsibility for sustainable development

Although there is a wider discourse about the responsibility of business for social welfare, responsibility in this context centres on two key concerns. First, critics contend that MNCs have a responsibility to be selective in their investment decisions in light of the prevailing sociopolitical conditions in LDCs. Second, having invested in an LDC, it is felt that MNCs have a responsibility to apply the highest prevailing standards necessary to minimize their environmental and social impacts, whatever the context of the operation.

The Decision to Invest in LDCs

Critics maintain that there are circumstances where business, out of principle, should not invest in an LDC. They further contend that, when an MNC invests in, or has prior investments in, an LDC with questionable human rights and democratic records, it has a moral responsibility, given its size and power, to pressure the relevant authorities for democratic reform and respect of civil rights. For instance, many felt that Shell should have intervened in the case of Ken Saro-wiwa in Nigeria, or at a minimum should have terminated their operations, as Pepsi did in Myanmar.

MNCs have in turn responded that, while they have a duty to behave in an environmentally and socially responsible manner, they have neither the power nor the internal mandate to influence broader political change. Moreover, their attempts to influence political processes, however well intentioned, can be interpreted as undue interference in the country's sovereign affairs. MNCs further contend that, if they themselves do not invest in a country, other lower profile and potentially less conscientious companies will do so.

The Application of Global Standards

Furthermore, critics maintain that MNCs have a responsibility to apply the same environmental and social standards wherever they operate – be it in a developed- or less developed country context. MNCs contest this point, with some claiming that they already apply global standards and others admitting that they do not, as it is not deemed an appropriate strategy.

Some MNCs are adamant that, through their internal health, safety and environmental policies, as well as internal audits, they already apply global principles.

These proclamations, however, are called into question. A number of cases, including Shell in Nigeria and Texaco in Ecuador, are used by critics to illustrate that, in practice, universal standards are not always applied. NGOs argue that MNCs behave far more responsibly in a developed country context where there is tighter legislation and greater public scrutiny.

Other MNCs maintain that standards and regulations *should* be developed at a local, rather than a global level, since conditions vary the world over. These MNCs feel that the task facing business is now to 'think locally and act globally'. Needless to say, NGOs dispute this approach.

Of those MNCs that do not believe in global standards, a number contend that their responsibility should primarily be to comply with local regulations and expectations. For instance, Disney Corporation justifies the low wages given to Haitian workers by its compliance with all relevant local legislation, including that pertaining to the minimum wage (see Cooper, 1997). While compliance with local legislation is considered important, critics of MNCs do not see this approach as reflecting responsible business practice. In many cases, social and environmental legislation in LDCs is weak and, even where strong, there is often an absence of enforcement mechanisms.

Moreover, critics argue that, where local regulation is weak, MNCs have a responsibility to lobby for legislation that protects both local communities and their environments. MNCs typically respond that they should not be considered 'agents of change' on issues such as strengthening weak environmental and social legislation. However, critics point out that, when in the *economic* interest of MNCs, they have shown themselves willing to exert considerable influence over legislation and policy. For instance, oil companies lobbied for the passage of the 1971 Alaskan Native Settlement Claims Act, which needed to be passed prior to oil extraction in the Prudhoe Bay area (see Chance and Andreeva, 1995).

2 – Repositories of power for sustainable development

A second important theme in the contemporary debate concerns which agents have the power to advance sustainable development in LDCs.

Power at the Host-Country Level
MNCs' feel strongly that the national government is ultimately the repository of power for promoting sustainable development. They argue that NGOs have a tendency to overestimate the power of MNCs and underestimate the ultimate power of the state. For example, governments can nationalize MNCs' assets at any time, as seen in the cases of ITT in Chile and the oil industries in Iran, Peru and Venezuela.

However, given the dependence of local economies on MNCs' investments and, more generally, international financial markets, NGOs contest that, in reality, host-country governments do not today retain the power to enforce sustainable business practices. They cite, for example, the case of Nigeria, where an overwhelming percentage of Nigeria's foreign exchange derives from oil, thereby limiting the government's power to intervene. In support of this claim, critics note that, although Nigeria's environmental laws are strong on paper, in practice a number of oil MNCs have ignored these laws without sanction.

It has also been suggested that other factors might limit, in practice, the powers of the host-country government. In a number of LDCs, critics maintain that legislation on environmental issues was and continues to be written in direct consultation with the very businesses whose interests are at stake. Moreover, they assert that business and government interests can become so aligned as to exclude the interests of local communities. For instance, it has been reported that representatives of the Nigerian government and Shell have routinely switched from one organization to the other, making it increasingly difficult to differentiate between the state and the MNC. MNCs counter that their internal operating procedures weed out corruption and that this provides an effective mechanism against undue influence on government decision-making.

Power at the Level of the International Community

Variations in environmental legislation between LDCs and developed countries have led NGOs to call for international regulation of MNCs. In an age of globalization, it is argued that laws at the purely national level do not lead to sustainable business practice and that it is necessary instead to regulate MNC activity at the international level. NGOs lament that there are no international standards, let alone an international enforcement regime to regulate MNC operations.

The MNC position, however, is that the global economy has a number of incentives for sustainable business practices – notably that negative public relations changes in consumer buying patterns and discontented employees generate competitive pressures for responsible behaviour. MNCs maintain that, as a consequence of this pressure, they now equate good environmental and social policies with good business, particularly in a world of global media and instantaneous communications.

Power at the Level of the Home Country

The NGO community feels that, in the absence of power at the level of the host-country government (where the MNC subsidiary operates) or the international community, there is scope for formal and informal enforcement at the home-country level (where the MNC headquarters are situated). They cite the precedents provided by Ecuador's indigenous peoples taking Texaco to court in the US and the consumer campaign against Shell in Europe regarding the disposal of the Brent Spar production rig at sea.

Power at the Local Level

Critics of MNCs contend that local communities are typically excluded by their own governments from any meaningful participation in projects in their own territories, citing cases such as RTZ in Madagascar and Elf in Peru. It is strongly felt that, if the local community does not want a project, they should have the power to stop it, or, at a minimum, to have an active involvement in its definition; this is the principle of prior informed consent. MNCs have responded that they accept the principle of prior informed consent, but are not explicit in explaining whether the power of veto rests solely with national government or includes the affected communities.

Even in those cases where consent has been obtained from local communities, NGOs point to the asymmetry in knowledge between the MNC and the local community with regard to the impacts of the project. Specifically, they question whether communities have adequate information and, critically, are able to understand this information in a manner that allows them to make an informed decision. MNCs, however, contend that, through the activities of NGOs and their lawyers, local communities now possess better resources to make informed decisions.

3 – Representation by sustainable development

The limited representation of affected communities in the project development process is a recurrent theme in the debate. In this regard, NGOs speak of a 'democracy gap' at the local level.

Representation by the Host Government
NGOs contest that the host-country government often does not represent the local interests. This is particularly the case in those countries with non-democratic regimes and excluded minorities. More profoundly, some representatives of the NGO community note that a universal feature of the development process within the nation-state has been the sacrifice of local interests for the sake of the so-called 'greater good'.

Nigeria is often cited as a case in point where, regardless of whether Shell was conforming with host-country legislation, the government, being a military dictatorship, was not representative of local community interests. It has been asked rhetorically: 'Why was Shell dealing with a military dictatorship? Why was it not dealing directly with the local people?'

MNCs counter that NGOs are expecting too much of business to bypass the national government and deal directly with more local communities. It has been asked: 'Who is business to decide that the national government does not legitimately represent the interests of the local people?'

Representation by the MNCs' National Subsidiaries
Critics further submit that in-country subsidiaries of MNCs do not adequately represent the interests of local communities. The case of RTZ Mining in Madagascar has been cited by members of the NGO and some members of the MNC community as an instance where the subsidiary did not adequately represent the views of the local community.

Furthermore, it is asserted that the restructuring and downsizing of many MNCs means that their subsidiaries have inadequate human resources to represent local community interests. MNCs respond that, with slimmer subsidiaries, decision-making has become less bureaucratic and more efficient and thus they are now better prepared to respond to and represent local community interests.

In their defence, MNCs explain that it can be difficult to identify the 'true' local interest and who represents it. One MNC representative has asked rhetorically: 'Is it a question of who talks the loudest?' This dilemma was illustrated by the follow-on question of: 'Who, for example, speaks for the local community on the issue of the Newbury Bypass?'[3] – the point being that, if you spoke to the local community in Newbury, you would probably receive widely differing views on the possible merits and disadvantages of the bypass. NGOs contend that, in situations of this complexity, the burden of responsibility lies with MNCs to communicate to *all* local stakeholders.

However, even within the NGO community, it is acknowledged that the above strategy is perhaps unrealistic: the question was raised as to whether business actually has the *time* to deal with the diversity of contrasting views at the local community level. Furthermore, the difference in values between the MNC subsidiary and local community may be so great as to block effective communication. The question remains: 'Can the distinct, possibly non-monetary values of a local community be effectively represented within an organization that values profit above all else?'

Representation by the NGO Community

Finally, NGOs assert that, since local community interests in developing countries cannot find representation in either the national government or MNC, it is ultimately left to NGOs to represent the views of the local community. A member of the NGO community has offered the example of Papua New Guinea, where an NGO arranged for legal representation of the affected community in the Australian courts.

4 – Reorganization for sustainable development

It is acknowledged by both MNCs and NGOs that there are a number of important organizational constraints that hinder MNCs' responsiveness to sustainable development in LDCs.

Issue Prioritization and Incentives

Critics contend that MNCs' practices are geared to maximize profits and growth and thus, in the course of doing business, local environmental and social interests are often sacrificed. MNCs themselves acknowledge that, traditionally, environmental and, in particular, social issues are not always given the priority they deserve. This situation has led to an absence of internal incentives and performance-related indicators for these issues. MNCs have identified the lack of incentives as a constraint at both the headquarters and subsidiary level, where performance still tends to be measured in terms of traditional financial and production criteria.

In particular, MNCs acknowledge that equal priority is not yet accorded to the issue of social responsibility. In the words of one MNC representative, community relations has traditionally been viewed as 'wallpapering on the wall', where the community relations department plays a 'sweeper, clean-up role', usually after the situation has already deteriorated. It is also recognized that, relative to environmental issues for which there are often technological solutions, it is perhaps more difficult to define the social responsibility of business and relevant standards.

The lack of priority given to social and environmental performance has traditionally been reflected in the organizational response from MNCs. These issues have been dealt with by autonomous departments, who are viewed as putting the brakes on financial gain. Consequently, they have not received the necessary financial and human resources and have lacked senior management support.

Inter-firm Communications

NGOs question whether the current communication channels used by MNCs limit their capacity to behave sustainably. It is contended that, in an effort to please head-quarters, there is a tendency for MNC subsidiaries to be economical with the truth regarding social and environmental impacts. While MNC headquarters may have the best environmental and social intentions, the feedback they receive from the field may not provide an accurate picture of reality Therefore, it is only after seri-ous and sometimes irreparable damage has occurred that headquarters become aware of the situation, such as the case of Shell in Nigeria and Union Carbide in Bhopal, India.

Possible Solutions

The previous section has identified four important themes in the current debate on sustainable business practice in LDCs. This final section seeks to explore a number of possible changes that could be made to advance the responsiveness of MNCs to their social and environmental impacts. These have been divided into solutions that are (1) external and (2) internal to the MNC.

1 – External to the MNC

A number of critics of the global economy and the role of MNCs therein advocate international regulation of MNCs on environmental and social issues, as in the European Union, where environmental and social standards are in the process of being harmonized. This approach has been advocated since the 1970s and, in spite of various initiatives within the United Nations, has been unsuccessful. Indeed, even where international conventions exist – notably, the International Labour Organi-sation's *Convention 169 Concerning Indigenous and Tribal Peoples in Independent Countries* – there has been inadequate compliance. In short, there would not ap-pear to be adequate support from MNCs or governments – North and South – to establish and enforce international regulation.

In the Absence of International Regulation

In the absence of international regulation of MNCs, a number of international vol-untary codes have been established – for instance, the 1976 OECD Guidelines for Multinational Enterprises (which does not explicitly address environmental and social issues), the Valdez Principles and the 1991 Business Charter for Sustainable Development established by the International Chamber of Commerce (Hagg, 1984; Sanyal and Neves, 1991; ICC, 1994). Yet the critics of MNCs feel that, without sanc-tioning powers, these voluntary codes do not adequately protect local communities and their environment (see Mayhew, 1997).

MNCs feel that international market forces can provide the necessary competi-tive pressures for sustainable business practices. NGOs share this view, but contend that this is conditional on their efforts to expose recalcitrant MNCs and mobilize consumer interest in the North. Moreover, international market forces would only appear to be effective for high-profile MNCs, such as oil companies with up- and downstream operations and MNCs that rely on their brand names, such as Levi Strauss, The Gap, Nike and Disney.

Home-Country Legislation

NGOs propose that, without international regulation and weak legislation in the host country, it should be possible to enforce responsible behaviour in the country of the MNC's headquarters. In this way, marginalized communities might find a voice in the courts of the North. NGOs point to the historic example of Ecuador's indigenous peoples taking Texaco to court in New York city.

Host-Country Legislation

There seems to be a consensus between NGOs and MNCs that there should be institutionalized mechanisms for representation and participation of the local community in the project development process. For this reason, the constitutional framework adopted by an LDC would seem highly relevant. In those countries where there are decentralized − as opposed to centralized − constitutional structures, such as Colombia and South Africa, affected communities are more likely to secure their rights through participation in the project development process.

Beyond the constitutional framework, the precise nature of environmental and social legislation appears to be important. Firstly LDC governments should enact laws that establish a strict set of environmental and social standards, but allow companies the flexibility to meet those standards as they see best. Secondly, governments should emphasize the compliance of industry with standards and avoid mandating numerous studies on how industry will meet those standards. Thirdly, governments should promote mechanisms that enable affected communities and NGOs to participate in the identification of environmental and social impacts and ensure MNC compliance with relevant mitigating measures.

The entity or entities responsible for environmental and social issues should be resourced adequately. In particular, they need to possess the relevant managerial and technical competence. For instance, in Colombia, as part of its 1991 constitution, a Ministry of Environment was established as an autonomous unit, with direct funding from central government and has since created a competent team of trained environmental and social specialists.

Partnerships

In the wake of pressure to respond to their direct environmental and social impacts, as well as to adopt a broader role in the development of their areas of operation, a number of MNCs have established partnerships with NGOs and local governments. MNCs have recognized that they often do not possess the necessary skills and human resources to meet these objectives. For example, MNCs have found that cooperation with local NGOs can be effective for independent environmental monitoring, for implementing community development projects such as education and health, and for ensuring that interested local communities are included in the Environmental Impact Assessment process.

2 – Internal to the MNC

The first challenge facing MNCs is how to structure themselves to better meet the demands of sustainable development. At the headquarter level, it has been suggested that MNCs appoint non-executive directors who are explicitly responsible for sustainable business practice (see PIRC, 1997). It is further suggested and acknowledged by many MNCs that line managers should be made directly responsible for environmental and social impacts, rather than delegating this responsibility to individual departments.

MNCs can also adapt their operating policies to better incorporate social and environmental issues. Senior management should be made aware that the failure to address environmental and social impacts can affect the MNC's bottom line and thus need to be incorporated into traditional investment and operating decisions. To encourage this change, incentives should be developed that reward and sanction company employees and contractors on the basis of their environmental and social performance. MNCs can link bonuses directly to these performance indicators. For instance, one oil multinational has introduced a 'no surprises' policy whereby senior management pay is linked to an absence of unreported social and environmental problems.

To measure their environmental and social impacts, MNCs can adopt relevant performance indicators. For instance, to monitor environmental impacts, they can adopt indicators that pertain to atmospheric emissions, spills, discharge into water supplies, recycling, use of toxic chemicals and overall environmental expenditure. On social issues, equivalent indicators are still largely to be developed, although MNCs such as The Body Shop are at the forefront of defining such indicators.

Traditional auditing techniques can largely be adapted to measure MNCs' environmental and social performance, as proposed by organizations such as Traidcraft plc and the New Economics Foundation for social issues. One means of assuring that auditing remains accurate is to establish parallel lines of communication with local communities. Under this arrangement, MNC headquarters would receive reports not only from their subsidiaries, but from representatives of the affected communities. This could provide a form of independent external auditing of subsidiary activities.

Conclusion

The contemporary debate on how to promote more sustainable business practice among MNCs in LDCs has tended to be dominated by individual cases. This chapter has shown, however, that four common themes transcend the individual cases. Each theme encapsulates some of the major challenges facing MNCs and other stakeholders in the pursuit of sustainable development in LDCs and could usefully serve as avenues for future research. This chapter has concluded with a number of possible solutions, external and internal to the MNC, in an effort to advance the debate and support the objective of more sustainable business practices in the developing world.

References

Cairncross, F (1992) *Costing the Earth: The Challenge for Governments, The Opportunities for Business*, Harvard Business School Press, Boston, MA

Chance, N A and Andreeva, E N (1995) 'Sustainability Equity and Natural Resource Development in Northwest Siberia and Arctic Alaska', in *Human Ecology*, vol 23, no 2, pp217–40

Choucri, N (1993) 'Multinational Corporations and the Global Environment', in N Choucri (ed) *Global Accord: Environmental Challenges and International Responses*, The MIT Press, Cambridge, MA

Cooper, G (1997) 'No Glamour for Disney's Sweatshop Toilers', in *The Independent*, 10 October, p3

Costanza, R, et al (1995) 'Sustainable Trade: A New Paradigm for World Welfare', in *Environment*, vol 37, no 5, pp17–20

Daly H and Cobb, J (1994) *For the Common Good: Redirecting the Economy Toward Community, the Environment and Sustainable Development*, Beacon Press, Boston, MA

Fairbanks, M and Lindsay, S (1997) *Plowing the Sea: Nurturing the Hidden Sources of Growth in the Developing World*, Harvard Business School Press, Boston, MA

French, H F (1997) 'When Foreign Investors Pay for Development', in *Worldwatch Magazine*, vol 10, no 3, pp9–17

Hadlock, C R (1994) 'Multinational Corporations and the Transfer of Environmental Technology to Developing Countries', in *Journal of International Environmental Affairs*, vol 6, no 2, pp149–174

Hagg, C (1984) 'The OECD Guidelines for Multinational Enterprises: A Critical Analysis', in *Journal of Business Ethics*, vol 3, pp71–76

Harrison, A (1994) 'The Role of Multinationals in Economic Development: The Benefits of FDI', in *The Colombia Journal of World Business*, winter, pp7–11

International Chamber of Commerce (1994) *The Business Charter for Sustainable Development*, ICC, Paris, France

Institute of International Finance (1997) *Capital Flows to Emerging Market Economies*, IIF, January, Washington, DC

Jackson, T (1997) 'Facing up to a Challenging Opposition', in the *Financial Times*, 31 October, p16

Korten, D C (1995) *When Corporations Rule the World*, Earthscan, London

Mayhew, N (1997) 'Fading to Grey: The Use and Abuse of Corporate Executives' Representational Power', in R Welford (ed) *Hijacking Environmentalism: The Corporate Response to Sustainable Development*, Earthscan, London

Pensions Investment Resources Consultancy Ltd (1997) *The Committee on Corporate Governance: A Response from PIRC Ltd*, PIRC, London

Redclift, M (1987) *Sustainable Development: Exploring the Contradictions*, Methuen, London, UK

Sanyal, R N and Neves, J S (1991) 'The Valdez Principles: Implications for Corporate Social Responsibility', in *Journal of Business Ethics*, vol 10, pp883–890

Schmidheiny, S and the Business Council for Sustainable Development (1992) *Changing Course*, Cambridge, MA

Tahija, J (1993) 'Swapping Business Skills for Oil', in *Harvard Business Review*, September–October, pp64–77

United Nations Conference on Trade and Development (1995) *Recent Trends in International Investment and Transnational Corporations*, United Nations, Geneva, Switzerland

World Commission on Environment and Development (1987) *Our Common Future*, Oxford University Press, Oxford

Wescott, W F (1992) 'Environmental Technology Co-operation: A Quid-Pro-Quo for Transnational Corporations and Developing Countries', in *The Colombia Journal of World Business*, autumn–winter, pp145–153

Notes

1   Organized by the Committee for Interdisciplinary Environmental Studies, Cambridge University. Tel: 01223 333366; e-mail: jhs15@cam.ac.uk
2   'Chatham House' rules were applied at this workshop, in which statements are made in confidence, without attribution
3   The Newbury Bypass is one of a number of government road-building projects to alleviate congestion in Britain's city centres These projects have generated public concern over their environmental impact as the proposed bypasses often run through ecologically sensitive areas

12

The Responsibility of Business to the Whole[1]

David C Korten

Business has become, in this last half century, the most powerful institution on the planet. The dominant institution in any society needs to take responsibility for the whole …

Willis W Harman, August 1990

In this widely quoted statement on business responsibility, Willis Harman issued a wake-up call. He pointed out that institutional changes have fundamentally realigned the power relationship between business and the rest of society, and called on business leaders to examine the profound, but largely neglected, implications of this reality.

Such an inquiry must address a number of basic questions. How did business come to be the dominant institution of society? Is this dominance consistent with the healthy function of society? Given the distinctive nature and competence of business, what is its appropriate role and responsibility vis-à-vis other institutions? What is the responsibility of business to the whole and what are the most appropriate ways to assure its accountability to the whole for the discharge of this responsibility? These seldom asked questions take us to the heart of the dilemmas created by the rise of business to its current position of dominant power.

The Rise and Concentration of Corporate Power

It is not really business per se, but rather a complex interlocking web of global financial markets and corporations, a subset of the institutions of business, that have become the planet's most powerful institution. The power issue centres on the global corporation as a distinctive form of business organization.

It is instructive to recall that the institution of the corporation was first created by kings to serve as an agent of colonial expansion. Some claim the American revolution was as much a revolution against the crown corporations as against the crown itself. As a consequence, corporations were treated with great caution in the early days of the new republic. The few corporate charters issued were generally for a limited duration to serve a carefully delineated public purpose. The crown has since

Reproduced by kind permission from the People-Centred Development Forum: http://iisd.ca/pcdf/1997/responsibility.htm

been replaced by the modern shareholder, and access to corporate charters has been democratized. Yet the original power and function of the corporation – concentrating wealth and power in the hands of an élite ruling class – have been largely restored.

Although a CEO may by choice organize the internal operations of a corporation around self-organizing networking structures that decentralize responsibility and make relationships more egalitarian, this does not change the corporation's formal structural overlay. Inherently one of the most authoritarian of human institutions, the structure of the corporation is designed to concentrate wealth and power at its apex. The CEO has the legal authority to reclaim at any time the power or authority previously delegated; hire, fire and reassign staff; open and close plants; add and drop product lines; and change transfer pricing almost at will with virtually no recourse by the people or communities affected, either inside or outside the organization. Nor is the CEO at liberty to relinquish this power. By law it goes with the position.

Historically, exercise of the regulatory powers of the state was the primary restraint on the expansion of corporate power. Together the processes of deregulation and globalization have effectively relieved that constraint by placing the power of global corporations and finance beyond the reach of the state. The hopeful claims of some business observers notwithstanding, the mega-corporations are not shedding their power. To the contrary, they continue to concentrate and consolidate it through mergers, acquisitions and strategic alliances. The statistics are sobering:

- Of the world's 100 largest economies, 51 are corporations. Only 49 are countries. The economy of Mitsubishi is larger than that of Indonesia, the world's fourth most populous country and a land of enormous natural wealth.
- The combined sales of the world's top 200 corporations are equal to 28 per cent of the world's GDP.
- These same 200 corporations employ only 18.8 million people, less than one-third of 1 per cent of the world's people – and the downsizing continues.
- In 1995 the total value of mergers and acquisitions for the world exceeded any prior year by 25 per cent.

The primary accountability of these corporations is to the global financial markets in which each day US$1.4 trillion in foreign exchange changes hands in the search for speculative profits wholly unrelated to any exchange of real goods or services.

Whose interests are represented by these financial markets to which the world's most powerful corporations are beholden? In the US 77 per cent of shareholder wealth is owned by a mere 5 per cent of households. The broader population that holds a beneficial ownership through pension funds is represented in corporate governance by a few hundred fund managers who have no accountability to the beneficial owners beyond protecting the security of their benefits. Globally the share of the world's population that has a consequential participation in corporate ownership is far less than 1 per cent. This concentration of corporate power, accountable only to a tiny global élite, denies the most basic principles of democratic governance. It also results in an ever increasing concentration of the world's wealth. *Forbes* magazine now identifies 447 billionaires in the world, up from only 274 in 1991.

Their combined assets are roughly equal to the total annual incomes of the poorest half of humanity.

It is axiomatic. In a healthy democratic society the dominant institution must be both *responsible for* the whole and *accountable to* the whole. Not long ago, nation states were our dominant institutions. The nation state had a clearly mandated responsibility for the whole and the institutions of democratic societies were structured to assure commensurate accountability to the whole.

By contrast, global corporations and financial markets serve financial bottom-line mandates that are as narrow as their constituencies. The deregulation and economic globalization that have increased their power, have done nothing to broaden their mandates and/or accountability. To replace the power of the state with the power of the global corporation is tantamount to an act of collective suicide.

We are experiencing the consequences in the form of six current tendencies of the global system identified by Willis and colleague Thomas Hurley in a co-authored paper written only days before Willis' cancer was diagnosed:

1   Destruction of the natural environment.
2   Destruction of community.
3   Transfer of wealth upward.
4   Marginalization of persons, communities and cultures.
5   Erosion and denial of the sense of the spiritual or sacred.
6   Creation of learned incapacity and helplessness.

Spiritually impoverished and on the brink of destroying the natural and social fabric on which human life and civilization depend, we are creating societies that diminish the human spirit and place our very survival at risk. Dominated by the power and values of global corporations and financial markets, the global economy bears a major responsibility.

It is ironic that the policies that have concentrated power in our most authoritarian and least accountable institution have been promoted in the name of human freedom, democracy and the market economy. In the true market economy envisioned by Adam Smith small producers compete for the favour of small consumers on the basis of price. We do not have an economy centrally planned by socialist governments to serve the party bosses, but what we do have is not so different as we might think – an economy centrally planned by the world's largest corporations to serve the interests of their wealthiest shareholders.

There is indeed a positive relationship between a market economy comprised of small independent producers and human freedom. However, corporate freedom is to human freedom and the market economy what monarchy is to democracy – they are fundamentally at odds. Confronting this conflict is key both to reversing the devastating trends that threaten our future and to defining the real challenge of socially responsible management. The perhaps startling implication is that the number one priority of socially responsible business leaders must be a commitment to create the conditions of a socially efficient market economy.

The Conditions for a Socially Efficient Market

The market is a powerful and indispensable mechanism for facilitating efficient economic choices. However, even Adam Smith was quite clear that the invisible hand of the market works to the larger benefit of society only to the extent that a number of specific conditions are met. A number of such conditions have been identified and elaborated by subsequent generations of market economists.

For example, the socially efficient market will be comprised of small locally owned enterprises that are rooted in place and operate within a framework of community norms and relationships. There should be no producers sufficiently large that they can artificially manipulate prices or consumer preferences nor associations through which producers may act in combination to set prices outside the market. Proprietary information is also a no-no. All market participants must have full access to relevant knowledge and technology.

One of the most basic principles of social market efficiency is that producers must bear the full cost of the products they sell. There must be no subsidies that distort market prices and allocation. And since markets respond only to money and the socially efficient market must respond to the needs of everyone, there must be reasonable equality of income and financial assets to assure everyone an opportunity to participate. There must also be an effective and democratically accountable government to perform functions to which business is not suited and to provide for the necessary regulation of the conduct of business. These are all conditions of the socially efficient market as envisioned by market theory. No serious student of this theory should be surprised by the social inefficiency of a global economy dominated by free floating capital and footloose corporations that command internal economies larger than those of most states, externalize their costs by bidding down environmental, work and safety standards, taxes and wages under threat of moving jobs elsewhere, own and control the public media, command advertising budgets that rival public spending on education, and use intellectual property rights to create government-protected monopolies. The existing global economy systematically violates every one of the conditions required to align the workings of the market with the public interest. It delinks the global corporation from meaningful public accountability, facilitates the externalization of costs and limits access by both consumers and investors to information essential to making informed decisions.

Market theory also embodies a number of basic assumptions regarding the fundamental responsibilities of the firm. Among others it should fully internalize its own costs, practise full disclosure with investors and consumers, avoid any form of anti-competitive practice or price fixing and obey the law. While these are nothing more than fundamentals of ethical business practice, they represent serious commitments indeed for a business operating in an unregulated global market economy that encourages and rewards the opposite behaviours. A commitment to honouring these principles represents the essential core of the firm's responsibility to the whole and should be the foundation of any social responsibility programme. To put it bluntly, a firm that is not seriously committed to meeting these standards has no legitimate claim to being socially responsible no matter how much it gives to charity or otherwise supports beneficial social causes.

Profits Earned vs Profits Extracted

According to market theory a firm's profits measure its value added contribution to the society. To the extent that this is true, it follows that a firm best maximizes its social contribution by maximizing the financial return to its shareholders. The catch here is that this same market theory also assumes that the firm fully internalizes the costs of its operation. To the extent that costs are externalized, however, the firm's profits represent not an addition by the firm to the wealth of society, but rather an expropriation by the firm of the community's existing wealth.

Sometimes the externalization takes the form of direct public subsidies – as, for example, the grant given by the state of Virginia to Motorola to locate a research and manufacturing facility in the state. It included a US$55.9 million grant, a US$1.6 billion tax credit and a reimbursement package worth US$5 million for employee training. Every dollar of this package represented a direct transfer of money from Virginia taxpayers to the profits of the Motorola corporation. Special property tax breaks given by New York City to private companies subsidized them to the tune of US$301.8 million in 1994 alone. Direct US government subsidies to tobacco growers will come to US$41 million in 1997. The oil and gas industry gets US$2.4 billion a year in federal subsidies in the form of oil depletion allowances. Over a ten-year period, the US government subsidized Cargil's foreign grain sales by US$1.3 billion. The US government is currently in the process of giving away spectrum rights to the broadcast industry that former Senator Robert Dole estimates are worth between US$12–70 billion. McDonald's receives US$1.6 million from the government each year to advertise its fast-food products overseas. The conservative Cato Institute estimates that such direct and tax-break corporate subsidies total US$135 billion a year.[2]

In the 1950s taxes on US corporations provided 31 per cent of the federal government's general revenues. Their share is now down to just 15 per cent. In 1957, corporations provided 45 per cent of local property tax revenues in the US. By 1987, their share had dropped to about 16 per cent. Since corporations rely on public services and infrastructure, expect the full protection of their assets by the US military and depend on workers educated at public expense, they rightly bear a fair share of the tax burden that is required to pay for these and other public services. When they are excepted from paying their fair share of taxes, the cost of the services they enjoy is shifted to other taxpayers.

There are also the costs imposed on society by the products that corporations sell. For example, the health consequences of the cigarettes from which corporations profit cost the public an estimated US$53.9 billion a year. Similarly, society bears a US$135.8 billion burden for the consequences of unsafe vehicles. There are as well the costs borne by workers who suffer injuries and accidents as a result of unsafe work places (US$141.6 billion) or die from workplace cancer (US$274.7 billion).[3]

These are all uncompensated costs imposed on society by the operations and activities of corporations. Every such externalized cost, whether in the form of a direct cash payment or in the form of diminished health and quality of life, involves privatizing a gain and socializing its associated costs on to the community. Each such externalized cost represents an unearned public subsidy to the firm's profits – a taking by the corporation from the society – and is properly deducted from reported financial profits when determining the value-added contribution of the corporation to society.

Ralph Estes, author of *Tyranny of the Bottom Line* and *Corporate Social Accounting*, has compiled estimates from a number of studies of the costs that corporations impose on US society. He came up with a conservative total annual figure of US$2.6 trillion based on 1994 dollars, not even including the direct cash subsidies and special tax breaks estimated by the Cato Institute.[4] This figure compares to total 1994 before tax corporate profits in the US of US$515 billion.[5] In other words, society subsidizes America's corporations by more than five times the amount of the profits they generate for their shareholders.

Some of the externalized costs might be considered a form of income transfer from society to the corporation and its owners. As disturbing as this may be, the truly tragic forms of cost externalization involve the absolute and sometimes permanent, destruction or depletion of the real productive capital of the society. For example, when a corporation:

- employs workers in insecure jobs with inadequate pay, the stress of economic insecurity and attempting to maintain self and family on less than a living family wage results in family breakdown and violence, depleting the social capital of society;
- hires young women in places like the Mexican maquiladoras under conditions that after three or four years leave the workers with eyesight problems, allergies, kidney problems and repetitive stress injuries that permanently impair their productive efficiency and render them unemployable, it both destroys individual lives and depletes society's human capital;
- strips mines, forests, fisheries and mineral deposits, dumps wastes and sells toxic chemicals that do not break down naturally in the environment, it depletes the earth's natural capital;
- funds campaigns against environmental and other regulations essential to protecting the long-term health and viability of the society and demands direct subsidies, subsidized infrastructure and relief from their fair share of taxes, it depletes society's institutional capital by undermining the credibility and legitimacy of the democratic governments that prove unable to enforce the laws and provide the services essential to protecting the long-term health and viability of society;
- cuts its own investments in research and employee training, downsizes workers and closes plants in denial of any responsibilities to once loyal and productive employees and supportive communities, it erodes the corporation's own physical, intellectual, social and moral capital.

These are not hypothetical concerns. Take the case of the Benguet Mining Company in the Philippines documented by Robin Broad and John Cavanagh in their book *Plundering Paradise* (University of California Press, 1994). In the quest for gold, Benguet Mining cut deep gashes into the mountains, stripped away trees and topsoil and dumped enormous piles of rock into local rivers. With their soils and water sources depleted, the indigenous Igorot people in the area can no longer grow rice and bananas, and have to go to the other side of the mountain for drinking water and to bathe. The cyanide used by the Benguet corporation to separate the gold from the rock poisons the local streams, kills cattle that drink from the streams and reduces rice yields of people in the lowlands who use the water for irrigation. When the tailings and cyanide empty into the oceans they kill the coral reefs and destroy the fishing on which thousands of coastal people depend.

While no specific estimates are available, the cost of the Benguet Mining operations is borne by the community almost certainly exceeds the amount of the company's profits and local payroll by a wide margin, resulting in a substantial net loss to society. Tragically there is nothing at all special about the Benguet case. It is much the same with Shell Oil in Nigeria, Texaco in Ecuador, Freeport-McMoRan in Indonesia, or countless other less publicized cases of predatory corporations devastating the lives and habitats of people who have no democratic voice, as they extract and destroy natural capital for a quick profit.

Or consider the report recently cited by Bob Herbert in the *New York Times*[6] on the working conditions endured by young women ages 15–28 working in factories that make Nike shoes in Vietnam. Three meals of rice with a little vegetable and perhaps some tofu costs the equivalent of US$2.10. Renting a room costs at least US$6 a month. Workers must cover these and all other expenses out of their wages of US$1.60 a day. Those interviewed complained that since starting work at the factory they have suffered frequent headaches, general fatigue and weight loss. Workers are allowed one toilet break and two drinks of water per eight-hour shift. Again, Nike is unfortunately not all that exceptional. It just happens to have become the poster child symbol of corporations that profit from worker exploitation.

The profitability of a good many of our largest corporations has little to do with efficiency. Their profits depend to a disturbing extent on their ability to use their extraordinary economic power to extract huge subsidies from the larger society. That in turn allows them to outbid their competitors for capital and to undercut their prices to consumers to further consolidate their power and to demand still more subsidies. As ecological economist Neva Goodwin bluntly explains: '*Power is largely what externalities are about. What's the point of having power, if you cannot use it to externalize your costs – to make them fall on someone else?*'[7]

Of course, there will be those who argue that the public benefits from these 'cost savings' in the form of lower prices. Here we must again come back to the concept of market efficiency. Where prices are lower due to a subsidy this distorts the market signals, giving the subsidized product an advantage over non-subsidized alternatives and increasing the hidden burden on society. The various subsidies enjoyed by the car have no doubt contributed to making it the dominant form of transportation in the US, at enormous cost to the country's quality of life. The removal of these subsidies would likely shift the balance in favour of more environmentally and socially efficient public transport and urban densities.

Corporations have long portrayed themselves as powerful engines of wealth creation for the benefit of the whole of society. This is a part of their reality. The corporation also presents a darker face to the world – a powerful engine of wealth extraction and concentration. Both faces are real, which defines a central dilemma of our time. How do we exorcize the dark side without destroying the essential and beneficial wealth-creation face of the business sector? Fortunately, there may be a truly market-based solution to this dilemma based on linking together two fundamental market principles: internalized costs and fully informed buyers.

A Market-based Approach to Corporate Responsibility

There has been a growing interest in various kinds of social accounting and auditing as a means of increasing the public accountability of corporations to their multiple stakeholders. A variety of initiatives seek to provide more information to the public on a host of concerns ranging from environmental performance, product safety, affirmative action, working conditions and community charities. All make an incremental contribution towards increasing corporate accountability. Most, however, are at once fragmented, detailed and partial. Beyond the quite valid idea that a corporation should serve more than the narrow financial interests of its shareholders, they are not grounded in a coherent theory of either the market or the corporation. The corporation was never intended to function as a public charity or policy advocate and is not by design suited to such functions.

It is important to note that, for all its power, the global corporation is a rather crude and simplistic organizational form. It is designed to be accountable to one constituency – its shareholders – for one thing – profit. Compare the corporation's accountability structures to the rich complexity and sophistication of the structures of modern democratic government designed to hold government accountable to the whole, for the whole.

To ask the corporation to be responsible in some way to a broader set of stakeholders for meeting a variety of often vague and fragmented standards is to deny its nature as an institution designed to pursue a single clearly defined objective for a single interest constituency. It essentially means asking the corporate CEO to be responsible for making value choices on behalf of the corporation's shareholders, customers and society beyond profit maximization. Even if the law and the corporate board were to grant a CEO such discretion, what reason do we have to expect that he or she will exercise it to the larger benefit of larger society? To whom and through what mechanisms is a corporate CEO accountable for the exercise of this discretion? Why should we assume that all persons who happen to head powerful corporations have the wisdom and the motivation to make decisions for the whole? And even for those who do have the wisdom and motivation, by what right do they hold such power over the rest of society?

Our efforts to correct the dysfunctions of unaccountable corporate power must be based on a more focused approach grounded in market theory and our understanding of the nature of the corporation and its accountability structures. A straightforward focus on internalizing costs and assuring all stakeholders free access to relevant information relating to cost internalization meets both these conditions and would offer a market-based approach to making the corporation a more socially responsible entity. Indeed, actualizing these two conditions of a socially efficient market should be the central focus of any corporate responsibility programme.

The centre piece of such a social responsibility initiative would be a corporate cost internalization audit. We might call it the market efficiency audit (MEA) to highlight the fact it implements a basic market principle. Some critics of environmental, health and safety regulations argue that such matters should be left up to the market to be arbitrated by investor and consumer choice. Of course, to exercise this choice intelligently requires access to the relevant information. Providing that information is the primary purpose of the MEA.

The MEA would not be a general social audit of all the things the firm might do to benefit society beyond its bottom line. Rather it would be a clear and specific measure of the corporation's externalized costs – the total public subsidy of its operations. As with financial accounting, market efficiency audit accounting should seek to arrive ultimately at a single bottom-line number. This figure could be compared to the corporation's total sales, profits and tax payments and to averages for the industry and for all corporations to assess the extent of the corporation's welfare dependency.[8]

The full audit report should be in the public domain and readily available to any interested party. A summary of the results should be included in the firm's financial prospectus for review by all actual and prospective shareholders. The basic results should also be included in the labelling of any of the corporation's products. Just as a shirt label might indicate the cotton content, it might also reveal that the public subsidy content is, say, US$15. Thus the buyer will know the uncompensated cost to society of his purchase and can make an informed choice to choose an item from a more socially efficient producer. The lower the public subsidy content of a given product, the more socially responsible the purchase.

Similarly, the lower the percentage of a corporation's subsidy to total sales, the more socially responsible it is to invest in that corporation. It would be a far more meaningful indicator for socially responsible investing than the crude yardsticks now applied. Corporations could be ranked by their percentage of cost internalization, just as they are now ranked by profit.

Firms seriously committed to being at the forefront of social responsibility may lead the way by undertaking MEAs on a voluntary basis as a demonstration of their commitment to serving the public good. However, an annual MEA should in due course be a legal requirement for any corporation with US$500 million or more in either sales or assets. The preparation of an MEA by smaller corporations and unincorporated businesses should be encouraged, but not necessarily required.

Some will surely argue that such an audit would be an unnecessary and expensive diversion of economic resources because the amount of externalized cost for their corporations is negligible. Any executive who really believes this should be an active proponent of the MEA and an early voluntary adopter. The audit should confirm the responsibility of their company and thereby strengthen its public legitimacy and good will. In any event, the public that has granted the privilege of a corporate charter has both the need and the right to know.

The MEA cannot rightfully be considered an unjustified socialist intrusion of the state into private affairs. It in no way denies shareholders of their right to profits commensurate with the contribution of their investment to increasing the wealth of society or the freedom of choice of consumers. It simply calls on the institutions of the market to play by the rules of the market so that consumers, investors and communities that are negotiating for corporate investments can make more fully informed market decisions.

Furthermore, the burden of proof to establish that it is producing a net benefit to society should rest with the corporation that enjoys the special privileges conveyed by the corporate charter. The idea that the corporation enjoys such privileges as a natural right is a legal fiction without moral foundation. If there is a cost involved in producing such proof, it should be considered a price paid for those privileges – a part of the normal cost of doing business as a corporation. In any event, the costs involved will rarely be more than a small fraction of the public subsidy the corporation enjoys. Any corporation that finds it an excessive burden would be free to avoid the scrutiny by giving up its corporate charter and the special privileges it bestows.

Maintaining the independence and integrity of the MEA will pose an important challenge. There will be need for a well-developed set of MEA accounting standards established by qualified and independent professional groups under public scrutiny. A corporation's MEA accounting system should be maintained by a special unit accountable directly to a committee of outside board members and be subject to audit by an accredited independent external agency. Ralph Estes has suggested that the ultimate governmental oversight might be the responsibility of the Securities and Exchange Commission.

The idea of MEA accounting is not new. Corporate social accounting was a lively topic, especially within the accounting profession, in the 1970s. With the current upsurge in public awareness and concern about corporate responsibility it is now an idea whose time has come.

It could become an organizing issue for various groups concerned with increasing corporate responsibility and accountability. Groups developing social auditing instruments might join with professional accounting groups to develop appropriate accounting and auditing standards. Advocacy groups campaigning on corporate issues can raise public consciousness of the extent and implications of cost externalization, and build political support for legislation mandating the implementation of MEA accounting. Business groups that have a serious commitment to increasing business responsibility should call on corporations to make cost internalization a basic principle in corporate codes of conduct.

Such measures can never be an adequate substitute for a strong and vigorously enforced regulatory framework designed to protect the public from the worst consequences of cost externalizing corporate practices. They can, however, be an important supplement to such measures consistent with sound market principles.

If MEA accounting were to become a standard feature of corporate management practice, it would bring to light vast hidden inefficiencies of a system of business that, in the name of the market, violates nearly every principle of an efficient market economy. It will almost surely lead to radical and much needed restructuring of the institutions of the business sector, as the market purges the truly inefficient and restores a needed institutional balance in society by significantly reducing the dominance of the largest and most subsidy-dependent global corporations and the disproportionate allocation of wealth to shareholders over workers.

It will also raise the prices and thereby reduce the use, of many harmful market goods. Traumatic as this may be for the corporate world during the transition period, the end result will be a healthier business community, healthier societies and an increase in both the legitimacy and efficiency of the world's market economies. In pressing forward this agenda, business leaders will be working to fulfil their social responsibility to the whole in ways that are both powerful in their positive implications for society and consistent with their roles and the nature of the institutions they head.

Notes

1   This chapter was written in memory of Willis W Harman – philosopher, teacher, writer, futurist and president of the Institute of Noetic Science, as well as my teacher, mentor and friend for some 35 years – who died of brain cancer on 30 January 1997. Willis long held two central beliefs about business. First, he believed that the future of humanity requires a basic rethinking of the relationship of business to the whole. And second, he had a deep faith in the readiness and ability of business people to lead this rethinking through a process of critical self-reflection and action

2   'The End of Corporate Welfare as We Know It?', *Business Week*, 10 February 1997, p36

3   Estimates are from Ralph Estes (1995) *Tyranny of the Bottom Line: Why Corporations Make Good People Do Bad Things*, Berrett-Koehler, San Francisco, pp177–185

4   ibid, p178

5   US Bureau of Economic Analysis, *Survey of Current Business*, June 1996, as reported. Otto Johnson (ed) (1996) *1997 Information Please Almanac*, Houghton Mifflin, New York, p64

6   31 March 1997, pA-5

7   Neva Goodwin (1994) 'Externalities and Economic Power', paper presented at the autumn retreat of the Environmental Grantmakers Association, Bretton Woods, N H, 13–15 October, p2

8   A related approach, the corporate 'Social Impact Statement,' is presented in Ralph Estes' *Corporate Social Accounting* (1996) John Wiley & Sons, Chapter 4. It

matches corporate social benefits against social costs to arrive at a net social surplus or deficit. Estes is now organizing a national Stakeholder Alliance to press for full corporate accountability

13

Global Spin

Sharon Beder

Introduction

This chapter examines the way that corporations have used their financial resources and power to counter gains made by environmentalists, to reshape public opinion and to persuade politicians against increased environmental regulation. Corporate activism, ignited in the 1970s and rejuvenated in the 1990s, has enabled a corporate agenda to dominate most debates about the state of the environment and what should be done about it. This situation poses grave dangers to the ability of democratic societies to respond to environmental threats.

Between 1965 and 1970 environmental groups proliferated; environmental protection, especially pollution control, rose dramatically as a public priority in many countries. *Time* magazine labelled it a 'national obsession' in America. A *'sense of urgency – even crisis – suddenly pervaded public discussion of environmental issues. The press was filled with stories of environmental trauma ...'* (Vogel, 1989, p65).

As environmental concern grew, so did distrust of business institutions, which were seen to be the primary cause of environmental problems such as air and water pollution. Public respect for business fell to an all-time low and *'for the first time since the Great Depression, the legitimacy of big business was being called into question by large sectors of the public'* (Parenti, 1986, p67). Surveys showed increasing percentages of people nominated 'factories and plants' as the major source of air pollution. The distrust of business and support for environmentalism was highest among the young and the college or university educated (Vogel, 1989, pp70, 98).

Governments worldwide responded with new forms of comprehensive environmental legislation, such as Clean Air Acts and Clean Water Acts and the establishment of environmental regulatory agencies. These new environmental laws were part of a general trend in legislation aimed at regulating corporate activities and constraining unwanted business activities. In the UK, new environmental legislation included a Clean Air Act in 1968, a Water Act in 1973 and the Control of Pollution Act in 1974. In the US, there was even more legislation:

> From 1969 through 1972, virtually the entire American business community experienced a series of political setbacks without parallel in the post-war period. In the space of only four years, Congress enacted a significant tax-reform bill, four major environmental laws,

Reproduced by kind permission of Green Books, from Sharon Beder (1997) *Global Spin*, Green Books, Tofnes *an occupational safety and health act and a series of additional consumer-protection statutes. The government also created a number of important new regulatory agencies, including the Environmental Protection Administration (EPA), the Occupational Safety and Health Administration (OSHA) and the Consumer Product Safety Commission (CPSC), investing them with broad powers over a wide range of business decisions* (Vogel, 1989, p59).

Businesses found that their past ways of dealing with government no longer sufficed. The scope of political conflict widened. '*For the first time since the 1930s, business found its political influence seriously challenged by a new set of interest groups*'(Vogel, 1989, p112). Grefe and Linsky describe the traditional business approach in their book *The New Corporate Activism*:

> *Back then, it was standard for organizations to conduct their government relations in accordance with a 'fix-it' mentality. They had a problem. They hired a lobbyist. They said, 'Fix-it!' What they meant was 'Kill it or make it go away' … It was 'influence peddling', quite simply – that is, finding the person who knew the legislator or regulator and getting him (it was always a 'him' in those days of the old-boy network) to bury the problem* (Grefe and Linsky, 1995, p2).

The First Wave of Corporate Activism in the US

In various business meetings, corporate executives lamented their decline in influence. '*The truth is that we've been clobbered*,' the Chief Executive Officer of General Motors told chiefs from other corporations. The Chairman of the Board of General Foods asked, '*How come we cannot get together and make our voices heard?*' (Vogel, 1989, p194) – which is, of course, what they did. Throughout the 1970s, US corporations became politically active, getting together to support a conservative anti-regulatory agenda and financing a vast public relations effort aimed at regaining public trust in corporate responsibility and freedom from government regulation.

According to David Vogel in his book *Fluctuating Fortunes: The Political Power of Business in America*, '*It took business about seven years to rediscover how to win in Washington*'. Once they realized how the political scene had changed, corporations began to adopt the strategies that public-interest activists had used so effectively against them – grassroots organizing and coalition building, telephone and letter-writing campaigns, using the media, research reports and testifying at hearings, '*to maximize political influence*' (Vogel, 1989, pp10–11). To these strategies, corporations added huge financial resources and professional advice. '*A new breed of public affairs professionals began emerging*' who could service corporations in their new activism (Grefe and Linski, 1995, p2):

> *For business, the turbulence of change was a nightmare of new regulations and increasingly vocal interest groups that needed pandering to. The rules of the game had changed and new ways had to be found to at once get what one needed from government, shout down the opposition and harness the power of interest groups for one's own benefit through persuasion* (Blyskal and Blyskal, 1985, p153).

They established 'public affairs' departments, increased the funding and staffing of those departments and allocated responsibility for public affairs to a senior company executive, such as a vice-president. The offices of these public affairs units were increasingly sited in Washington. Chief Executive Officers also devoted increasing amounts of their time to government relations. A survey of 400 public affairs units in large and medium-sized firms in 1981 found that most received more than US$1/2 million each year in funding and more than half had been set up after 1970 (Saloma, 1984, p67; Vogel, 1989, pp195–197).

The number of business lobbyists in Washington increased rapidly through the 1970s. By 1982, 2445 firms *'had some form of political representation in Washington'* compared with 175 in 1971. Trade associations also moved to Washington, often being restructured and given increased budgets (Vogel, 1989, p197).

> *All told, as of 1980 there were in Washington 12,000 lawyers representing business before federal regulatory agencies and the federal courts, 9,000 business lobbyists, 50,000 trade-association personnel, 8,000 public relations specialists, 1,300 public-affairs consultants and 12,000 specialized journalists reporting to particular industries on government developments affecting them. The number of individuals employed by the 'private sector industry' exceeded the number of federal employers in the Washington metropolitan area for the first time since before the New Deal* (Vogel, 1989, p198).

In response to government regulations brought on by the activities of environmentalists and public interest groups, businesses began to cooperate in a way that was unprecedented, building coalitions and alliances and putting aside competitive rivalries. This was facilitated by the introduction of legislation such as the Clean Air Act that affected large numbers of industries as opposed to one industry at a time. *'They learned to find people who were similarly situated and form ad hoc committees with these people and have a concerted, organized effort across the board of a number of industries who were similarly situated to fight the thing together'* (Vogel, 1989, p200).

Broad coalitions of business people sought to affect *'a reorientation of American politics'.* The Chamber of Commerce and the National Association of Manufacturers were resurrected and rejuvenated and new organizations such as the Business Roundtable (for large corporations) and the Small Business Legislative Council (for small businesses) were formed to lobby government. The Business Roundtable, established in 1972, consisted of the CEOs of almost 200 corporations. It *'cranked out smooth public-relations messages'* warning of the costs of environmentalism. One of the Roundtable's early successes was its opposition to the Consumer Protection Agency in which it used strategically designed polling techniques and employed a public relations firm to distribute editorials and cartoons to thousands of papers and magazines (Himmelstein, 1990, p132; Ricci, 1993, p156; Sherrill, 1990, p374).

This trend towards corporate activism could be observed in other countries too. In Australia, corporations *'substantially increased their level of resources and commitment to monitoring and influencing the political environment'*; ensured that their senior executives were effective political operatives in their dealings with politicians and bureaucrats; hired consulting firms to help with government sub-missions; and established government relations units within their companies with direct access to the Chief Executive Officer. Also, as in the US, *'concerted efforts were made to improve and centralize business representation at the national level'* so as to mobilize and increase their power (Bell and Warhurst 1992, pp58–59, Wanna, 1992, p61).

The Confederation of Australian Industry (CAI) was established in 1970 and the National Farmers Federation in 1977. The Australian Business Roundtable, modelled on the US Business Roundtable and made up of chief executives of 20 of Australia's largest companies, was founded in 1980. The Business Council of Aus-tralia was formed in 1983 by the chief executives of 66 large corporations, following what they perceived as a weak showing by business at the Economic Summit or-ganized by the newly elected Labour government. The Business Council now represents big business in Australia (Wanna, 1992, p74).

Rejuvenation of the activism of business in the US happened at a time when political power in Congress was becoming more decentralized and fragmented and party loyalty was weakening. Individual politicians were increasingly susceptible to pressure from interest groups. Whereas previously business leaders could effec-tively lobby key people in Congress, they now had to adopt a new lobbying strategy that focused on a wide number of individual members of Congress. This required organizing support in a number of electorates so that *'by 1978, corporations and trade associations were spending between US$850 million and US$900 million a year on mobilizing their supporters throughout the United States'* (Vogel, 1989, p204). Trade associations did this by organizing the owners of large numbers of small businesses to lobby their Congress representative while large corporations mobi-lized shareholders, suppliers, customers and employees.

The War of Ideas

Far more important than the money invested in political campaigns, however, was the money invested in other forms of political influence, particularly in influenc-ing the political agenda through the dissemination and selling of ideas:

> *Right-wing businessmen like Richard Mellon Scaife and Joseph Coors and conservative treasuries like the Mobil and Olin foundations, poured money into ad campaigns, law-suits, elections and books and articles protesting 'Big Government' and 'strangulation by regulation', blaming environmentalists for all the nation's ills from the energy crisis to the sexual revolution* (Sale, 1993, p49).

Corporations put large amounts of money into advertising and sponsorships aimed at improving the corporate image and putting forward corporate views. Much of this advertising was on environmental issues. One 1974 survey of 114 large compa-nies *'found that thirty to thirty-five per cent of corporate advertising addressed environmentalism, energy-related issues, or the capitalist system'*. During the mid-1970s over US$100 million was being spent each year on this sort of advocacy advertising, particularly by oil companies, electrical utility companies and the chemical industry (Vogel, 1989, p217).

The Advertising Council also became active: using funds from the US Department of Commerce, it attempted to educate the public about the benefits of free enterprise, distributing millions of booklets to schools, workplaces and communities. It blamed inflation on government regulation. The idea for this campaign came from the chairman of the board of Procter and Gamble, the largest advertiser in the US, in a speech in which he called for American people to be better educated about the free enterprise system, so that business people need not be defensive about their work (Parenti, 1986, p73, Sethi, 1977, p61).

In Australia, after the election of a 'progressive' Labour government in 1972, the Australian Chamber of Commerce reacted with a nationwide 'economic education campaign' to promote free enterprise; and in 1975 Enterprise Australia was established by the Free Enterprise Association (funded by multinational companies such as Esso, Kodak, IBM and Ford Motors) to take part in the *'propaganda warfare for capitalism'*. In 1977, the president of the Institute of Directors in Australia told his fellow directors that the Institute should, in conjunction with Enterprise Australia, *'publicise and sell the benefits of the system it espouses'* (Carey, 1995, pp87–88, 105, 112, 114).

Another area of corporate investment in the US, Britain and Australia was to support scholars whose views were compatible with the corporate view by funding them in universities or non-university research institutes, otherwise known as think-tanks. This was seen as a way of countering some of the anti-business research that was being produced in universities, particularly in the social sciences. Irving Kristol, one of those widely credited with persuading the US business community of the merits of this strategy, argued: *'You can only beat an idea with another idea and the war of ideas and ideologies will be won or lost within the 'new class', not against it'* (Vogel, 1989, p221). The 'new class' comprised people, such as government bureaucrats, academics and journalists, who dealt in ideas rather than products.

Another person who persuasively made these arguments was William Simon, head of the Olin Foundation. He argued that rather than fight each piece of legislation as it came up or spend money getting particular candidates elected, business people should foster a 'counterintelligentsia' *'in the foundations, universities and the media that would regain ideological dominance for business'*. Three of the wealthiest US foundations funded the establishment of the Institute for Educational Affairs (IEA), which was conceived by Kristol and Simon to coordinate the flow of money from corporations into the production of conservative ideas. Millions of corporate dollars were distributed each year in this way (Himmelstein, 1990, pp146, 149–150).

Corporations continued to fund the sciences and engineering, but became much more political in other university funding, endowing 40 chairs of 'free enterprise' between 1974 and 1978, to promote business values to undergraduate students at colleges perceived to be liberal. They also spent millions *'to influence the teaching of business and economics in the nation's high schools'*. They sponsored or funded educational films promoting free-market economics and screened on public television, such as Milton Friedman's series *Free to Choose* and five films on American

Enterprise supported by Phillips Petroleum Company. The Business Roundtable also sponsored economics courses in primary and secondary schools (Vogel, 1989, p 223, Saloma, 1984, p74).

In Australia, the Australian Chamber of Commerce and Enterprise Australia used surveys of school leavers to find the 'deficiencies' in their attitudes to the free enterprise system and then circulated corrective material through schools. They also produced 15 videos and films with titles such as *Profits, Advertising and The Market Economy*. Their material was made available to school resource centres with the approval of the departments of education in each state (Carey, 1995, pp112–113).

Enterprise Australia produced a series of television programmes called *Making it Together*, distributed a textbook by one of its directors entitled *The World of Business*, presented awards to young achievers and broadcast commercials promoting the benefits of free enterprise on over 100 radio stations. Business groups such as chambers of commerce, the Australian Bankers Association and the Australian Mining Industry Council ran conferences and made presentations to teachers, business people and school students (Carey, 1995, pp88, 119, 125).

Part of the aim of all this 'education' was to get people used to the idea that '*it is an appropriate part of business's role in democracy to judge what beliefs we must hold in order to be "economically educated"*'. They juxtaposed personal, political and economic freedom, arguing that constraints on economic freedom were tantamount to reducing personal and political freedom and that those who sought to '*intervene excessively in the play of market forces*', however well-intentioned they might be, posed a major threat to those freedoms. Criticism of the economic system amounted to subversion of the political system (Carey, 1995, p88, 119, 125).

Think-tanks also took a leading part in the war of ideas in various countries. In the US in particular, conservative foundations and large corporations established and/or funded a new set of think-tanks which were ideologically compatible with right-wing causes and corporate interests, promoting the free market and attacking government regulation:

> *Funded by eccentric billionaires, conservative foundations and politically motivated multinational corporations, right-wing policy entrepreneurs founded think-tanks, university centers and political journals and developed the social and political networks necessary to tie this nascent empire together. The end product was a tidal wave of money, ideas and self-promotion that carried the Reaganites to power* (Alterman, 1994, p59).

This influx of money meant not only that conservative think-tanks proliferated but that other think-tanks moved towards the right. As Jerome Himmelstein points out in his book *To the Right*: '*The political mobilization of big business in the mid-1970s gave conservatives greater access to money and channels of political influence. These helped turn conservative personnel into political leaders and advisers and conservative ideas, especially economic ones, into public policy*' (Himmelstein, 1990, pp129, 146).

In the mid-1970s the corporate-owned media announced that a conservative mood had set in. Although there was indeed a 'backlash' from conservative groups, the media exaggerated what was happening by portraying it as a widespread change in public mood. This in turn helped shape public opinion into a conservative mould. Michael Parenti, in his book on the politics of the mass media, says:

> *In discovering a 'conservative mood', the news media had to overlook a great deal about the 1970s and 1980s including the various polls conducted during that period – which showed a shift in a progressive direction (even among many who labelled themselves conservative) on issues such as military spending, environmental protection, care for the elderly, tax reform and race relations ... By crediting conservative policies with a popular support they did not have, the press did its part in shifting the political agenda in a rightward direction* (Parenti, 1986, pp91, 93).

Robert Entman, in his book *Democracy Without Citizens*, agrees that the public's policy preferences had not changed much but *'the media-fed perception that they had swung right influenced politics'*, legitimizing the conservatism of Reagan's administration and allowing him to implement a policy agenda that lacked majority support (Entman, 1989, p86). During the late 1970s and early 1980s, protest activities by environmental and other public interest groups were mostly either unreported or dismissively reported as being a hangover from the past.

Vogel argues that by 1978 US business had *'clearly regained the political initiative'* and defeated many of the regulatory measures hard won by public interest activists. They achieved the abolition of the Consumer Protection Agency, the reduction of emissions standards, the deregulation of energy prices and the lowering of corporate taxes (Vogel, 1989, p193). In the late 1970s US business was spending a billion dollars each year on propaganda of various sorts *'aimed at persuading the American public that their interests were the same as business's interests'*. The result of all this expenditure showed in the polls when the percentage of people who thought that there was too much regulation soared from 22 per cent in 1975 to 60 per cent in 1980 (Carey, 1995, p89; Parenti, 1986, p74).

Ronald Reagan, who was elected president in 1980, owed his success partly to conservative corporate interests, which he served faithfully once in power through a combination of deregulation and political appointments and by directing funding away from agencies such as the EPA. During the 1980s, under Reagan's administration, the number of trade and professional associations, corporations and interest groups with offices in Washington continued to grow. By 1985 an estimated 80,000 employees of these associations were being serviced by accountants, lobbyists, lawyers, trade paper journalists, public relations advisers, direct mail consultants, economists and think-tanks (Sale, 1993, pp49–51; Ricci, 1993, p43). It was a huge information industry and all this information was shaped and presented to promote the interests of the associations and corporations generating it.

The New Corporate Activism

Corporations managed to achieve a virtual moratorium on new environmental legislation in many countries throughout the late 1970s and most of the 1980s. However, towards the end of the 1980s public concern about the environment rose again, reinforced by scientific discoveries regarding phenomena such as ozone depletion and weather patterns that seemed to indicate that global warming had already begun. Local pollution events, such as medical waste washing up on New York beaches and sewage pollution on Sydney beaches, also contributed to the public perception of an environment in decline.

A 1989 *New York Times*/CBS poll found that 80 per cent of people surveyed agreed that '*protecting the environment is so important that standards cannot be too high and continuing environmental improvements must be made regardless of cost*'. Green parties in Europe attracted 15 per cent of the vote, while 16 per cent of Canadians surveyed said that the environment was the most important problem in Canada – more important even than unemployment – and most people felt that solving environmental problems required government action. An Australian survey found that 59 per cent of people believed that protecting the environment was more important than other issues, including the economy and 81 per cent said they were prepared to pay for environmental protection (Rowell, 1996, p22; Winward, 1991, p107; Doern and Conway, 1994, p118; Perkins, 1990, p34).

A Saulwick poll in 1990 also found that 67 per cent of people thought that Australia should '*concentrate on protecting the environment even if it means some reduction in economic growth*' (McIntosh, 1990). Similarly, a 1991 Gallup poll found that 75 per cent said that environmental protection should be given priority, '*even at the risk of curbing economic growth*'. In this poll, 80 per cent of those surveyed called themselves environmentalists (O'Keefe and Daley, 1993).

Amidst all this public concern, regulatory agencies in various countries got tougher and new laws were enacted. In the US, the highest-ever number of environmental convictions were recorded by the EPA in 1989 and half of those convicted received jail sentences. Environmental indictments by the Justice Department increased by 30 per cent in 1990 over the previous year (Harrison, 1993, p6). In New South Wales, Australia, an Environmental Offences and Penalties Act was introduced in 1989 which provided for jail terms and million dollar fines for senior executives of polluting companies.

This heightening of public anxiety in response to scientific confirmation of environmental deterioration induced a new wave of corporate political activity. This time the corporate backlash was able to utilize the techniques and organizations that had been established in the 1970s for the same purpose. With their activist machinery already in place, corporations were able to take advantage of the new PR techniques and information technologies available for raising money, building coalitions, manipulating public opinion and lobbying politicians. And this time, rather than focusing on defending the free enterprise system and opposing labour unions, the attack was primarily targeted at environmentalists. For example, in 1991 Bob Williams, a consultant to the oil and gas industry, wrote in his book *US Petroleum Strategies in the Decade of the Environment* that the industry needed '*to put the environmental lobby out of business ... There is no greater imperative ... If the petroleum industry is to survive, it must render the environmental lobby superfluous, an anachronism*' (Rowell, 1996, p71). Similarly, Ron Arnold, another industry consultant, told a meeting of the Ontario Forest Industries Association: '*You must turn the public against environmentalists or you will lose your environmental battle as surely as the US timber industry has lost theirs'* (O'Callaghan, 1992, p86).

Frank Mankiewicz, a senior executive at transnational PR firm Hill and Knowlton, observed:

> *The big corporations, our clients, are scared shitless of the environmental movement …*
> *They sense that there's a majority out there and that the emotions are all on the other*
> *side – if they can be heard. They think the politicians are going to yield up to the emo-*
> *tions. I think the corporations are wrong about that. I think the companies will have to*
> *give in only at insignificant levels. Because the companies are too strong, they are the*
> *establishment. The environmentalists are going to have to be like the mob in the square*
> *in Romania before they prevail* (Greider, 1992, p24).

Having observed the rise in environmental consciousness and the defensiveness of US industry, C J Silas, CEO for Phillips Petroleum Company, wrote in *Public Affairs Journal* at the beginning of 1990: '*There's no reason we cannot make the environmental issue our issue. If we wait to be told what to do – if we offer no initiatives of our own and react defensively – we're playing not to lose and that is not good enough*' (Silas, 1990, p34).

During the 1990s the application of public relations to environmental concerns really came into its own. Environmentalism was labelled 'the life and death PR battle of the 1990s' and 'the issue of the decade' by public relations personnel. Activist Brian Tokar suggests that the rise in environmental PR was because, with the collapse of communism in many parts of the world, '*the growth of ecological awareness in the industrialized countries may be one of the last internal obstacles to the complete hegemony of transnational corporate capitalism*' (Nelson, 1993, p27).

The coalition building which began in the 1970s continues to grow. A survey of 30 of the largest firms in the US found that each firm was involved in an average of 5.7 coalitions such as the Business Roundtable; most of them '*formed for legislative and regulatory purposes and focused primarily on national issues*' such as the environment. More than a third of the corporations surveyed spend over a million dollars each year on '*coalition activity*' (Bovet, 1994).

Some corporations have gone beyond their corporate allies in their organizing efforts, hiring specialized public relations firms to set up front groups that promote the corporate agenda but pose as public interest groups. Public relations firms also have become adept at creating the impression of grassroots support for corporate causes so as to convince politicians to oppose environmental reforms. A 1992 survey by the US Public Affairs Council found that 73 per cent of the 163 large companies surveyed had a senior executive responsible for grassroots organizing, a newly acquired responsibility growing at a rate second only to environmental affairs (Grefe and Linsky, 1995, p244). There are now also several firms in the US which specialize in creating grassroots support for industry causes.

Industry interests have been able to turn the disaffection of rural and resource industry workers, farmers and small business people into anti-environmental sentiment. Nowhere has this been more spectacularly achieved than in the US with its Wise Use Movement. The Wise Use Movement has attained grassroots support by enrolling thousands of people who are worried about their future and feel individually powerless to do anything about it. A similar coalition has been formed in Canada, called the Share Movement and elements of this type of movement are spreading to Australia.

Those who oppose undesirable developments and unfettered resource extraction are now finding that they are not only subject to the abuse of industry-funded anti-environmental groups, but they are also vulnerable to a new wave of law suits filed against them for exercising their democratic rights to circulate petitions, write to public officials, attend public meetings, organize boycotts and engage in peaceful demonstrations. Every year thousands of environmentalists and ordinary citizens are sued for speaking out against governments and corporations.

Corporate political donations have also increased. Organizations involved in influencing environmental legislation in the US since 1989 have included the American Farm Bureau Federation, which has contributed almost US$1 million to congressional candidates between 1989 and 1994 in its efforts to get the Clean Water Act controls on factory farms removed – the Republicans have introduced a bill that does just that. Oil corporation and land developer Chevron Corporation, which is a member of the Alliance for Reasonable Regulation, has spent over US$1 million on congressional candidates during the same period and managed to introduce the concept of 'plausible risk' into the same bill so that acceptable toxicity levels would be reduced. According to the EPA's Toxics Release Inventory, Chevron releases millions of pounds of toxic material into the environment each year (Levathes, 1995, p18).

Exxon, with a similar annual discharge of toxic material, has also been a member of the Alliance for Reasonable Regulation and also spent over US$1 million in that same period on lobbying congressional candidates in its efforts to prevent the Clean Air Act being strengthened. Dow Chemical and its affiliates have also given over US$1 million and opposed the strengthening of the Clean Air Act, as well as pushing for cost-benefit analysis to be incorporated into the Clean Water Act. Chevron, Exxon and Dow Chemical all give financial support to a range of front groups, including the Alliance to Keep Americans Working, the American Council on Science and Health, and the National Wetlands Coalition (Levathes, 1995, p19; Megalli and Friedman, 1991, p184).

In Europe, lobbyists and corporate consultants are flocking to Brussels to influence policy-making by the European Parliament:

> *Leading the most recent wave of arrivals are large US law firms with strong Washington, DC, lobbying experience. They join an international armada of advocates already active in Brussels, including ... public relations groups, confederations of European trade associations, representatives of US states, German lander and British municipalities, small 'boutique' consultancies, in-house representatives of individual US, European and Japanese companies, European trade unions, agricultural groups and a growing number of public-interest associations* (Gardner, 1991).

Conservative think-tanks, having been instrumental in bringing Ronald Reagan to power in the US and Margaret Thatcher to power in the UK, have turned their attention to environmental issues and the defeat of environmental regulations. They have sought to cast doubt on the very features of the environmental crisis that had heightened public concerns at the end of the 1980s, including ozone depletion, greenhouse warming and industrial pollution.

Think-tanks have opposed environmental legislation in a variety of ways. In the US they have attempted to hamstring the regulatory process by advocating legislation which would ensure that regulatory efforts become too expensive and difficult to implement, by insisting on cost-benefit analyses and risk assessments of proposed legislation, and compensation to state governments and property owners for the costs of complying with the legislation. Throughout the Western world, these think-tanks have promoted free-market techniques such as tradable property and pollution rights, pricing mechanisms, tax incentives and voluntary agreements for dealing with environmental degradation. These have been taken seriously by governments and in some cases accepted by environmentalists as a valid alternative to tougher legislation.

Corporations have also turned their attention to the next generation, through the development and distribution of 'educational' material to schools. The potential to shape environmental perceptions and improve corporate images at the same time has attracted many customers to the firms designing educational materials for corporations. These materials inevitably give a corporate view of environmental problems and avoid solutions that would involve reduced consumption, increased regulation or reduced corporate profits.

The combination of activist techniques and corporate money is a powerful weapon in the battle of ideas. In the US, opinion polling indicates corporate-funded anti-environmental efforts produced a major shift in public opinion within the space of a single year. In 1992, 51 per cent of those surveyed agreed that environmentalists had 'gone too far', compared with 17 per cent the year before (Rowell, 1996, p22).

Andrew Rowell, in his book *Green Backlash*, dates the arrival of the anti-environmentalist backlash in Britain as spring 1995, when the media took up the 'anti-green tune' and a number of books were published that attacked environmentalism. These included a book by Richard North whose research, according to Rowell, was funded by British chemical company ICI and another published by the Conservative UK think-tank, the Institute of Economic Affairs (Rowell, 1996, p320).

The corporate muscle of multinational (also known as transnational) corporations is formidable. In 1995, the UN Conference on Trade and Development (UNCTAD) reported that these corporations – 40,000 of them – controlled two-thirds of the world's trade in goods and services (Raghavan, 1995, p31). According to *New Internationalist* magazine in 1993:

> *The combined sales of the world's largest 350 multinationals total nearly one third of the combined gross national products of all industrialized countries and exceed the individual gross national products of all Third World countries* (Anon, 1993, p18).

Many of the largest multinational corporations are headquartered in the US and it is not surprising that the strategies they have pioneered there to combat environmental regulations are now being used in other countries. The remainder of this chapter looks at the implications for democracy of this second wave of corporate activism.

Declining Democracy

Surveys show that the majority of people in most countries are not only concerned about the environment; they think environmental protection should be regulated by governments and given priority over economic growth (Dunlap et al, 1993). Yet this widespread public concern is not translating into government action because of the activities of large corporations that are seeking to subvert or manipulate the popular will.

A recent *ABC News/Washington Post* survey, for instance, found that nearly three-quarters of people in the US didn't think government was doing enough to protect the environment; an *NBC News/Wall Street Journal* survey found that a majority of respondents wanted environmental regulations strengthened (compared to less than one in five people who thought they should be weakened). Similarly, a *Time/CNN* poll found that a majority of people wanted environmental expenditure by government increased, with only 16 per cent wanting it reduced. A Harris survey found that most people would be willing to pay more taxes and higher prices if the money was spent 'to protect and restore endangered species'. And a Gallup poll in 1995 found that two-thirds of people agreed that 'protection of the environment should be given a priority, even at the risk of curbing economic growth', a result mirrored in a 1994 *Times Mirror* magazines survey (Pettinico, 1995, p28–30; Rockland and Fletcher, 1994).

Despite such public opinion, the Republican-dominated Congress has actually been dismantling and weakening existing environmental regulations, with devastating consequences for the environment. *The Economist* recently reported an OECD study that found the environment was deteriorating in the US:

> *Wetlands, good for wildlife, are being mopped up by developers; extinctions are increasing ... Municipal waste accumulates: each American now jettisons 2kg of rubbish a day, more than any other people on earth. Nuclear waste and used nuclear fuel pile up in temporary stores. The number of vehicles on the roads has doubled since 1970 and drivers cover twice as many miles ... Some 15 per cent of rivers and 10 per cent of lakes are still too grubby for people to swim or fish in. Some 59m people still live in areas where the air is dirtier than the government thinks safe. And the United States remains the world's largest producer of carbon dioxide, which may be causing global warming* (Anon, 1995a).

Yet the corporate-generated Congressional attack on environmental legislation goes on relentlessly. Industry groups have used their lobbyists, their political contributions, their coalitions and front groups to achieve this result:

> *Lobbyists for the coalitions have provided staff to Republican lawmakers, drafted parts of bills and sat on the dais with congressmembers during committee meetings; they even*

set up an office adjacent to the House floor to write amendments during the floor debate
last March ... 267 political action committees (dubbed the Dirty Water PACs because
of their anti-environmental agenda) contributed US$57 million to political candidates
between 1989 and 1994 (Levathes, 1995, p16).

The pattern of public concern and government inaction is repeated in other countries. For example, whilst Australians are among the world's most environmentally
concerned people, their government's environmental record is one of the worst for
OECD countries. A 1994 *Sydney Morning Herald* Saulwick poll found that 57 per
cent of people surveyed thought environmental protection should have a higher
priority than economic growth (Beale, 1994a; Southam, 1994, p28), while a New
South Wales EPA survey, which also found high levels of environmental concern,
discovered a '*strong community perception that the politicians are out of touch with*
voters on environmental issues' (Beale, 1994b, p7a).

The London-based New Economics Foundation, in comparing the environmental
performance of 21 OECD countries, found that Australia, Canada and the US were
at the bottom of the list, with Australia at number 18, Canada at 20 and the US last
at 21 (the UK was at number 10). Australians rivalled Americans in terms of gar-
bage production and carbon dioxide emissions per head. Australia also scored badly,
as did the US, on energy efficiency, species extinctions and private vehicle use
(Southam, 1994, p28). The influence of the industrial lobby in Australia is clearest
on the greenhouse issue, where the government relies on coal and mining industry-
funded studies in its decision-making. This led to the situation where the Australian
government lobbied (unsuccessfully) to obstruct an international climate agreement
in Berlin in 1995, even after the US supported it (Gilchrist, 1995). In 1997, Australia continued to lobby Japan and other countries to oppose European proposals
for uniform international greenhouse gas reductions.

The media can give a distorted impression of public opinion on environmental
and other issues. Michael Parenti, in his book *Inventing Reality: The Politics of the*
Mass Media, argues:

> *Public opinion is not just an expression of sentiment; it is a democratic power resource*
> *that sometimes constrains and directs policymakers who otherwise spend their time*
> *responding to the demands and enticements of moneyed interests ... The media short-*
> *circuit the process by which public preference may otherwise be translated into*
> *government policy* (Parenti, 1986, p93).

The gap between what the majority wants and what government delivers would seem
to indicate a failure of democracy. Yet, ironically, the corporate subversion of the
green movement has been a response to the effective exercise of democratic power
by citizens and environmental activists two decades earlier. Although robber barons
of a much earlier era like William Vanderbilt could declare '*The public be damned!*'
(Seitel, 1995, p32), modern corporate executives cannot afford to take this attitude.

Alex Carey, author of *Taking the Risk out of Democracy*, argued that the 20th
century has seen three related developments: '*the growth of democracy, the growth of*
corporate power and the growth of corporate propaganda as a means of protecting

corporate power against democracy' (Carey, 1995, p18). Similarly, Noam Chomsky argues in his book *Necessary Illusions*:

> *In the democratic system, the necessary illusions cannot be imposed by force. Rather, they must be instilled in the public mind by more subtle means. A totalitarian state can be satisfied with lesser degrees of allegiance to required truths. It is sufficient that people obey; what they think is of secondary concern. But in a democratic political order, there is always the danger that independent thought might be translated into political action, so it is important to eliminate the threat at its root* (Chomsky, 1989, p48).

Corporate Power

Corporate power has various dimensions. Traditionally, it has been institutional-ized in government decision-making structures as a result of the importance of corporate investment to economic growth and the provision of employment. Indi-vidual companies can threaten to withdraw that investment if they do not get their way. It is in the interests of government, therefore, to negotiate and consult exten-sively with corporate representatives on all policy matters that may affect them. This gives corporations privileged access to government policy-making. In many countries such as Britain and Australia, '*policy-making occurs not so much in par-liament or indeed even in cabinet, but in a more decentralized pattern of policy* communities *involving institutionalized interaction between key departments, rel-evant statutory authorities, advisory committees and a range of select, client interest groups*' (Wanna, 1992, p105).

Clearly the bargaining power that any particular company can exercise will depend on its size, the number of people it employs, its ability to move offshore and the state of the economy in the country where the company is exercising that power (Bell, 1992, p51). The more that corporations can cooperate and present a coherent and united political agenda, the more power they will have. The degree of corporate influence can fluctuate over time and in the late 1960s and 1970s corpo-rate power was particularly weak. However, since that time corporations have consciously built coalitions, set aside individual differences and become more politically active and consequently more powerful.

Another traditional form of influence has been through financial contributions to parties and candidates; it costs millions of dollars just to run for office in the US, and most of that comes from corporations, including 70 per cent of contribu-tions to the Democrat and the Republican parties (Carothers, 1993, p15). In the UK, corporate donations seem to account for over half of all donations to the Con-servative Party (£4.3 million out of £7.3 million in 1992–1993). But donations don't have to be made public; almost two-thirds of donations received between 1987 and 1991 cannot be traced to their donors by outsiders to the party. According to Paul Anderson and Nyta Mann in the *New Statesman & Society* in 1994:

> *The Tories' finances are one of the great unsolved mysteries of British politics ... What is known about the Tories is that they have received substantial sums from companies*

and individuals with commercial interests in government spending and policy decisions. The big corporate donors of the past fifteen years include defence, engineering and construction companies that have benefited from large government contracts, tobacco companies that want to prevent legal constraints on advertising their products and privatized utilities (Anderson and Mann, 1994).

In Australia, business directly sponsors political party campaigns rather than individual candidates and the major parties, Labour, Liberal and National, receive the majority of their financial support in this way (Wanna, 1992, p71).

However, politicians are concerned with getting re-elected and this means that public opinion matters. Citizens generally do not like the idea that government is run to suit those with economic power and resources. With the rise of public interest groups in the 1960s and 1970s, the closed policy-making arrangements between industry and government were 'forced open' and governments had to listen to other voices. Environmental groups and others gathered their own information, some of it from government files using Freedom of Information Acts. This information could be used effectively in hearings and in the media and decision-makers learned to take account of a greater range of interests and to justify their decisions on rational grounds (Ricci, 1993, p8, 152–153; Gellner, 1995, p501; Greider, 1992, p47).

This need for 'rational' decisions meant that bureaucrats '*churned out an endless stream of statistics, reports, hearings, bulletins, journals, rulings, proposals, statements, press reports and other forms of information*' on every issue (Ricci, 1993, p41). Politicians were now exposed to a far greater range of information from more sources and had to appear to be making informed decisions. A new market was thus created for a particular kind of information which enabled politicians to justify decisions that were often still being influenced by financial donations and corporate pressure (Greider, 1992, p50).

In response, the major corporations opened up public affairs offices. Public relations firms, lobbyists and think-tanks proliferated, shaping and moulding information and manufacturing expertise on behalf of their clients and offering it to the politicians. Although caught somewhat off-guard at first, in many ways the move towards information-based decisions has suited business interests because of their ability to hire experts – scientists, economists and statisticians – and their fear of losing the 'emotional' battle.

Clearly not all interest groups have equal resources at their disposal and in their efforts to persuade government some groups have more bargaining power, time, resources and energy (Johnson, 1993, pp98-99). As William Greider asks in his book *Who Will Tell the People: The Betrayal of American Democracy*, '*Who can afford to show up at all these public hearings? Who will be able to deploy their own lawyers or scientists or economists to testify expertly on behalf of their agenda? Who is going to hire the lobbyists to track the legislative debate at every laborious stage? Most citizens do not qualify*' (Greider, 1992, p50). Public-interest groups, such as environmental groups, find it impossible to keep up with all the public hearings and submissions.

Corporations clearly have far greater financial resources at their disposal. As pressure groups, they can invest millions of dollars into grassroots organizing, polls, lawyers, computer and satellite technology, video news releases and professional advice to put their case directly to politicians and government officials, and to garner public support.

The greater power of corporations in a democratic system has long been recognized. In 1978 an effort to regulate the amount of money that corporations could spend on propaganda was defeated in the US Supreme Court. A dissenting judge observed:

> *Corporations are artificial entities created by law for the purpose of furthering certain economic goals. It has long been recognized, however, that the special status of corporations has placed them in a position to control vast amounts of economic power which may, if not regulated, dominate not only the economy but also the very heart of our democracy, the electoral process* (Carey, 1995, p105).

Since that time, corporations have indeed set out to use their economic power to dominate the machinery of democracy. Greider argues that a new industry has emerged in Washington that he calls '*democracy for hire*'. He says this involves the packaging and sale of democratic expression and '*guarantees the exclusion of most Americans from the debate*' (Greider, 1993, pp8–9; Greider, 1992). He points out that:

> *Only those who have accumulated lots of money are free to play in this version of democracy ... Modern methodologies of persuasion have created a new hierarchy of influence over government decisions – a new way in which organized money dominates the action while the unorganized voices of citizens are inhibited from speaking* (Greider, 1992, pp35–36).

The traditional pluralist account of competing interest groups gives a veneer of democratic respectability to what is in reality a corporate rout: '*The steady diffusion of authority has simply multiplied the opportunities for power to work its will ... pluralist deal-making continues in the guise of governing – but now the entrenched monied interests are back in charge of the marketplace, running the tables in the grand bazaar*' (Greider, 1992, pp108–109). Governments, rather than weighing the demands of various interests, are less and less responsive to public opinion and more and more influenced by these corporations and monied interests.

A primary assumption of democracy is that there is no collusion of interests between government and the groups trying to lobby them, but in practice this is not the case. During the 1980s a close and at times unethical relationship developed in the US between lobbyists and the Reagan administration:

> *Members of Congress worked in tandem with lobbyists to generate 'grassroots' support for pet issues. Lobbyists formed coalitions to support the White House's favorite issues. The White House recruited lobbyists to help with controversial appointees needing Senate confirmation. The Congressional committees or the White House Commissions that were supposed to be looking out for the people's interests, who were to oversee the agencies, who were to clean up the 'messes' when discovered, worked with and were often comprised of lobbyists and publicists. The very organizations*

designed to protect America from an abusive system had become part of the system
(Roschwalb, 1994, p270).

Yet despite their huge influence, or perhaps because of it, there is almost no government scrutiny or regulation of lobbying activities (Carlisle, 1993, p25). John
Stauber, editor of *PR Watch*, says: '*The corporate flacks, hacks, lobbyists and influence peddlers, the practitioners of modern PR ... have become a kind of occupation
army in our democracy*' (Montague, 1993).

The revolving-door syndrome further weakens the separation between government and corporate interests. The creation of a senior executive service in the US
and in countries like Australia has enabled business people and those whom they
have funded in think-tanks to penetrate the top layers of government bureaucracy.
Each new administration appoints the top levels of the agencies and departments
such as State, Defense and Treasury. These appointments often come from the corporate sector, '*corporate leaders who sever their numerous directorships to serve in
government for two or three years, then return to the corporate community in a same
or different capacity*' (Domhoff, 1985, p21). In Australia they retain their corporate
shareholdings whilst in government unless there is an obvious conflict of interest
with their ministerial duties. In any case, it is unlikely that they lose their corporate perspective during their period of office.

Similarly, senior bureaucrats and politicians are often employed by corporations, think-tanks, the media and lobbying firms when they lose office or retire from
it. In Australia, key politicians from the previous Labour government have moved
into organizations such as the plastics industry Trade Association and into consultancies which help developers gain government approval for environmentally
damaging projects. To have this opportunity, these former government officials need
to service corporate interests whilst in office. The same is true of top public servants. Similarly, in the US, there is a regular flow of personnel between government
administrations and think-tanks, the media and public relations firms. Some think-
tanks, such as the Heritage Foundation, actively select and train young people with
this in mind. Robert Sherrill, in the fifth edition of his well-used university text
Why They Call it Politics: A Guide to America's Government, points out:

> *The revolving door between government and industry is oiled by money. Former high-
> level bureaucrats and politicians leave government to become well-paid lobbyists for big
> business – often the same big-business elements that they were allegedly regulating when
> they entered government. (Many were alumni of big business at the time they entered
> government; revolving doors, after all, do go in a circle)* (Sherrill, 1990, p363).

The shareholdings of politicians provide another mechanism by which corporate
interests are protected. In 1996 there was a major controversy in Australia over the
shareholdings of the newly elected Liberal government (Gordon and Megalogenis,
1996, p1) and their potential to create conflicts of interest. However, this seems to
be accepted practice in the UK where, in 1995, 389 out of 566 MPs had registered
financial interests '*in outside bodies, directly related to being an MP*' (Rowell, 1996,
p78). Liberal Democrat MP David Alton noted:

Prime Ministers soon find solace in directorships and consultancies outside government. On the backbenches the same holds true. One hundred and thirty-five Conservative MPs hold 287 directorships and 146 consultancies between them and the other parties are not immune. Twenty-nine Labour members share sixty directorships and forty-three consultancies; while Liberal Democrats hold a total of fifteen (Rowell, 1996, p78).

The UK adds another dimension to the relationship between business and government by enabling big corporate donors to have their directors knighted; they may subsequently be placed in the House of Lords, where they become part of the legislative system. According to Alton, a donation of more than £500,000 has a 50 per cent chance of earning a knighthood for a company director (Rowell, 1996, p80).

Close relationships between politicians and industry executives can affect environmental legislation in other ways. Not only do politicians find their way on to corporate boards during and after their terms in government, but industry executives are also often placed on government committees where they can help make and implement government policy. In 1995 Sir Ron Dearing, director of the corporation IMI, which donated £30,000 to the Tories in 1993, was appointed chairman of the National Curriculum Council; he was recently responsible for a report into higher education in the UK (Anderson and Mann, 1994).

In 1995 the UK committee which set pollution limits for the cement industry had a membership that included people from the British Cement Association, the British Association of Cement Manufacturers, British Pre-Cast Concrete Federation, ARC Southern, Castle Cement, Pioneer Aggregates and the British Ready Mixed Concrete Association (Anon, 1995b). Two years later a House of Commons Select Committee, set up following public concerns about the increased use by cement kilns of industrial waste as a fuel source, found that the control of cement kiln emissions by the Environment Agency had been, according to *New Scientist*, 'lax and secretive' (Anon, 1997, p11).

The close relationship between corporations and governments is especially important when it comes to the implementation of laws. Once a law is enacted, politicians feel satisfied that they have been seen to be doing something and the media spotlight tends to be removed. Yet it is then that the real negotiations begin. In Washington, for example, tens of thousands of lawyers, lobbyists, trade associations, consultants and business people then engage in a struggle '*over the content of federal regulations – the precise meaning that will flow from the laws that Congress has enacted*' (Greider, 1992, p107).

Covert Power

The structural power of corporations through their ownership and control of a large part of any modern nation's economy and their power as a highly resourced and powerful pressure group with close ties to government, are supplemented by a third form of power which is far more covert: the power to set the political agenda and shape perceptions (Bell, 1992, p47). Corporations seek not only to influence legislation and regulation but also to define the agenda – what it is legitimate for government to consider and what can be discussed in the political arena – thereby rendering those groups who have other agendas ineffective. '*Everybody is compelled to work within a system of values and institutional rules which restricts the formal political process to making the current system work, even though the system only benefits the few*' (Williamson, 1989, p57). Even the defeats suffered by individual corporations can be seen as '*set within a wider political context – an outer frame-work – which invariably serves the system needs of capitalism*' (Bell, 1992, p56).

Setting the agenda means deciding not only what will be discussed, but also what will not be. Covert power covers the area of 'non-decisions' as well as decisions (Ball and Millard, 1986, p24). For example, environmental issues can be debated so long as the system of decision-making that gives autonomy to corporations to decide what they produce and how they produce it is maintained. Decision-making and political debate is therefore confined to the relatively safe areas of waste discharge, packaging and product safety. So effective is the manufacture of the new corporate consensus that many have accepted the assumption that unless corporations are happy, then the economy will suffer and the working and the poor will be worse off. '*For the homeless in the streets, then, the highest priority must be to ensure that the dwellers in the mansions are reasonably content*' (Chomsky, 1989, p22).

Corporations use their economic power and resources to shape public opinion through the think-tanks, public relations and propaganda. But this shaping is designed to go unnoticed, '*to alter perception, reshape reality and manufacture consent*' (Dowie, 1995, p2) without their targets being even aware that it is happening. Says one PR executive: '*You never know when a PR agency is being effective; you'll just find your views slowly shifting*' (Stauber and Rampton, 1995, p14).

Corporations also use institutions such as the media to shape cultural understandings, meanings and values and '*if not usurping the whole of ideological space, still significantly limiting what is thought throughout the society*' (Ryan, 1991, p18). True democracy would require easy access for all points of view to be communicated with mass audiences on topics of debate, but the media portrays a very restricted range of views. 'Photo opportunities' and spectacles replace lively political debate (Kellner, 1990, p94).

Education is another obvious arena in which to shape public perceptions and cultural expectations. Through pervasive advertising on television and in schools and through specially designed educational materials distributed to schools, corporations have quite consciously set about ensuring that future generations are big consumers, share corporate values and view environmental problems from a corporate point of view. Advertising and the television programming it supports also reinforce the idea that personal, social and environmental problems can be solved through purchasing corporate products and services.

Democracy has become dominated by a vast information industry aimed at attaining the consent of the public to the goals and values of those who can best afford the experts:

> *The ascendancy of the PR industry and the collapse of American participatory democracy are the same phenomenon. The growing concentration of economic power in fewer and fewer hands, combined with sophisticated marketing techniques and radical new*

electronic technologies, have come together in the past decade to fundamentally re-shape our social and political landscape ... (Montague, 1993).

The aim is not to eliminate debate or prevent controversy, because controversy reinforces the perception of a healthy democracy. What is important is the power to limit the subject, scope and boundaries of the controversy (Chomsky, 1989, p48).

This results in, and is reinforced by, minimal differences between major political parties. In the US, Britain and Australia there has been a merging of agendas and a decline in difference between parties (Sherrill, 1990, p351). The sameness of the parties, the emptiness of the campaign rituals and commercials and the feeling that their votes don't count for much, has contributed to massive voter apathy in the US and Britain, where voting is voluntary.

At a time of rising citizen participation in environmental and public interest groups, less than half of US citizens even bother to vote. At the regional and local level a candidate usually only needs 20–30 per cent of the votes of the eligible electorate to get elected. At the 1994 Congressional elections when the Republicans gained a majority, only a third of those eligible to vote did so. Even among those who vote, apathy is high. One survey found that only 10 per cent of those who voted thought their vote made a difference and only 17 per cent thought the election was important (Stauber and Rampton, 1995, p78; Tokar, 1995, p155; Sherrill 1990, pp359–360).

In the UK, participation in general elections tends to be higher – generally, between 70 and 80 per cent. However *Freedom's Children*, a 1995 study by Helen Wilkinson and Geoff Mulgan of UK voters between 18 and 35 years old, found that young people are increasingly alienated from party politics. They are less likely to register to vote than older people, *'less likely to vote for or join a political party and less likely to be politically active'*:

> *The overwhelming story emerging from our research, both quantitative and qualitative, is of an historic political disconnection. In effect, an entire generation has opted out of party politics* (Smith, 1996).

Whilst they are concerned about particular issues, including the environment, they do not see that voting for a particular party will do much to address them.

The Media and Democracy

The media's bland diet of superficial material does not encourage participation in the political process, but rather depoliticizes the audience. Political scientist Lance Bennett argues that the *'parade of disjointed spectacles'* that fill news programmes *'relegate citizens to spectator roles, leaving a residue of powerlessness after the drama and entertainment of the moment have faded'* (Bennett, 1992, p402). This is done by avoiding larger questions of power and institutional reform, by focusing on individual actors, appealing to the *'concerns of individual viewers'* and severing the connection between political information (as received from the media) and political organization and participation (Bennett, 1992, p404). The media present politics *'as a depressing spectacle rather than as a vital activity in which citizens can and should be engaged'* (Rosen, 1996).

Television, in particular, tends to depoliticize its viewers by filling their time with mindless passive entertainment which portrays the existing system of free enterprise and consumption as generally beneficial and gives only limited air play to protest groups, usually the more moderate of these. The TV entertainment format tends to shorten viewers' attention spans, so that they have less patience for listening to ideas that take a while to explain (Kellner, 1990, p105; Ricci, 1993, p88).

Joe Saltzman, an editor of *USA Today*, argues that the media practice of replacing complex information with symbols, images and catchwords, has trained the audience to want nothing else and that this threatens democracy:

> *Citizens become conditioned to respond to the facile stereotype, to the symbols they trust or fear and they become incapable of understanding and acting on real debate and questioning. They even grow to resent such discussion, wanting instead a quick fix, a fast image, an easy-to-grasp phrase* (Saltzman, 1989, p87).

'The overwhelming conclusion is that the media generally operate in ways that promote apathy, cynicism and quiescence, rather than active citizenship and participation' (Gamson et al, 1992, p373). Writing about the British media in his book *Packaging Politics*, Bob Franklin notes that most citizens glean their political knowledge from the media, but at the same time the media packaging of politics has emphasized *'image and appearance'* and the reduction of political discourse to sound bites. Audiences have therefore grown *'increasingly sceptical, uninterested and cynical about media presentations of politics'*. This has resulted in *'an increasingly widespread lack of interest in politics'*:

> *In media democracy, politics (like football) has become an armchair activity. Watching the match from a ringside seat at home has replaced the need to play the game. Participation in a media democracy is essentially ersatz and vicarious* (Franklin, 1994, p11).

Similarly, Jacobson and Mazur, from the Centre for the Study of Commercialism, argue that television undermines democracy:

> *Democracy demands an informed citizenry; TV reduces information to oversimplified factoids. Democracy demands involvement; television keeps us glued to the couch. Democracy depends on the freedom of the press; television is controlled by a handful of private interests. Democracy thrives in strong communities; television keeps us isolated in our separate living rooms* (Jacobson and Mazur, 1995, pp47–48).

At the same time that the media are turning the public away from politics, politicians increasingly are using the media, rather than the public, *'as a source of issues and as a source of support'*. The media have become the most significant audience for politicians (Ryan, 1991, pp7, 130). Noam Chomsky divides the media into 'mass popular' and 'élite'. The latter, for example the *New York Times* and the *Washington Post*, are aimed at decision-makers – the *'more educated, wealthy, articulate part of the population*' (Szykowny, 1991, p28). Of the mass popular media, Chomsky says:

> For the large mass of the population, I suspect that the main impact of television comes not through the news but through mechanisms to divert their attention. That means network programming – everything from sports to sitcoms to fanciful pictures of the way life is 'supposed' to be. Anything that has the effect of isolating people – keeping them separated from one another and focused on the tube – will make people passive observers ... The role of the public, then, is to be spectators, not participants; their role is just to watch and occasionally to ratify (Szykowny, 1991, p28).

Implications for Environmentalism

Nevertheless, the media plays a part in creating mass movements through its ability to present images of protest and alternative lifestyles to masses of people. No matter how negatively it portrays such groups and their leaders, it cannot prevent people from being attracted to the values and lifestyles of those being portrayed. In the 1960s, television *'might have inadvertently advanced counter-cultural and radical values'* (Kellner, 1990, p119).

The periodic emergence of counter-cultural movements and strong public activism is a sign that even the underlying realm of cultural understandings and meanings is fluid and changeable. This fluidity and changeability means that the opportunity to break free from corporate definitions of what is possible and feasible is always there. John Stauber and Sheldon Rampton, in their book *Toxic Sludge is Good For You!: Lies, Damn Lies and the Public Relations Industry*, put their faith for the future in the emergence of a new, genuine, democratic movement. They say that the existence of such a vast public relations industry *'proves it is possible. The fact that corporations and governments feel compelled to spend billions of dollars every year manipulating the public is a perverse tribute to human nature and our own moral values'* (Stauber and Rampton, 1995, p206).

But to influence the covert realm of cultural constructions and ideology requires going beyond the superficial jockeying for influence that occurs in the realm of policy debate. Environmentalists, particularly those in the major environmental groups, tend to concentrate their efforts in the public realm of pressure-group politics and ignore the ideological sphere where corporations set the agenda. It is in this ideological sphere that environmentalists need to devote their energies if they want to win.

Jim Hightower argues in *Earth Island Journal* that environmentalists are not doing much good as lobbyists in Washington, where the boundaries of the debate and its rules of etiquette are already clearly drawn:

> We've simply got to get the hogs out of the creek. As Aunt Eula knew, this is not a chore to undertake in your best trousers, politely pleading: 'Here hog, here hog ... pretty please.' To get hogs out of the creek, you have to put your shoulders to them – and shove ... Yet most national environmental organisations today are indeed dressed

in their Sunday trousers, engaged in the soft-hands work of lawyers and lobbyists in Washington, sincerely but futilely attempting to negotiate the relative positions of hogs (Hightower, 1995, p32).

A new wave of environmentalism is now called for: one that will engage in the task of exposing corporate myths and methods of manipulation. One that opens up new areas and ideas to public debate rather than following an old agenda set by corporations.

References

Alterman, Eric (1994) 'Fighting Smart', *Mother Jones*, vol 19, no 4, pp59–61

Anderson, Paul and Mann, Nyta (1994) 'A Cure of Sleaze?', *New Statesman & Society*, vol 7, no 327, pp14–16

Anon (1993) 'Going Global', *New Internationalist*, August, pp18–19

Anon (1995a) 'Environmental Policy: Could Try Harder', *The Economist*, 21 October, pp32–33

Anon (1995b) 'Cement Mixers', Campaigns and Updates, *The Ecologist*, November–December, p2

Anon (1997) 'Soft on Cement', *New Scientist*, 15 March, p11

Ball, Alan R and Millard, Frances (1986) *Pressure Groups and the Distribution of Power: A Comparative Introduction*, Macmillan, London

Beale, Bob (1994a) 'Most Say Environment More Important than Economy', *Sydney Morning Herald*, 12 April

Beale, Bob (1994b) 'We're All Going Green', *Sydney Morning Herald*, 11 June, p7a

Bell, Stephen and Warhurst, John (1992) 'Political Activism Among Large Firms', in S Bell and J Wanna (eds) *Business-Government Relations in Australia*, Harcourt Brace Jovanovich, Sydney

Bennett, W Lance (1992) 'White Noise: The Perils of Mass Mediated Democracy', *Communication Monographs*, no 59, December, pp401–406

Blyskal, Jeff and Marie (1985) *PR: How the Public Relations Industry Writes the News*, William Morrow and Co, New York

Bovet, Susan Fry (1994) 'Leading Companies Turn to Trade Associations for Lobbying', *Public Relations Journal*, vol 50, no 7, pp13–14

Carey, Alex (1995) *Taking the Risk Out of Democracy*, A Lohrey (ed) UNSW Press, Sydney

Carlisle, Johan (1993) 'Public Relationships: Hill and Knowlton, Robert Gray and the CIA', *CovertAction*, no 44, pp19–25

Carothers, Andre (1993) 'The Green Machine', *New Internationalist*, August, pp14–16

Chomsky, Noam (1989) *Necessary Illusions: Thought Control in Democratic Societies*, Pluto Press, London

Doern, G Bruce and Conway, Thomas (1994) *The Greening of Canada: Federal Institutions and Decisions*, University of Toronto Press, Toronto

Domhoff, G William (1985) 'The Power Elite and Government' in G McKenna and S Feingold (eds) *Taking Sides: Clashing Views on Controversial Political Issues*, Dushkin Publishing Group, Guildford, Connecticut

Dowie, Mark (1995) 'Introduction: Torches of Liberty', in J Stauber and S Rampton (eds) *Toxic Sludge is Good For You! Lies, Damn Lies and the Public Relations Industry*, Common Courage Press, Monroe, Maine

Dunlap, Riley E, Gallup Jr, George H and Gallup, Alec M (1993) 'Of Global Concern: Results on the Health of the Planet Survey', *Environment*, vol 35, no 9, pp6–15, 33–39

Entman, Robert M (1989) *Democracy Without Citizens: Media and the Decay of American Politics*, Oxford University Press, New York

Franklin, Bob (1994) *Packaging Politics: Political Communications in Britain's Media Democracy*, Edward Arnold, London

Gamson, William A, Croteau, David, Hoynes, William and Sasson, Theodore (1992) 'Media Images and the Social Construction of Reality', *Annual Review of Sociology*, no 18, pp373–393

Gardner, James N (1991) 'Lobbying, European-Style', *Europe*, November, pp29–30

Gellner, Winand (1995) 'The Politics of Policy 'Political Think Tanks' and their Markets in the U.S.-Institutional Environment', *Presidential Studies Quarterly*, vol 25, no 3, pp497–510

Gilchrist, Gavin (1995) 'Secret Strategy Undermines Greenhouse Fight', *Sydney Morning Herald*, 7 August, p1

Gordon, M and Megalogonis, G (1996) 'PM Forced to Review Code', *The Australian*, 16 October

Grefe, Edward A and Linsky, Marty (1995) *The New Corporate Activism: Harnessing the Power of Grassroots Tactics for Your Organization*, McGraw-Hill, New York

Greider, William (1992) *Who Will Tell the People: The Betrayal of American Democracy*, Simon & Schuster, New York

Greider, William (1993) 'Grassroots Organizing, PR-style: Democracy for Hire', *PR Watch*, vol 1, no 1, pp8–9

Harrison, E Bruce (1993) *Going Green: How to Communicate Your Company's Environmental Commitment*, Business One Irwin, Homewood, Illinois

Hightower, Jim (1995) 'Get the Hogs Out of the Creek!', *Earth Island Journal*, vol 11, no 1, p32

Himmelstein, Jerome L (1990) *To the Right: The Transformation of American Conservatism*, University of California Press, Berkeley

Jacobson, Michael F and Mazur, Laurie Ann (1995) *Marketing Madness*, Westview Press, Boulder, Colorado

Johnson, David (1993) 'The Canadian Regulatory System and Corporatism: Empirical Findings and Analytical Implications', *Canadian Journal of Law and Society*, vol 8, no 1, pp95–120

Kellner, Douglas (1990) *Television and the Crisis of Democracy*, Westview Press, Boulder, Colorado

Levathes, Louise (1995) 'Easy Money: How Congressional Candidates are Cleaning up with the Dirty Water PACs', *Audubon*, November–December, pp16–22

McIntosh, Philip (1990) 'Most Prepared to Put Environment Ahead of Growth', *Sydney Morning Herald*, 15 June

Megalli, M and Friedman, A (1991) *Masks of Deception: Corporate Front Groups in America*, Essential Information

Montague, Peter (1993) 'PR Firms for Hire to Undermine Democracy', *Rachel's Hazardous Waste News*, no 361

Nelson, Joyce (1993a) 'Great Global Greenwash: Burson-Marsteller, Pax Trilateral and the Brundtland Gang vs the Environment', *CovertAction*, no 44, pp26–33, 57–8

O'Callaghan, Kate (1992) 'Whose Agenda for America?', *Audubon*, September–October, pp80–91

O'Keefe, M and Daley, K (1993) 'Checking the Right', *Buzzworm*, vol 5, no 3, pp38–44

Parenti, M (1986) *Inventing Reality: The Politics of the Mass Media*, St Martin's Press, New York

Perkins, Peter (1990) 'Developing a Program to Satisfy the Community's Concerns', paper read at NSW Agriculture & Fisheries DAs Conference

Pettinico, George (1995) 'The Public Opinion Paradox', *Sierra*, November–December, pp28–31

Raghavan, Chakravarthi (1995) 'TNCs Control Two-thirds of the World Economy', *Third World Resurgence*, nos 65/66, pp31–32

Ricci, David (1993) *The Transformation of American Politics: The New Washington and the Rise of Think Tanks*, Yale University Press, New Haven

Rockland, David B and Fletcher, Gwyn L (1994) 'The Economy, the Environment and Public opinion', *EPA Journal*, vol 20, nos 3–4, pp39–40

Roschwalb, Susanne A (1994) 'The Hill & Knowlton Cases: A Brief on the Controversy', *Public Relations Review*, vol 20, no 3, pp267–276

Rosen, J (1996) 'Breaking the News: How the Media Undermine American Democracy', *The Nation*, 5 February, pp25–28

Rowell, Andrew (1996) *Green Backlash: Global Subversion of the Environment Movement*, Routledge, London and New York

Ryan, Charlotte (1991) *Prime Time Activism: Media Strategies for Grassroots Organizing*, South End Press, Boston, MA

Sale, Kirkpatrick (1993) *The Green Revolution: The American Environmental Movement, 1962–1992*, Hill & Wang, New York

Saloma, John S (1984) *Ominous Politics: The New Conservative Labyrinth*, Hill & Wang, New York

Saltzman, Joe (1989) 'Style vs Substance', *USA Today*, January, p87

Seitel, Fraser P (1995) *The Practice of Public Relations*, 6th edn, Prentice-Hall, Englewood Cliffs, New Jersey

Sethi, S Prakesh (1977) *Advocacy Advertising and Large Corporations*, Lexington Books, Lexington, MA

Sherrill, Robert (1990) *Why They Call it Politics: A Guide to America's Government*, 5th edn, Harcourt Brace Jovanovich, San Diego

Silas, C J (1990) 'The Environment: Playing to Win', *Public Relations Journal*, January, pp10, 34

Sloan, Pat (1995) 'P&G/Paramount Deal to be Mimicked', *Advertising Age*, 66, 6 March, p2

Smith, Trevor (1996) 'Citizenship, Community and Constitutionalism', *Parliamentary Affairs*, vol 49, no 2, pp262–272

Southam, Kate (1994) 'Why Green Australia Got Such a Black Mark', *Sydney Morning Herald*, 12 February, p28

Stauber, J and Rampton, S (1995) *Toxic Sludge is Good For You! Lies, Damn Lies and the Public Relations Industry*, Common Courage Press, Monroe, Maine

Szykowny, Rick (1991) 'Manipulating People: The Role of the Media is Serving Power', *Third World Resurgence*, no 12, August, pp27–30

Tokar, Brian (1995) 'The 'Wise Use' Backlash: Responding to Militant Anti-Environmentalism', *The Ecologist*, vol 25, no 4, pp150–156

Vogel, David (1989) *Fluctuating Fortunes: The Political Power of Business in America*, Basic Books, New York

Wanna, John (1992) 'Furthering Business Interests: Business Associations and Political Representation', in S Bell and J Wanna (eds) *Business-Government Relations in Australia*, Harcourt Brace Jovanovich, Sydney

Williamson, Peter (1989) *Corporatism in Perspective: An Introductory Guide to Corporatist Theory* (Sage Studies in Neo-Corporatism) Sage Publications, London

Winward, John (1991) 'Consumer Preferences and the Environment', in T Baker (ed) *Green Futures for Economic Growth: Britain in 2010*, Cambridge Econometrics, Cambridge

14

Mixed Messages

Carl Frankel

The human face is really like one of those Oriental gods: a whole group of faces juxta-posed on different planes; it is impossible to see them all simultaneously.

Marcel Proust

In the 1951 film classic *Rashomon*, a merchant and his wife are attacked by a bandit. The merchant is killed and the woman is raped. The movie retells the story four times, through the eyes of the three protagonists and a woodcutter who witnessed the event and each time a sharply different story emerges. Director Akira Kurosawa seems to be saying that all we have is our perceptions, that there is no single, objective reality. Certainly the Rashomon principle holds true in the world of sustainable business. Companies are not 'good' or 'bad' so much as complex, multi-faceted entities – much like humans, actually – whose 'true identity', such as it is, is in the eyes of the beholder.

Consider, for instance, Asea Brown Boveri (ABB), which, with annual orders in excess of US$35 billion, is one of the world's largest engineering and energy technology businesses. The company has been called '*one of the founding fathers of corporate environmentalism*,' and with good reason.[1] Former CEO Percy Barnevik was an early and ardent supporter of the World Business Council on Sustainable Development. Billionaire Stephan Schmidheiny, name author of *Changing Course* and (with Federico J L Zorraquin) the subsequent *Financing Change*, sits on ABB's board of directors and is one of the company's leading stockholders. The company was one of the first companies to publish a freestanding environmental report and continues to position itself as a strong advocate of sustainable development. In a 1994 document, the company asserted: '*ABB is committed to sustainable development. Protection of the environment is among our top corporate priorities. We address environmental issues in all our operations and public policy.*'[2]

For many members of the sustainability community, however, one word puts the lie to ABB's environmental commitment – Bakun, a giant Malaysian hydro-electric venture intended to transport power from the Eastern Malaysian state of Sarawak across the South China Sea to peninsula Malaysia via an 800-mile (1300 kilometre) long, 500 kilowatt cable.[3] The list of question marks about the project runs almost as long as the cable. Start with the fact that Malaysia doesn't even need the additional capacity. In 1995 the country generated an energy surplus of almost 64 per cent and by the time Bakun comes on line – slated for around 2003 – renewable energy

Reproduced by kind permission of New Society Publishers from Carl Frankel (1998) *In Earth's Company*, New Society Publishers, Gabriola Island, Canada alternatives such as solar will be cost-competitive with conventional energy sources. Not only that, but the projected increase in capacity discourages energy-efficiency and demand-side management initiatives, locking Malaysian officials into precisely the 'consume more' mentality that contributes so heavily to our current crisis of unsustainability. When Ani Arope, the outgoing chairman of the Malaysian power authority, publicly complained about excess power supplies following a 1996 blackout, he was publicly rebuked by prime minister Mohammed Mahathir: *'When you have a product, you have to go out and sell. If you sit down and say you have too much, you will not be able to'.*[4] So much for energy conservation.

Credible experts have attacked the economic and financial assumptions under-lying Bakun as far too optimistic. According to Mark Mansley, author of *Bakun: High Dam – High Risk?* and a specialist in Asian energy issues with the firm Delphi International, *'There's a huge amount of capital going into a project which is eco-nomically dubious and where the financial returns are at best uncertain'.*[5] The project has also been criticized as being environmentally destructive – over 400 square miles (1000 square kilometres) of rainforest will be flooded and there is also the possi-bility of increased greenhouse gas emissions from rotting vegetation in the reservoir – and socially insensitive too – around 10,000 people, many of them indigenous tribespeople, will be forcibly relocated. Small wonder, then, that Gabungan, a 40-member coalition of Malaysian NGOs, has condemned Bakun as *'socially destructive, environmentally disastrous and economically misconceived'*, or that the project has been targeted by virtually every major transnational campaign group, including Friends of the Earth, Greenpeace and the World Wide Fund For Nature.[6]

What does all this have to do with ABB? Simply this: until it was abruptly and unexpectedly relieved of its assignment by the Malaysian authorities – for reasons reportedly having nothing to do with the environment – the Swiss–Swedish con-glomerate was to have been the leading outside contractor on the project, responsible for overall project management and the supply of electrical equipment. Bakun had been expected to contribute about US$3 billion to ABB's coffers.

How did the company's intended participation in this dubious project square with its commitment, as stated in its formal environmental policy, to *'involve itself in international activities devoted to solving global environmental problems and promoting sustainable development'* and to *'play its part in the transfer of environ-mentally sound technologies and methods to developing countries'?* And how did its commitment to *'foster openness and dialogue with employees and the public on environmental matters'* square with the forcible relocation of 10,000 Malaysians?

The answers to those questions depend on who you ask. ABB's president and CEO Göran Lindahl has argued that his company has no duty to second-guess a decision made by the sovereign state of Malaysia:

> *I put a clear borderline between what is the responsibility of the Sarawak and Malaysian authorities and what is ABB's responsibility. Malaysia is like a sovereign state: we can-not go in there like a colonial power and try to take over. I must emphasize this point: it is the Malaysian government which has taken the decision to build the dam. Our job is to carry out the project.*[7]

Critics of ABB have dismissed this as the corporate equivalent of the infamous World War II 'I was only obeying orders' defence and argued that for projects like Bakun, which so directly and powerfully affect the global problematique, this argument no longer (so to speak) holds water. Tom Gladwin, director of the Global Environment Program at New York University's Stern School of Business, bluntly calls arguments like Lindahl's '… *just a convenient smoke screen. Multinational corporations like ABB are among the most powerful institutions on the planet and up to their eyeballs in the political and legal affairs of sovereign states when it suits their corporate interest*'.[8]

Lindahl has also argued that, given that the Bakun dam will in fact be built, it is best to have an environmentally sensitive company as project manager. ABB had intended to require all suppliers to get ISO 14001 certification, for instance – a not insignificant commitment. But even if you buy into Lindahl's arguments, there's no getting around the fact that ABB's willing – no, eager – participation in Bakun at a minimum raises questions about the depth of its commitment to sustainable development.

So will the 'real' ABB please stand up? That is easier said than done. Environmentalists who like to keep things simple dismiss the pro-sustainability behaviour of companies like ABB as so much greenwashing, but that's disingenuous. Corporate identity is more aptly viewed as one of those figure-ground images that allow a person to see one of two images – a vase, say, or a crone – but never both simultaneously. Only, in ABB's case the two images are a white hat and a black one.

The company is not at all atypical in this regard. The Roman god Janus had two faces, each looking in an opposite direction. So do most corporations.

General Motors (GM), the world's largest industrial corporation, provides another example of how this is so. In 1994, the company became the third Fortune 500 company (and first Fortune 500 manufacturing company) to endorse the Coalition for Environmentally Responsible Economies (CERES) principles, a step that earned the company much favourable press coverage and with good reason. For the company to sign a set of environmental principles that had been formulated by environmentalists and that required it to commit to regular, extensive public disclosure represented a courageous break from corporate business-as-usual.

Ask GM spokespeople and the company's commitment to the CERES principles is one more star in what has long been an illustrious environmental firmament. '*GM has had a strong environmental program since the early 1970s,*' declares Dennis Minano, the company's senior environmental officer.[9] Glossy promotional materials sing the same song.

And indeed there is much that is positive in GM's environmental track record. Toxic Chemical Release Inventory (TRI) emissions have been reduced by over 40 per cent since 1988. Packing used by suppliers to ship materials for GM cars and trucks has been reduced by over 500 per cent and nearly 60 per cent of all packing waste is now recycled. Statistics like these, plus its commitment to driving eco-efficiency down the supplier chain, led to the company's receiving *Business Ethics* magazine's 1996 Award for Environmental Excellence.

GM has also been a leader in electric vehicle research and development. *Popular Mechanics* magazine called its Impact '*the first real-world, practical electric-powered passenger car for the 21st Century'.*[10] *Popular Science* also heaped encomiums on it, calling it the *'world's best electric car'.*[11]

But there is another side to the story. Even while the company was forging ahead with research and development into Impact, it was working overtime to quash electric vehicle incentives in the northeast US. A 1992 report by the New York city-based Council on Economic Priorities painted an unflattering portrait of GM. While acknowledging that the company was *'in some ways an innovator'*, the study noted that *'in other respects, GM's environmental policy is a troubling one'.* Among the problems identified: extensive criticism for making exaggerated claims about its environmental record; potential involvement at upwards of 200 Superfund toxic waste disposal sites; and extensive Political Action Committee (PAC) contributions to members of Congress with below-average environmental voting records.

For Paul Billings, Director of State/Government Relations at the American Lung Association, the environment has no bigger enemy than GM: *'For years, the company has led the industry's opposition to good environmental controls in automobiles. They've been quick to take credit for every compromise they've been dragged into, but they've fought us kicking and screaming every step of the way. When you consider them environmentally, you have to take into account their products on the road and their campaigns in the public-policy arena against environmental improvements.'*[12]

With the rest of the car industry, General Motors has announced its support for a higher gasoline tax as an alternative to higher fuel economy standards. According to Chris Calwell, a consultant to the Natural Resources Defense Council, there are two schools of thought on the reasons for the car industry's stance – because they genuinely believe that it would be better for the environment and business, or because they know it will never happen. Either way, he goes on to note, *'Talk is cheap and the industry has yet to back up its talk with any real action – no lobbying, no money spent to get a gas tax passed'.*[13]

GM has good reason to be ambivalent. By more actively supporting higher fuel taxes, the company risks breaching its fiduciary duty to its shareholders – basic economics tells us that if it costs more to drive, people will drive less and less driving means fewer sales of GM cars and trucks. In addition, the company's customers don't want higher fuel economy standards and if GM has taken anything to heart in recent years, it is the Total Quality Management (TQM) maxim about listening to your customers. For years the company did not do that, a non-starter of a strategy that brought it perilously close to bankruptcy in 1992.

The running battle over fuel-efficiency incentives has been waged primarily in California. In 1991, the legislature passed a bill that would fund rebates on fuel-efficient cars with fees on inefficient ones. It was designed to solve the exact problem that the industry complains about – the lack of economic incentives for people to buy more fuel-efficient cars. Nevertheless, governor Wilson refused to sign the bill and since then car industry lobbying has kept it from clearing the legislature.

Again, the industry position is that regulators have no business getting between them and their customers. In addition, they argue that by giving energy efficiency such a high profile, the government is actually helping Japanese car manufacturers who have a better reputation in this area.

Another black mark against GM came to light in late 1995, when the EPA and the Department of Justice announced that the company would spend approximately US$45 million to settle charges that it had illegally defeated pollution control devices inside nearly 500,000 Cadillacs since 1991, resulting in carbon monoxide emissions of up to three times the legal limit. That is hardly the behaviour one would associate with an endorser of the CERES principles.

Another sensitive issue revolves around so-called 'light trucks' – sports utility vehicles, vans, minivans and pick-up trucks. These vehicles are much less fuel-efficient than passenger cars, but that hasn't kept General Motors and other car manufacturers from marketing them with such gusto that in November 1997 their light truck sales exceeded those of cars for the first time.[14] This shift in momentum has been fuelled by the booming demand for sports utility vehicles: in the decade from 1986–1996, US retail sales of those yuppie paeans to rugged individualism climbed from 5.0 per cent to 13.8 per cent of all US sales.[15] On an annual basis, light trucks now account for over 40 per cent of new vehicle sales.[16]

This trend is a gross negative for the environment. Light trucks mean significantly lower fuel-efficiency and that much more carbon spewing skyward. '*The biggest single step we can take against global warming,*' says Dan Becker, director of the Sierra Club's energy and global warming programme, '*is to make more fuel-efficient vehicles.*'[17] Whereas the federal corporate average fuel economy (CAFE) standard for cars is 27.5 miles per gallon, for light trucks it is a much more paltry 20.7 mpg – and sports utility vehicles as a rule are much less fuel-efficient than that. The differential was created to give a break to workhorse trucks, but it also offered the industry a loophole, which it was quick to spot and exploit. And so, enter the sports utility vehicle, that playtoy for people with money to burn and an oxymoronic fantasy about getting back to nature in their car. '*The industry exploited the law,*' says Becker. '*The development of the light truck was a way to escape CAFE.*'[18]

Thus a core – and hugely successful – marketing strategy by General Motors and other car manufacturers has directly and substantially increased greenhouse gas emissions.[19] Nor is this the only way in which company policies have been counterproductive. In 1997, the chief executives of General Motors, Ford and Chrysler met with President Clinton, to whom they delivered, according to the *New York Times*, '*an earful of complaints about the administration's interest in limited emissions of greenhouse gases that may contribute to global warming*' – not a stance that is consistent with a commitment to environmental protection.[20]

Monsanto provides yet another example of the Janus face of business. The company has two spectacular sustainability feathers in its cap, having been the first US company to formally commit to going 'beyond compliance', and also the first one to formally commit to sustainable development as a core business strategy. The company has conducted two 'Million Dollar Challenges' to spur development of innovative wastewater treatment technologies and has received Presidential Awards for Green Chemistry and for Sustainable Development.

Over the past few years, a steady stream of the nation's 'greenerati' – the leading visionaries and spokespeople for a sustainable industrial system – has paraded through the company's executive suites, taking senior management through the paces of what's wrong with the world and how to fix it: author and entrepreneur Paul

Hawken; green designer and architect William McDonough; botanist Peter Raven; even David Korten, author of *When Corporations Rule the World* and a staunch foe of transnationals like Monsanto – the list of progressive sustainability thinkers who have provided input to Monsanto goes on and on. CEO Robert Shapiro now ranks as one of the world's foremost industry advocates of fourth-era corporate environmentalism, having delivered his message, among other forums, in a wave-making 1997 interview in the *Harvard Business Review*.[21]

Monsanto warrants kudos for more quiet initiatives as well, such as its support of micro-credit, a breakthrough strategy pioneered by Muhammad Yunus of the Grameen Bank in Bangladesh that provides modest loans to people who normally would not qualify for bank financing. Monsanto recently helped sponsor a major international conference on micro-credit that was held in Washington, DC. The company also hosted a follow-up conference in St Louis in June 1997 to bring corporations and NGOs together to explore the possibility of creating partnerships for micro-credit in regions around the world. Monsanto's CEO, Robert Shapiro, is the co-chair of the Council of Corporations, the goal of which is to reach 100 million of the world's poorest families through credit by the year 2005.

Seen through another lens, however, the company is nothing but trouble. Part of the problem lies with the company's embrace of biotechnology, a stance that horrifies some observers. '*The rush into biotech rivals the rush into nuclear power 50 years ago,*' says Ronnie Cummins, national director of the Pure Food Campaign. '*It is creating the conditions for an environmental Auschwitz or Chernobyl.*'[22]

Monsanto has also taken hits for a variety of research and regulatory shenanigans. In the 1980s the company was accused of manipulating research into the health effects of dioxin and, more recently, of muscling its genetically engineered bovine growth hormone through regulatory channels, despite unresolved concerns about its impact on human health. It has opposed labelling bills that would allow companies to notify consumers that the milk in their products came from cows that hadn't been treated with bovine growth hormone. It has also been implicated in the notorious 'circle of poison' whereby chemicals banned in the US are sold overseas and then make their way back into the country on the backs, so to speak, of treated products.

The bottom line is that Monsanto ranks high on standard lists of corporate environmental heroes and of corporate villains, too – which actually isn't all that unusual. Several years ago, I asked several experts to informally rate the environmental performance of 20 major corporations. The scores varied widely. In one instance, expert no 1 gave DuPont the highest possible rating, while expert no 2 gave it the lowest. DuPont had recently conducted an environmental image campaign, with one particularly memorable advertisement showing a sequence of applauding animals. The expert who gave DuPont low marks confessed that he viewed these advertisements as a tacit admission of wrongdoing.[23]

The mixed messages that corporations deliver are of two basic types. The first can be characterized as black-hatted business-as-usual – that is, good old corporate duplicity. It's a shopworn tale – companies doing their utmost to water down environmental regulations, often under cover of night, while loudly proclaiming their environmental commitment to all who will listen. One is put in mind of the professional wrestling villain who does something awful to his opponent and then, wide-eyed, protests his innocence to the scowling referee. In these cases, charges of greenwashing are well founded.

Our first example of corporate duplicity comes from the pharmaceutical industry. The issue involves ozone-depleting substances (ODSs) which, for the most part, were banned by the Montreal Protocol. The agreement, however, did allow for certain exceptions, specifically for *'essential uses'* where an ODS is deemed *'necessary for the health, safety or is critical for the functioning of society'*, and *'there are no available technically and economically feasible alternatives or substitutes that are acceptable from the standpoint of environment and health'*. Such an exemption was carved out for the use of CFC-11, -12 and -114 as propellants in so-called 'metered dose inhalers' (MDIs), which are used in the treatment of asthma and other respiratory ailments.

The market for MDIs is quite substantial – about US$4 billion – and growing rapidly, in large measure because of the rise in pollution-related lung disease. About 440 million MDIs were in use as of 1996, with the number expected to climb to 800 million by the turn of the century. With the stakes this high, it is not surprising, if discouraging, that major players in the pharmaceutical industry have done their best to slow down the phase-out of ODS-based MDIs.[24]

The effort was triggered by the introduction by 3M in 1995 of a non-CFC MDI, the first of its kind to reach the market. While less than ideal environmentally – it used the propellant HFC-134a, a rather potent greenhouse gas – the new product represented a significant improvement over the CFC-based products on the market. For rival vendors, moreover, it posed a significant competitive threat: it was priced at or below the level of CFC-propelled MDIs and estimates gave it the potential to replace over half the existing MDI market.

Unlike rival suppliers, the administrators of the Montreal Protocol were delighted to learn of the new product. A report by the organization's Technology and Economic Assessment Panel (TEAP) suggested that, given the 3M introduction and other promising developments, the phase-out of CFC-propelled MDIs could be accelerated sharply. Kate Victory, editor of *Business and the Environment*, a trade newsletter, reports what happened next:

> *TEAP's proposal was presented for discussion at the … Montreal Protocol's Open Ended Working Group, held from 26–29 August [1996] in Geneva, Switzerland. To the surprise of many observers, however, the proposal was vehemently opposed by a handful of developing countries – namely, India, South Africa and Kenya. The countries cited concerns over the implications for health in developing countries as well as the potential cost of alternatives. As a result, no decision was reached at the meeting…*
>
> *Several observers felt that the objections expressed by Kenya and other countries were actually a result of lobbying by pharmaceutical companies opposed to the phaseout of CFC-propelled MDIs…*[25]

Pharmaceutical companies took other steps as well. Glaxo Wellcome hired a public relations firm, GPC Connect, which was quoted in a trade publication as saying that it had been *'appointed by Glaxo Wellcome to run an international lobbying drive to delay the ban on* [CFC-containing] *MDIs as used by asthma sufferers. Glaxo*

Wellcome is hoping to delay an eventual ban on [CFC-containing] *MDIs to allow it time to develop alternatives*.[26] A Glaxo Wellcome executive subsequently attempted to explain away this unfortunate foray into candour by writing that the company had '*asked GPC Connect to advise on internal communications procedures to help facilitate the complex transition from CFC to non-CFC MDIs internationally*' – an exercise in corporate gibberish that only lent credence to the original GPC Connect assertion.[27]

Pharmaceutical companies also took action inside the nation's capitol. Writes Victory:

> *Sources told BATE* [Business and the Environment] *that pharmaceutical companies wishing to delay the transition successfully lobbied in the US Congress to attach a CFC tax repeal rider to unrelated legislation. Buried deep in the 'Small Business Job Protection Act of 1996' (HR 3448) is Section 1803, which repeals the US$5.80 per pound tax on CFCs used as propellants in MDIs. The bill became law on 20 August* [1996]. *The cost of producing a pound of CFCs ranges from US$0.50 to US$2.00, so the tax was clearly an incentive to cut back on CFC production and use. Changing the rules makes it harder for manufacturers of new alternatives to realize a timely return on investment.*[28]

Our second example of corporate anti-environmentalism isn't industry-specific. It is about how the corporate community as a whole responded to the Republican takeover of the US Congress in 1994. Readers will recall that the conservative uprising set into motion a no-holds-barred assault on business-as-usual in the federal government. Among the targets were substantial portions of the system of environmental protection that had been built up painstakingly over the previous 20 years. For the most part, the corporate community responded with silence, or applause.

The Republican campaign had two faces – one relatively centrist, the other extremist. The more moderate one focused, legitimately, on regulatory reform. You don't have to be a Republican to believe that the country's regulatory system needs fixing; the question is how to do so without dismantling its safeguards. The so-called Dole bill proposed to achieve this by requiring cost-benefit analyses for regulation. The very thought produced howls from environmentalists who argued that regulatory oversight would drown under a sea of red tape and endless litigation. But defenders argued, with some justification, that the bill would only impose the same logic on regulatory processes that businesses already apply to their own operations. '*It would help federal agencies prioritize more effectively*,' argued John Cohen, executive director of the Alliance for Reasonable Regulation (ARR), an industry group that supported the Dole bill.[29]

A substantial majority of the business community favoured the Dole bill. ARR members included companies with excellent environmental reputations, such as AT&T and CERES principles endorsers General Motors and the Sun Company. Industry lobbyists worked closely with legislators to help make the Dole bill a reality. Indeed, rarely, if ever, has the collaborative process been so overt. In one memorable instance, three lobbyists with the law firm of Hunton & Williams sat beside the staff director of the Senate Judiciary Committee and answered questions as if they were themselves staff members. In another, a lobbyist represented herself to a federal agency as speaking for an aide of one of the senators who was drafting the bill. This boundary-blurring behaviour invited the perception that, as one critic put it to the *New York Times*, the Dole bill was '*by big business, for big business and of big business*'.[30]

For Republican extremists, 'regulatory reform' was essentially a pretext for rolling back environmental regulation. Tom Delay, who, as the majority whip in the House of Representatives is one of Newt Gingrich's chief deputies, is not one to control his rhetoric: he has called the EPA the '*Gestapo of government*' and labelled the Nobel Prize, which was awarded in 1995 to two researchers for their work on CFCs, the '*Nobel appeasement prize*'. Many Republican proposals reflected this unrepentant anti-environmentalism.

Did the corporate community resist this backlash? No. Many businesses and trade associations were only too eager to leap aboard the anti-environmental bandwagon. Big business had a big hand in writing the House revision of the Clean Water Act which, if passed, would have reduced substantially protection for wetlands and controls on polluted run-off from farms and city streets. The paper industry successfully inserted a provision calling for the EPA to give greater weight to cost-benefit analysis and risk assessment in determining what technologies should be used to meet water quality goals. The Chemical Manufacturers Association (CMA) won a clause softening pollution discharge requirements. These and other pro-business provisions came to legislative aides via a lengthy memorandum from an industry group that was headed by a so-called 'environmental manager' with the US Chamber of Commerce.

In fairness, it must be added that there was the occasional corporate objection to Congressional extremism – not many, but a few. DuPont spoke out against attempts to repeal or postpone the country's phaseout of CFCs and the Chemical Manufacturers Association objected to early proposals to cut the EPA's budget by an enormous 34 per cent. Mort Mullins, vice president of regulatory affairs for CMA, told *Fortune Magazine*, '*That much of a cut in one year would be disruptive and counter-productive. We must protect the EPA's core programs that are essential to the credibility of the agency*'.[31]

Sceptics would argue that positions like these come from enlightened self-interest, not genuine environmental commitment and they have a point. Du Pont has invested heavily in CFC alternatives, while the CMA may have been concerned that attempts to roll back too much too soon might backfire – as indeed they did: the Republicans managed to pass remarkably few of their environmental rewrites, largely because the extremist rhetoric and proposals produced a powerful backlash. Overall, however, the impression one got from corporate America during these heady times for conservatives was unabashed 'delight at the goings-on in the nation's capital.

How is one to make sense of the apparent inconsistency between corporate claims of environmental commitment and their behaviour inside the Beltway? In a phrase: cognitive dissonance. Corporations are made up of, and also operate within, a host of different cultures and value systems. In the words of Nigel Roome, a professor specializing in business and the environment then at York University's Schulich School of Business, they function in '*interdependent systems which operate at different scales in time and place*'.[32] Far from being integrated entities, corporations contain what amount to multiple, parallel and often unaligned universes, with each responding to different – and often contradictory – rules of engagement. As a result it is the rule, not the exception, for environmental management and lobbying to occupy entirely separate tracks within a corporation – for the two to have nothing whatsoever to do with each other. And that seems to be what happened as Environmental Health and Safety Departments went one way and Regulatory Affairs Departments another, during the conservative Republican uprising of 1994–1995.

A glaring case in point comes from a Fortune 500 company with a strong environmental profile whose chief environmental officer was genuinely shocked when I told him that his company belonged to the Alliance for Reasonable Regulation. A few days later he called to tell me that the company's name was being removed from the list of ARR supporters.

And so, when Bob Banks, the chief environmental officer at Sun Company, points out that '*the regulatory initiatives in Washington DC are having no effect on our overall commitment*', and when Paul Tebo, vice president of safety, health and environment at DuPont, says that '*you need to look at the whole spectrum of what companies are doing*', they're probably not engaging in greenwashing so much as communicating their sincere assessment of this complex state of affairs.[33] All of which is to suggest that companies can be green inside their factories and in their environmental-management policies and brown inside the Beltway.

The bottom line is that businesses are complex organisms with often conflicting agendas – it is unreasonable to expect consistency from them. The fact that the corporate community didn't rally en masse against the Republican initiatives in Washington doesn't quite put the lie to its environmental commitment. But it doesn't sing hosannas to it, either.

A more recent example of reactionary corporate thinking comes from the broad-based industry opposition to the movement for a strong United Nations treaty imposing meaningful limits on greenhouse gas emissions. In the US, much of the campaigning has been conducted via the neutral-sounding Global Climate Information Project (GCIP), which includes among its members such powerful trade organizations as the American Automobile Manufacturers Association, the American Petroleum Institute, the US Chamber of Commerce, the National Association of Manufacturers, Edison Electric Institute and a host of others as well. The organization objected to President Clinton's cautious acknowledgement of the need for binding emission limits because it '*is not fair to consumers, workers, farmers, seniors and small businesses*', and it opposed the proposed treaty that was ultimately agreed upon in Kyoto in December 1997 on the grounds that it would '*have little or no environmental benefit*'.[34] The GCIP spent an estimated US$13 million on an advertising campaign designed to pressure the Clinton Administration into watering down its position on the climate-change issue.[35] And the Global Climate Coalition, another industry organization, has for years been funding efforts to undermine the global scientific and public dialogue about global climate change.[36]

There have been some breaks in the ranks – Robert Campbell, CEO of Sun Oil Company, came out in favour of binding emissions and executives at British Petroleum and Royal Dutch/Shell have expressed a similar readiness to take climate change seriously – but positions like these are very much the exception. Overall, business has done its level best to scuttle the United Nations' climate-change treaty.

The second type of mixed message is more subtle. Sometimes an organization's conduct comes across as environmentally favourable from one perspective and as obstructionist from another. Duplicity isn't the issue here, perspective is. These framing issues are tricky and don't readily lend themselves to clear judgements of right or wrong. They do, however, lend notes of ambiguity and complexity to the dialogue and they also remind us to be sceptical in the face of corporate claims that a given position demonstrates environmental commitment. It is always useful to ask: 'What position and actions could have been taken but weren't?' and 'How might the issue be reframed to create a less favourable interpretation of the corporate position?' Not to put the corporation in the wrong, but because framing country is spin country and questions like these serve as ritual incantations whose effect is to keep our heads clear and ward off the magic of ... the spin.

One example of a framing issue comes out of the forest products industry. No one questions the hugely important role that forests play in our global ecosystem. International forestry practices raise a *Who's Who* of environmental issues – rainforest devastation, soil depletion, water pollution, fishery preservation, global warming and loss of biodiversity, to name just a few.

Ask environmentalists and representatives of the forest-products industry how to address these issues and both sides offer the same solution: sustainable forestry. However, they disagree on what the term means. Environmentalists argue for a broad definition that takes into account the long-term nurturing of the forest resource (*'focusing on what's left, not what's taken'* is how one expert puts it), and that more expansively still addresses social issues such as the treatment of local communities and indigenous peoples. Historically, industry representatives have tended to favour a more limited definition, preferring to focus on what's quantifiable – that is, on having a positive growth-to-harvest ratio and no net loss of forest land. In other words, cut one, plant one. They have used a similar rationale to argue against including biodiversity in the sustainable-forestry calculus – again, because it is not quantifiable.

The future of sustainable forestry hinges in large part on the outcome of this debate. There's no doubt that the future lies with sustainable forestry, but will this include monoculture or mean a quantum shift in forest management practices?

The American Forest & Paper Association (AFPA), the leading wood products trade association in the US, stepped into the fray in 1994 when it announced that beginning in 1996, compliance with a set of sustainable forestry principles would be a condition of membership. Whether the move was progressive or reactionary is largely a matter of interpretation. On the one hand, the AFPA's Sustainable Forestry Principles are a public commitment to environmental responsibility and there is much that is specifically positive in them. For instance, they require clear-cuts to be blended into the landscape and they also limit the size of a company's clear-cuts to an average of 150 acres (60 hectares), a requirement that will put constraints on companies operating in flat pinewood forests where much larger clear-cuts are possible.

Most importantly of all, the principles go beyond the industry's 'cut-one-plant-one' definition of sustainable forestry. Objective Four of the AFPA's Implementation Guidelines requires companies to *'enhance the quality of wildlife habitat by*

*developing and implementing measures that promote habitat diversity and the con-
servation of plant and animal populations found in forest communities*.[37] In other
words: *sayonara*, monoculture.

Does this mean that the AFPA has sided with the progressives? Not necessarily.
The principles contain more than a few grey areas. For instance, the 'special sites'
principle calls for companies to '*manage* [their] *forests and lands of special significance (for example, biologically, geologically, or historically significant) in a
manner that takes into account their unique qualities*'.[37] Precisely what this means
is unclear. Does it preclude selective cutting of an old-growth forest? Not necessarily. Nowhere do the principles require member companies to keep old-growth forests
off-limits.

Furthermore, the AFPA's initiative can be viewed as an ill-disguised effort to
stunt the growth of the sustainable forestry certification movement, which is rapidly building up a considerable head of steam in North America. The American Society
for Testing Materials (ASTM), a leading US standards organization, is developing
what it calls a 'Standard Guide for the Assessment of Sustainably Harvested Wood',
while, on a less theoretical front, the Rainforest Alliance's SmartWood initiative,
the world's oldest timber certification programme with over 50 certified enterprises,
is expanding its expertise into North America through its SmartWood Network, which
links regional non-profit certification organizations in the US, Canada and worldwide. The National Wildlife Federation, the largest US environmental group, has
agreed to provide certification services for the SmartWood Network in the northeast United States – potentially a significant move, given the organization's excellent
name recognition and its direct access to a 1.6 million-person membership base.
SmartWood programme certifiers will be accredited by the Forest Stewardship
Council, an Oaxaca, Mexico-based organization that in the brief few years of its
existence has managed to impose the beginnings of order on the burgeoning forest-products certification industry.

All these certifiers apply a much more holistic definition of 'sustainable' than
the AFPA. To the extent that the association succeeds through its principles in creating the perception that its members practice sustainable forestry, it obviates the
need for certification, blunts the movement's momentum and ensures that the power
to determine how they manage their resources remains in the hands of the forest-
product companies themselves.

So are the AFPA's Sustainable Forestry Principles 'green?' Yes; no; maybe – you
decide.

Another interesting framing issue is presented by Wal-Mart, the enormously
successful mass-market retailer, with close to US$105 billion in annual revenue.
Over the years, Wal-Mart Stores has developed an excellent reputation for environmental commitment and its Lawrence, Kansas, eco-store is widely viewed as the
jewel in its green crown. In many ways it is an impressive achievement, with features that include a 1200 square foot (110 square metres) permanent environmental
education centre and a one-stop recycling centre for tin, glass, paper and sorted plastics. More striking still is the extent to which environmental considerations have been
incorporated into the building's design. Although steel is the usual roofing material
for Wal-Mart stores, sustainably harvested wood was utilized for the Lawrence store's

roof and ceiling structure. Altogether, 750,000 board feet of sustainably harvested wood were used, making it the largest amount of wood ever certified as sustainably harvested for a single project. The Lawrence skylight system operates in tandem with the building's fluorescent lighting system to minimize energy consumption. Photo sensors mounted at the base of the skylight walls continuously monitor the amount of light entering the building and automatically adjust the level of the dimmable light fixtures accordingly. In this way, only the exact amount of electrical light needed is provided beneath the skylight area. The parking lot contains recycled asphalt. Bumper blocks and directional signs are made of recycled plastic. Trolley bays are either made from recycled plastic or are 'recycled' from other stores. Even Wal-Mart's road sign is solar-powered.

Does all this make Wal-Mart, or Wal-Mart's eco-store, an environmental winner? Not if you ask David Morris of the non-profit Institute for Local Self-Reliance:

> *Wal-Mart's Kansas eco-store has received enormous publicity but the context for the store is egregious. Wal-Mart has done the same thing everywhere. It moves into an area, drives out small businesses, drives out diversity – in short, undermines community. The fact that the Wal-Mart operation in Lawrence is an eco-store does not undo any of that.*[38]

In Morris' opinion, even if you leave out the social component, the Wal-Mart eco-store fails on strictly environmental grounds:

> *If you compare a Lawrence, Kansas with a Wal-Mart store against a Lawrence without one, having no Wal-Mart wins hands down. The environmental costs of building a Wal-Mart store and parking lot are immense, even if you build environmentally. So is the mileage logged by people traveling to shop there. There is only one benefit in having a Wal-Mart in your town: you pay less. That does not make up for the social and environmental costs.*[39]

Morris' critique serves as a valuable reminder that whether we hold something as good or bad, as favourable or unfavourable, in large measure depends on our frame of reference. It is also consistent with one of the core principles of fourth-era corporate environmentalism – the need to 'remember sustainable development'. For Morris, sustainability requires us to look beyond relative environmental impacts and to consider other issues such as the quality of life and the impact on the community. Not only that, but he believes scale itself is intrinsically problematic. As green as it is, even the Lawrence, Kansas, Wal-Mart is still a superstore and Wal-Mart is still a megacompany. For Morris, big is unsustainable, period.

Yet another set of framing issues might collectively be called the 'curious incident of the dog in the nighttime'. The phrase comes from a passage in a Sherlock Holmes story called *Silver Blaze*:

> *'Is there any other point to which you wish to draw my attention?'* [asked Watson].
> *'To the curious incident of the dog in the nighttime.'*
> *'The dog did nothing in the nighttime.'*
> *'That was the curious incident,' remarked Sherlock Holmes.*[40]

The business/sustainability community is replete with similar 'curious incidents'. Behind the veil of corporate actions there lies another story – what companies choose not to do; products and initiatives they do not follow up on; the white spaces in the text.

The 'Greening-Up' Line in the Sand

Mainstream consumer-goods companies have devoted much time and expense to improving the environmental performance of their established product lines. Most detergent companies have introduced 'Ultras', which substantially reduce packaging. The major soda companies have introduced two-litre soda bottles containing post-consumer recycled plastic. Packaging has been eliminated entirely for some deodorants, toothpaste and other products. Many established products have been relaunched as refills.

The consumer-goods majors tend to position steps like these as proof of their environmental commitment and from one perspective this claim is warranted. These exercises in product 'greening-up' do indeed reduce materials consumption and waste. But their actions have a shadow side. In choosing to green up their products, the consumer-product majors have elected to steer clear of 'deep-green' products – radically reformulated offerings whose core identities are built around their environmental assets. Moreover, their position entirely fails to address the even more fundamental issue of sustainable consumption.

One effect of the corporate embrace of product 'greening-up' has been to diffuse and in the process defuse consumer concerns about the environment. This in turn has reduced the marketplace appeal of deep-green alternatives, which for all intents and purposes have been foreclosed from mainstream distribution channels.

The consumer-goods majors have ample reason to want to keep the consumer marketplace from becoming very green. They have made substantial investments in capital equipment for their established non-green (or greened-up) product lines. In addition, by introducing 'deep-green' products, they would be inviting a more critical appraisal of the environmental performance of their established brands. Moreover, by shifting the consumer-goods centre of gravity to a point where the environment was a much more important buying consideration, the majors would run the risk of letting fresh air into a market structure that is pretty well sealed now, and tilted very much in their favour. By going 'deep-green', in other words, they would open the door to a new buying culture, with potentially grievous consequences for their established franchises.

These business reasons mitigate against the consumer-goods majors making the leap into deep-green products. But the fact remains that they could have chosen to do so.

Plastics Is As Plastics Does

Currently, two types of plastic – polyethylene terephthalate (PET) soda bottles and high-density polyethylene (HDPE) milk jugs – are being recycled at high rates in the US, while all the other frequently used resins are hardly recycled at all. For Richard Denison, a senior scientist with the Environmental Defense Fund (EDF), the consumer-products industry is a prime culprit for the failure to expand plastics recycling beyond PET and HDPE – again, not for what it has done so much as for what it hasn't. He writes:

> Consider two reasons why recycling of soft drink bottles and milk jugs is working:
> **Single vs multiple types of plastic** *Soft drink bottles are all made from the same type of plastic – easily identified by people and easily reprocessed. The same goes for milk jugs. In contrast, many other consumer products come in different types of plastic that look alike but cannot be recycled together (except for low-grade uses such as making plastic lumber). This hodgepodge results not from any functional requirement but from short-term economics: these packagers buy the cheapest plastic available at a given time.*
> *EDF supermarket surveys found at least four different plastics used to make shampoo bottles and five or more for all-purpose cleansers. Colgate-Palmolive dishwashing liquid and Lysol disinfectant each come in three different plastics.*
> **Clear vs colored** *Soft drink bottles and milk jugs are clear, in contrast to the broad palette of pigments used in most plastic bottles for purely cosmetic reasons. Companies like Procter & Gamble and Lever Brothers have won praise for using recycled plastic in their bottles. Ironically, they have done so by cornering the market on clear milk jugs, to which they add their trademarked pigments. The next time around, the bottles are lucky to be used even as plastic lumber – and far more likely to end up as trash.*[41]

In Denison's view, the consumer-goods companies are perpetuating the plastics recycling status quo (or rather the plastics non-recycling status quo) by not giving environmental considerations enough weight in their plastics buying and processing decisions:

> Procter & Gamble has a color called Tide Red. It is its own color – no other company can use it. The company buys clear plastic and dyes it Tide Red. Theoretically it could use clear HDPE and a large Tide Red sticker but it does not. Instead it has chosen to link its brand image to a specific plastics processing technology.[42]

Does Procter & Gamble have good reason to stick with its 'tide-and-true' Tide Red marketing strategy? Absolutely. But it's also true that P&G could have elected to lead a shift in the packaging paradigm to clear plastic and big labels. It hasn't, opting instead for the lesser course of increasing its use of recycled plastic. And so we have another instance of a greener road not taken.

Twilight of the Champions

There are basically two types of corporate environmentalism. The first, which we might think of as Corporate Environmentalism no 1, is largely operational and compliance-oriented – Environment Health & Safety business-as-usual, essentially, with a handful of eco-efficiency electrons circling around a nucleus of regulatory compliance. The second, Corporate Environmentalism no 2, is more aggressive, more creative, more unorthodox. It is the sort of corporate environmentalism that can lead to substantial breakthroughs, if it is given a home where it can endure and flourish.

Unfortunately, Corporate Environmentalism no 1 – corporate environmentalism in its safe form – has proven to be the default option for virtually every company, while Corporate Environmentalism no 2, and its champions, are at risk.

At the Canadian utility Ontario Hydro, Brian Kelly and his team tried to make sustainable development a part of the core business strategy. At retailer Home Depot, Mark Eisen concentrated on motivating suppliers to deliver environmentally superior products. At consumer products company Church & Dwight, Bryan Thomlison's focus was on driving change through complex multi-stakeholder partnerships.

Unfortunately, all three champions of Corporate Environmentalism no 2 were let go. In Kelly's case, it was because his champion, CEO Maurice Strong, left the company. Home Depot's Eisen fell victim to an organizational shuffle and a subsequent decision to focus on more strictly operational issues. At Church & Dwight, Thomlison got axed as part of a broader corporate downsizing. All these companies had the opportunity to do something dramatic and opted instead to go back to their EH&S knitting. That is hardly a surprise, but it is disappointing. Corporate Environmentalism no 1 is the rule. The bolder, potentially more significant Corporate Environmentalism no 2 is vulnerable and the rare exception – still more testimony to how much could be done and isn't.[43]

Who's Up First? The 'After You, Alphonse' Syndrome

It is the rare company that goes against the business grain. It does happen occasionally, though. For instance, in 1990 Esprit International ran a Plea for Responsible Consumption in *Utne Reader* magazine:

> *Today, more than ever, the direction of an environmentally conscious style is not to have luxury or conspicuous consumption written all over your attire. This is still our message. We believe this could best be achieved by simply asking yourself before you buy something (from us or any other company) whether this is really something you need. It could be you'll buy more or less from us, but only what you need. We'll be happy to adjust our business up or down accordingly, because we'll feel we are then contributing to a healthier attitude about consumption ...*[44]

More recently, the recreational clothing manufacturer Patagonia announced its intention to limit its growth in defiance of the hallowed capitalist tenet, 'expand or perish'. To that end it has reduced its product lines, accompanying its move with printed materials asking consumers pointed questions about how many sets of outdoor clothes they really need.

But examples like these, which invariably come from privately held companies with progressive political agendas, are very much the exception. If a publicly held company tried something similar, a rash of stockholder lawsuits would surely follow.

In some cases, however, the reluctance to lead by example cannot be fobbed off on fear of litigation. Consider, for instance, the case of Dow Chemical's Corporate Environmental Advisory Council (CEAC). The CEAC is an environmental management innovation of the first order. It brings together a group of highly respected and indisputably independent environmental specialists for regular meetings, who advise Dow on environmental-management and related governance issues.

When Dow's CEAC was formed in 1991, it was met with some resistance by company managers who were dubious about the wisdom of opening the corporate doors to outsiders. But those doubts dissolved over time as the CEAC proved to be a valuable management tool.

When companies make decisions without soliciting outside opinion, they run two risks. The first involves institutional parochialism – every corporate culture has its own biases and blinders. Second, the understandable desire of employees to stay on the right side of the boss can stifle dialogue. The CEAC kills both these birds with a single green stone. Indeed, about the only argument that can be mustered against the CEAC is the chestnut that you shouldn't give outsiders strolling rights within the corporate compound.[45]

In Dow's CEAC we have a proven idea and an idea, moreover, whose time has come – one can scarcely imagine an initiative more in tune with the emerging values of collaboration and disclosure. Yet in the six years since Dow founded the CEAC, not a single mainstream company has followed suit.

The CERES principles provide another example of excessive corporate caution. In 1993 the Sun Company became the first company to endorse the principles. Since then only seven more Fortune 500 companies have come aboard. That's a mighty slow rate of acceptance, especially for a document that is not even legally binding. Here, as in other environmental areas, companies want to be first to be second, or first to be third – or better yet, first to be thirtieth.

Over time, the recurring exposure to these mixed messages can get discouraging. We are clearly getting something less from the corporate community than the wholehearted engagement that the global problematique requires. No matter how we explain this unfortunate situation – as a function of unresolved internal conflicts – that is, of having to operate within Nigel Roome's '*interdependent systems which operate at different scales in time and place*', or as the inevitable consequence of the imperatives of global corporate capitalism, as per critics like David Korten – we keep returning to the same picture: of a corporate sector that is playing both sides against the middle and continues to be largely in denial about the severity of the crisis.

One veteran of the corporate environmental wars, a person who spent years working diligently and ultimately unsuccessfully to get a public company to adopt an aggressive pro-environmental strategy, recently confided: '*I have concluded that any corporation that is publicly traded is the enemy. We have to rebuild from the ground up, at the local level with neighborhood-driven, "Mom-and-Pop" capitalism.*'[46]

My friend's despair is understandable – and widespread too, as evidenced by the emergence of a still small but growing, and socially significant, global movement that favours such things as local self-reliance (keeping businesses small and ownership local) and voluntary simplicity (redefining happiness outside the context of Western-style consumption). But while it is easy to sympathize with the impulse to put all one's eggs into the basket of local self-reliance, such a step would be misguided. Clearly there is a place for substantially more local self-reliance and such initiatives need to be encouraged, but we just as clearly need to devote substantial amounts of time and energy to seeking points of leverage within the current industrial system. Whether the prospect pleases or pains you, the fact is that transnational companies are going to be with us for some time. And what this calls for from sustainability activists is, among other things, a sort of corporate strategic aikido – that is, an approach that uses the language and values of mainstream corporate culture to create a business case so compelling that companies are left with little choice but to adopt more sustainable policies and practices.

True, corporations are working within significant constraints, but within those limitations individuals often have substantial freedom of choice and can and do make a difference – not always, but sometimes. In making sustainability a core business strategy, Monsanto's Robert Shapiro is making a considerable difference – that is true even if you take issue with the company's pro-biotechnology interpretation of sustainable development.[47] Ditto for executives like Claude Fussler at Dow Chemical and a whole host of other hard-working – and often under-appreciated (indeed, to the public eye largely invisible) – corporate sustainability champions. Is the road often rocky for them? Absolutely. But change does happen.

Not only can the sustainability initiatives of individuals like this have a positive impact inside their own organizations, but their efforts – if successful by the measure of business culture – can have a domino effect, inspiring other companies to follow suit and at a deeper level driving a shift in the dominant business culture towards ever greater levels of sustainability.

Let's say a progressive foundation were to underwrite the development of a sustainability master plan. Such a document, in my opinion, would have three distinct components. One would be relatively radical: work to build a strong foundation for alternative economic strategies and structures. A second would focus on reversing the considerable structural constraints that the global financial and economic system currently imposes on individual corporations and executives.[48] And the third would be the aforementioned corporate strategic aikido. Such an approach, it seems to me, would be sound practically and at the same time the best possible prescription against despair. And in fact this strategy already is being pursued by sustainability activists around the world, albeit in a random, chaotic, self-generating sort of way. While the precise outcome of their efforts remains to be seen, one thing is certain:

everyone has their own path, their own 'best strategy', and it is all these paths together that create change.

Notes

1   Martin Wright (1997) 'Energy, Economics and Ethics Collide', *Tomorrow* magazine, January/February, p28

2   The document was 'ABB Environmental Management Programme', Initial Review (1996) It was cited in a press release by International Rivers Network, 'NGOs Urge ABB to Quit Malaysian Dam', 5 July

3   In late 1997, the Bakun project was put on hold, for financial not environmental reasons

4   Quoted in Martin Wright (1997) 'Green Energy or White Elephant?', *Tomorrow* magazine, January/February, p34. The comment was outlandish enough to earn Mahathir a place on *Tomorrow's* list of 'environmental chumps' for 1997

5   ibid, p35

6   Quoted in Martin Wright, *Energy, Economics and Ethics*, p28

7   Quoted in Martin Wright (1997) 'Backing Up Bakun', *Tomorrow* magazine, January/February, p29

8   See Carl Frankel (1997) 'Corporate Responsibility Head-Butting', *Tomorrow* magazine, May/June, p27

9   Personal communication, 1994

10   Cliff Gromer (1994) 'New Age of the Electric Car', *Popular Mechanics*, February, p38

11   Dan McCosh (1994) 'We Drive the World's Best Electric Car', *Popular Science*, January, p52

12   Personal communication, 1994

13   Personal communication, 1995

14   Personal communication (1997) Paul Zajac, American Automobile Manufacturers Association, December

15   These data come from a table entitled 'US Retail Sales of Sport Utility Vehicles, 1986–1996', with the credited sources being the American Automobile Manufacturers Association and Ward's Automotive Reports

16   Vince Bielski, 'Fuel Deficiency', from *Sierra* magazine and the Sierra Club website. See http://www.sierraclub.org/sierra/

17   Personal communication, December 1997

18   Quoted in Bielski, *Fuel Deficiency*

19   Responding to widespread criticism, Ford and Chrysler announced in early 1998 that they would refine popular models of their sports utility vehicles so that they would produce no more air pollution than cars. See Keith Bradsher (1998) 'Ford, Chrysler to Cut Emissions of Sport Utility Vehicles, Minivans', *New York Times*, 6 January

20   Keith Bradsher (1997) 'Car Makers Voice Complaints about Limiting Gas Emissions', *New York Times*, 3 October, pD2

21   Joan Magretta (1997) 'Growth Through Global Sustainability: An Interview with Monsanto's CEO, Robert B Shapiro', *Harvard Business Review*, January/February, pp79–88

22   Quoted in Carl Frankel (1996) 'Monsanto Breaks the Mold', *Tomorrow* magazine, May/June, p63

23   See Carl Frankel (1992) 'Consumers Rate Environmental Performance', *Green Market Alert*, February, pp5–6

24   The following case study is drawn from excellent reportage by Kate Victory in the trade newsletter *Business and the Environment*. See Kate Victory (1996) 'Pharmaceutical Firms Get Mixed Market Signals on CFC-Free Inhalers', *Business and the Environment*, October

25   ibid, p2

26   ibid, p3

27   ibid

28   ibid

29   Personal communication, 1995

30   Stephen Engelberg (1997) 'Business Leaves the Lobby and Sits at Congress's Table', *New York Times*, 31 March, ppA1, A26. The Dole bill was not enacted, although efforts continue to enact similar legislation

31   Faye Rice (1995) 'Hands off the EPA! Did We Really Say That?', *Fortune Magazine*, 18 September, p22

32   Quoted in Carl Frankel and Martin Wright (1997) 'The Business Dilemma', *Tomorrow* magazine, January/February, p36

33   Personal communications, 1996

34   See Global Climate Information Project website, http://www.climatefacts.org

35   See Joby Warrick (1997) 'Trade Groups Move to Blunt UN Push for Pollutant Treaty', *Washington Post*, 10 September, pA02

36   The efforts of the Global Climate Coalition have been detailed in Ross Gelbspan (1997) *The Heat Is On: The High Stakes Battle over Earth's Threatened Climate*, Addison-Wesley Publishing Company, New York

37   See American Forest Paper Association (1994) *Sustainable Forestry Initiative*, Washington, DC

38   Personal communication, 1995

39   ibid

40   What this told Holmes, clever soul that he was, was that someone known to the dog had perpetrated the crime in question

41   Richard A Denison (1993) 'It's Time to Take Another Look at Plastics Recycling', *EDF Letter*, vol 24, no 6, November 1993

42   Personal communication, 1995

43   The travails of these sustainability champions are discussed in greater detail in Carl Frankel (1997) 'Twilight of the Champions', *Tomorrow* magazine, September/October, pp28–30

44   *Utne Reader*, July/August 1990, inside cover and p1

45   In point of fact, Dow's secrets are safe with CEAC members who are required to sign confidentiality agreements

46   Personal communication, 1997

47   I use this example not to argue that Monsanto's vision of sustainable development is the correct one – I am undecided on that question – but to make the more limited point that individuals within corporations can be effective change agents. If Monsanto's Shapiro can steer his company toward a version of 'sustainability', with large quotation marks, then in principle there is nothing to keep another executive from guiding his or her company toward a less troublesome version of sustainable development

48   The work of Richard Grossman and Ward Morehouse at the Massachusetts-based Program on Corporations, Law & Democracy is representative of this sort of effort. Grossman and Morehouse argue that a sovereign people should be able to revoke corporate charters (or otherwise place strict limits on corporate behaviour) when that conduct is detrimental to the general welfare and that statutes on the books in many states make it legally appropriate to do so

15

Getting Engaged: Business–NGO Relations on Sustainable Development

David F Murphy and Jem Bendell

Introduction

Monsanto's [cotton] *field trials in Karnataka* [India] *will be reduced to ashes in a few days. These actions will start a movement of direct action by farmers against biotechnology, which will not stop until all the corporate killers like Monsanto, Novartis, Pioneer etc. leave the country.* [If] *we play our cards right at the global level and co-ordinate our work, these actions can also pose a major challenge to the survival of these corporations in the stock markets. Who wants to invest in a mountain of ashes, in offices that are constantly being squatted (and if necessary even destroyed) by activists?*

Professor Nanjundaswamy, of the Karnataka State Farmers Association, November 1998 (quoted in Cummins, 1998, p1)

On 28 November 1998 and again on 2 December, contingents of Indian farmers in the Karnataka region, chanting 'Cremate Monsanto' and 'Stop Genetic Engineering', uprooted and burned genetically engineered cotton fields in front of a bank of television cameras and news reporters. NGOs, including the Karnataka State Farmers Association, have called on the biotechnology company Monsanto to 'get out of India' and for the government to ban field tests and imports of genetically engineered seeds and crops. In Manila, later that year, under the slogans of 'Stop the Terminator Seeds' and 'Put a Face on the Enemy', the Southeast Asia Regional Institute for Community Education and 12 other NGOs organized a militant mass demonstration outside Monsanto's corporate offices (Cummins, 1998, p1).

This sort of antagonism between business and NGOs is not a new phenomenon. In 1962, Rachel Carson's *Silent Spring* launched the contemporary northern environmental movement with an exposé on the harmful effects of pesticides on people and their natural environments. The chemical industry responded with a scathing attack on environmentalists, branding them '*a motley lot ranging from superstitious illiterates and cultists to educated scientists*' (Hoffman, 1996, p53). Thirty years later, in the lead up to the 1992 Rio Earth Summit, Stephan Schmidheiny's *Changing Course* was intended as a clarion call for global business to see environmental pressures as new business opportunities. *Changing Course* launched the Business Council for Sustainable Development (BCSD) and offered 38 case studies of best environmental practice, including chemical producers such as Ciba-Geigy, Dow, DuPont and Shell. Greenpeace responded with a pre-emptive attack on *Changing Course* hours before its official launch in May 1992. Weeks later at the Rio Earth Summit, the NGO released *The Greenpeace Book of Greenwash* (Bruno, 1992) which castigated nine of the BCSD companies for their poor environmental records. From *Silent Spring* to the present day, relations between representatives of business and the NGO movement have, for the most part, remained strongly antagonistic.

The mid-1995 confrontation between Shell and Greenpeace over the disposal of the Brent Spar offshore oil installation confirmed the long-standing image of two tribes engaged in perpetual war over values, words and ideas. Yet this was not the end of the story. Eventually the protests led Shell-UK to engage the Environment Council, a British NGO, to facilitate a series of European-wide 'Dialogue Forums' between the company and a wide range of NGOs and other stakeholders on alternative disposal options for the Brent Spar. In late 1996, Shell-UK's Chief Executive Chris Fay said that his company *'had no option but to pursue the goal of sustainable development'* (Cowe, 1996, p17). Similarly, since the outcry over Shell's operations in Ogoniland, both before and after the Nigerian government executed environmental activist Ken Saro-Wiwa, the company has consulted with Amnesty International on its business principles and new corporate human rights policy.

Why are the relations between business and NGOs important to our understanding of business' role in sustainable development? For three reasons. First, as the business community turns to consider the social aspects of sustainable development and broadens its conceptualization of environmental management (Elkington, 1997), so engaging stakeholders, including NGOs, becomes central to business strategy. Second, the relations between business and NGOs remind us of the social construction of environmental issues (Hannigan, 1995) and the social and political dimensions to business. Drawing on the ideas of the Italian political theorist Antonio Gramsci, David Levy (1997) argues that most environmental management is an exercise in political, not environmental, sustainability. This is a negative critique of the political role of what are unaccountable and undemocratic organizations. In a related vein, Uwe Schneidewind and Holger Petersen (1998) draw on the ideas of British sociologist Anthony Giddens, to argue that as transnational corporations are *architects*, as much as servants, of the political and economic system they operate within, society should demand more overt political responsibility from them.

Increasingly, managers share this new self-awareness. For example, in the past Shell argued that *'politics is the business of governments'* and that the company should not interfere with government policies (NGO Taskforce on Business and Industry, 1997, p19). Since the Brent Spar and Nigeria episodes, senior managers within Shell have begun to change their approach. In 1996, the Shell Group's Chief Executive Cor Herkströter said he wanted the company to replace its *'technological arrogance'* with a more cooperative approach, which recognizes that environmental issues are *'social and political dilemmas'* with *'a range of possible answers'* (Herkströter, 1996, p9). Whereas in the past, a faith in science and certainty governed business decisions, the emerging approach of senior management in international companies is to put people and their organizations, at the centre of the debate – and therefore to acknowledge the political nature of corporate environmentalism and social responsibility.

The third reason and the main focus of this chapter, is that NGOs are increasingly turning to business and the market to pursue their social and environmental objectives. We believe this affects the operating environment of business and its role in the sustainable development of less industrialized countries. In this chapter, therefore, we provide an overview of the different types of NGOs that promote sustainable development, the ways they are affecting business and examine some of the macro-level reasons why this is happening. We conceptualize the changes as a strengthening consumer politics (effecting political and social change through consumer activism) and a system of civil regulation (the 'regulation' of business by NGOs and other organizations of civil society).

Who Are We Talking About?
NGOs and Sustainable Development

Michael M Cernea (1988) argues that the term non-governmental organization (NGO) '*seems deceptively simple*' in that it '*offers a broad umbrella for a kaleidoscopic collection of organizations*' (p9). The 'NGO' acronym is now so ubiquitously used that similar to 'MTV' or 'CNN', it is increasingly taken as understood.

The total number of international, national and local NGOs worldwide is unknown. The Union of International Associations estimated in the early 1990s that there were more than 20,000 international or transnational NGOs. This total included some 1000 NGOs that have consultative status with the UN Economic and Social Council (Willetts, 1998). Within many nation states, the number of national and local NGOs is often much higher. At the end of 1998, there were 188,476 registered 'non-governmental' charities in England and Wales.[1] Ten years ago, Rajesh Tandon (1989) estimated that there were several thousand voluntary agencies in India, including relief and rehabilitation agencies, philanthropic, charity-owned NGOs, social action groups and intermediary organizations.[2] Anand Srinivasan (1999) cites recent estimates of 25,000–30,000 active Indian NGOs, although he acknowledges that there has been no complete census to date.

Unlike CNN or MTV, what is and what is not an NGO is widely debated. Cernea captures the diversity of NGOs rather well:

> *Nongovernmental organizations can be arrayed along a broad spectrum that ranges from strong to very fragile and weak; from international and central to local and peripheral; from very large and federated to small and isolated, from durable and growing to ephemeral and short-lived* (1988, p3).

Organizations as diverse as an international, multi-million dollar operation such as the World Wide Fund For Nature (WWF) and a local farmers' group such as the Association of Sarva Seva Farms (ASSEFA) in India are both described as an NGO. The common understanding about NGOs is that they are non-profit as well as non-governmental. However, 'non-profit' is not an appropriate descriptor, as it could include organizations that lobby on behalf of commercial interests, such as the International Chamber of Commerce (ICC) and other trade or industry associations. Despite the enormous diversity of NGOs worldwide, a general definition of NGOs is none the less possible within the context of this discussion. NGOs are organizations that have as their primary purpose the promotion of social and/or environmental goals rather than the achievement or protection of economic power in the marketplace or political power through the electoral process.

Many NGOs receive both public and private funding, tax breaks and access to the negotiating table of governments, multilateral agencies and, increasingly, corporations. NGOs are gaining greater recognition and power at international, national and local policy levels. The growing participation of large numbers of different NGOs in UN conferences, meetings and other official processes confirms this trend (Krut, 1997). At the same time, many NGOs are finding themselves with a growing responsibility as corporate watchdogs and agents of sustainable development. All NGOs, however, do not have the same global political access and recognition, nor do they all have the same opportunity or inclination to influence business behaviour via either protest or partnership.

Given that the global NGO movement remains exceedingly diverse, largely disorganized and quite often divided, what is it that we can say NGOs stand for, and what is it that we can say NGOs do? To help answer this, we focus on shifts in thinking and action within three broad categories of NGO – environment, development and Southern.

Four waves of environmental NGOs

In the North, environmental NGOs have evolved towards a sustainable development orientation through three waves of environmentalism (Murphy and Bendell, 1997). The first wave of environmentalism began in the 1900s as a residue of the Romantic Movement, which championed a return to nature in the wake of the Industrial Revolution. Therefore, people were primarily concerned with preserving what was 'wild' or 'natural'. It was a Western-centric concept of a divide between humans and nature that led to the creation of the first national parks.

The second wave in most Northern, industrialized countries began in the 1960s. Due in part to the socio-economic changes that supported a variety of new social movements at the time, this environmentalism stressed the oneness of humans and our environment. The emerging science of ecology and the Apollo pictures of the earth in space helped to create this environmental consciousness. The first major environmental campaigning groups were set up around this time and focused primarily on increasing regulation to protect people from industrial pollution.

The third wave began in the mid–late 1980s. With increasing resources but insufficient progress at the international and national policy levels, environmental NGOs began to seek practical ways of moving things forward and implementing solutions. The global environmental problematique began to be broken down into everyday issues with practical remedies. Third-wave environmentalism places increasing emphasis on market-oriented campaigns and seeking workable solutions to environmental problems.

Recently there have been calls for a fourth wave of environmentalism, particularly from Mark Dowie, who describes the fourth wave as:

> *a broad-based, multi-ethnic movement that takes a long-term global view, challenges prevailing economic assumptions, promotes environmental protection as an extension of human rights and engages in direct action when necessary* (1991–1992, p90).

We accept Dowie's suggestion that Northern environmental groups should integrate '*the lessons of the grassroots*' into their strategies (ibid, p90). However, in many respects third-wave environmentalism has already begun to adopt environmental justice and sustainability ideals and strategies, the latter including direct action, consumer boycotts, corporate dialogue and North–South NGO alliances.

Four generations of development NGOs

Many development NGOs based in the North have also begun to embrace the sustainability agenda and the advocacy route. Korten (1990) describes three generations of development NGO strategies. First generation development NGOs focus on the provision of disaster relief and welfare – the original role of Northern NGOs such as Oxfam; second generation strategies focus on promoting small-scale, self-reliant community development; and third generation strategies involve increasingly large and sophisticated NGOs '*working in a catalytic, foundation-like role rather than an operational service-delivery role … facilitating … other organisations* [to develop] *the capacities, linkages and commitments required to address designated needs on a sustained basis*' (Korten, 1987, p149).

Korten goes on to describe the need for fourth-generation NGOs which aim to build '*a critical mass of independent, decentralised initiatives in support of a social vision*' (1990, p127). Part of this strategy is building links between different NGOs and addressing the more structural issues at the heart of social and environmental problems. Whereas third-generation NGOs '*seek changes in specific policies and institutions*', Korten suggests that fourth-generation NGOs will facilitate the coming together of loosely defined networks of people and organizations, across national borders in the North and South, to transform the institutions of global society (1990, p123).

Southern NGOs

The typologies outlined above are particularly relevant for understanding the role of Northern-based NGOs in promoting sustainable development. Despite recent efforts by both development and environmental NGOs in the North to broaden their respective agendas, for the most part they remain distinctive NGO categories. For many Southern NGOs, community and activist groups, however, the division between environment and development is not so clear. For example, the Malaysia-based Third World Network or the Mexican Coalition on Environment and Development embrace a broader sustainable development agenda than Northern NGOs such as WWF or Oxfam. While many Southern environmental NGOs remain urban, middle-class membership organizations with limited grassroots connections, there are numerous examples of environmental NGO collaboration with peasant organizations and indigenous peoples, particularly in Latin America and Asia (Reilly, 1995; Heyzer et al, 1995).

When local Southern groups protest against their lands being acquired or their rivers being poisoned, they are fighting for their mutual, material interests (Collinson, 1996). The environmental problems faced by peoples of developing countries often have far more severe effects on their livelihoods than for people in the North. In recent years, many Southern groups have begun to assume the language of Northern environmental NGOs and present their dilemmas in environmental terms. Martin Khor of the Third World Network captures this phenomenon well with the following comments:

> *Our goals in the South are about survival, humanity and dignity. And democracy. A great deal of energy has been spent in the South ... in helping social movements regain their right to land and other resources, in order to promote their rights to good health and adequate nutrition, to safety, to housing and to a sustainable environment. All these changes are necessary for both social justice and a sound environmental and development policy* (1993, p223).

The global NGO movement remains extremely heterogeneous, not merely in relation to environment–development or North–South differences. Whether one compares NGOs on a global or even on a national basis, there are as many differences in NGO philosophy, purpose and strategy as there are similarities. To paraphrase Rubem C Fernandes, common wisdom on a global scale may be unattainable given such '*highly diverse hierarchies of values*' (1994, pp319–320), although there is evidence of an emergent, shared, discourse based around a critique of economic globalization (Lynch, 1998).

What Are We Talking About? Conflict and Collaboration

The aspect of NGO work that we concern ourselves with in this chapter is that which is of concern to business. Our research has found that both managers and campaigners believe that NGOs are affecting corporate policies on social and environmental issues. This influence has major implications for the sustainable development of local communities worldwide. NGOs are influencing these communities, via business, in three key ways: forcing change, through boycotts, direct action and lobbying; facilitating change though various forms of partnership; and sustaining change by establishing alternative trading systems and 'regulatory' mechanisms. To illustrate these strategies we provide a short case study of relations between NGOs and the timber trade.

The case of deforestation and NGO relations with the timber trade

Deforestation arrived as a significant international policy issue and major Northern media story in the mid-1980s (Humphreys, 1997). Since that time the rates of forest degradation have shown little evidence of slowing. Despite lengthy consultations among governments and rising concerns from the public reaching a peak at the 1992 Rio Earth Summit, deforestation has increased dramatically over the last five years. Tropical forests are disappearing at the rate of nearly 1 per cent per year, with the annual deforestation rate in the Brazilian Amazon increasing 34 per cent between 1991 and 1994 (United Nations, 1997; Serrill, 1997).

One of the major stages for deforestation and conflict between business and local groups in the 1980s was Amazonia. Unions of rubber tappers led the fight against cattle ranchers and loggers. Meagre rubber-tapper livelihoods were being threatened because rubber barons realized they could make more money cutting down the trees and grazing cattle. Accordingly the tappers decided to stage 'empates', direct action protests whereby chain-saw gangs were confronted and asked to leave the land they were clearing. These protests raised the attention of the international media so that '*by the mid-1980s … indigenous groups and tappers were considered legitimate participants in the debate*' (Dore, 1996, p15).

One protester who rose to international fame was Chico Mendes, the leader of the Xapuri Rural Workers Union. He soon became a symbol of the human-dimension to the deforestation issue:

> *With Mendes' involvement with the rubber tappers, the authorities could no longer dismiss efforts to save the rain forests as foreigners interfering with Brazilian affairs* (Rowell, 1996a, p214).

In December 1988 Mendes was the ninetieth rural activist to be murdered in Brazil that year (Hall, 1996). After his death the world's news media reverberated with headlines and leading stories on the rubber tappers and deforestation. With increased NGO campaigning and media coverage, the profile of environmental issues rose in most Northern countries in the late 1980s. As the struggles of indigenous peoples against tropical deforestation became known, the role of the timber trade became a key consumer concern. For example, a wooden product such as a mahogany table came to be associated with the murder of forest dwellers. At this time, local, largely autonomous Rainforest Action Groups (RAGs) in North America, Europe and Australia were formed.

In Britain, beginning in the spring of 1991, various RAGs started to take direct action against wood-product retailers. These groups organized mock chainsaw massacres outside do-it-yourself (DIY) home improvement and furniture stores with protesters dressed as loggers graphically depicting the destruction of the world's rainforests. Protesters leafleted customers and delivered anti-tropical timber pledges to store managers. The intention was to discourage customers from buying tropical timber products.

Later in 1991, local Friends of the Earth (FoE-UK) groups built upon the initial RAG protests. On one November weekend, there were over a hundred demonstrations, including 25–30 demonstrations outside the outlets of DIY market leader B&Q plc. Subsequently, on 11 December, FoE-UK claimed in a press release that its protests had prompted dramatic policy developments in the DIY retailers B&Q, Texas Homecare and Homebase, who were now committed to '*stop selling environmentally damaging tropical rainforest timber*' (FoE-UK, 1991). The anti-DIY demonstrations proved to be highly successful and garnered considerable media and public attention. Customers began to write letters to the retailers and to confront store managers and employees with tough questions about timber sourcing. For the most part, the companies took both the protests and customer letters very seriously.

Meanwhile, WWF-International was itself beginning to turn to industry, having become disillusioned with protracted international negotiations on a global forest convention and other international policy initiatives. In 1989, WWF had already announced its own 1995 target for the world's timber trade to be sustainable. At the 1992 Rio Earth Summit, governments could only produce the 'toothless' 'Non-legally Binding Authoritative Statement of Principles for a Global Consensus on the Management, Conservation and Sustainable Development of all Types of Forests'. Francis Sullivan, then WWF-UK forest officer, believed '*you cannot just sit back and wait for governments to agree, because this could take forever*' (1994). He felt certain it was right to try and work with people and companies who might be able to get things done.

For the DIY trade, WWF-UK appeared to offer a solution to a mounting business problem. Following WWF-UK's 'Forests Are Your Business' seminar in December 1991, ten companies committed themselves to reaching the WWF-UK 1995 target and launched the so-called 1995 Group. The cumulative effects of direct action and boycotts had forced change from companies and now it was the turn of WWF to facilitate further change.

To join the 1995 Group, the companies had to agree to phase out by 1995, the purchase and sale of all wood and wood products not sourced from well-managed forests. It soon became apparent, however, that the participating companies needed a credible system for defining good forest management and for ensuring that products were from such forests. What was needed was a standard-setting body with a system for verifying product claims. Following 18 months of preparatory work, the Forest Stewardship Council (FSC) was launched in 1993. The Founding Group consisted of environmental NGOs, forest industry representatives, community forestry groups and forest product certification organizations. Both WWF-International and B&Q, among other organizations, provided financial and logistical support.

The FSC mission statement commits members to '*promote management of the world's forests that is environmentally appropriate, socially beneficial and economically viable*' – language consistent with the principles of sustainable development. The FSC accredits certification bodies to ensure that they adhere to FSC principles and criteria when certifying forests as well managed and allows them to issue the FSC logo once a chain of custody has been recorded from the forest to the company selling the end product. Becoming fully operational in early 1996, the FSC represented the first global mechanism for denoting responsible forest management.[3] Through its establishment, NGOs like WWF were effectively institutionalizing changes to the existing 'regulatory' framework for the timber trade. Later in the chapter, we explore further the emergence of this new form of regulation.

By the end of 1995, commercial support for the FSC had spiralled in the UK. The WWF-UK 1995 Group had reached 47 members, accounting for about a quarter of the British consumption of wood products. Although many of the companies did not reach the 1995 target, a significant number had purchased certified timber and had specified where most if not all their timber was coming from. The 1995 Group was consequently extended with the revised target that companies would purchase wood only from certified forests by the year 2000. By 1999, there were over 90 members in the renamed 1995+ Group. The UK experience with business–NGO partnership in the forest products sector has provided a basis for sustaining change in forest management practices around the world.

Partnerships between the timber industry and NGOs are growing in other countries. There are similar timber buyers groups or business–NGO partnerships committed to the FSC in Australia, Austria, Belgium, France, Germany, The Netherlands, North America, Spain, Scandanavia and Switzerland. The Dutch 'Hart Voor Hout' initiative dates back to early 1992 and many of its developments paralleled the British experience – namely, the catalytic role of protest in leading DIY retailers to seek NGO partners (Murphy, 1997).

The impetus for Northern buyers groups, of course, comes from Northern consumers, campaigners, corporations and NGOs. However, members of Southern civil society also have a voice in the process, through the FSC. Representatives of NGOs such as the Foundation of the Peoples of the South Pacific (Papua New Guinea), FUDENA (Venezuela) and SKEPHI (Indonesia) participate in the FSC as either board representatives or members of specialist working groups. At the national level in the South, FSC working groups have been established to ensure that the global principles and criteria are adapted to the local context – for example, Brazil and Cameroon. Although only 25 per cent of current FSC members are from the South, the organization is supporting efforts to increase this number. Furthermore, a special working group on social aspects of certification is attempting to find ways in which the social performance of the FSC could be improved (Colchester, 1997).

The case of deforestation and the timber trade illustrates the three key ways NGOs are influencing business: forcing change, facilitating change and sustaining change. We now describe these relations in more detail.

Forcing change

NGOs appear to be able to force corporations to change their policies and practices through boycotts, direct action and lobbying. The deforestation case study illustrates the way that NGOs can force change in corporate practice. There are numerous other examples of boycotts (in the North) and direct action (in the North and South) leading to changes in policy with implications for sustainable development in the South.

For example, the fracas over Shell's proposed dumping of the oil platform Brent Spar, mentioned at the start of this chapter, subsequently led the media to turn its attention to Shell Nigeria's use of lower environmental standards in the West African country's Delta region. From 1982 to 1992, 1.6 million gallons of oil were spilled from Shell's Nigerian fields in 27 separate incidents. Various Niger Delta communities had experienced Shell's gas flaring 24 hours a day for 30 years (Rowell, 1995). The company was also accused of implicitly supporting human rights abuses, given its perceived close association with the repressive Nigerian military regime. For example, at one of the many demonstrations against the company in Ogoniland, 80 villagers were killed by the Nigerian Mobile Police Force. In addition, in late 1995 the government executed the leader of the Movement for the Survival of the Ogoni People (MOSOP), Ken Saro-Wiwa and eight other Ogoni activists.

The protests, which had been ignored for years before they went global and which involved such violent repression, finally forced the company to change its policies and practice. In March 1997 Shell released its revised business principles, which included for the first time explicit support for human rights, and in May, Shell published its first public report on community and environmental issues in Nigeria. That report established new targets, including an end to gas flaring within ten years. A year earlier Shell's former group chief executive offered an indication of the company's new stance:

> *We must remain sensitive to the evolving needs and concerns of all our stakeholders. I fully accept that, in this process, we must be prepared to engage in wider debates – including on human rights issues* (Herkströter, 1996, p14).

There are many other examples of protests, their initial repression and then policy change from the corporations being criticized (see Murphy and Bendell, 1997). In 1995, NGO activists campaigned against chemical company DuPont's plan to build Asia's largest nylon factory in Goa, India. The activists alleged that the US$200 million plant would pollute rivers, deplete drinking-water supplies and desecrate sacred Hindu land. At one demonstration in January 1995, police fired on protesters, killing one. Reportedly enraged at the death, the protesters went on the rampage and burnt down DuPont's project office. Later that year, amid continuing protest, DuPont announced that it was moving its plant to the neighbouring state of Tamil Nadu (Rowell, 1996a).

In the North, activist attendance at annual shareholder meetings to demonstrate or table controversial motions is another forcing mechanism, as is the growing NGO support for ethical investment, now worth £15 billion in the UK, where investments are screened against social and environmental criteria. Although these tactics have worldwide implications, they do not yet appear to be a viable option for NGOs in countries where consumer and investment power is less influential.

Of course, NGOs are not always successful in forcing change. Nestlé's experience with infant formula boycotts since the late 1970s is a case in point. Despite the company's commitment in 1984 to abide by the marketing code of the World Health Organization, Nestlé has continued to face NGO pressure since 1988. Nestlé insists that it is abiding by the code, but NGOs such as Action for Corporate Accountability argue that the company continues to promote bottle feeding over breast feeding, thereby contributing to infant deaths and disease (*Business and Society Review*, 1992). Although NGOs may not be successful in realizing change in corporate policy, by putting an issue on the agenda, conflict can lead to governmental intervention, as appears to be the case with the issue of biotechnology in India. After the protests of farmers, mentioned at the beginning of this chapter, the Andhra Pradesh provincial government asked Monsanto to halt all field trials of genetically modified cotton in the state. Government officials in New Delhi also reiterated that the so-called 'Terminator Technology' seeds, patented by the company Monsanto, will not be allowed into the country (Cummins, 1998).

Facilitating change

As the timber trade case illustrated, conflict between business and NGOs can often lead to collaboration. By partnering with industry, NGOs are facilitating change in corporate social and environmental practice, with major implications for sustainable development in the South. These business–NGO collaborations differ from the close relationships of the past, as they are not based on corporate philanthropy but on strategic partnerships dealing with the internal operational issues of participating businesses.

The experience of WWF's partnership with timber companies in the WWF 1995 Group has led to a similar initiative to conserve the world's fisheries. In 1996 WWF-International launched a partnership with the Unilever Corporation, the world's largest buyer of frozen fish, to create economic incentives within the seafood industry for sustainable fishing throughout the world. The new Marine Stewardship Council (MSC) is the result of their endeavours.

Development NGOs are also beginning to facilitate the contribution of major companies to sustainable development in the South. For example, in the UK the Fairtrade Foundation, a coalition of international development, consumer and fair trade organizations, launched a pilot project in 1997 to work with British companies to develop codes of practice to guide relationships with their Southern suppliers. A similar initiative, but with a broader mandate and with government financing was launched in early 1998:

> The ETI is an alliance of companies, non-governmental organisations (NGOs) and trade union organisations committed to working together to identify and promote good practice in the implementation of codes of labour practice, including the monitoring and independent verification of the observance of code provisions (ETI, 1999).

By late 1999, the Ethical Trading Initiative (ETI) had 14 corporate members, including supermarket chains such as Asda, J Sainsbury and Tesco and leading garment industry players such as Levi Strauss and the Pentland Group. Sixteen NGOs including Oxfam (UK/I), and Save the Children Fund are involved, along with three trade union organizations. The ETI is supported by the UK government's Department for International Development.

Meanwhile, many Southern NGOs have limited experience of collaborative relations with big business, either national or global. There is also little evidence of Southern business embracing civil society as allies. Mutual prejudices will take time to overcome. Nicanor Perlas of the Philippine Council for Sustainable Development explains:

The thawing of the lines between business and civil society is fairly recent. Bridges are still being built. Trust is still being developed. Common policy agendas are still being nurtured (Perlas 1997).

Despite this there are some examples of southern NGOs facilitating change in corporate practice: two examples from India and Zimbabwe are noted below.

The Peddireddy Thimma Reddy Farm Foundation in Hyderabad, India, is dedicated to the protection and strengthening of farming and farm communities. Inspired by Gandhian concepts, the NGO promotes a vigorous agricultural industry that embraces rural development and international markets. The director, P Chengal Reddy, is both an advocate of the farmer and a facilitator for agri-business. In 1996, Peddireddy received a grant from the US-based Asia Foundation to work with Suvera Processed Foods Private Limited, a local agri-processing company, to address pollution in the mango-processing industry. Each of Suvera's 27 mango pulp-processing factories in India's Chittoor District dump 2000 tons of waste every harvest season. To reduce Suvera's processing wastes and convert remaining wastes into new products, Peddireddy focused on clean production research, training, consultation and technical analysis. Initial training in clean production was given to selected workers and managers. The NGO identified opportunities to reduce pollution and extend the company's season of employment into the off-season by converting mango waste into new products such as fuel, cocoa-extender, cattle feed and fertilizer. As an addition, machinery manufacturers were involved in discussions to reduce large energy losses in the processing plant.

Suvera benefited from Peddireddy's familiarity with local environmental conditions and its research capabilities, training and social expertise. By working with the NGO, Suvera Foods achieved a 95 per cent reduction in waste, leading to minimized waste-hauling costs and the new by-products resulted in new sales for Suvera. As a consequence, interest in clean production has expanded among NGOs and industries in other parts of India (Plante and Bendell, 1998).

In Zimbabwe, the development NGO Organization of Rural Associations for Progress (ORAP) and Central African Batteries (CAB) have been working together since 1992. ORAP initially provided CAB with foreign currency to enable a consortium of Zimbabwean business people to purchase the company which was a multinational subsidiary at the time. In exchange, ORAP was reimbursed in Zimbabwe dollars, given 10 per cent of CAB's shares, granted a place on the company's board and guaranteed an annual income of Z$100,000. ORAP in turn agreed to use these funds to promote income-generating projects. The ongoing ORAP–CAB partnership is a formal joint venture that creates small businesses to sell or lease batteries to households and to develop solar-powered recharging centres. This helps to promote a more regular and sustainable energy source for local lighting (UNEP/PWBLF, 1994).

From a business point of view, the reasons for collaboration fall into three broad categories. First, there is the management of corporate responsibility. Major corporations need to interact with and respond to NGOs as a means of demonstrating corporate accountability and thus their legitimacy as powerful global economic and political actors. A second motivation for collaboration is the need for corporations

---

Box 15.1 NGOs as a New 'Asset' for Business

Credibility A recent study by the Investor Responsibility Research Centre outlines how environmental reports and claims by companies continue to suffer from a credibility gap in the eyes of a variety of stakeholders (SustainAbility and UNEP, 1996). *'Faced with this credibility challenge, active dialogue and stakeholder partnerships assume unprecedented importance'* (ibid, p21). Northern retailers of products from Southern countries are particularly in need of credible information to reassure consumers, as illustrated by our case study of the WWF 1995 Group and the Forest Stewardship Council. Southern producers also require credibility for their social and environmental claims in order to access ethically sensitive markets in the North.

Marketing Greater credibility can facilitate sensitive promotion of products, services or companies in relation to sustainable development issues. By working with NGOs, some companies are generating a level of interest in their environmental policies which hitherto has only been experienced by the likes of the eco-conscious Body Shop.

Expertise NGOs have a wealth of expertise on sustainable development issues. For example, our timber trade case study showed that with complex supply chains and often strained buyer–supplier relations, the DIY retailers benefited from WWF-UK's free advice in implementing their forest product sourcing and certification programmes.

Ideas Related to expertise is the resource of ideas and critical thinking that NGOs can provide. If profit-making organizations are to meet growing social and environmental demands, they will need to undergo profound organizational change. In future, business needs to consider fundamental questions such as: 'Who really needs this product?' and 'Will the community be healthy and prosperous enough to produce and to buy our products in the future?' In order to address such concerns, business needs to work with other sectors of society and to share ideas.

Networks Northern companies can tap into NGO networks in order to address sustainable development issues on the ground in countries where their suppliers are operating. International NGO networks also offer opportunities for Southern suppliers to access socially and environmentally progressive markets in the North.

---

to manage conflict and protect corporate reputation. For reasons of marketing, recruitment, employee motivation and risk management (preventing store boycotts and protecting share prices), it is prudent to cultivate the public impression of a socially and environmentally responsible business in a society with established consumer politics. The third reason, for managers acting on the sustainable development agenda, is that companies can access new resources by partnering NGOs. These 'resources' relate to credibility, expertise, marketing, ideas and networks (Box 15.1).

Sustaining change

In addition to forcing and facilitating change in business behaviour, NGOs are actually sustaining change in the marketplace by 'going it alone' and establishing new trading relationships and even new systems of 'regulation'. These changes have an impact on the operating environment of business, as the following examples illustrate.

New 'fair trade' relationships have been established by NGOs in the North and producers of commodities in the South. These alternative trading relationships have captured market share from other companies and demonstrated that responsible, sustainable, business is workable. One example is Cafédirect, a UK-based marketing company which promotes the Cafédirect brand of fairly traded coffee. As of early 1999, Cafédirect had a 4 per cent share of the UK roasted coffee market and 2 per cent of the freeze-dried market.

In addition to establishing alternative supply chains, where NGOs own, or partly own, the trade, NGOs are also establishing alternative 'regulatory' systems, where NGOs 'own', or partly own, the rules of trade. For example, in the timber trade case study, NGOs such as WWF helped set up a new globally applicable system for the endorsement of products from well-managed forests: the FSC accreditation, certification and labelling scheme. Instead of waiting for intergovernmental regulatory agreements or better implementation of existing governmental regulations, the NGOs established their own system. With increasing numbers of companies demanding FSC-endorsed products, the NGOs have really begun to change the rules of the timber trade.

Of course, the development of the FSC has much to do with the earlier campaign work of NGOs. Without RAG and FoE-UK forcing change through protests against DIY retailers, WWF would not necessarily have had the opportunity to facilitate change in the timber trade. Then, without WWF facilitating a market demand for well-managed forest products, the FSC would not have been effective in sustaining change through providing a new regulatory mechanism for such products. Conversely, without strategies for facilitating and sustaining change, the forced changes in corporate behaviour would not necessarily be meaningful or durable. Thus we see how the three types of market-oriented NGO strategy are not mutually exclusive; rather, each strategy is more or less dependent on NGOs pursuing the other strategies at the same time.

In describing the three types of market-oriented NGO strategy we do not mean to imply that there is a similar situation with business–NGO relations globally: there is a great deal of regional differentiation in the types of NGOs and business. To date, there appears to be greater evidence of NGOs forcing or facilitating change in corporate policy in the North than in the South. There is limited evidence of business–NGO partnerships in the South. This is partly due to the fact that most NGOs in the South have *'allied themselves with popular movements to oppose the state, while for all practical purposes, ignoring the market and its institutions'* (de Oliveira and Tandon 1994, p7). In the face of globalization and state deregulation, however, Southern NGOs are increasingly engaging business. We now discuss why this is the case.

Why Now? The Politics of Pressure in a Globalizing Economy

From the examples provided, it is evident that NGOs are developing more coherent market-oriented strategies to pursue their objectives. A number of dynamics are combining to generate these new strategies, including economic globalization, developments in telecommunications and information technology, the emergence of global brands and a strengthened form of 'consumer politics'. We deal with each in turn.

The first dynamic is the emergence of the global economy and the perceived decline in the role of the nation state. Supported by the new communication technologies, '*alliances of various kinds have given rise to the stateless corporation in which people, assets and transactions move freely across international borders*' (Snow and Coleman, 1992, p8). The 1990s have also seen the rapid development of global money markets. Private investment in the developing world spiralled from US$44 billion in 1990 to over US$167 billion in 1995 (World Bank, 1996). During the same period, official development assistance (ODA) fell slightly to a total of US$59 billion by 1995 (OECD DAC, 1996). Today, private money is influencing the levels of environmental protection and social welfare in the South as much as, if not more than, the ODA:

> [H]ow the hundreds of billions of private capital are spent matters far more than how the few billion dollars of official assistance devoted to environmental investments [and development programmes] gets dispensed (Esty and Gentry, 1997, p2).

The globalization of trade and finance may be proceeding at a pace but the globalization of governance, as expressed through 'government', is not (Schiavone, 1997). With increasingly large and mobile capital and industry, the power of governments to set their own policy agendas has weakened (Camilleri and Falk, 1992; Korten, 1995; Strange, 1996). In a global market, if a TNC does not favour the policies of a particular government it can choose to locate elsewhere. These types of investment decisions by TNCs are increasingly important as they control 33 per cent of the world's productive assets (UNRISD, 1995). If the international money markets anticipate a withdrawal by a number of TNCs, then confidence in a country's economic performance and therefore its currency may decline, leading to an economic downturn. Hence the international economy is determining state monetary and fiscal policy, propelling governments into a process of competitive deregulation.

At the international policy level, the predominance of global trade matters appears to be undermining efforts to promote international environmental and labour standards and sustainable development. Many international negotiations on new sustainable development policies have resulted in an impasse typified by the failure of Earth Summit II delegates in 1997 to agree on either a forest convention or a joint political statement on forest protection. Even when consensus is achieved around new conventions and protocols, such legally-binding international agreements typically include loopholes and take decades to ratify and implement, not to mention ensuring compliance (Ryle, 1997). Lending impetus to the need for policy alternatives, Miguel de Oliveira and Rajesh Tandon suggest that *'the same processes that globalize problems also globalize solutions'* (1994, p5).

The undermining of state authority does not necessarily mean that the market rules, as it also provides *'unprecedented opportunities for the global emergence of a third sector'* (de Oliveira and Tandon, 1994, p4). These opportunities arise from developments in telecommunications and information technology. Global access to computers, fax machines, modems, satellite communications, solar-powered battery packs and hand-held video cameras has provided many NGOs with greater knowledge, voice and power. Although the vast majority of the world's poor and powerless do not have direct access to information technology, growing numbers of NGOs and activist groups do. The flow of information around the world during political uprisings and following the disappearances or murders of notable campaigners lends added political weight to these events. *'Thanks to cyberspace, absolute control over information access is no longer possible'* (Johnston, 1997, p336). Consequently, risk-management consultant John Bray notes that *'in an Internet-connected world, companies are coming to realise that there is no hiding place for poor performance on environmental and social issues'* (1998, p128).

A third factor relates to the role that major corporations are beginning to assume in the psyche of people in developed and developing countries. With global expansion, certain brands have become well known throughout the world. A brand image is an aggregate of the thoughts of customers or investors associated with a particular company symbol, from a product logo to a stock market listing. Brand image and therefore corporate reputation, have become so important that changes to them can have significant effects on company profitability or value (Griffith and Ryans, 1997). Environmental and social issues hold both positive and negative potentials for companies with global brand images. Meanwhile, many NGOs carry public opinion with them on environmental and social issues, which means that they have the ability to affect corporate brand image in these areas.

In addition to these global or Northern processes, there is a factor peculiar to Southern NGOs which is leading them to focus their advocacy efforts on the market. In many countries, the pressures of foreign debt and structural adjustment programmes often limit the scope of governments to act on ethical issues such as environmental protection and fair pay. Consequently, governments do not have sufficient resources to respond to NGOs and to implement policies for sustainable development.

With a variety of campaigning tools at their disposal, NGOs – North and South – are creating a new politics of pressure to which business must respond. In her review of the state of the environment and human rights at the end of the millennium, Barbara Rose Johnston concludes that:

> *Perhaps the strongest evidence of progressive political change is found in the informal 'civic organization' sector, where the ability to organize, communicate, create networks and form coalitions has meant the emergence of a political force whose power and impact cannot be overstated* (1997, p332).

The emergence of this new political force requires analysis within the context of historical political movements. Thus it is time to consider a final dynamic – the growth of consumer politics.

What Can It Mean? The Emergence of 'Consumer Politics' and 'Civil Regulation'

It is widely understood that worker unrest with factory owners and other capitalists in most Northern industrialized countries at the turn of the last century led to the establishment and legal protection of trade unions and a democratic political force for workers. Critics of capitalism argued for the development of a 'producer politics' where workers unite in order to control capitalist access to labour. The social democracies that emerged from this period embodied the notion that capitalism worked best if there was a counterbalancing force to capitalists through strong government and trade unions: capitalists needed the workers while workers, it was argued, needed the capitalists.

At the close of the century this balance has been lost. This social democratic system has led to, or coincided with, a huge expansion of many economies during the 20th century. Neo-liberal governments have largely rejected the social democratic model, rolling back the state, privatizing state industries and promoting greater international free trade. Trade union power and influence has also declined. The result is that global business does not have an effective counterbalancing force of globally organized workers. Increasingly the offer of the lowest pay and working conditions wins capitalist investment.

The decline in trade unions in most Northern countries is linked to the way work has changed. People are changing jobs more quickly than before. Family members no longer do what their parents did. For many people, personal identity is not determined so much by one's work but increasingly by how one spends one's money and spare time. Many people have more money and spare time. This, in turn, has seen a rise in consumerism and the emergence of consumers as socio-economic and political actors. In Northern industrialized countries, environmental concern has not led to workers uniting to demand better corporate performance, but to consumers uniting to do so. Whereas the establishment of trade unions and powerful political parties arose from the workers' movement, the establishment of NGOs arose from the environmental movement. Usually supported by financial donations and voluntary labour, NGOs can be regarded as the organizational expression of 'consumer politics'.

Whereas producer politics gained its power through controlling access to labour, consumer politics gains its power through controlling access to customers. Corporate boycotts and direct action protests are the confrontational outcomes of consumer politics, in contrast to the strikes and lockouts of producer politics. Business–NGO partnerships are the cooperative tools of consumer politics, in contrast to the social dialogue and business–union deals of producer politics. Whether consumer politics can exert the same counterbalancing force as producer politics did in the past is still open to question. Dialogue between businesses and NGOs about consumer concerns may offer an opportunity to build meaningful partnerships for sustainable development.

Consumers and their NGO advocates, however, need power to force companies to enter into genuine dialogue and partnership. Certain groups of consumers (and their advocates) do not have the same power as other consumers. Consumer power is often linked to spending power. In consumer politics it is one dollar, one vote, not one person, one vote. This poses major problems for people with little, or no, consumer power: citizens of Southern countries have far less of this political power than their counterparts in the North. However, with producer politics, power is not gained by an individual's worth as a worker but is gained through collective action and collective bargaining. In the same way, cooperation and camaraderie between NGOs in the North and South may be able to deliver the necessary counterbalance to international business and create a favourable socio-economic environment for sustainable development. Indeed, such a counterbalancing force from NGOs could even be considered as a new form of 'regulation'.

Positive corporate responses to the tactics of NGOs could be characterized as voluntary initiatives and therefore be examples of self-regulation. Self-regulation has been championed as a way of promoting sustainable development by allowing flexibility in addressing environmental issues and by creating incentives for environmental innovations (WBCSD, 1997). However, self-regulation is criticized by both environmentalists and academics for not going far enough and for being used by industry as a means of discouraging new environmental legislation (Welford, 1997; FoE-UK, 1995). The United Nations Research Institute for Social Development (UNRISD) contends that *'international business cannot be expected to author their own regulation: this is the job of good governance'* (UNRISD, 1995, p19).

Positive corporate engagement with NGOs is not merely self-regulation. Certainly, some of the impetus for the changes is coming from the business community itself, through organizations such as the World Business Council for Sustainable Development (WBCSD) and the ICC. Key individuals within companies are also playing instrumental roles in the change process. However, the catalytic roles of Northern and Southern NGOs as business provocateurs and partners are also driving these changes.

We are witnessing the emergence of a different model of business regulation which we call civil regulation (Bendell, 1998; Zadek, 1999). Civil regulation is defined as a situation where organizations of civil society,[1] such as NGOs, set the standards for business behaviour. Companies may then choose to adopt or not to adopt these standards. For those that adopt the standards and treat NGOs as potential assets instead of threats, a number of commercial and non-commercial benefits are available (see Box 15.1). For those companies that choose not to adopt these standards, the forcing tactics of consumer politics can be expected from NGOs (boycotts, direct action, etc), with deleterious effects on corporate reputation, sales and costs. Whereas government fines for pollution violations now rarely affect company value, consumer politics brings greater financial risks. Although governments may have the purported monopoly on force – and therefore the 'final say' – in reality, the ability of NGOs to regulate business behaviour through carrots and sticks is rapidly becoming more

---

Box 15.2 Reconsidering Regulation

The use of the term 'regulation' may seem strange, but not when you consider the classical concept. From a reworking of Kantian writings (Kant, 1964), a regulatory framework can be defined as a norm-creating and norm-enforcing system which must exhibit the following five components:

1   an agent, or agents, which can make choices between alternative norms of behaviour;
2   alternative norms of behaviour between which to choose;
3   a subject, be it something or someone, upon which a chosen norm is imposed;
4   a resolution regarding which of the alternative norms should apply to the subject;
5   a mechanism for ensuring that the chosen norm is adhered to by the subject(s).

In terms of national government and the legislature the resolution regarding which norm to choose is called 'legislation' and the preferred norm is called a 'law'. However, it is wrong to assume national government to be the only agent considering different norms of behaviour and making resolutions about which should apply to different subjects and then using a mechanism to ensure compliance.

In civil regulation the agent is civil society, where, given concerns with sustainable development, different norms of behaviour for corporations are debated. NGOs then make resolutions about the standards that should be upheld by the subjects of the regulation, the corporations. The mechanism for compliance is provided by consumer politics. Therefore, from a reworking of the classical roots of modern thought about government and the rule of law we find that whereas legal regulation is in decline, civil regulation is a valid depiction of modern business–NGO relations.

---

powerful. Consequently, we believe that the use of the term regulation is justified (Box 15.2).

The business case for active compliance with civil regulation, 'civil compliance', is clear: avoiding the costs of conflict and tapping into the assets of civil society, as we outlined above. Further to this there is a more strategic reason why companies should welcome the emergence of civil regulation. Companies are caught in a prisoners' dilemma which makes them externalize as many social and environmental costs as possible: the worry is that if they do not externalize these costs, they will not be as competitive as the company that does. While profitability may rise in the short-term as a result of lax regulation, this is not a stable social climate for business in the longer term. Civil unrest in the South can be understood as a reaction to the inadequacy of the state and to corporate malfeasance. The only escape can come from working together and tipping the market in favour of responsible business. To achieve this, business requires an external force to push reluctant companies forward. In the 21st century, it does not appear that governments will have sufficient capacity to play this role. Instead, intergovernmental bodies and civil society organizations must take on greater responsibility for maintaining a level playing-field. This is the business case for new global governance mechanisms and, consequently, civil regulation.

What's the Catch? Limitations of Civil Regulation

In this chapter we have suggested that the regulatory vacuum created by economic globalization is being filled, to some extent, by NGOs. Yet the archaic nature of civil regulation suggests that it will not be sufficient on its own to deliver environmental security and socio-economic justice. Key questions remain.

What is the potential for the civil regulation of businesses involved in trade where there are markets with less developed consumer politics? For example, in the case of forestry, Northern business support for the FSC has not stopped Asian companies with poor management practices from increasing their logging activities in tropical forests. This is because the growing demand for timber in the emerging economies has not yet been matched by a growing consumer politics. Even as Northern-based companies in other sectors develop higher social and environmental standards for their operations in the South, their Asian or Latin American competitors are likely to continue to cut corners when supplying Southern markets. This means that civil regulation, as expressed through certification and labelling schemes, may merely serve to shift international trading patterns and have little affect on environmental protection or sustainable development in the South.

What is the potential of civil regulation in countries where the ability to organize, take direct action and speak freely is not protected by government? Without the ability to wield the 'stick', Southern NGOs and communities will not be able to realize the benefits of civil regulation. The ability to do this relies on government protecting civil liberties, which is not the situation in all countries:

> *One reason why Latin American environmental campaigners are more vulnerable than their fellow activists in Europe or North America is that Latin America's democratic and judicial institutions are still weak and protesters often have limited recourse to the law* (Collinson, 1996, p1).

This reminds us that NGOs do not have the same power as governments, as they do not have a universal legal monopoly on the use of force. They do not have the ability to impose fines or other penalties.

The answer might lie in North–South linkages. From the examples provided, it appears that, to become active in civil regulation, Southern NGOs need to be linked with supportive NGOs in countries with developed consumer politics. The Shell Nigeria example also reminds us that Southern campaigning on its own is not always effective in changing corporate practices. Protests by local Delta communities against Shell began in the late 1980s, but it only became an issue in the North much later when Northern NGOs, companies and the media joined the cause.

What is the legitimacy and accountability of Northern NGOs in regulating the market on behalf of Southern producers? The need for North–South NGO alliances is an indication of the democratic deficit Southern peoples face: the power to regulate corporate activity in the South resides in the North. To influence the behaviour of global corporations or their subsidiaries, Southern NGOs must make contact with Northern NGOs and then persuade them of their grievances and their alternatives. Many Southern NGO campaigners argue that Northern NGOs impose solutions on them, demonstrating an approach that could be described as ethical imperialism. In order to overcome this problem, Southern NGO participation in policy development must be facilitated. This poses a logistical and financial challenge that many Northern NGOs appear reluctant to meet. However, as the civil regulation agenda develops, more questions will be asked of Northern NGOs relating to their legitimacy in negotiating on behalf of developing country communities. Therefore NGOs seeking greater legitimacy for collaborative business campaigns will need to demonstrate greater accountability to Southern civil society in the future.

Conclusion

This chapter has provided an overview of business–NGO relations on sustainable development, particularly in the South. There is a spectrum of NGO activity worldwide aimed at forcing and facilitating change in corporate practice and in sustaining change via alternative trading models and civil regulation schemes. These changes are occurring within the context of globalization where increased corporate power and influence over governments undermine the regulatory role of governments and intergovernmental bodies. The global reach of corporate brands such as Nike, McDonald's and Nestlé is now well established. The flip-side of globalization is that it also offers NGOs unprecedented opportunities to effect political and economic change via new technologies, particularly the Internet. The emergence of civil regulation has meant that NGOs are beginning to offer innovative global responses to state deregulation and corporate malpractice. However, there are questions about the extent to which civil regulation will work in countries where consumer politics is less prevalent and where civil liberties often are not protected by governments.

A recent report by the director-general of the International Labour Organization (ILO) argues that '*[g]lobalization cannot be left to its own devices. Rather, economic progress ... should be accompanied by social progress*' (ILO, 1997, p1). In a related vein, at the 1999 World Economic Forum, UN Secretary General Kofi Annan challenged the world's largest and most powerful companies '*to enact and uphold standards on human rights, labor and the environment in their operations in developing countries*':

> *The spread of markets far outpaces the ability of societies and their political systems to adjust to them, let alone to guide the course they take ... History teaches us that such an imbalance between the economic, social and political realms can never be sustained for very long ... Without your active commitment and support* [for a code of conduct],

there is a danger that universal values will remain little more than fine words ... and unless those values are really seen to be taking hold, I fear we may find it increasingly difficult to make a persuasive case for the open global market (Swardson, 1999, pA15).

Annan's words echo many NGO critiques of economic globalization, yet more calls for voluntary corporate commitment via codes of conduct, as Annan suggests, will not be enough. NGOs will continue to force, facilitate and, in some cases, sustain change in business practice. However, the limits of civil regulation mean that NGO and corporate action must be backed up by legally-binding, intergovernmental agreements linked to supportive national policies. Sustainable development may ultimately depend on '*the transformation of local, national and global policy processes in order to challenge business to accept culpability for the environmental and social problems it has helped to create. Whether the catalyst is policy, protest or partnership, in a globalised economy business must be willing to assume a greater share of the responsibility for resolving the consequences of its actions*' (Murphy, 1997, p293).

References

Bendell, J (1998) *Citizens' Cane: Relations Between Business and Civil Society*, paper presented at the third international conference of the International Society for Third Sector Research (ISTR), Geneva, June. Available at: www.mailbase.ac.uk/lists/business-ngo-relations/files/citizenscane

Bray, J (1998) 'Web Wars: NGOs, Companies and Governments in an Internet-connected World', in *Greener Management International*, winter, no 24, pp115–129

Bruno, K (1992) *The Greenpeace Book of Greenwash*, Greenpeace-International, Amsterdam

Business and Society Review (1992) 'Nestlé', in *Business and Society Review*, no 80, spring, p76

Camilleri, J A and Falk, J (1992) *The End of Sovereignty: Politics of a Shrinking and Fragmenting World*, Hants E Elgar, Aldershot

Carson, R (1962) *Silent Spring*, Houghton Miflin, Boston

Cernea, M M (1988) *Nongovernmental Organizations and Local Development*, World Bank discussion paper, no 40, The World Bank, Washington, DC

Cohen, J (1995) 'Interpreting the Notion of Civil Society', in M Walzer, *Toward Global Civil Society*, Berghahn Books, USA

Colchester, M (1997) *Social Aspects of Certification*, a report of the first meeting of the FSC Social Working Group held in San Pedro, Brazil, 25–26 April, Forest Peoples Programme, Moreton-in-Marsh, England

Collinson, H (ed) (1996) *Green Guerrillas: Environmental Conflicts and Initiatives in Latin America and the Caribbean*, Latin American Bureau, London

Cowe, R (1996) 'Shell Comes Clean to its Green Critics', in *The Guardian*, 26 November, p17

Cummins, R (1998) '"Cremate Monsanto": Global Opposition Intensifies', *Food Bytes*, no 15, 7 December, http://www.purefood.org

de Oliveira, M D and Tandon, R (eds) (1994) *Citizens: Strengthening Global Civil Society*, Washington, CIVICUS (Worldwide Alliance for Citizen Participation)

Dore, E (1996) 'Capitalism and Ecological Crisis: Legacy of the 1980s', in H Collinson (ed) *Green Guerrillas: Environmental Conflicts and Initiatives in Latin America and the Caribbean*, Latin American Bureau, London

Dowie, M (1991–1992) 'American Environmentalism: A Movement Courting Irrelevance' in *World Policy Journal*, vol IX, no 1, winter, pp67–92

Elkington, J (1997) *Cannibals With Forks: The Triple Bottom Line of 21st Century Business*, Capstone, Oxford

Esty, D C and Gentry, B S (1997) *Foreign Investment, Globalization and the Environment*, New Haven, Yale Centre for Environmental Law and Policy, Con

ETI (1998) *Ethical Trading Initiative Website*, http://www.ethicaltrade.org

Fernandes, R C (1994) 'Threads of Planetary Citizenship', in de Oliveira, M D and Tandon, R (eds) *Citizens: Strengthening Global Civil Society*, Washington, CIVICUS

FoE-UK (1991b) 'Friends of the Earth brings DIY Stores into Line', press release, 11 December, FoE-UK, London

FoE-UK (1995) *A Superficial Attraction: the Voluntary Approach and Sustainable Development*, December, FoE-UK, London

Griffith, D A and Ryans Jr, J K (1997) 'Organising Global Communications to Minimize Private Spill-Over Damage to Brand Equity', *Journal of World Business*, vol 32, no 3, autumn

Hall, A (1996) 'Did Chico Mendes Die in Vain? Brazilian Rubber Tappers in the 1990s', in H Collinson (ed) *Green Guerrillas: Environmental Conflicts and Initiatives in Latin America and the Caribbean*, Latin American Bureau, London

Hannigan, J (1995) *Environmentalism: A Social Constructivist Perspective*, Routledge, London

Herkströter, C A J (1996) 'Dealing with Contradictory Expectations – the Dilemmas Facing Multinationals', speech by the president of the Royal Dutch Petroleum Company in Amsterdam, 11 October, Shell International, The Hague

Hoffman, A (1996) 'Trends in Corporate Environmentalism: the Chemical and Petroleum Industries, 1960–1993', in *Society & Natural Resources*, no 9, pp47–64

Heyzer, N, Riker, J V and Quizon, A (eds) (1995) *Government-NGO Relations in Asia: Prospects and Challenges for People-Centred Development*, Macmillan Press, London

Humphreys, D (1997) *Forest Politics: The Evolution of International Cooperation*, Earthscan, London

ILO (1997) *The ILO, Standard Setting and Globalization*, executive summary of the report of the director-general, International Labour Conference 85th Session, ILO, Geneva

Johnston, B R (ed) (1997) *Life and Death Matters: Human Rights and the Environment at the End of the Millennium*, AltaMira Press, California

Kant, I, *Groundwork of the Metaphysic of Morals*, H J Paton (trans) (1964) Harper & Row, New York

Khor, M (1993) 'Economics and Environmental Justice: Rethinking North–South Relations', in R Hofrichter (ed) *Toxic Struggles: The Theory and Practice of Environmental Justice*, New Society Publishers, Philadelphia

Korten, D (1987) 'Third Generation NGO Strategies: A Key to People-centred Development' in *World Development*, vol 15, supplement, pp145–59

Korten, D (1990) *Getting to the 21st Century*, Kumarian Press, Hartford, Conn

Korten, D (1995) *When Corporations Rule the World*, Earthscan, London

Krut, R (1997) *Globalization and Civil Society: NGO Influences in International Decision-Making*, UNRISD, Geneva

Levy, D L (1997) 'Environmental Management as Political Sustainability', *Organisation and Environment*, vol 10, no 2, pp126–47

Lynch, C (1998) 'Social Movements and the Problem of Globalisation', *Alternatives*, vol 23, pp149 – 173

Murphy, D F (1997) 'The Partnership Paradox: Business–NGO Relations on Sustainable Development in the International Policy Arena', unpublished PhD thesis, School for Policy Studies, University of Bristol

Murphy, D F (1998) 'Partnership for Sustainable Development: Business–NGO Relations in a Changing World', paper prepared for the UNCTAD *Partners for Development Summit*, Lyon, France, 9–12 November

Murphy, D F and Bendell, J (1997) *In the Company of Partners: Business, Environmental Groups and Sustainable Development Post-Rio*, The Policy Press, Bristol

Murphy, D F and Bendell, J (1999) *Partners in Time? Business, NGOs and Sustainable Development*, UNRISD discussion paper, no 109, UN Research Institute for Social Development, Geneva

NGO Task Force on Business and Industry (1997) *Minding Our Business: The Role of Corporate Accountability in Sustainable Development*, an independent assessment submitted to the UN Commission on Sustainable Development, prepared by J Barber, Integrative Strategies Forum, Washington, DC

OECD Development Assistance Committee (1996) 'News Release' SG/COM/NEW, vol 96, no 64, 11 June

Perlas, N (1997) personal communication with Jem Bendell, May

Plante, C and Bendell, J (1998) 'The Art of Collaboration: Lessons from Emerging Business–NGO Partnerships in Asia', in *Greener Management International*, winter, no 24, pp91–104

Reilly, C A (ed) (1995) *New Paths to Democratic Development in Latin America: The Rise of NGO-Municipal Collaboration*, Lynne Rienner, London

Rowell, A (1995) 'Oil, Shell and Nigeria: Ken Saro-Wiwa Calls for a Boycott', in *The Ecologist*, vol 25, no 6, November–December, pp210–213

Rowell, A (1996a) *Green Backlash: Global Subversion of the Environment Movement*, Routledge, London

Rowell, A (1996b) 'Sleeping With the Enemy', in *The Village Voice*, 23 January

Ryle, J (1997) 'Arms Campaigners Enter Political Minefield', in *The Guardian Weekly*, vol 157, no 24, 14 December, p23

Schiavone, G (1997) *International Organisations: A Dictionary*, Macmillan Reference, London

Schneidewind, U and Petersen, H (1998) 'Changing the Rules: Business–NGO Relations and Structuration Theory', *Greener Management International*, winter, no 24, pp105–114

Schmidheiny, S (1992) *Changing Course: a Global Business Perspective on Development and Environment*, The MIT Press, London

Serrill, M S (1997) 'Ghosts of the Forest', in *Time*, vol 150, no 17A, November, special issue, pp50–55

Snow, C C, Miles, R E and Coleman, H S (1992) 'Managing 21st Century Network Organisations', in *Organisational Dynamics*, winter

Srinivasan, A (1999) 'Non-Governmental Organizations', http://www.anand.to/india/ngo.html, [17/9/99]

Strange, S (1996) *The Retreat of the State: The Diffusion of Power in the World Economy*, Cambridge University Press, Cambridge

Sullivan, F (1994) personal communication with D F Murphy, 11 November

SustainAbility, NEF and UNEP (1996) *Engaging Stakeholders*, SustainAbility, London

Swardson, A (1999) 'Annan Urges Conduct Code for Businesses' in *The Washington Post*, 1 February, pA15

Tandon, R (1989) 'The State and Voluntary Agencies in India' in R Holloway (ed) *Doing Development: Governments, NGOs and the Rural Poor in Asia*, Earthscan in association with CUSO, London

United Nations (1997) 'WWF/The World Bank', press release, no 97, 25 June, United Nations, New York

UNEP and PWBLF (1994) *Partnerships for Sustainable Development: The Role of Business and Industry*, Prince of Wales Business Leaders Forum (PWBLF), London

UNRISD (1995) *States of Disarray: The Social Effects of Globalization*, UNRISD, Geneva

Walzer, M (ed) (1995) *Toward a Global Civil Society*, World Bank, Berghahn Books, USA

WBCSD (1997) *Signals for Change*, WBCSD, Geneva

Welford, R (1997) *Hijacking Environmentalism: Corporate Responses to Sustainable Development*, Earthscan, London

Willets, P (1998) 'Political Globalization and the Impact of NGOs upon Transnational Companies', in J Mitchell, *Companies in a World of Conflict*, Royal Institute for International Affairs and Earthscan, London

World Bank (1996) *World Debt Tables 1996*, World Bank, Washington

Zadek, S (1999) *Can Corporations be Civil?*, paper presented at the conference 'NGOs in a Global Future', Birmingham, January

Notes

1   The Charity Commission for England and Wales defines a charity as '*an organisation created to provide something of benefit to others in society*' (see http://www.charity-commission.gov.uk)

2   At the end of 1989, there were 12,313 NGOs registered with the government of India's Ministry of Home Affairs

3   Between mid-1994 when the FSC Secretariat was established and early 1996, staff developed the FSC accreditation system which included extensive negotiation with prospective certifiers. The first FSC certifications were approved in February 1996 when the first four FSC accredited-certifiers signed their contracts with the FSC (Soil Association, SGS Forestry, Scientific Certification Systems and Rainforest Alliance)

4   We do not go into the debate about the concept 'civil society' in this chapter because of its highly theoretical nature. The term is not new, with Hegel and Marx writing about civil society in the 18th and 19th centuries, but there are various usages of the term today. Political activists in Eastern Europe before and during the revolutions of the late 1980s and early 1990s spoke of it as the networks and markets which existed outside the totalitarian state (Walzer, 1995). Others, however, believe that no element of '*the two part model … whereby civil society includes everything outside the state sector, is useful today*' (Cohen, 1995 p35). Instead a three-sector model can be proposed which draws on the work of Antonio Gramsci to differentiate between civil society, the state and the economy (Cohen, 1995). Within this three-sector model there are maximalist and minimalist usages of the term. Maximalist conceptions of civil society include all voluntary associations (from development groups to the local choir), while minimalist conceptions try to focus on the role of the organization in society. Recently, it has been argued that civil society is best considered as a movement of people (and their organizations) involved in the democratization of autocratic organizations, whether they are governmental, business or sociocultural (Bendell, 1998). This conception of civil society is the one most closely allied to our concept of civil regulation. For a further discussion, see Bendell (1998)

Section 5

Trade and Sustainable Development

Introduction

As the protests around the World Trade Organization Ministerial Conference held in Seattle in December 1999 clearly demonstrated, trade is a topic about which passions run high and over which opinion is sharply divided. On the one hand, there are those who regard the current global trading system as a force for good, whilst on the other there are those who see it as anything but.

The World Trade Organization, the body responsible for overseeing international trade, argues that the current global trading system *'offers a range of benefits'* and that *'there are many over-riding reasons why we're better off with the system than we would be without it'* (WTO, 1999a, p2). According to the WTO, the trading system cuts the cost of living, stimulates economic growth and job creation, gives a voice to smaller countries, allows trade disputes to be handled fairly and even helps to keep the peace. As the system lowers trade barriers, production costs are reduced, which means cheaper goods and services and a lower cost of living. Lower trade barriers also increase the volume of trade, which leads to increased economic growth and employment. Within the WTO, smaller countries have a voice and some bargaining power, whereas if such a forum did not exist, more powerful countries would be freer simply to impose their will unilaterally on their smaller trading partners. With increased trade, there are more opportunities for disputes between trading partners. However, the WTO's disputes settlement process enables any disputes that arise to be settled constructively. And by helping trade to flow smoothly and providing a forum for resolving disputes, the WTO minimizes the chances of trade issues leading to armed conflict and so plays a part in maintaining international peace.

The WTO argues that it is a misunderstanding on the part of its critics to claim that the current trading system prioritizes commercial interests over development and the environment. On the contrary, the preamble to the Marrakesh Agreement (which established the WTO) includes among its objectives, optimal use of the world's resources, sustainable development and environmental protection. And it is also a misunderstanding to believe that the WTO is the tool of powerful lobbies. The WTO offers two reasons why this is the case. First, it is only governments that take part in trade negotiations, and so business and other groups can only exert influence on WTO decisions through their government. And second, *'the outcome of a trade round has to be a balance of interests. Governments can find it easier to reject pressure from particular lobby groups by arguing that it had to accept the overall package in the interests of the country as a whole'* (WTO, 1999b). And as trade negotiations reach decisions by consensus, they are democratic (even more so than if majority voting was used) and so to claim that the WTO is undemocratic represents yet a further misunderstanding.

However, there are many who see things rather differently. Take, for instance, the issue of democracy within the WTO. There was a great deal of criticism of the proceedings at the Seattle Ministerial Conference which many felt were anything but democratic. In fact, according to one commentator, *'The rhetoric that the WTO was a consensus organisation with participation by all was exposed as a complete sham'* (Coates, 1999). It was reported that most of the important negotiations at the Conference took place in 'green room' meetings to which most of the developing countries were not invited. The view expressed by Ghana's minister of trade and industry was that *'There is no transparency in the proceedings and African countries are being marginalized and generally excluded on issues of vital importance for our peoples and their future'* (Aslam, 1999).

In addition, many feel that the current trading system is not a level playing-field but one which the developed countries in the WTO have tilted in their favour. As one newspaper website put it *'Critics say the WTO and its agreements are skewed in favour of rich industrial countries; the west may preach trade liberalisation, but it has used negotiations to prise open third-world markets while keeping its own barriers intact'* (*Guardian Unlimited*, 1999). Many of those who hold this view believe that this situation has arisen as a result of the undue influence of large corporations. For instance, Martin Khor, director of the Third World Network, describes how a number of trade experts have expressed concern that governments of the dominant trading countries are *'being overly influenced by the narrow commerical interests of their large corporations, which are now in the driving seat of trade policy'* (Khor, 1999, p1). And the noted environmentalist Vandana Shiva expresses her concerns more forcefully (Shiva, 1999) when she says that:

> the rules of the WTO are driven by the objectives of establishing corporate control over every dimension of our lives – our food, our health, our environment, our work and our future... The centralised, undemocratic rules and structures of the WTO that are establishing global corporate rule based on monopolies and monocultures need to give way to an earth democracy supported by decentralisation and diversity. The rights of all species and the rights of all people must come before the rights of corporations to make limitless profits through limitless destruction.

In Chapter 16, Paul Ekins enters into the debate over trade and the environment. His view is that the WTO rules, designed to promote trade liberalization, place unnecessary constraints on the efforts of individual nations to deal with environmental issues. He argues that it is very much in the interests of the business community that this conflict be resolved in a way that allows environmental issues to be addressed fully because, if this does not happen the conditions in which business can continue to do business may well disappear. As he puts it: *'environmental unsustainability has the potential not only to destroy market stability at the global level ... but also to engender large scale social chaos.'*

Having summarized those articles of the General Agreement on Tariffs and Trade (GATT) that apply to the environment, Ekins outlines, using informative examples, the three types of policy for environmental protection that may be constrained by trade-related concerns:

1 International, environment treaties which envisage trade measures as part of their enforcement system.
2 Environmental policies which act as non-tariff barriers to trade or which include trade measures.
3 Environmental policies which are perceived to impair domestic competitiveness.

What follows is a discussion about how the WTO articles could be amended to solve these problems and Ekins emphasizes that only fairly minor amendments are needed along with a reinterpretation of existing articles. (Interestingly, he notes how surprising it is that a set of rules dating from just after the Second World War, when the environment was hardly on the political agenda, need so little alteration to make them suitable for an age in which sustainable development has become a global concern.) Ekins closes by reiterating how much it is in the interest of business that this conflict between trade and environment be solved and urging business to use its influence to bring this about. '*Business should start to put its weight behind the kind of minimum global regulation of world trade that would ensure that its playing field is stable and green, as well as level and much less prone than at present to disruption by environmentally induced disintegration in society at large.*'

In the final chapter of the Reader, Nick Robins and Sarah Roberts examine the export opportunities available to businesses in developing countries that have resulted from moves towards sustainability in the developed world. Whilst exports are a major source of revenue for developing countries, producers in these countries are having to meet ever more stringent environmental requirements in key export markets, '*resulting from tightening regulations, new corporate practices and changes in consumer values and lifestyles*'. A small number of pioneering businesses in the developing world have responded positively to these developments and are able to obtain premium prices and increased market share through meeting these requirements. A large number of these pioneering businesses are from the forestry, food and textiles sectors, and the authors describe the developments in these sectors which are illustrated with a number of informative case studies. The chapter concludes by distilling the lessons that can be learned from these pioneering enterprises so that more businesses in the developing world can follow in their footsteps, thus not only boosting economic development but ensuring that '*sustainable consumption moves out of the margins and into the mainstream*'.

References

Aslam, A (1999) 'Developing Countries Assail WTO "Dictatorship"', press release, http://www.twnside.org.sg/souths/twn/title/assail-cn.htm, [17/12/99]

Coates, B (1999) 'Friends Fall Out', *The Guardian*, 8 December

Guardian Unlimited (1999) 'Seattle Summit', http://www.newsunlimited.co.uk/wto/article/0,2763,111671,00.html, [17/12/99]

Khor, M (1999) 'WTO Hijacked by Big Corporations, South Countries the Victims', http://www.twnside.org.sg/souths/twn/title/mk3-cn.htm, [17/12/99]

Shiva, V (1999) 'This Round to the Citizens', *The Guardian*, 8 December
World Trade Organization – WTO (1999a) '10 Benefits of the WTO Trading System', http://www.wto.org/wto/10ben/10ben00.htm, [20/12/99]
World Trade Organization – WTO (1999b) '10 Common Misunderstandings About the WTO', http://www.wto.org/wto/10mis/10mis08.htm, [17/12/99]

16

Business, Trade and the Environment: an Agenda for Stability in World Trade

Paul Ekins

Introduction

There are two elements of the context in which the majority of businesses operate today which present quite new challenges to the corporate world: globalization of economic activity and the liberalization of trade which is both its cause and consequence; and growing evidence of environmental damage and threat, on a global scale, for which business is sometimes blamed and to which it is increasingly expected to make a sensitive response.

Trade liberalization presents business with both threats and opportunities. The opportunities come from an expanding market, with associated possibilities of economies of scale. The threats come from intensified competition as tariff and non-tariff barriers to trade, which give protection to domestic industries, are removed in a business environment that is changing at an accelerating pace. The stakes, in terms of both the risks and the potential rewards, are high.

The negotiations on trade liberalization that have been pursued, first under the auspices of the General Agreement on Tariffs and Trade (GATT) and now under the World Trade Organization, entail complex calculations of national advantage. Industrial protection at home is given up for gains in market access abroad in a trade-off which always involves winners and losers. Deals are only possible because of a perception that liberalization will result in a bigger cake overall, in the division of which all national participants will be made better off in aggregate, although the restructuring that is required to produce the bigger cake is not painless. Trade negotiations are among the most sensitive areas of national politics.

Those businesses that are well placed to take advantage of global markets are, not surprisingly, among the most enthusiastic promoters of trade liberalization. Business associations and publications have generally argued strongly that free trade is one of the principal stimulants to global economic growth – for example, *Business Week* in 1993 opined: '*[F]reer markets and freer trade in the new global economic system are what will ultimately put an end to slow growth and high unemployment in the industrial world*', while business and environment groups such as the Business Council for Sustainable Development (now the World Business Council for Sustainable Development) have added that it can also be a force for environmental improvement – for example, Schmidheiny (1992, p69) considers that '*free trade has a role to play in progress towards sustainable development*'. These arguments found their way without qualification into the Agenda 21 document of the 1992 Rio Earth Summit, which adopted as one of its objectives: '*To promote an open, non-discriminatory and equitable multilateral trading system that will enable all countries ... to improve their economic structures and improve the standard of living of their populations through sustained economic development*' (*Earth Summit '92*, p50).

There is now a substantial literature which contests the claim that free trade is necessarily beneficial either for the environment or for society as a whole (see, for example, Ekins et al, 1994 and some of the other articles in this special journal issue on trade and environment – Brack, 1995, Andersson et al, 1995). Some writers go further and cast trade liberalization as a major threat to the environment (for example, Daly and Goodland, 1994). Still others regard globalization as a process of the intensification of corporate hegemonic power at the expense of both the environment and ordinary people (for example, Korten, 1995).

This chapter is principally concerned with the conflicts between trade liberalization and environmental protection, whether perceived, potential or actual. Whatever the causes or ultimate implications of the powerful social, economic and technological forces that are driving globalization, the trend towards freer trade is likely to continue. At the same time the governments, especially in the North, that are involved in trade negotiations are now under increasing pressure to deliver environmental improvements, arising from both their international commitments to move towards sustainable development and domestic demands for improved environmental quality. Only rarely will the environmental policy which they adopt as a result be trade neutral. Sometimes it will impose costs on domestic business. Sometimes it can create business openings and competitive advantage by stimulating innovation, by tightening up management or by developing capacity in the environmental sector. Sometimes the policies will act as a barrier to trade. Policies of the last type may be expected to be especially attractive to governments, for they enable them simultaneously to satisfy their environment and business lobbies, while not adversely affecting prospects for their exporters. On the other hand, if generalized, such policies could do much to negate the painstaking removal of tariff and non-tariff barriers that have been the result of eight hard rounds of GATT negotiations.

For business the most important desirable characteristic of globalization is the orderly development of world markets in a climate of economic stability. Environmental unsustainability has the potential not only to destroy market stability at the global level (an impact it has already had on some parts of the insurance industry – see Schmidheiny and Zorraquin, 1996, pp117–119, 121–125), but also to engender large-scale social chaos. The World Resources Institute (WRI), in collaboration with both the Development and Environment Programmes of the United Nations, has concluded, on the basis of one of the world's most extensive environmental databases, that '*The world is not now headed toward a sustainable future, but rather toward a variety of potential human and environmental disasters*' (WRI, 1992, p2).

The trade–environment debate is therefore of profound importance to business. Its outcomes will affect not only the nature and extent of environmental policy, but also the marketplace within which business, especially international business, is conducted. This chapter makes some pragmatic suggestions of ways in which the worst of the conflicts between trade liberalization and environmental protection can be resolved in favour of the environment. The suggestions fall far short of 'the new protectionism' which, for example, Lang and Hines (1993) see as necessary if sustainable development is to become a reality. The danger to business is that, if trade and development continue to proceed in an environmentally unsustainable manner, even the new protectionism may seem utopian compared to the economic turmoil to which this unsustainability could give rise. Business is thus well advised to engage in the trade–environment debate, the outcomes of which could have profound implications not only for the slope of the playing-field on which it finds itself playing, but whether there is a playing-field at all.

The Gatt Articles and the Environment

The GATT Articles are founded on the principle of non-discrimination in trade with regard to:

1 Trading partners: any country that is a GATT signatory must accord all other GATT signatories the same trading conditions as it accords to its 'most favoured nation'.
2 National treatment: like products, these must be treated in the same way irrespective of their country of origin.

Article XX permits limited exceptions to these 'most favoured nation' and 'like product' principles, including exceptions related to the conservation of natural resources, but so far there has never been an environmental dispute under GATT in which an exception on these grounds has been upheld.

In 1992, the GATT Secretariat spelt out what environmental protection is compatible with current trade rules:

> *GATT rules ... place essentially no constraints on a country's right to protect its own environment against damage from either domestic production or the consumption of domestically produced or imported products. Generally speaking, a country can do anything to imports or exports that it does to its own products and it can do anything it considers necessary to its production processes* (GATT, 1992, p23).

Following the Uruguay Round agreement in 1994, this formulation somewhat overstates a country's discretion on policy towards the environment and human health, for the new agreement requires policies in these areas that have trade effects to be based on 'scientific evidence' if they are not to be open to challenge from another country which feels them to be too stringent. Given substantial scientific uncertainty in many issues related to the environment, there is likely to be a wide margin of interpretation of what constitutes 'scientific evidence' in these cases. Nor is it clear that the WTO possesses the scientific expertise to make judgements in this area.

In a related area, that of food safety, considerable influence on scientific issues and therefore power to adjudicate on food safety, has been granted by the WTO to the Codex Alimentarius Commission. Although Codex is jointly financed by the UN Food and Agriculture Organization (FAO) and the World Health Organization (WHO), concern has been expressed that it is unduly influenced by transnational corporations (Evans and Walsh, 1994, p23, Lang and Hines, pp100–103, NCC, 1998, pp96–97). It may be more attuned, therefore, to business and trade priorities than to safeguarding human and animal health and either discourage or disallow regulations stricter than Codex-agreed international standards, which some countries and interest groups perceive as being too lax.

Even leaving to one side the problem of what constitutes 'scientific evidence', the GATT pronouncement quoted above about what a country *can* do to protect the environment throws into sharp relief what it *cannot* do under GATT rules:

- It may not use trade policy to protect its environment from foreign production. It could not impose trade sanctions, for example, on a neighbouring country which persistently exported air or water pollution, no matter how damaging its effects.
- It may not use trade policy to protect the environment outside its own jurisdiction, whether a global commons or the territory of another country. GATT rules do not currently envisage the possibility of trade measures being applied in support of, for example, the provisions of the Montreal Protocol (discussed below), the Framework Convention on Climate Change or the Law of the Sea.
- It may not impose on imports charges or other restrictions related to their process and production methods (PPMs), even when it is imposing identical treatment on its own production – that is, its policy is non-discriminatory). This obviously acts as a major discouragement to apply strict environmental policy measures to production processes where it is perceived that such measures may have a negative effect on the competitiveness of domestic business.
- Some environmental regulations may be deemed inadmissible as technical (or non-tariff) barriers to trade. GATT rules require such regulations to be the least GATT-inconsistent that are available. Esty (1994, p48) comments: '*This sets an almost impossibly high hurdle for environmental policy, because a policy approach that intrudes less on trade is almost always conceivable and therefore in some sense "available".*'

From an environmental point of view these GATT prohibitions impose considerable constraints on environmental policy. There follow some examples which illustrate how such provisions under GATT have either brought trade liberalization, trade rules and environmental policy into conflict or might do so.

Examples of Trade/Environment Interactions

The US–Mexico tuna–dolphin dispute

In 1991 the US banned Mexican-caught tuna from the US market on the grounds that the Mexican fishermen killed an excessive number of dolphins when fishing for tuna in the eastern tropical Pacific Ocean. Further to a challenge from Mexico, a GATT panel ruled that the US ban was GATT illegal because it related to process and production methods (PPMs) and resulted in discrimination against 'like products' (tuna) and because the US was seeking to apply its laws outside its jurisdiction.

In fact, the way that the US applied the regulation which led to the ban was also clearly discriminatory against Mexico (as the GATT panel also found) in that the permissible dolphin-kill ratio (number of dolphins killed per net dropped) was defined retrospectively based on what the US fishermen had achieved. There was thus no way that Mexican fishermen could know in advance how many dolphins they could kill without triggering the US ban. This aspect of the case raises the clearest suspicions that the US action was at least partially motivated by commercial and not environmental considerations. Its trade measure could easily have either specified a maximum dolphin kill ratio, equally applicable to Mexican and US fishermen; or banned tuna caught with certain kinds of nets (whether by US or Mexican fishermen) from the US market and insisted on inspection and certification arrangements to validate this. Had it done so, the measure might still have been deemed GATT incompatible (on grounds of extrajurisdictionality and the irrelevance of PPMs), but at least it would be clear that the US was seeking purely environmental and not commercial, gain.

Another GATT ruling went against the US when it was challenged in 1992 for seeking to ban tuna imports from third countries that had first imported the tuna from Mexico. This time the panel called into question the ability of any country to use the GATT exemptions clause, Article XX, for any kind of unilateral trade restriction (for further discussion of the tuna–dolphin case, see Esty, 1994, pp30–31, 268–269, and Brack, 1995, pp501–502).

In the event, neither of the judgements was adopted by the GATT council, but they infuriated environmentalists and did much to provide the political impetus for the environment–trade campaign, which resulted in the North American Free Trade Agreement (NAFTA) incorporating an environmental side agreement and which turned trade and the environment into a major international issue.

The trade provisions in the Montreal Protocol

A number of international environmental agreements contain trade provisions (listed in Andersson et al, 1995, pp117–119), of which the most important are probably the Convention on International Trade in Endangered Species (CITES, 1973), the Montreal Protocol on Substances that Deplete the Ozone Layer (1987) and the Basel Convention on the Control of Transboundary Movements of Hazardous Wastes (1989), of which the second is discussed briefly here.

The Montreal Protocol contains trade provisions relating to parties to the protocol, in so far as imports of ozone-depleting substances (ODS) are subject to the control schedules and relating to non-parties with regard to trade in ODS themselves, in products containing them and, potentially, in products manufactured with them. These provisions are complex and have been examined in detail elsewhere (Brack, 1996). Here it need only be noted that the reports of the GATT tuna–dolphin panels '*appeared to cast considerable doubts over the GATT-compatibility of the Montreal Protocol. Its control measures lead to quantitative restrictions on trade; its trade provisions directed against non-parties can be applied against WTO members who are not Protocol signatories and envisage trade restrictions on the basis of process and production methods (PPMs); and both sets of measures could be regarded as extrajurisdictional*' (Brack, 1996, p72).

The Montreal Protocol has gained the accession of the great majority of countries (150 by 1995) and has fixed stringent controls on the production of ODS which have greatly reduced the quantities which would otherwise be in circulation. Many observers of, and participants in, the protocol process believe that the trade provisions made an important contribution to these achievements. Clearly the uncertainty which still surrounds them does not help with the negotiation of future international environmental agreements which might benefit from such provisions and it reinforces the perception of environmental insensitivity with which the WTO is sometimes regarded.

The US–Venezuela gasoline reformulation dispute

New rules made by the US Environmental Protection Agency under the 1990 Clean Air Act Amendment required that from 1995 all gasoline sold in the US had to be of an equal or greater cleanliness than that sold in 1990. Domestic refiners were allowed to qualify for an individual baseline standard derived from documentation of their gasoline formulations in and after 1990. Importers, however, had to meet an imposed standard based on the average for the US industry.

Venezuela, later joined by Brazil, appealed to the WTO in 1995, alleging discrimination. The US sought to defend itself with the Article XX exceptions relating to health and the conservation of resources (in this case, clean air). The final WTO judgement accepted that air was a 'depletable resource' under the terms of Article XX and accepted the relevance of the health exception in this case, but found in favour of Venezuela and Brazil because the US could have achieved its environmental goals in a less discriminatory way – namely, by setting a single standard for domestic producers and importers (ITLR, 1996).

Because, unlike the tuna–dolphin case, the regulation was applied to a product, there was no challenge to the US setting the standard. But, as with tuna–dolphin, the unnecessarily discriminatory way in which the regulation was formulated leads to suspicion that commercial as well as environmental protection was an objective of the measure.

The Danish bottles case

In the early 1980s Denmark instituted a mandatory deposit-refund system for drinks containers and, to facilitate their reuse, stipulated that container designs would need to be approved by the government. Foreign producers objected that the regulation was discriminatory against them because the system effectively ruled out containers other than glass, which were more expensive to transport and prevented product differentiation through innovative packaging design. On challenge the European Court ruled in 1988 that the deposit-refund was a legitimate means for Denmark's pursuit of its environmental objectives, which were in turn justified by the European Community's commitment to environmental protection. However, it also ruled that the stipulation on container designs acted as a disproportionate restraint on trade compared to the environmental benefit it yielded and so it was disallowed (Esty and Geradin, 1997, pp297–299). Had the challenge been brought to GATT, it may well be that the deposit-refund system would have been disallowed as well because GATT had no general commitment to environmental protection and the system may well have been found disproportionately trade-restrictive.

The Finnish carbon tax

Finland was the first country to introduce a carbon tax, in 1990, which has evolved into a wide-ranging carbon-energy tax. Economic theory suggests and Finland's own studies confirm, that a carbon tax would be the most effective instrument to curb carbon emissions, which was the aim of the tax. Thus coal, the most carbon-intensive fossil fuel, bore a carbon-energy tax that was 78 per cent carbon related (Teir, 1996, p246).

Ten per cent of Finland's electricity is imported and the marginal generating fuel is coal, so that the Finnish carbon-energy tax had potentially serious implications for the competitiveness of domestic coal-fired generation. To address this issue, Finland levied a tax on imported electricity at a rate which was the average of the Finnish carbon-energy tax on electricity overall, but still only about half that on coal-generated electricity. However, even this tax on imported electricity is considered to run counter to the Treaty of Rome because Finnish electricity, as such, is untaxed. Neither European nor WTO trade regulations permit a tax on imports to balance input taxes on domestic production.

The result has been that, at the end of 1995, the Finnish government decided to remove its carbon tax and replace it with an overall tax on electricity, which would comply with the trade rules. However, the electricity tax will be substantially less effective at reducing carbon emissions because it will do nothing to encourage switching to low carbon fuels in electricity generation which, in other countries, is one of the principal ways in which carbon dioxide reductions have been achieved.

The European Commission's carbon-energy tax

In 1992, just prior to the Rio Earth Summit, the European Commission introduced its proposal for a carbon-energy tax as one of its proposed measures to reduce carbon emissions in order to mitigate climate change. The proposal exempted the six most energy-intensive industrial sectors, was made conditional on a similar tax being introduced in North America and Japan and recommended both that governments should introduce it on a revenue-neutral basis and that tax rebates should be given against investments in energy efficiency. Nevertheless, the tax was vehemently opposed by the business community. '*Activities undertaken independently by companies, national trade associations, European trade association and industry confederations such as Union of Industrial and Employers' Confederation of Europe (UNICE) added up to a major anti-tax campaign*' (Ikwue and Skea, 1996, p100).

The principal argument employed by business in its campaign was that the tax would impact negatively on corporate and national competitiveness. In fact, the exemptions and other proposals would have rendered the economic impacts minimal in practically all sectors. According to Ikwue and Skea (1996, pp101–102): '*The key issue remains one of trust. Industry does not trust governments to introduce such a measure without turning it into a revenue-raising device at some point in the future. The tax is seen as "the thin end of a wedge"*.' Reduction in competitiveness was the most important threat that such a wedge represented. Notwithstanding the growing rhetoric in favour of environmental taxation, this will be very difficult to introduce in a systematic and broad-based way while such a threat is still perceived to exist. The next section examines the extent to which such a perception is soundly based.

Business Competitiveness and Environmental Policy

Where environmental policies cause companies to incur costs or otherwise result in the prices of their products being raised, both economic theory and common sense suggest that this will impair companies' competitiveness and therefore that of the countries in which they are located. However, there are a number of reasons why corporate responses to environmental policy may, in fact, confer economic benefits rather than costs:

- Preventing pollution at source can save money in materials and in end-of-pipe remediation.
- Voluntary action in the present can minimize future risks and liabilities and make costly retrofits unnecessary.
- Companies staying ahead of regulations can have a competitive edge over those struggling to keep up.
- New 'green' products and processes can increase consumer appeal and open up new business opportunities.
- An environmentally progressive reputation can improve recruitment, employee morale, investor support, acceptance by the host community and management's self-respect.

Smart (1992) gives many examples of firms which have benefited financially for these reasons from voluntary environmental management initiatives. A similar view of the possibly beneficial effects of corporate environmental action, also illustrated by a number of examples, came from the Business Council for Sustainable Development (BCSD), which stated: '*Many of the waste reduction and environmentally positive programs in business are economically viable and are providing positive rates of return in relatively short time periods*' (Schmidheiny, 1992, p96). De Andraca and McCready (1994, p70), also of the BCSD, emphasize the competitive benefits to be gained by innovation and eco-efficiency induced by stringent regulations and high prices of environmental resources.

This generally positive view about the way in which environmental policy has so far impacted on firms is reflected at the macroeconomic level in a perception that the competitiveness effects of environmental policy have not been great. In 1996 the OECD review of this issue concluded: '*The trade and investment impacts which have been measured empirically are almost negligible*' (OECD, 1996, p45). Similarly, Pearce (1992, p27) has claimed that '*there is no evidence that industrial competitiveness has been affected by environmental regulation*'.

But, however slight the past effect of environmental regulations on competitiveness, three observations are pertinent. The first is that past environmental policies have not resulted in a diminution of environmental concern and the new goal of sustainable development seems to be requiring more stringent policy, with more potential effects on competitiveness, than in the past.

Second, there is widespread agreement that in today's global economy '*ever fiercer competition prevails*' (HMSO, 1993, p1) which, according to the US Office of Technology Assessment, raises the possibility that '*environmental regulations could be more of a competitive disadvantage than before*' (OTA, 1992, p8).

Finally, it seems likely that environmental policy in the future will make more use of environmental taxes than in the past. Such taxes have distinctive implications for competitiveness, which need to be examined separately from an assessment of the impacts of an environmental policy which has so far relied largely on regulation.

Although they allow society as a whole to achieve environmental goals more cost effectively than total reliance on regulation, in one way environmental taxes and charges raise more serious competitiveness issues than regulations for firms that are in particularly environmentally intensive sectors. This is because, after compliance with regulations, firms may use the environment without further payment; with environmental taxes firms pay for *all* use of the environment, even that which is within the limits specified by society. Of course, it is this continuing payment which gives the incentive for continual improvement which is a feature of environmental taxes.

Because of fear of their potential effects on competitiveness, most countries that have introduced environmental taxes have given vulnerable firms or sectors tax exemptions or concessions. These reduce the economic efficiency of the environmental tax and reduce the economic advantage to be gained from clean production systems. They also slow down the process of structural change in the economy such that energy- and environment-intensive economic sectors both become less intensive and less important economically relative to less environment-intensive sectors. It is therefore important to note that the overall effects on business competitiveness from the tax will depend on how the tax revenues are recycled through the economy: while environmentally intensive sectors may end up worse off, clean businesses are likely actually to benefit from it.

In fact, the effect on competitiveness of a carbon tax will be determined by a number of influences, including:

- the size of the carbon tax and the nature and extent of the offsets (how the revenues are recycled through the economy);
- the carbon intensity of the product;
- the trade intensity of the product (ratio of exports plus imports to production).

Pezzey (1991) calculated the cost impact on ten different sectors of a carbon tax of US$100 per tonne of carbon levied on the fuel inputs. He found that as long as the revenues are returned to industry, losses of price-competitiveness in the four relatively carbon-intensive sectors will be counterbalanced by gains in the six non-carbon intensive sectors. Moreover, the carbon-intensive sectors will only lose competitiveness to the extent that they do not reduce their carbon-intensity at a rate equal to the tax being applied. This point is discussed further below.

International competitiveness depends not only on cost increases but also on the trade intensity of the affected products. Relative price rises of untraded goods may affect demand for those goods in domestic markets, but they will not affect international trade. In Pezzey's simulation the low-trade intensity of iron and steel and non-metallic minerals (both sectors comprising heavy, bulky goods, including iron and cement) substantially reduces the trade impacts that these sectors will suffer from the carbon tax. Indeed, the trade impacts on chemicals are also reduced by the medium-trade intensity of this sector, leaving non-ferrous metals as the only sector in which a high-trade intensity and high-cost increase from the tax may cause significant trade effects from the tax. Against this it may be noted that 57 per cent of UK exports in 1995 were to EU countries, so that if the carbon tax was imposed on an EU-wide basis (as was the proposal from the European Commission in 1991), all the trade effects for these sectors would be much attenuated.

While such a simulation only takes account of immediate, first-round effects of the relative price-changes, rather than eventual adjustments to equilibrium, the main mechanisms through which imposing environmental taxes influences sectoral competitiveness are clear, as is the difference between the impacts from environmental taxes on sectoral and national competitiveness. The cost increases in the four most affected sectors will impair their position in domestic markets with respect to the products of other sectors. The six sectors whose costs are decreased by the revenue recycling will be particular beneficiaries from the shift in relative prices. For the country as a whole, however, there is no reason for thinking that its competitiveness will be affected at all by the shift. More sophisticated modelling of a tax shift from labour to the use of natural resources – for example, DIW, 1994, Barker, 1995, WIFO, 1995, INFRAS, 1996) comes to much the same conclusion for a number of European countries.

This also seems to have been true of the actual experience of Denmark, which has a small, open economy and which has been a pioneer in the area of environmental taxation. According to its Ministry of Economic Affairs: '*Danish experience through many years is that we have not damaged our competitiveness because of green taxes. In addition, we have developed new exports in the environmental area*' (Kristensen, 1996, p126). The study of the Norwegian Green Tax Commission (1996, p90) has also endorsed this essential conclusion: '*Reduced competitiveness of an individual industry is not necessarily a problem for the economy as a whole... It is hardly possible to avoid loss of competitiveness and trade effects in individual sectors as a result of policy measures if a country has a more ambitious environmental policy than other countries or wishes to be an instigator in environmental policy. On the other hand, competitiveness and profitability will improve in other industries as a result of a revenue neutral tax reform.*'

However, this does not resolve the problem of the fear of competitiveness getting in the way of environmental policy, because the individual sectors threatened by such effects can be expected to lobby vociferously against any measures that are perceived to be likely to cause them and it is quite possible that they will have enough political influence for the measures to be changed or abandoned.

For example, at the time of the debate on the European carbon/energy tax the *Financial Times* (*FT*, 1994) reported on why 'European Chemical Companies are Shifting Bulk Capacity to Asia': '[They] *are being driven away from their home bases by high costs and what manufacturers perceive as an ever-tightening regulatory stranglehold.*' The paper quotes two top executives from the industry in this vein.

Policy-makers in industrial countries take these kinds of statements seriously and in a number of countries regulatory structures are regularly reviewed in an effort to reduce costs on business. In the case of the carbon-energy tax proposal discussed earlier, not only did the proposal, against all environmental–economic logic, exempt the energy-intensive industries from the proposed tax on grounds of competitiveness, but the proposal was made conditional on North America and Japan introducing a similar measure of their own. In the event, of course, the tax was not introduced at all. In Finland, as also discussed earlier, the tax was introduced and retained, but was made less environmentally effective so as to allow the government to compensate for effects on competitiveness under trade rules.

It is little wonder that environmentalists are alarmed by what is variously called the 'political drag' or 'regulatory chill' on environmental policy of concern over competitiveness. Esty (1994, p162) notes: '*This political dimension of competitiveness is a reality in almost all environmental policy debates.*' It is hard to avoid the conclusion that if countries are not to shy away from difficult environmental policy because of fears of competitiveness, if such fears are not to present serious obstacles to environmental policy, the issue must be addressed head on, in such a way that trade rules are amended to allow competitiveness to be explicitly addressed and neutralized.

Reconciling Trade Rules with Environmental Policy

It is encouraging that the Preamble to the Agreement to establish the WTO places the central objective of the new organization – raising living standards – in the context of '*optimal use of the world's resources in accordance with the objective of sustainable development, seeking both to protect and preserve the environment and enhance the means for doing so in a manner consistent with* [countries'] *respective needs and concerns at different levels of economic development*'. However, this form of words need mean very little in practice. In order for it to do so, the WTO will have to consider how to deal constructively with the three types of policies for environmental protection which, as seen from the earlier examples and discussion, may be constrained by trade-related concerns:

1   International environmental treaties which envisage trade measures as part of their enforcement system.
2   Environmental policies which act as non-tariff barriers to trade or which include trade measures.
3   Environmental policies which are perceived to impair domestic competitiveness.

If trade is to be supportive of sustainable development, it is essential that policies of these kinds are not militated against by trade rules. They are discussed in turn to see how this might be achieved.

International treaties

It is generally agreed that international or transboundary environmental problems should be addressed by international agreement or treaties involving all affected parties (GATT, 1992, p35). However, such agreements are notoriously difficult to conclude, especially when large numbers of countries are involved so that international agreements on transboundary environmental problems involving all affected parties have proved elusive, leaving national policies or agreements between a subset of the relevant parties to fill the gap.

Once concluded, there are relatively few ways in which international environmental agreements can be enforced. Trade measures rank high among these few ways, whether in the form of concessions to encourage participation in, and observance of, the agreement, or restrictions and sanctions to discourage cheating and free-riding. At present, as was seen with the Montreal Protocol, trade measures to help to enforce multilateral environmental agreements, are of at least doubtful GATT validity. This is clearly unsatisfactory if the trading system is to be seriously concerned to promote sustainable development. A necessary reform is that the GATT rules must permit trade measures explicitly to back up widely supported international agreements.

Environmental regulations as non-tariff barriers and trade measures

The purpose of environmental regulations is to prevent, mitigate or remedy environmental damage. Such damage can ensue from the consumption of products or from their processes and methods of production. Ecologically there is no meaningful distinction to be drawn between the environmental harm deriving from products or from their processes and production methods. Sustainable development demands that regulations be equally available to address both sources of environmental damage.

Yet, at present, even voluntary eco-labels that give information to consumers about PPMs in other countries have been under attack as constituting GATT-invalid constraints on trade. The WTO Committee on Trade and the Environment notes in its 1996 report of its first two years' discussions that, on this issue, '*many delegations expressed the view that voluntary standards based on* [non-product related] *PPMs are inconsistent with the* [Technical Barriers to Trade] *Agreement as well as with other provisions of GATT*' (WTO, 1996, paragraph 70, p14). Mandatory eco-labels would appear to be even further beyond the pale. When in 1992 the Austrian parliament passed a regulation requiring all tropical timber to be labelled, a threat of trade sanctions and of a GATT challenge by Malaysia resulted in the regulation being withdrawn (Cairncross, 1995, pp230–231).

It should not be impossible to design conditions under which countries can pursue sustainable development to their desired extent within an orderly multilateral trading system, but without constraint from it on their environmental policy-making. Such conditions might require that:

* The policies must be specific with regard to the seriousness of the environmental damage they are seeking to address and where this damage is being or will be felt.
* Esty (1994, p283) adopts a three-point categorization of environmental harms: serious (rapid, major, certain irreversible harms); moderate (less rapid, major and certain or reversible harms); limited (least certain, slower, reversible or narrower harms). Provided the environmental damage physically affected the country concerned or the global commons and unless the damage is both limited and reversible, both the policy necessary to address it and the trade measures to enforce it, should be deemed legitimate. No distinction with regard to these environmental policies need be drawn between those directed at products and those directed at PPMs.
* Eco-labels to facilitate the provision of information to consumers concerning the life-cycle environmental impacts of goods and services, with regard to the products themselves and their PPMs should be considered fully compatible with WTO articles.
* The environmental policies and measures derived from them must be legislatively non-discriminatory between foreign and domestic producers or products. With regard to eco-labels, for example, it is possible that, in the Austrian case mentioned above, the proposed eco-label would have been less controversial if

it had been applied to temperate as well as tropical timber. The policies should also be introduced only after due notice – for example, 12 months – has been given, during which the international agreement with potentially affected parties should be sought that would make the measures unnecessary.

If the GATT rules had been consistent with these suggestions, clearly the arguments in the case studies discussed earlier would have been very different, but it is interesting to note that the trade measures involved would still not necessarily have been immune from challenge. For example, in the tuna–dolphin case it was noted above that the GATT panel ruled that the US ban was GATT-illegal because it related to PPMs and not to products and because the US was seeking to apply its laws outside its jurisdiction.

Under the proposals above neither of these reasons would have invalidated the US ban. However, Mexico would have had several other possible grounds of challenge:

1   The killing of the dolphins could be considered a 'limited and reversible' environmental harm. Dolphins are not classed as an endangered species and it could be argued that the taking of 30,000 dolphins per year out of a population numbered in millions (Esty, 1994, p188) is sustainable.
2   The application of the US ban could be deemed discriminatory (and the GATT panel ruled it so) in that, as noted above, the permissible dolphin-kill ratio (number of dolphins killed per net dropped) was defined retrospectively based on what the US fishermen had achieved.
3   The US proceeded to its ban without giving formal notice to Mexico of its intent to do so, nor did it try less drastic measures first. Interestingly, Esty (1994, p251) observes: '*The US tuna ban ... had very little practical effect on Mexican exports to the United States because the demand for Mexican tuna had collapsed as a result of commercial and consumer pressures, intensified by the US tuna-packers voluntary dolphin-safe labelling scheme. The market for tuna lacking the dolphin-safe label almost completely dried up.*'

Under the terms of the proposals set out above, the GATT panel could well have come to the same conclusion about the US ban, but for different reasons.

Similar considerations apply to the petrol reformulation dispute. It would have been quite possible to design the detailed regulation differently so that it attained the same level of environmental protection but did not discriminate against non-US refineries. Only in the Danish bottles case, given that the regulation addressed a Danish physical environmental problem, would the above suggestions have made the regulation unequivocally GATT compatible.

Threats to competitiveness

One approach to seeking to allay fears of competitiveness from environmental policies involves the progressive harmonization of environmental standards or policies. There is undoubtedly some scope for this and Esty and Geradin (1997, pp283–294) explore in some detail various approaches to potential harmonization which still takes some account of differences between countries. However, such a process is bound to be slow in a global community in which these differences – economic, social and environmental – are so profound.

Another approach is to seek to minimize effects on competitiveness by announcing the policies well in advance and introducing them gradually enough to give industry time to adjust to them. This is standard good practice for policy-making in general, but may not allow environmental problems to be addressed quickly enough, or may give too much time for organized interests that are profiting from unsustainability to mobilize against or water down policy proposals.

Finally, there is the possibility of allowing border tax adjustments (countervailing duties (CVDs) on imports or export rebates for exports) to offset the effects of environmental policies on competitiveness in both domestic and foreign markets. This response is the one generally favoured by environmental organizations (see, for example, Arden-Clarke, 1993), when it is often coupled to a suggestion to return the revenues raised by CVDs to developing countries to help to finance environmental improvements. The practical problems associated with this response are formidable: the cost-internalization approach to calculating the level of CVDs is often infeasible because of the complexity of the environmental effects concerned; the proposal raises the keenest fears among developing countries of an environmental smokescreen for commercial protectionism; its implementation could involve a substantial bureaucracy; and the means of disbursement to developing countries of funds collected would be difficult to design, establish and control.

However, if it is true that the political drag from competitiveness is proving a serious impediment to environmental policy-making, then a commitment to sustainable development may require the introduction of a way of mitigating effects from environmental policy on competitiveness that does not undermine world trading rules. For example, the ability to levy countervailing duties on imported products (or to give export rebates to exported products), where these have been given a competitive advantage (or disadvantage) by domestic environmental legislation, could be subject to provisos such as the following:

- The environmental legislation must be seeking to address a global or physical transboundary environmental problem and represent more stringent policy than in the past.
- The CVD or export rebate can only be levied or granted for a strictly limited period – for example, three years – after the introduction of the environmental legislation.
- The amounts of the CVD or rebate must be based on independently audited estimates by the industries concerned of the cost to them of the environmental legislation and the consequent rise in the prices of their products. A minimum threshold of competitive disadvantage might need to be shown – for example, 5 per cent on the price of a product – before CVDs or rebates would be allowable.
- The estimates should again be subject to independent scrutiny one year after the introduction of the legislation to verify that a competitive disadvantage had

in fact been incurred because of compliance. Should this not be the case, the CVD or rebate must be immediately revoked.
- The CVD or rebate would have to be announced in advance of their introduction and be open to challenge. CVDs should be placed in a fund to help developing countries to improve the environmental performance of their economies.

The purpose of permitting such a procedure would be to remove the influence of arguments about competitiveness from environmental policy-making by permitting companies that can show genuine disadvantage from it to be protected from its effects for a limited period while they adjust to the new reality. A concerned company would have to go to considerable trouble and show significant disadvantage, which should deter frivolous applications and insignificant CVDs or rebates. The environmental legislation would have to deal with a genuine transboundary grievance, and the whole procedure would be open to challenge.

Surprisingly, the actual textual changes to the WTO articles that would be required to implement the foregoing proposals on international environmental agreements, environmental regulations and CVDs are very few. What is overwhelmingly required is a change of interpretation of the current WTO articles, rather than their wholesale redrafting. This principally applies to Article XX which appears to give significant scope for the protection of the environment and the health of living things, but various restrictive interpretations have significantly narrowed this scope. To bring them into line with the proposals made earlier would require the following changes:

1   In Article XXg the words 'and the environment' should be added after '*natural resources*'.
2   Clarification should be issued that henceforth non-discriminatory action to protect the environment with regard to transboundary physical spillovers and the global commons, whether unilateral or not or related to PPMs or not, would not per se be ruled incompatible with GATT. Rather the key test will be the seriousness of the environmental harm addressed in relation to the disruption caused to trade.
3   The extent of disruption to trade from environmental measures taken under 2 should only be a criterion for challenge when the environmental harm being addressed was limited and reversible.
4   The need for sound science in the application of environmental policy should be interpreted in accordance with the Precautionary Principle (see, for example, O'Riordan, 1993) by an independent group of experts, which is open to the receipt of submissions from interested parties and gives a detailed account of its procedures and decisions.
5   Similar procedures of openness, transparency and public involvement should be adopted by the WTO itself, especially in its resolution of disputes.

The suggestion about permitting a levying of CVDs to give limited protection against competitive disadvantage arising from environmental protection would require a new sub-clause in Clause 8 of Article III (on national treatment of like products), to the effect that the provisions of Article III would not apply to the kinds of limited protection described above.

The fact that it is predominantly reinterpretation of the WTO rules rather than their redrafting that is required does not mean that the changes will be easily implemented. Almost certainly the changes in interpretation will need to be accompanied by financial provisions to ease the transition to sustainability for poorer countries, which will otherwise continue to be suspicious that the greening of the WTO is protectionism in disguise. Richer countries have the choice whether to make this investment in sustainability now or wait until the pressures of unsustainability in an ecologically interdependent world erode the possibilities of global cooperation and security and, perhaps, of civilized life itself.

Conclusion: How Should Business Respond?

The world trading system stands at a crossroads. Global economic integration and the intensification of economic competition have brought new issues on to the trading agenda and re-emphasized the importance of some old ones. These issues include the environment, human rights, labour standards, the maintenance of competitive markets and other issues concerned with the regulation of corporate conduct.

It will not be easy for the WTO to address these issues in a way that both wins international consensus and satisfies those who are concerned with them. There will be a temptation to try to proceed with business-as-usual and avoid the full negotiations on the issues that are increasingly seen to be necessary. The complete failure of the work to date of the WTO's Committee on Trade and Environment to make any substantial progress on the environmental issues it has considered has already done much to confirm in environmentalists' eyes the essential insensitivity of the WTO to the environment. This in turn contributes to the growth of protectionist forces which are inclined to reject the objective of a broadly open international trading regime altogether.

For business, three of the possible outcomes of the debate between trade and social and environmental issues are likely to be distinctly uncomfortable:

1 A failure to take the necessary measures to move towards sustainable development seems increasingly likely to bring about environmental disruption on an unprecedented scale. The insurance industry is the first to find that past environmental errors can result in huge liabilities. For example: '*The estimated bill for hazardous waste and asbestos damages and remediation in the United States is US$2 trillion, based purely on the projected costs of meeting US claims against general liability insurance policies written by US and European insurers*' (Schmidheiny and Zorraquín, 1996, p120). The same source quotes the president of the Reinsurance Association as saying that climate change could bankrupt the industry. Insurance is one of the core institutions of capitalism, allowing risks to be spread to reduce the exposure of individual entrepreneurs. Higher cost or, at the limit, unavailable insurance, would constitute a serious brake on business activity.

2   A resurgence of protectionism that put globalization into reverse would cause market and financial chaos. There are real and theoretically well-founded fears that considerations of competitiveness will result in '*a race to the bottom*' (Korten, 1995, pp229–237) as a result of competitive social and environmental deregulation. There is little evidence as yet of such a race in industrial countries, but should it begin to bring about falling social and environmental standards, or should competitive pressures be widely perceived to be blocking necessary regulations in the face of growing environmental crises, a 'new protectionist' alliance between labour, environmental and social interests could make international business activity anything from more costly to infeasible.

3   Attempts by individual countries to implement the policies necessary for sustainable development while exposed to the full competitive rigour of globalized markets could cause industrial and economic pain, or perceptions of such pain, beyond social and political endurance. Although, as discussed above (and in more detail in Ekins and Speck, 1998), there is little evidence that environmental policy in the past has had a significant impact on competitiveness, business consistently opposes environmental policies and especially environmental taxes, on competitiveness grounds and even threatens relocation. Such threats, whatever their basis, make policy-making fraught and uncertain. Most governments back down in the face of such corporate opposition, increasing the likelihood of major disruption from unaddressed environmental problems, as discussed in the previous paragraph.

This chapter has made some suggestions as to how the WTO rules could accommodate environmental policy-making for sustainable development. The suggested changes are not revolutionary. It is in fact rather surprising that the WTO rules, formulated just after the Second World War when environmental issues were not even on the agenda of most organizations, should be so easily adapted to an era when the achievement of environmental sustainability has become one of the principal global challenges. As already noted, this does not mean that the changes will be uncontroversial or easily effected. It is all too possible that, left to itself, the WTO Trade and Environment Committee will stretch its discussions interminably and inconsequentially into the next millennium. Each of the three possible consequences sketched in the previous paragraph suggests that is not in the interests of business to allow this to happen. Business now has the global reach and influence which would enable it to help to bring these discussions to a more positive conclusion, if it chose to get involved. It should start to draw a clear distinction between non-discrimination, which is the foundation of free trade and of the GATT and WTO which promote it and indiscriminate deregulation, which is a recipe for environmental and social unsustainability. Business should start to put its weight behind the kind of minimum global regulation of world trade that would ensure that its playing-field is stable and green, as well as level and much less prone than at present to disruption by environmentally induced disintegration in society at large.

References

Andersson, T, Folke, C and Nyström, S (1995) *Trading with the Environment*, Earthscan, London

Arden-Clarke, C (1993) 'Environment, Competitiveness and Countervailing Measures', paper presented to the OECD Workshop on Environmental Policies and Industrial Competitiveness, January 28–29, Paris, mimeo, WWF International, Gland, Switzerland

Barker, T (1995) 'Taxing Pollution Instead of Employment: Greenhouse Gas Abatement Through Fiscal Policy in the UK', *Energy and Environment*, vol 6, no 1, pp1–28

Brack, D (1995) 'Balancing Trade and the Environment', *International Affairs*, vol 71, no 3, pp497–514

Brack, D (1996) *International Trade and the Montreal Protocol*, Royal Institute of International Affairs/Earthscan, London

Business Week (1993) 'What's Wrong?', *Business Week*, 2 August, p59

Cairncross, F (1995) *Green, Inc.: a Guide to Business and the Environment*, Earthscan, London

Daly, H and Goodland, R (1994) 'An Ecological-economic Assessment of Deregulation of International Commerce under GATT', *Ecological Economics*, no 9, pp73–92

De Andraca, R and McCready, K (1994) *Internalizing Environmental Costs to Promote Eco-Efficiency*, Business Council for Sustainable Development, Geneva

DIW (Deutsches Institut für Wirtschaftsforschung; German Institute for Economic Research) (1994) *Wirtschaftliche Auswirkungen einer ökologischen Steuerreform*, DIW, Berlin

Earth Summit '92, Regency Press Corporation, London (this publication comprises an abridged version of Agenda 21 and some introductory articles)

Ekins, P, Folke, C and Costanza, R (1994) 'Trade, Environment and Development: the Issues in Perspective', *Ecological Economics*, vol 9, pp1–12 (special issue on trade and environment co-edited by the authors)

Ekins, P and Speck, S (1998) 'The Impacts of Environmental Policy on Competitiveness: Theory and Evidence' in T Barker and J Köhler (1998) *International Competitiveness and Environmental Policies*, Edward Elgar, Cheltenham, pp33–69

Esty, D (1994) *Greening the GATT: Trade, the Environment and the Future*, Institute for International Economics, Washington, DC

Esty, D and Geradin, D (1997) 'Market Access, Competitiveness and Harmonisation: Environmental Protection in Regional Trade Agreements', *The Harvard Environmental Law Review*, vol 21, no 2, pp265–336

Evans, P and Walsh, J (1994) *The EIU Guide to the New GATT*, Economist Intelligence Unit (EIU), London

Financial Times (*FT*) (1994) 'The Dye is Cast by Growth and Costs' by Paul Abrahams, *Financial Times*, London, 31 May

General Agreement on Tariffs and Trade (GATT) (1992) 'Trade and the Environment' in *International Trade 1990–91*, GATT, pp19–48, Geneva

Her Majesty's Stationery Office (HMSO) (1993) *Realising Our Potential: a Strategy for Science, Engineering and Technology*, Cm.2250, HMSO, London

Ikwue, A and Skea, J (1996) 'The Energy Sector Response to European Combustion Emission Regulations' in F Lévêque (1996) *Environmental Policy in Europe: Industry, Competition and the Policy Process*, Edward Elgar, Cheltenham, UK, pp75–111

INFRAS (1996) *Economic Impact Analysis of Ecotax Proposals*, Zürich, Switzerland

International Trade Law Reports (ITLR) (1996) *United States Standards for Reformulated and Conventional Gasoline: Commentary, Report of the Panel (17th January 1996), Report of the Appellate Body (29th April 1996)*, ITLR, vol 1, Cameron May, London

Korten, D (1995) *When Corporations Rule the World*, Kumarian Press, West Hartford, CN/
  Berrett-Koehler Publishers, San Francisco/Earthscan, London

Kristensen, J P (1996) 'Environmental Taxes, Tax Reform and the Internal Market – Some
  Danish Experiences and Possible Community Initiatives' in *Environmental Taxes and
  Charges: NATIONAL Experiences and Plans*, European Foundation for the Improvement
  of Living and Working Conditions, Dublin, and Office for Official Publications of the European Communities, Luxembourg

Lang, T and Hines, C (1993) *The New Protectionism: Protecting the Future Against Free Trade*,
  Earthscan, London

NCC (National Consumer Council) (1998) *Farm Policies and Our Food: the Need for Change*,
  NCC, London

Norwegian Green Tax Commission (1996) '*Policies for a Better Environment and High Employment*', Oslo

OECD (1996) *Implementation Strategies for Environmental Taxes*, OECD, Paris

O'Riordan, T (1993) 'Interpreting the Precautionary Principle', CSERGE working paper PA
  93–03, CSERGE, University of East Anglia, Norwich

Office of Technology Assessment (OTA) (1992) *Trade and Environment: Conflicts and Opportunities*, OTA, Washington, DC

Pearce, D (1992) 'Should the GATT be Reformed for Environmental Reasons?', CSERGE working paper GEC 92–06, CSERGE, University of East Anglia/University College, London

Pezzey, J (1991) *Impacts on Greenhouse Gas Control Strategies on UK Competitiveness*, Department of Trade and Industry, HMSO, London

Schmidheiny, S (with the Business Council for Sustainable Development) (1992) *Changing
  Course: a Global Business Perspective on Development and the Environment*, The MIT Press,
  Cambridge, MA

Schmidheiny, S and Zorraquin, F (with the World Business Council for Sustainable Development) (1996) *Financing Change: The Financial Community, Eco-Efficiency and Sustainable
  Development*, The MIT Press, Cambridge, MA/London

Smart, B (ed) (1992) *Beyond Compliance: a New Industry View of the Environment*, World
  Resources Institute, Washington, DC

Teir, G (1996) 'The Evolution of CO_2/Energy Taxes in Finland' in *Environmental Taxes and
  Charges: National Experiences and Plans*, papers from the Dublin Workshop, 7–8 Febru-
  ary 1996, European Foundation for the Improvement of Living and Working Conditions,
  Dublin, and Office for Official Publications of the European Community, Luxembourg

WIFO (Austrian Institute of Economic Research) (1995) *Makroökonomische und sektorale
  Auswirkungen einer umweltorientierten Energiebesteuerung in Österreich*, Vienna

World Resources Institute (WRI) (with UNDP and UNEP) (1992) *World Resources, 1992–93*,
  Oxford University Press, Oxford/New York

World Trade Organization (WTO) (1996) *Report of the WTO Committee on Trade and the Environment*, adopted 8 November, WTO, Geneva

17

Reaping the Benefits: Trade Opportunities for Developing-country Producers from Sustainable Consumption and Production

Nick Robins and Sarah Roberts

Introduction

In today's globalizing world, export success is one of the major routes to economic progress for developing countries. But the conditions for success are changing as producers face rising environmental expectations in key export markets, resulting from tightening regulations, new corporate practices and changes in consumer values and lifestyles. These new expectations reflect the growing recognition that current patterns of consumption, particularly in the richer, industrialized world, are environmentally unsustainable. In the 21st century, profound changes in the ways in which goods and services are produced, traded and consumed will be required both to reduce the burden on the global environment and to ensure that a growing population has the resources to meet its needs.

The primary responsibility for taking the lead in making these changes lies with the industrialized economies of North America, Western Europe and East Asia. For developing-country producers seeking to succeed in these markets, sustainable consumption presents a number of new and often complex challenges. For those that can adapt to these requirements and start moving to anticipate trends, there could be new opportunities to capture market share, generating financial, environmental and social benefits in the process. Across the developing world, a small number of pioneering companies are gaining premium prices and increased market share by providing goods and services that meet these new expectations. This chapter looks at the lessons to be learned from these pioneers to ensure that sustainable consumption moves out of the margins and into the mainstream.

Reproduced in full from W Wehrmeyer and Y Mulugetta (eds) (1999) *Gracing Pains: Environmental Management in Developing Countries*, pp219–231, by kind permission of Greenleaf Publishing, Sheffield, UK

Setting the Agenda

Sustainable consumption and production came of age as an international policy priority at the United Nations Conference on Environment and Development (UNCED) in June 1992. After strenuous bargaining, during which the US had declared that '*the American way of life is not up for negotiation*', the Agenda 21 action programme agreed by the world's governments concluded that '*the major cause of the continued deterioration of the global environment is the unsustainable pattern of consumption and production, particularly in industrialised nations*' (Agenda 21, Chapter 4).

The Rio Earth Summit highlighted the deep divide in consumption and pollution between North and South, whereby the 20 per cent of the world's population in the rich 'North' account for 50–90 per cent of consumption and pollution. To remedy this, Agenda 21 called on the industrialized world to take the lead in making the shift towards more sustainable consumption and production patterns. It also called for a new balance to be struck to make international trade flows, development needs and environmental sustainability mutually reinforcing.

Since Rio, much attention has been focused on trying to understand the implications of changing production and consumption patterns for the global economy. Essentially, sustainable production and consumption present two sides of the same coin. The emphasis of sustainable production is on the supply side of the equation, focusing on improving environmental performance in key economic sectors, such as agriculture, energy, industry, tourism and transport. Sustainable consumption addresses the demand side, looking at how the goods and services required to meet basic needs and improve quality of life – such as food and health, shelter, clothing, leisure and mobility – can be delivered in ways that reduce the burden on the earth's carrying capacity.

Both sides are, of course, inextricably linked and a life-cycle perspective is required to pinpoint where action can best be taken along the product chain to reduce environmental damage to levels within the earth's carrying capacity. Traditionally, most efforts have been directed at cleaning up the production process, particularly in industrialized countries. Now attention is shifting to finding new ways to change consumption so that the conventional links between meeting needs and improving the quality of life with pollution, resource use and waste can be broken. Doing this is, of course, highly complex, with many structural factors combining to make up the patterns of consumption, which then determine the choice and use of goods and services. Key factors include market dynamics, technological innovation, physical infrastructure, the regulatory framework and cultural values.

Experience has shown that sustainable consumption and production presents four critical challenges at the international level:

1 *Restructure the economy over the long term* Given the current pressures being placed on the world's environment and the prospects of further expansion in both affluence and human numbers, there is a growing consensus in international policy circles that tough targets for environmental improvement will have

to be achieved in the years ahead. The European Union has now adopted the goal first proposed by the Wuppertal Institut for a 'Factor 10' improvement in resource productivity and pollution reduction over the next 30 years; there is also growing enthusiasm for a more short-term 'Factor 4' improvement over the next decade (see von Weizsäcker et al, 1997).

2 *Rethink core ethical values* Much of the sustainable consumption agenda has been driven by citizens and non-governmental environment, development and consumer organizations promoting more sustainable lifestyles. Indeed, for many, sustainable consumption is not a scientific or a technical question, but is first and foremost a question of values, requiring a new *'ethic of living sustainably'*. For environmental organizations such as Friends of the Earth, this means designing strategies for sustainable production and consumption on the basis that each person should have equal access to the natural resources required to meet their needs (see FoEE, 1996).

3 *Reform the policy framework* The scale of change required means that action cannot be left up to market or voluntary efforts alone. Governments have a major responsibility for putting in place an assertive policy and regulatory framework that rewards producers and consumers whose actions contribute to long-term sustainability and penalizes those who deplete natural capital (see Box 17.1).

BOX 17.1 POLICY INNOVATION FOR SUSTAINABLE PRODUCTION AND CONSUMPTION

Industrialized-country policy-makers and regulators have been taking action in six main areas with impacts for developing-country producers:

1 *Product regulation* Limiting and phasing out the use of toxic chemicals that have adverse health effects for consumers has remained a critical area of activity. A prominent example has been Germany's ban on the import of textiles and other products treated with potentially damaging azo dyes. Uncertainty about the requirements, coupled with a lack of approved testing systems meant that the German ban caused real difficulties for many developing-country textile producers.

2 *Waste legislation* Governments are now placing greater emphasis on the duties of corporations to reduce consumer wastes through the 'extended producer responsibility' approach. For example, Germany's new Closed Substance Cycle and Waste Management Act, which came into force at the end of 1996, will mean that whoever produces, markets and consumes goods is now responsible for the avoidance, recycling, reuse and environmentally sound disposal of waste. These take-back requirements can have significant implications for the packaging used by producers in the South, favouring materials easy to collect and recycle in the industrialized world, rather than traditional materials.

3 *Economic instruments* Between 1989 and 1994, the number of economic instruments used for environmental policy purposes, such as taxes, charges,

Box 17.1 Continued

deposit–refund systems and tradable permits, increased by 50 per cent in the OECD. These include a new landfill charge on waste in the UK, a new energy levy in The Netherlands and federal taxes on ozone-depleting substances in the US. One of the challenges for the future is the degree to which industrialized countries, particularly in Europe, will make border-tax adustments for climate change.

4   *Product information* Considerable heat has been generated by the growth in environmental labelling schemes in the industrialized world, notably the European Union's eco-label scheme. For example, the EU's eco-label criteria for paper have been attacked by developing-country exporters for placing too high a premium on recycled content, thereby making it almost impossible for them to gain the label for their products made from sustainably harvested wood (see IIED, 1996). Elsewhere, positive steps are being taken to improve the access of developing-country products to eco-labels. Building on its 20-year experience with the Blue Angel scheme, Germany's Federal Environmental Agency is now developing a new initiative to improve communication and cooperation with developing countries to produce goods with high environmental and social standards.

5   *Public procurement* Governments in North America, Europe and Japan are moving to integrate environmental provisions into their purchasing programmes. In October 1993, President Clinton issued an Executive Order on Federal Acquisition, Recycling and Waste Prevention to guide government agencies in the choice and purchase of environmentally preferable products. All federal government agencies are now also required to purchase Energy Star computers, monitors and printers. In Japan, a 'Green Purchase Network' was established in 1996, comprising 400 companies, 100 governmental bodies and 100 private agencies. As public procurement becomes more liberalized, government efforts to raise the environmental performance of the goods and services they buy could become a major bone of contention in international trade.

6   *Trade policy* Trade policies are also being changed in the industrialized world to give positive encouragement to sustainably produced goods from developing countries. For example, when the European Union updated its Generalized System of Preferences agreement with Asian and Latin American countries in 1994, it included a special incentive arrangement to provide additional preferences to countries implementing international agreements on sustainable forestry management. Some governments are supplementing their formal trade policies with additional efforts to transfer information both on new environmental regulations and on clean technology. One notable example is the GREENBUSS database launched by the Dutch Centre for the Promotion of Imports from Developing Countries (CBI). GREENBUSS is accessible online via the Internet and is used by trade associations and export promotion agencies in developing countries to find the latest information on regulatory requirements throughout the European Union.

Source: Robins and Roberts, 1997

BOX 17.2 TRADE, SUSTAINABLE CONSUMPTION AND THE
ENVIRONMENT

The creation of a global economy is taking place at a time when the ecological impacts of production and consumption are increasingly spilling over national frontiers. However, the world currently lacks a clear system for resolving the tensions that this creates. One thing is sure: sovereign nations alone cannot take decisions in the best interest of the global environment.

Recent disputes over trade and environment have exemplified this problem. Developing countries have strongly opposed efforts by developed countries to introduce new environmental regulations that seek to alter the ways in which exports are produced. Thus in 1991, the US banned imports of tuna and tuna products from Mexico on the grounds that the numbers of dolphin killed were far greater than by the US fish industry. But under international trade law such non-tariff barriers dealing with production processes are not allowed, so a GATT dispute panel ruled against the US. India and other developing nations have more recently challenged a similar US ban on shrimp imports that have been caught in ways that damage turtle populations. While, on moral grounds, it is hard for any country to argue that it has the right to develop its economy on an unsustainable basis, there is a real fear in developing countries that new environmental regulations could be used as a way of reducing market access and increasing production costs, thereby harming their competitiveness. Developing countries also argue that trade measures are inherently unfair, as they can be used only by the economically powerful against the economically weak: what trade instrument can be used by Bangladesh or the Maldives to ensure that the US does not export products that have been produced with very high carbon emissions?

Source: Robins and Roberts, 1997

4 *Renew international co-operation* Shifting the global economy on to a sustainable path will require an unprecedented degree of international cooperation. The requirements of an open world trade system need to be carefully balanced with the imperatives of environmental sustainability and poverty reduction. Transitional support will be required to support developing countries in the move to sustainable production and consumption methods, providing a new role for development assistance agencies. Already, international agencies are also supporting both sustainable production initiatives and efforts to promote trade in more sustainably produced goods and services. These range from the network of national cleaner production centres, supported by the UN Environment Programme (UNEP) and the UN Industrial Development Organisation (UNIDO) in Brazil, China, India, Mexico, Tanzania and Zimbabwe to Germany's GTZ Biotrade initiative for promoting exports of organic agriculture from almost 20 developing countries.

To date, however, international policy efforts to address sustainable consumption have resulted in much frustration and suspicion. There are genuine fears in many developing countries that much of the environmental criteria adopted in richer countries is protectionism in another guise, implemented to reduce the competitiveness of developing-country exports. Globalization, increasing trade liberalization and the establishment of the World Trade Organization have raised the stakes. Consumption patterns and their 'footprints' are now increasingly international, as are aspirations. Environmentalists fear that the current trade rules, which mean that countries cannot discriminate against a product on the grounds of the way in which it was produced, will reduce the impact of many hard-won environmental regulations, ultimately leading to the lowest common denominator of environmental protection in the name of open markets and free trade. Sunita Narain and Anil Agarwal from the Centre for Science and Environment in India set out the dilemmas clearly in Box 17.2.

Threat or Opportunity for Developing-country Exporters?

An increasing number of businesses are viewing these changes in a positive light, seeing new growth markets opening up. The *Harvard Business Review* in its January–February 1997 edition described the business implications of a sustainable world as '*one of the biggest opportunities in the history of commerce*'. For business, this means going beyond compliance with environmental regulations and engaging in pollution prevention in their factories, product stewardship for their goods and services, and investing in the new generation of sustainable technologies. In Europe and North America, a small committed group of companies has been experimenting with new ways of producing and selling goods and services which create new market dynamics for developing-country exporters and suppliers. Three sectors have been particularly affected to date: forestry, food and textiles.

Forestry

For over a decade, high-profile campaigns have been waged to highlight global deforestation, particularly in the tropical rainforests, with the aim of pressurizing governments to introduce effective regulation. Campaigners urged individuals and institutions in industrialized countries to cut their consumption of wood-based products and to boycott tropical timber in particular. Protests were staged outside shops identified as selling unsustainable timber. In Europe, environmental campaigns have certainly been one factor in the recent decline in imports of tropical timber. But when it became clear that regulation could not deliver sustainable forestry quickly enough, the focus shifted to the marketplace.

One example is the establishment of the Forest Stewardship Council, set up by a global coalition of environmental and social interest groups. The FSC has developed principles and criteria for sustainable forest management, which producers can voluntarily use to certify their products. Simultaneously, the FSC has formed buyers' groups in a number of countries of companies who pledge to phase out all

---

Box 17.3 Demand for Sustainable Timber Creates Market Advantages for Southern Producers

Gaining International Market Advantage through Certification
When PIQRO Laminated Flooring Company, originally set up by the Mexican government, was sold, its new owners saw exports as the key to their future success. The company began sourcing its wood from Plan Piloto Forestal, a nearby community forest project, part of which had been FSC-certified and became the first company to export certified tropical timber flooring to the US. It was sold through a number of independent distributors and, after a few months of marketing, PIQRO products were picked up by a national store due to their certification. This attracted the attention of a number of large flooring distributors, including International Hardwood Flooring (IHF), the largest tropical flooring importer in the US. IHF, which was seeking to differentiate its position in the market, negotiated to buy and distribute all PIQRO's export-grade products. In exchange for this exclusivity, IHF is investing in PIQRO to enable it to meet world standards, essentially becoming a strategic partner in PIQRO, helping PIQRO to complete the metamorphosis from an unprofitable state-owned company serving the regional flooring market to a world-class exporter of high-quality sustainable products.

European Demand Supports Small Producers in the Solomon Islands
Forests are being exploited at a wholly unsustainable rate in the Solomon Islands as foreign timber companies buy up communal logging rights. Communities were finding the incentives offered difficult to resist in a country with few employment options and services, until NGOs in the Solomons and Europe began working together to develop trade in timber which would offer communities long-term sustainable livelihoods while maintaining the forest resource. NGOs are working with producer groups in the Solomons to develop sustainable management systems for the forests and gain FSC certification. The timber that they produce is being sold through alternative trading organizations in Europe where there is high awareness of the impacts of unsustainable logging and willingness from individual and institutional consumers to seek out alternatives and, in some cases, pay a premium for wood products that are guaranteed as coming from sustainable sources. Producers receive 40 times more per tree than if they had sold their logging rights and they are provided with a decent long-term income.

Source: Robins and Roberts, 1997

---

non-FSC-certified wood producers by a certain date. The FSC is thus using business concerns about reputation, risk management and customer loyalty to develop a new market in sustainable timber. Interestingly, one of the most fervent business supporters of the FSC in the UK is B&Q, a DIY chain previously targeted by environmental groups. With support from NGOs and businesses, some developing-country producers are tapping into the lucrative international market for sustainable wood, thereby gaining higher prices and secure livelihoods (see Box 17.3).

Food

Agriculture has long been the mainstay of South–North trade flows, but the long-term decline in the real price for many commodities and the volatility of the commodity markets has resulted in highly insecure livelihoods for many developing-country producers. Now, however, some are gaining higher prices and long-term income security by selling their products into environmentally friendly or fair-trade markets in the North.

Concern about the environmental and animal welfare implications of intensive agriculture combined with some very well-publicized health scares – for example, pesticide residues and BSE – has led to soaring demand for organic produce in many Northern countries. The European Union market for organic goods was estimated to be worth nearly 3 billion ECU in 1993, over half of which is met by imports. In the US, demand for organic food is growing at over 20 per cent per year, providing lucrative markets for developing countries who can make up the shortfall between demand and domestic production.

And organic markets can indeed be lucrative. Although yields can be lower and labour costs higher than for conventional production, food that is certified organic fetches premiums of between 50 per cent and 200 per cent. In total, it is estimated that Northern consumers currently spend US$500 million on organic produce from developing countries, over and above what they would pay for conventional foodstuffs.

Latin American producers have been particularly quick to tap into these markets. The organic sector in Mexico is now estimated to be worth US$500 million and Argentina is making serious efforts to develop its organic sector, with sales rising from US$1.5 million in 1992 to a projected US$20 million in 1996. This rapid development has been supported by efforts to overcome the bureaucracy surrounding EU recognition of imported organic goods. By requesting equivalency status for its certification system, Argentina became the first developing country to obtain a place in the EU provisional list, thereby gaining market advantages.

Organic certification is one of the most widely recognized and trusted labels and essential for consumer confidence and the payment of premiums. However, certification can be a slow, laborious and relatively costly process and a particular challenge to small developing-country producers. A common solution is to form cooperatives to bring down the costs and to develop domestic certification systems. Costs remain, however and national legislation is required for full compliance with the EU requirements which can be an insurmountable hurdle for many developing countries.

The fair-trade movement has been taking practical action to try to increase trade from developing countries for over 20 years, focusing on providing secure sales, fair prices and decent working conditions for poor producers. Over the last 10 years, a variety of organizations have developed independent certification processes for a number of agricultural goods. The provision of quality control and marketing support for producers and easily recognizable fair-trade marks combined with some strenuous market development work, has brought certain fair-trade goods out of the margins of health-food shops and on to the mainstream shelves of the majority

---

BOX 17.4 FAIR TRADE COFFEE: AN INSTANT SUCCESS

A number of organizations have been working with coffee producers' groups in developing countries for many years to develop fair international trade in this commodity. In recent years, these efforts have received a major boost with the development of recognizable fair-trade marks and the development of brands of instant coffee which are sold in mainstream retailers.

Cafédirect is one such brand, developed by a partnership of four fair-trade organizations with the aim of building an instantly recognizable, generally available brand of fair-trade coffee to which buyers would find it easy to switch. It is now sold in 1700 supermarkets across the UK and sales have increased dramatically over the last five years, with Cafédirect now accounting for 3 per cent of the roast and ground market and 2 per cent of the instant market. It has become the third best-selling brand of coffee in Safeway's, one of Britain's leading supermarkets, despite being 10 per cent more expensive than conventional brands.

Fourteen producer organizations from Mexico, Costa Rica, Peru, Nicaragua, the Dominican Republic, Uganda and Tanzania supply Cafédirect and the farmers and their families have benefited from higher price and secure sales. For some producer organizations, fair trade has provided secure foundations from which to convert to organic production-generating environmental benefits.

Source: Robins and Roberts, 1997

---

of supermarkets in many countries. The most well-known fair-trade commodity is coffee (see Box 17.4), but a more recent success story is the fair-trade banana which has seized 12 per cent of the Swiss market and 9 per cent of the Dutch market since its launch in 1996 (see Smith, 1997).

Fair trade can also bring environmental benefits. Ethical trading organizations encourage the producers with whom they work to improve the environmental sustainability of their production and reduce the use of external inputs such as pesticides and fertilizers. A number of initiatives with the producers of other beverages, such as tea and cocoa, which originally aimed to improve their economic and social conditions have also resulted in environmental benefits as these producers convert to organic production.

Textiles

Textiles is another sector where attention has been focused on the environmental and social issues associated with production, leading to changing market conditions for developing-country producers.

NGO campaigns on the conditions of Southern workers who produce goods for Northern retailers have led to a number of firms developing codes of conduct for their suppliers. Examples include Nike and The Gap, who were both targeted after poor working conditions at their developing-country subcontractors were revealed and the code of practice negotiated between FIFA (International Soccer Federation) and international trade unions to improve conditions in the production of

---

BOX 17.5 INCORPORATING ETHICS INTO MAINSTREAM COMPANY POLICY

Patagonia is a fast-growing outdoor clothing company based in California, which has taken an assertive stance on environmental and ethical issues since its foundation. The company started to introduce organic cotton to its products in 1991 and, although it did not meet with much consumer interest, in 1994 the board of directors decided that the environmental impacts associated with conventional cotton were severe enough to justify requiring that Patagonia's entire cotton range should be organic by 1996.

Patagonia worked with their suppliers to help them make the change. One of these was a Thai company that had never used organic cotton before but were willing to try. According to Michael Brown, head of environmental assessment at Patagonia, both sides gained from the changes: '*We've benefited from their sophistication and willingness to engage in development with us; they've developed expertise in organic cotton which may be marketable elsewhere.*' Patagonia reports buoyant sales and, as the company's founder Yvon Chouinard says, '*it is possible to apply our environmental principles and be successful*'.

However, they believe that their products have sold well primarily for the traditional reasons that people buy their products. '*Our customers wanted the value in our products that they had always sought from us: durability, performance, fit, timeless styling.*' The message is clear: ethical products can be highly desirable, but they have to meet all the other product criteria as well.

Source: Robins and Roberts, 1997

---

sportswear and footballs after the use of child labour in the manufacture of footballs was revealed at the time of the 1994 World Cup.

Most of these codes of conduct have tended to focus on labour conditions, but some include broader social and environmental issues. Levi-Strauss, the US clothing manufacturer, has developed 'Terms of Engagement' with its potential business partners, which include environment, ethical, health and safety, legal, employment (including child labour) and community development conditions.

Other clothing companies have implemented ethical policies despite little consumer interest or public pressure (see Box 17.5).

Government policy and regulation have also forced producers to make some significant changes to their production processes in order to keep their markets. A prime example of how industrial innovation and government support turned a potential threat to exports into an opportunity for growth and environmental improvement is given by the Indian response to the German ban on azo dyes.

In 1994, Germany prohibited the import of textiles containing certain azo dyes on health grounds, which had direct repercussions for exporters to the German market, particularly in India where textiles account for nearly half of all exports to Germany. Similar regulations have now been introduced by other European countries, such as The Netherlands and in the future it is likely that the whole

---

Box 17.6 Turning Bans into Dividends: The Case of Century Textiles

Century textiles, India's largest textile producer, managed to turn the new requirements into a market advantage through early awareness of the development of the regulations, good relationships with their customers and independent certification. In 1994, one of Century's major German clients sent through details of the new standards that they required, which essentially meant that Century had to find substitutes for a number of their dyes and become Eco-Tex certified.

The chemical technology manager, Mahesh Sharma, declared: '*I went through hell, but then there were dividends.*' These dividends included the optimization of the dyeing process, so that, although most of the substitute dyes cost 10–15 per cent more than their predecessors, overall production costs only rose marginally and significant market advantages ensued. Eco-Tex certification enabled Century to charge an 8–10 per cent premium and bought them new buyers, particularly from the US and UK who re-export to Germany, increasing their market by 10 per cent in the first year.

Source: Robins and Roberts, 1997

European Union will adopt such regulations. This is exactly the type of regulation that many developing-country producers fear, potentially requiring costly use of new materials and changes in production processes if they are to keep their export markets.

The Indian government responded in two ways. Firstly, having decided that there were sufficient domestic health concerns, they matched the German restrictions on azo dyes; secondly, they provided support in terms of information and technical assistance to small mills, which were likely to find it the most difficult to adjust. The industry themselves took steps to meet or surpass these new requirements. One company that managed to incorporate sustainability requirements and remain internationally competitive is Century Textiles (see Box 17.6).

Opportunities in other sectors

It is not just in traditional developing-country export sectors where Southern producers are benefiting from moves towards more sustainable production and consumption. In higher value-added manufacturing sectors, such as consumer durables and electronics, Southern producers are increasingly having to meet higher production standards and energy-efficiency targets if they are to access export markets.

Take the case of refrigerators. Under the Montreal Protocol which regulates the production, import and export of ozone-depleting substances, industrialized countries were required to phase out the production of CFCs by 1996, while developing countries have until 2006. However, for Southern refrigerator manufacturers to export to Northern markets, they need to meet the higher environmental standards

---

BOX 17.7 GAINING NEW MARKETS FROM PROTECTING THE OZONE LAYER: FRIDGEMASTER, SWAZILAND

FridgeMaster in Swaziland is the largest manufacturer of refrigeration products in Southern Africa and was instrumental in Swaziland becoming a signatory to the Montreal Protocol in 1992. By 1993, the company had become the first producer of CFC-free goods in Africa. Currently, its major market is regional, with the bulk of its products being sold through outlets in South Africa, but it also exports to Mozambique, Botswana, Zimbabwe and further afield to Mauritius, Malta, Dubai, Turkey and Russia. By phasing out CFCs long before the international deadline, FridgeMaster hopes to enhance sales in existing markets and access new markets, particularly in Europe.

Although converting to CFC-free production cost the company US$4 million in operating costs – 6 per cent of turnover – this has been more than recovered through accelerated sales and the company has expanded significantly since it switched to CFC-free production, with sales through its major South African retailer, Hyperama, trebling in one year. In order to reach its target of 15 per cent growth over five years, FridgeMaster is investing close to 4 per cent of its profits in research and development, seeing this as the only way to maintain its competitiveness in world markets. The company is also focusing on reducing the energy consumption of its products as a way of appealing to European consumers willing to pay a premium for energy efficiency. Thus, rather than being a barrier to exports, the high expectations of European consumers fits with FridgeMaster's ambition to tap new markets and continually add value to their products.

Source: Robins and Roberts, 1997

---

now. For a number of companies, this accelerated schedule has provided the route for market development (see Box 17.7).

Sourcing from the South: Lessons for the Future

The Earth Summit +5 meeting in June 1997 concluded bleakly that *'Five years after UNCED, the state of the global environment continues to deteriorate... Marginal progress has been made in addressing unsustainable production and consumption patterns'* (UNCSD, 1997).

There is no doubting the truth of this statement, but there is much that producers and consumers can do that will immediately contribute to improving the sustainability of production and consumption. The more that both consumers and producers can benefit from such efforts, the greater the progress that will be made; and this means high-quality products being produced, used and disposed of in a sustainable way. Business has an important role to play, and pioneering companies are already taking advantage of the new trade opportunities generated by changing consumption and production patterns in their export markets. The challenge now is to build on the success of practical lessons, and target policy and market action towards removing barriers to change and enhancing further innovation.

Pioneers can make a difference

Pioneering companies, such as those profiled above, demonstrate that sustainable production and profitability can be combined and that the potential threat of changing markets can be turned into a business opportunity. Their success has come from a combination of long-term commitment and the development of the necessary capacity to make the transition.

No one can do it on their own

However, few companies will be able to make this transition on their own. What has proved central to success is new partnerships along the product chain. Support from NGOs, government agencies or close relationships with their buyers in the North is generally crucial to support the transition to more sustainable practices. This is particularly important for small and medium-sized firms who may face considerable information, skills and resource gaps. However, as the fair-trade movement has illustrated, relatively small amounts of support at the initial stages can result in significant dividends in the future.

Combining quality with sustainability

One fundamental element that is required if sustainability is to be combined with profitability is the need to retain high standards of quality. Few people will buy inferior products in return for sustainability benefits. As Flip van Helden said of the sustainable timber project in the Solomon Islands: '*Sustainable timber is a beautiful concept but we cannot sell a concept only, we are selling a product.*' Century Textiles cloth, FridgeMaster refrigerators and FSC-certified timber all demonstrate that sustainability can mean high-quality products that meet all usual buyer specifications as well as delivering environmental and social benefits.

Independent verification and performance guarantees

Central to the credibility of sustainable products is a trustworthy labelling system, particularly if premium prices are being charged. Independent certification schemes provide buyers with a guarantee that the claims about the product can be substantiated and have proved central to the development of many markets, including organic products, sustainable timber, environmentally friendly textiles and refrigerators and fairly traded goods. However, the certification process can prove to be a severe managerial and cost burden. Initiatives such as the training of local inspectors and the development of group certification schemes are essential if certification is not to become a barrier to small producers generally and producers in developing countries.

Moving sustainability into the mainstream

Supplier codes of conduct and sustainable procurement criteria can help to ensure that more sustainable practices go beyond the certified niches and enter the mainstream of trade. Ultimately, all commercial and institutional buyers should implement supplier criteria that can be independently verified. Ideally, such codes of conduct should cover both environmental and social issues. It is essential that retailers work with their suppliers to help them improve their performance rather than simply dropping those who cannot meet the standards immediately. Initiatives such as the UK Ethical Trading Initiative, a partnership of companies and NGOs that is working to develop a common system of monitoring and verification, are important developments in making the use of these codes more widespread and credible.

A supportive policy framework

Positive policy choices can make a difference to the ease with which sustainable initiatives can emerge and spread. The response of the Indian government to the German legislation on azo dyes helped turn a potential threat into an export opportunity for their textile producers. Governments in export markets have responsibilities to ensure that their policy-making processes are transparent to exporting countries and that new regulations are phased in in such a way that producers have time to make the necessary changes. Government procurement criteria can help to develop the market for more sustainable products, as can support for practical mechanisms for implementing sustainable production and consumption. In her support for the UK Ethical Trading Initiative, Clare Short, the UK Minister for International Development, has stressed the importance of partnerships between governments, business, consumers and pressure groups, and especially the role of business since private trade and investment now dwarfs aid flows. These types of partnerships are likely to play an even more important role in the future.

References

Friends of the Earth, Europe (1996) *Sustainable Europe*, FoEE, Brussels, Belgium

International Institute for Environmental Development (1996) *Towards a Sustainable Paper Cycle*, IIED, London

Robins, N and Roberts, S (1997) *Unlocking Trade Opportunities*, report by IIED for the UN Department of Policy Coordination and Sustainable Development, IIED, London

Smith, A (1997) 'Bananas: Straightening up a Bent World', in *Ethical Consumer*, vol 49, October–November

United Nations Council for Sustainable Development (1997) *Overall Progress Achieved since the United Nations Conference on Environment and Development: Report of the Secretary General. Addendum: Changing Consumption and Production Patterns, Chapter 4, Agenda 21*, UNCSD, New York, NY

von Weizsäcker, E, Lovins, A and Lovins, L H (1997) *Factor Four: Doubling Wealth, Halving Resource Use*, Earthscan, London

Conclusion

Win–Win Revisited: a Buddhist Perspective

Richard Starkey and Richard Welford

Cast your eye over any of the weighty reports that set out to give you 'the state of the world', and I defy you not to be depressed. Forests, poverty, fresh water, population, climate change, species loss, environmental refugees, soil fertility; cut it which way you will, all the global indicators still show we're travelling in the wrong direction.

Then again, feel the breadth and depth of those who are now enlisted in the cause of addressing this crisis. In business, academia, local government and the media, an unskilled observer might assume that the Greenies were already taking over.

They'd be wrong, of course. Or rather premature. There has indeed been enormous progress on all fronts over the last decade, but rarely proportionate to the accelerating destruction of the natural and social capital on which all our lives depend. If anything the gap between need (what has to be done to take our aberrant species forward into a genuinely sustainable way of life) and response is growing.

The politicians all know that becoming sustainable is a non-negotiable imperative, but they are not convinced that they are the ones who've got to do it. It's all about mind sets in transition and a chronic lack of leadership. There are so many other problems that politicians have to address, apparently more immediate. Most of them see the environment as gloomy territory to engage in, with few tangible returns...

In business ... again it is usually the environment that ends up on the losing end, as a combination of economic benefits (usually construed as the indirect benefits that new jobs bring) demand that the environment be sacrificed yet again.

No-one should be too surprised by this. Few businesses anywhere in the world have yet re-engineered their innovation processes to embed sustainability as a core element in new product development.

So wrote Jonathon Porritt (2000) in *A New Century, a New Resolution,* a short booklet issued by the World Wide Fund For Nature on the first day of the new millennium as a reminder of what remains to be done if sustainable development is to become a reality. Porritt's piece is an eloquent and succinct summary of the problem. Whilst he acknowledges that politicians have woken up to the issues and whilst he is rightly excited by the fact that certain businesses are beginning to engage, sometimes at a deep level, with both the environmental and social dimensions of sustainable development, his core message is that not nearly enough is being done. And his views regarding business are echoed by Carl Frankel in Chapter 14 who sums things up in a single sentence: '*We are clearly getting something less from the corporate community than the wholehearted engagement that the global problematique requires.*'

How to explain this? How is it that politicians and the business community – and for that matter we as consumers and citizens – are not doing more? What is it about '*our aberrant species*', as Porritt calls us, that stops us engaging wholeheartedly with the global problematique – with social injustice in its many guises and the suffering it brings. The question as to why social injustice persists is one of the all-time big questions, one which has exercized the minds of a great many religious and social thinkers over the centuries. As we both have a long-standing interest in Buddhism and believe that a Buddhist perspective can throw some light on this fundamental question, this is the perspective we adopt here. However, in doing so, we fully recognize that what we say has much in common with other religious traditions as well as with Western philosophical and humanist traditions – all of which, we believe, have a contribution to make to the realization of sustainable development.

The Buddhist perspective is succinctly set out by the Tibetan monk, Professor Samdong Rinpoche, in a collection of essays published by the United Nations Environment Programme entitled *Moral Implications of a Global Consensus: Ethics and Agenda 21*. His key point is that what is happening in and to our outer environment is very much a reflection of what is happening in our minds or, as he put it, in our 'inner environment'. He certainly does not pull any punches when he says (Samdong Rinpoche, pp104–105).

> *The basic cause of our problems including the fear of annihilation of the planet is created by our own ... greed and selfishness and lack of compassion. In this context, my view is that there is no way out to save ourselves from disaster ... unless we ... realize and change our attitudes and abandon the nature of selfishness and greed and develop loving-kindness.*[1]

Uncomfortable reading though this might be, it has to be admitted that he has a point. For it is undoubtedly the case that if we were able to abandon our less endearing traits and develop a more caring, concerned attitude towards others, the world would be a better place. If our minds were imbued with the loving kindness and compassion that Samdong Rinpoche refers to, then the social injustice that now exists would simply not be tolerated. Achieving sustainable development would not be a problem.

So if by changing our minds we can bring about sustainable development, the big question is, how do we do this? How do we as a species go about developing more caring, considerate attitudes? The Buddhist answer to this question is very simple: given that such attitudes do not arise naturally in most of the situations we find ourselves, we need to practise![2] For whilst Buddhism is very clear that we all have the capacity to develop caring, considerate attitudes, it is equally clear that in order to develop this capacity we need to work at it.

Of course, in order to make the effort to practise in this way, it is important both to understand why we need to practise and to feel motivated to do so. The Buddhist perspective on why we need to develop such attitudes is summed up in the following meditation offered by the Buddhist teacher Geshe Kelsang Gyatso (1995, p425):

> *I myself have not the slightest wish to experience suffering and I am not content with the happiness I enjoy, but this is equally true for everyone else … I want happiness and so do others. I want freedom from misery, but so do others. Since we all want the same thing, I will regard others in the same way as I regard myself.*

And our motivation to practise arises from the realization that by doing so, we ourselves actually benefit. As David Edwards (1998, p186) puts it, actions *'inspired by kindness have a delightfully positive effect on our state of mind: they actually make us happy'*. In short – and to borrow the terminology used in Section 2 – Buddhists argue that developing attitudes of caring and concern constitutes a win–win opportunity! By doing so, we help others and at the same time help ourselves.

Interestingly, this view has been confirmed by a number of studies. For instance, a study carried out by James House at the University of Michigan found that doing regular volunteer work and interacting with others in a compassionate way dramatically increased life expectancy. And a 30-year study of Harvard graduates carried out by George Vaillant concluded that adopting an altruistic lifestyle is a critical component of good health (Dalai Lama and Cutler, 1999). In a survey of several thousand people who were regularly involved in volunteer work that helped others carried out by Allan Luks, it was found that these volunteers consistently reported better health than peers in their age group. Many also said that their health markedly improved when they began volunteer work. In addition many volunteers reported long-term effects of greater calm and relaxation. Reviewing the work of Luks, Dr Herbert Benson of the Harvard Medical School noted *'one of the healthiest things you can do for yourself is to volunteer to help your community'* (Edwards, 1998, p188).

And it is interesting to note the sense of dissatisfaction that can develop in situations where caring and concern are stifled. The Buddhist monk Lama Yeshe runs the Samye Ling monastery in Scotland, and in 1998 was invited to address 600 of Shell's top executives at its global meeting in Maastricht. He was such a success there that in 1999 he was invited to participate in a week-long seminar organized by the San Francisco-based Global Business Network and attended by 150 senior staff from some of the world's biggest companies. Lama Yeshe and his assistant, Buddhist nun Rinchen Khandro, organized early morning meditation sessions for the participants. Rinchen Khandro relates what they observed (Bunting, 1999, p1):

> *A lot of them expressed dissatisfaction in their lives. They talked about the meaninglessness of their work, about balance between work and family, between caring for the environment and people and the pursuit of profit. They were clever people who lacked the experience of love.*

In his wonderful book *The Ecology of Commerce*, Paul Hawken (1995, p1) writes:

> *I have come to believe that we in America and in the rest of the industrialized West do not know what business really is, or therefore, what it can become. Perhaps this is a strange remark, given that free-market capitalism is now largely unchallenged as the economic and social credo of just about every society on earth, but I believe it is correct. Despite our management schools, despite the thousands of books written about business, despite the legions of economists who tinker with the trimtabs of the US$21 trillion world economy, despite and maybe because of the victory of free-market capitalism over socialism worldwide, our understanding of business – what makes for healthy commerce, what the role of such commerce should be within society as a whole – is stuck at the primitive level.*

Here Hawken poses the most fundamental business question of all: what ultimately is the purpose of business? For him it is something far more than simply making money through buying and selling. For Hawken, the true purpose of business is to increase the general wellbeing of humankind through service – that is, through activities motivated by what Samdong Rinpoche refers to as loving-kindness and compassion and what we have called caring and concern for others. In the final analysis, then, the task for the business community – indeed it is the task for all of us – is to learn to develop our attitudes of caring and concern. This is the 'values revolution' to which John Elkington refers in Chapter 2. Not for a moment is this to suggest that caring attitudes don't exist within the business community. They do. The increasing number of environmental and social initiatives we are seeing from business are evidence of more than a self-interested desire to curry favour with stakeholders. They are evidence of a genuine commitment to making a real difference. As Simon Zadek pointed out in Chapter 10, '*Anyone working with the business community will have been impressed by the commitment of many people working within this community to improving the social and environmental footprint of the companies in which they work*'. The problem is not that these attitudes don't exist, but that they do not exist frequently enough. So, in the words of the song, business needs to accentuate the positive and eliminate the negative – and it can do so by taking advantage of pervasive and previously unexploited win–win opportunities!

The Dalai Lama has said (Dalai Lama and Cutler, 1999, p47):

> *Let us reflect on what is truly of value in life, what gives meaning to our lives and set our priorities on the basis of that. The purpose of our life needs to be positive. We weren't born with the purpose of causing trouble, harming others. For our life to be of value, I think we must develop basic good human qualities – warmth, kindness, compassion.*

And it is perhaps fitting to end this Reader with another remark made by the Dalai Lama (Dass and Bush, 1992):[3] '*Love and compassion are necessities, not luxuries. Without them, humanity cannot survive.*'

References

Bunting, M (1999) 'Holy New Alliance', *The Guardian*, G2, p1, September

Dalai Lama and Cutler, H (1999) *The Art of Happiness: A Handbook for Living*, Coronet Books, London

Dass, R and Bush, M (1992) *Compassion in Action: Setting Out on the Path of Service*, Bell Tower, New York

Edwards, D (1998) *The Compassionate Revolution: Radical Politics and Buddhism*, Green Books, Totnes

Gyatso, K (1995) *Joyful Path of Good Fortune: The Complete Guide to the Buddhist Path to Enlightenment*, Tharpa Publications, London

Hawken, P (1995) *The Ecology of Commerce: A Declaration of Sustainability*, Phoenix, London

Porritt, J (2000) 'Optimism of the Will' in WWF (ed) *A New Century: A New Resolution*, WWF and *The Guardian*, 1 January

Samdong Rinpoche (1994) 'Preservation of Inner Environment', in Brown, N and Quiblier (eds) *Moral Implications of a Global Consensus: Ethics and Agenda 21*, United Nations Environment Programme, New York

Notes

1   Loving-kindness, or wishing love, as the Buddhist teacher Geshe Kelsang Gyatso calls it, is a mind that wishes all other living beings to be perfectly happy. He says:

> *When we develop wishing love for all living beings, at the same time we develop great compassion – a mind that cannot bear others to experience any pain and desires their complete freedom from every kind of suffering. The realizations of wishing love and great compassion are like two sides of the same coin* (Gyatso, 1995, p409).

2   In Buddhism, as in many other spiritual traditions, one practises developing care and concern through meditation. Geshe Kelsang Gyatso (1995) describes meditation as a method for acquainting ourselves with positive states of mind. Very briefly , the idea is to practise generating and holding a particular positive state of mind within a meditation session in order to become familiar with it. By gaining this familiarity within a meditation session one is then more able to access that particular state of mind outside of meditation

3   This quotation was taken from the back cover of the book

Index